Prentice Hall Mainframe Software Series

DATA DICTIONARY

Implementation, Use, and Maintenance

ROM NARAYAN

PRENTICE HALL, Englewood Cliffs, New Jersey 07632

Library of Congress Cataloging-in-Publication Data

NARAYAN, ROM
    Data dictionary: implementation, use, and maintenance

    p.   cm.—(Prentice Hall mainframe software series)
    Bibliography: p.
    Includes index.
    ISBN 0-13-197351-7
       1. Data base management.   2. Data dictionaries.   I. Title.
    II. Series.
    QA76.9.D3N34   1988   88-4139
    005.74 '2—dc19   CIP

Editorial/production supervision and interior design: Rennie Rieger/John Fleming
Cover design: Ben Santora
Manufacturing buyer: Paula Massenaro

*To my wife,
Geetha*

Prentice Hall Mainframe Software Series

 © 1988 by Rom Narayan
Published by Prentice-Hall, Inc.
A Division of Simon & Schuster
Englewood Cliffs, New Jersey 07632

The publisher offers discounts on this book when ordered
in bulk quantities. For more information, write:
  Special Sales/College Marketing
  College Technical and Reference Division
  Prentice Hall
  Englewood Cliffs, NJ 07632

IBM is a registered trademark of International
Business Machines Corporation.
DATAMANAGER is a registered trademark of
MSP Ltd.

Printed in the United States of America
10 9 8 7 6 5 4 3 2 1

ISBN 0-13-197351-7

PRENTICE-HALL INTERNATIONAL (UK) LIMITED, *London*
PRENTICE-HALL OF AUSTRALIA PTY. LIMITED, *Sydney*
PRENTICE-HALL CANADA INC., *Toronto*
PRENTICE-HALL HISPANOAMERICANA, S.A., *Mexico*
PRENTICE-HALL OF INDIA PRIVATE LIMITED, *New Delhi*
PRENTICE-HALL OF JAPAN, INC., *Tokyo*
SIMON & SCHUSTER ASIA PTE. LTD., *Singapore*
EDITORA PRENTICE-HALL DO BRASIL, LTDA., *Rio de Janeiro*

Contents

040210

CHAPTER 3   **DATA DICTIONARY CONCEPTS**   **33**

CHAPTER 4   **ORGANIZATIONAL IMPLICATIONS**   **55**

Preface

AUTHOR'S PURPOSE

The ideas presented in this book are the results of the author's experience in implementing data dictionary systems during a nine-year period. The book is intended for persons within the MIS departments of companies who are interested in understanding and implementing a data dictionary. The managements of such companies recognize that information is a resource that can be deployed as a competitive weapon in strategies to gain an increasing market share, growth, and profitability. This recognition is translated into action items that result in the creation of data administration and data base administration functions within the MIS department. Managers of smaller companies that are looking to get into information management will definitely benefit by understanding and perhaps selectively applying the concepts and practices suggested in this book, depending on the amount of resources that can be allocated to this effort.

Additionally, funding is authorized to purchase or develop a data dictionary system. In many cases, the implementation of a data dictionary becomes a peripheral effort at systems development instead of the central activity that precedes and then supports systems development and end-user computing. If the principles and exhortations in this book were followed and supported by top management, dictionary implementation and maintenance would indeed become a crucial part of the MIS effort, as it should be. The benefits from this effort would flow in all directions—to the benefit of the entire organization, not just MIS. This book attempts to define the concept and the context of the data dictionary, and takes the reader through an exposition of the benefits of having a fully populated data dictionary. It then describes how to prepare a proposal for implementing a dictionary, selling the benefits to the various constituencies, and maintaining the data in the dictionary. By reading this book, the reader would get an insight into what a dictionary is, how it is related to other things being done in an MIS department, how it ties into a dictionary as a major project within an organization.

Normally, MIS projects have sponsors in the user segments of the business and are driven by sets of requirements or needs that can be quantified and are tangible; such may not be the case with a dictionary project. This is because there are several beneficiaries of the dictionary, and any one group may not possess the clout to sponsor and support the project in the long run. Even if a group takes on this role, as most data base administration groups tend to do, there is the danger that it may drive the dictionary implementation in such a way that it may not produce the desirable consequences for the entire organization. The way out of this situation is to have a sponsor in the organization at a high-enough level that that person can see the entire picture and drive the implementation through its gestation period, which can be anywhere from 12 months to 3 years. Once the Dictionary is self-sustaining, it can be subject to the project development and implementation process that prevails in the organization. This book will help the would-be sponsor to visualize the benefits and define a strategy that could be used to sell the project to other beneficiaries and provide direction to the implementation team. Examples of sponsors of the dictionary project include the director of MIS, manager of information resources, manager of data base administration, manager of end-user computing, and manager of systems development.

Success builds on success—and a dictionary project is no exception to this rule. This book proceeds on the assumption that in a project with a long gestation period, the ability to provide successes to the beneficiaries along the way is a key ingredient in ensuring the success of the total project. This book goes over the process of identifying the overall objectives of the project, the subobjectives as they apply to different constituent groups, and ways of identifying and reaching these goals.

Implementing the dictionary requires a combination of knowledge and skill that requires more than what is taught in college courses. Knowledge of the organization, its managers, and their objectives is of crucial importance in developing a strategy. Furthermore, a knowledge of dictionary concepts, installation and maintenance procedures, and benefits is important in communicating the pros and cons of dictionary use to users. This book attempts to give the reader a knowledge of dictionary use with which to communicate intelligently with different users, such as application system developers and operations personnel. The book does this through the liberal use of real-life examples, so that the reader is made aware of the various facets of dictionary usage and its consequences.

For the person who has the responsibility for developing the implementation plan and overseeing its implementation, the book offers the experiences of others who have gone through a similar process. The book is replete with examples from different systems and the procedures that have been used successfully in different sites. This information can be used and/or modified to suit the needs of the site and the strategies of the implementation manager.

For the individual or group with the responsibility for maintaining a dictionary and monitoring adherence to its policies, the book offers techniques and approaches that can be used to maintain the integrity of the data in the dictionary. In the area of initial population and maintenance of the dictionary, questions relating to the responsibility and accountability of individuals and groups often arise. These questions can be answered in only a general way because they are dependent on the specifics of the situation. Thus an environmental assessment is suggested before specific recommendations in the book can be put into action.

A comprehensive set of applications for a dictionary is described in this book. The purpose is to provide readers from different functional areas within MIS with a common base of concepts and information from which to draw. The book is organized such that different groups can benefit from reading sections of the book without having to read the entire book. Suggested reading sequences are provided for different classes of readers.

The methods proposed in this book are intended to be guidelines that can be used by a site administrator to develop an implementation strategy. There are many pitfalls that can be avoided in implementing a dictionary, and if this book leads to a smoother implementation by eliminating a misstep here and there, the author's purpose will be served.

For those readers who need an overall understanding of a dictionary as well as the know-how to interact with it, this book will serve as a reference. Application system developers, data base administrators, and operations personnel who need to use a dictionary during the system development life cycle will find detailed step-by-step procedures to help them achieve their objectives.

It is worth repeating that a dictionary is a tool, not a solution in and of itself. Properly implemented and used, it can be of considerable help, but used improperly, it can negate the very goals for which it was created.

AUDIENCE

There are three audiences for this book: MIS professionals involved with implementing and maintaining a data dictionary, users (both readers and updaters) of a data dictionary, and college students who need to understand a data dictionary from a practical viewpoint.

Implementers—The MIS or DP manager, systems development manager, operations manager, data base administration manager, and systems planning manager of an installation that is planning to install a dictionary. After a quick rundown of dictionary concepts, this book addresses the specifics of hands-on implementation. The person responsible for installing and administering the dictionary would find the material on entity models extremely helpful in planning the implementation.

Users—Individuals in the MIS department and in the user departments who will interface with the dictionary will find in this book both basic concepts and implementation details for their specific function. These people can read the first few chapters to get an understanding of the dictionary, and then move onto the chapters that deal with the application of the dictionary to a specific area. The application examples are intended to give the reader a perspective on what to expect from the dictionary, and to generate support for the implementation.

Students—Although this book is targeted at the MIS practitioner, this book would prove useful as an additional text in the second semester of a data base management systems (DBMS) course within an MIS or computer science curriculum. The chapters dealing with entity modeling, data planning, and systems development life cycle (SDLC) reinforce concepts gained in DBMS courses. The practical nature of the book could be exploited by instructors who wish to assign students a practicum involving the development of a dictionary implementation at a company.

SCOPE AND LIMITATIONS

The scope of this book is the set of constructs and ideas needed to define the objectives and formulate the policies for implementing a data dictionary. The book is based on the experiences of the author in implementing dictionaries in a practical environment. It is believed that the ideas presented in this book can be implemented in any computer hardware/software environment (i.e., IBM, DEC, Honeywell, Data General, etc.).

The reader of this book is assumed to have some understanding of the way in which business organizations function and the ways in which people anticipate and react to change. This is a book about implementing a disciplined approach to information management, through the implementation of a dictionary system and its associated procedures. The reader is asked to keep in mind the following statement by Machiavelli: "There is nothing more difficult to take in hand, more perilous to conduct or more uncertain in its success, than to take the lead in the introduction of a new order of things'' (*The Prince,* 1513).

SUGGESTED READING SEQUENCES

Chapters 1–3 serve to provide an understanding of Data Dictionaries and their role in information management. Chapter 4 outlines the organizational conditions that would support the implementation of a Dictionary. Chapters 5–12 focus on the details of Dictionary requirements analysis and implementation planning, population and maintenance strategies and procedures, selection of a Dictionary, training users, and monitoring performance of the Dictionary. Chapters 13–18 cover Dictionary applications from the user perspective. They cover Data Planning, Data Base Administration, System Development Life Cycle, Operations, Security, and End–User Computing.

Senior managers within the company seeking to move into information management should read Chapters 1–4. This will give them the overview plus the organizational requirements for a successful Dictionary project implementation. Information System managers and others responsible for information processing should read Chapters 1–4, 7, and 13–18. This would give them the perspectives that users of the Dictionary have. End users should read Chapters 1–3, 5, 6, and 18. This sequence would give them the overview, entity model concepts, naming conventions and standards, and use of the Dictionary for End-user Computing. Functional groups within the Information Systems organization should read Chapters 1–3, 5, 6, 9, 10, and the appropriate chapter pertaining to Data Planning, DBA, Systems Development, and Operations. It is important to grasp the use of the Dictionary over the course of the System Development Life Cycle, even though one is in a specialized functional area such as DBA or Operations. Finally, those directly associated with the implementation and on-going administration of the Dictionary should not only read the entire book, but also apply the concepts and use the examples to make their implementation a success.

ACKNOWLEDGMENTS

The material collected in this book reflects not only my experience with the implementation and use of dictionaries, but also the result of many, many discussions with people at Honeywell and Data General involved with various aspects of system design and development.

I would like to thank Steve Davidovich of the Ontario Civil Service for his encouragement in challenging ''conventional wisdom'' and looking beyond what is self-evident. A number of the implementation alternatives proposed in this book arose out of a quest for better methods of implementing a data dictionary.

I would also like to thank Hazel Dodds for assistance with initial editing of the manuscript, and the team at Prentice Hall, headed by Paul Becker, who have done an excellent job of producing the book.

Finally, I would like to thank my family for being patient with me during the many evenings and weekends that it took to complete the manuscript.

Additional Resources

The author conducts a training course called "Using Data Dictionary Effectively". The two main objectives of this course are:

1. To provide an overview of dictionary capabilities and usage, so that managers, systems and programming staff, data base administrators, and operations personnel can understand its potential and communicate on dictionary issues using a common framework.
2. To identify the key objectives of dictionary implementation, and show the steps that have to be taken to achieve those objectives.

It is taught several times a year, in major cities across the U.S. It is also available for on-site presentations.

A computer assisted instruction (CAI) package using the TRAINER 4000 CAI authoring system off Computer Systems Research Inc., of Avon, Connecticut, is available, and covers data dictionary fundamentals in an attractive interactive format. This course requires an IBM PC or compatible, and uses this book as the text.

This course is geared to functional users of the dictionary, who need to understand basic concepts, and specifically how they would interact with the dictionary during the system development life cycle. It will prove useful to those organizations that need to familiarize many people with dictionary concepts and practices in a short period of time.

To order a CAI diskette, send your name and address with a check, money-order, or company P.O., for $49 per copy ($55 for orders outside the U.S.) to the address shown below. Checks must be in U.S. funds and be drawn on a U.S. bank, or on a U.S. branch of a foreign bank. The CAI diskette is available in the 5¼ inch version or in the 3½ inch version. You must specify which version you want shipped, and also whether you will operate it from the "A" drive (diskette) or the "C" drive (hard disk).

Also, the author publishes a newsletter called the Data Dictionary User Group Newsletter. It is published quarterly and contains articles and features of interest to professionals who are involved in applying data base and data dictionary concepts and tools in business, education, government, and non-profit organizations.

To obtain further information on the training course, CAI package, or newsletter, address correspondence to:

NARAYAN SYSTEMS CONSULTANTS, INC.
955 Main Street
Winchester, MA 01890
(617) 721-0249

chapter 1

Introduction

WHAT IS A DATA DICTIONARY?

When a user or computer application requests data, the computer must know what data are stored in the data base, how they are organized, and how to access them from the data base so that the correct data are returned to the requester. These rules may be contained in a file layout, an "include" file, a copybook, a subschema, a relational table, or a data dictionary. To give a primitive example, a file layout that is part of an application program (i.e., an FD in a COBOL program) contains rules that could be sourced from a data dictionary. The FD contains basic information about each data element, including the size, the relative position within a record and file, and the access methods. However, all this information is embedded within a section of the application program source. For other persons to make use of this information, they would not only have to know the specific programs that contained the FD, but also the rules coded within those programs. Figure 1–1 shows the posi-

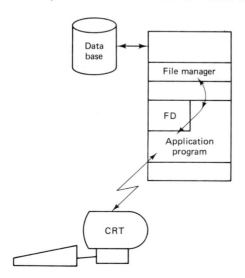

Figure 1–1 FD within application program.

1

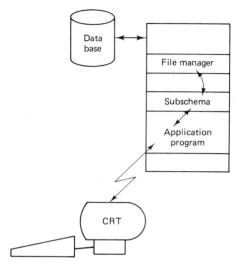

Figure 1–2 Subschema or application view.

tion of the FD within an application program; note how each application program has its own area for the FD.

In a typical data base management system (DBMS), the subschema (or user view of the data) may be located in a separate file and occupy a different segment of memory. Changes to the subschema can be made only by authorized personnel, and more rules, such as security access, can be incorporated. Thus the subschema that is sourced from a dictionary has more controls built into it. This is shown in Figure 1–2.

In the complex case, the data dictionary is the focal point for all data access; the data dictionary not only tells the computer where the data are located in the data base, but also which application programs process the data, and closely coordinates with the DBMS in controlling access to the data base. Figure 1–3 illustrates this situation.

As the number of computer applications grows and the data bases increase, the number of data dictionaries in the organization will continue to grow substantially; however, if the dictionaries are not synchronized to a common set of rules, they will tend to be different from one another. Thus a data base system that follows one set of data dictionary rules will not be able to communicate with another data base system

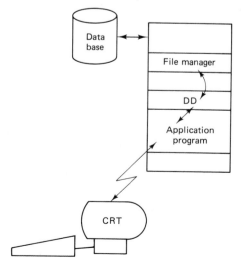

Figure 1–3 Data dictionary independent of application.

that follows another set of data base rules. There are two major problems when this occurs:

1. Users tend to lose confidence when the data follows different rules in different data bases.
2. Data-based systems tend to be duplicated, and proliferate unnecessarily, because it is often easier to create a new version of the data element than to resolve conflicts between existing ones.

PERSPECTIVES

Information Management

The importance of information management grows with the need to organize and control an organization's important asset—its information. Information management requires a long-term view of the situation and the commitment of the time and resources required to create the strategies that will be the basis on which a corporate base of information will be created.

Information management starts with the premise that the key information in the organization can be identified and cataloged. The information may be in the form of computerized data files, text files, electronic messages, source programs, run instructions, operating procedures, standards and policies, and so on. The data may reside on different types of media such as disk, tape, microfiche, laser, and file cabinets. The information about the information in the organization is often referred to as *metadata*, that is, data about data.

The data dictionary system is a tool that facilitates storage of the metadata as entities, and the capability to relate entities together in such a way that the organized metadata serve a useful purpose. For example, data about computer programs could be stored in the dictionary in an entity category called "program," while data about reports can be stored in an entity category called "report." Thus individual instances of programs such as CDR0102.CB or CONSRT0105 would be stored as entity category "program," whereas individual instances of reports such as DISPATCH RPT 01 or CONTRACT STATUS RPT 01 would be stored as entity category "report."

One of the primary purposes of organizing the metadata is to be able to describe and communicate that information to persons within the organization who are seeking information about reports or programs or any other entity that is stored in the dictionary; if the metadata were not organized in a central data base such as the data dictionary, it would be much more difficult to go to the many persons who may have different pieces of the information and search for that information.

Another important feature that the dictionary provides is the ability to link or relate two instances of the different entity categories. For example, if the program called CONSRT0105 produced the report called CONTRACT STATUS RPT 01, a link could be established in the dictionary that essentially connects the two instances. The reason for doing this is to make it easy to answer questions such as "Which program does this report come from?"

These functions are similar to the role played by the Dow Jones News/Retrieval Service, which maintains a current and up-to-date data base of current business and financial information. Data from various sources are collected, summarized, and presented in a user-friendly format to users with minimal computer training, who are allowed to query the data base of information. The data dictionary system can be viewed as a collection of up-to-date data on the various "things" that constitute the "data processing" environment of the company.

Data Resource Management

The term "data resource management" refers to the process of building and implementing data models that reflect the ongoing functions of the business. The physical implementation, support, and maintenance of these data models requires a solid dictionary foundation.

The data dictionary is useful in the following specific tasks that arise as a result of the decision to implement data resource management, that is, the standardization of data structures (both logical and physical) as well as the definition, quality, and protection of the data resource.

- Identification of the entities that go into making up the business, and the associations of these entities
- Establishment of naming standards and guidelines
- Provision of information on the availability of data for shared use
- Overall planning for applications so that the reuse of data structures wherever possible is ensured
- Provision and enforcement of security procedures
- Provision and implementation of procedures to maintain the integrity of data bases

Software Utility

The data dictionary is a software utility that catalogs an organization's data resources: what data exist, where they originate, who uses them, their format, and so on. Data dictionaries produce various reports based on the catalog as well as data description code for inclusion in application programs.

The data dictionary is an automated repository of all definitive information about an organization's data resources. This includes the key data elements that are used in conducting a business enterprise, generating standard names, mnemonics and sizes, and enforcing the use of these standards in all application programs. The data dictionary provides information about the meaning of data elements, system components, and machine configurations where they are located and used. The definitions in the dictionary are meaningful and useful to personnel who are engaged in the systems development life cycle, maintenance of computer systems, and the operational aspects of computer systems.

Documentation Role

Since the dictionary contains information that will be referenced often during the system development and operations personnel, it is crucial to keep these people's needs for information in mind when deciding on the quality and quantity of information that is entered into the dictionary. The data dictionary system should not be viewed as on-line storage of all system documentation; instead, the data dictionary should be viewed as the repository of key information that assists the users on the spot and provides a pointer to where additional information could be found.

For example, the information needed by the programmer trying to fix a software problem, in addition to a program source listing, includes the following:

- System specification
- System narrative
- System flowchart
- System data flow
- Program data flow

- Program narrative
- Program specification
- Edit and validation criteria for data items
- Where-used information about data items

The data dictionary provides much of this information, detailing definitions and relationships as well as general operation data.

Information Contained in the Data Dictionary

The data dictionary is a very useful tool within the data base approach. The dictionary contains all descriptive information needed in the data base environment: English-language name and description, COBOL name and picture, alias, source, and so on.

Hierarchical structures such as items within a record, records in a file, and so on, can be maintained in the dictionary so that file descriptions can be generated directly from the dictionary. This ensures that standard names and definitions are spread throughout the data processing environment. Thus the dictionary becomes a valuable point of reference when many people are involved in a large project using common data.

The dictionary also maintains cross-references. Almost any kind of relationship can be maintained in the dictionary; Figure 1–4 shows some of the relationships that exist in a typical dictionary. These cross-references allow the effects of a proposed change to be recognized before the change is made. The cross-reference capability also aids in the data base planning process. Key data items can be identified and their usage in various systems and programs can be portrayed in the dictionary. Data base planning can be carried out at the logical level and translated into physical data base structures, which can then be implemented directly from the dictionary.

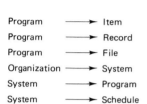

Figure 1–4 Relationships in a typical dictionary.

Queries That the Data Dictionary Can Answer

What are some of the queries that are likely to be directed against the data dictionary that one must be prepared to deal with? Here are some examples:

- What are the names by which a data item is known [i.e., its standard name, its colloquial name, its machine-readable name (COBOL), its name as it appears in report headings, etc.]?
- What is the definition of a data item (i.e., a narrative of useful information that would help the reader understand its meaning and usage and assist in formulating a strategy to incorporate its use)?
- What is the size of the data item (i.e., number of characters allowed or maximum value in terms of bytes of storage)?
- Who is the originator of the data item (i.e., the authoritative source of the data item in the organization and the keeper of the integrity of the values of the data item)?
- Where does this data item exist (i.e., reports, files, forms, screens, etc.)?
- What are the creation and validation rules for the data item (i.e., range of values, integrity checks with reference files, precedence conditions, machine code, etc.)?
- Which programs access a particular data item or file?
- Which programs use a particular subschema?
- Which programs run on a particular machine?
- What information is available about the subsystems, jobs, and programs that are part of a system?
- Which users receive a particular report?

Extensibility

The questions above addressed those entities (i.e., programs, reports, files, etc.) that are found in any MIS environment. The data dictionary allows the user to store data about entities that are important to the user's unique business need, above and beyond the MIS requirements. This is done by using the "extensibility" feature within the dictionary. This feature allows the user to define additional metadata entities, store information corresponding to these entities, and use the reporting capability of the dictionary to have queries answered.

The extensibility feature of the dictionary can be illustrated with the following example. Suppose that the installation wishes to store information about the responsibilities within the MIS department: who has responsibility for the various programs, the backup person in case of production problems, the qualifications of the individual, and so on. A representation of the model is shown in Figure 1-5. In this model the DEPT entity has one or many programmers (PGMR) and each programmer is responsible for many programs and has certain skills. In addition, the recursive arrow in the PGMR indicates the fact that each programmer could be related to other programmers to signify a backup in case the primary programmer is not available.

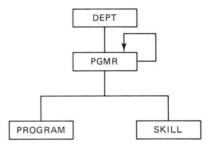

Figure 1-5 Extensibility model.

That these entities can be added to the dictionary, connected to existing entities such as PROGRAM, is a measure of the extensibility of the dictionary. Dictionary functions like the report generator will process the structure as has been defined by the dictionary administrator.

Data Dictionary Role in Information Management

In an information management context, the dictionary's central role is one of maintaining current information about the metadata, so that users can be directed to appropriate locations where actual occurrences of the data are stored. The inputs that go into making up the information content of the dictionary require the efforts of many persons in the organization; the benefits that result from a credible dictionary go beyond the MIS department where the dictionary generally resides.

Through the dictionary facilities, it is possible for end users to specify and obtain data from the company's production data systems, and perform the analyses to assist in decision making. The implementation of a dictionary is the first step toward an information management environment.

DATA DICTIONARY FUNCTIONS AND BENEFITS

The following is a list of data dictionary functions and their benefits.

- Summary documentation about systems
  - Quick look-up by maintenance personnel
  - Training new hires
  - Centralized summary documentation

- Relationships between program and data variables
  — Plan the impact of changes in data size, definition, etc.
  — Reduce the amount of redundancy as a result of using existing data items
  — Reduce development expenditures by using existing programs to obtain the data, if possible
- What information is where
  — Reduce time spent in searching for data about different entities
- Sources and users of data
  — Assign responsibility for data, thus enhancing integrity
  — Save time and avoid duplication of effort
- Edit and validation criteria
  — Ensure consistency of values in data items
  — Provide better intersystem communication because standard processing rules applied
  — Provide better control of data
- File and subschema definitions
  — Ensure consistency of presentation of file structures
  — Lead to standardization and centralized control of files by data base administration
- Interactive access to data dictionary
  — Leads to resolution of terminology conflicts
  — Identifies redundant entities
  — Settles issues regarding name, abbreviation, size, etc.
  — Results in consistency and control
- Jobs, programs, time and machine resource utilization
  — Is information that can be used for producing a schedule
  — Leads to better machine utilization

SUMMARY

Definition

The data dictionary is both a means and an end, a tool and a resource. While you are using it as a tool, you are creating a resource. As a tool, the dictionary allows you to document, organize, and control an organization's information resource. (Information resources include all manual and automated data, such as data elements, reports, screens, forms, etc., and all methods used for conveying information, such as programs, processes, machines, networks, transactions, etc.) It is a tool for people who need to know what the information processing resources of the organization are (typically, data processing resources such as programs, data bases, and application systems) and how these resources are used by different users. As a resource, the dictionary is an organized repository of information describing the source, use, edit criteria, control, user responsibility, and content of data within an organization.

Structure

The dictionary consists of the data base and an application system. The data base stores the organization's metadata, and the application system (set of programs and procedures) provides a user interface to this data base. In the remainder of this book, references to the dictionary will imply both the data base and the application system surrounding it.

Uses

The data dictionary is used in many ways.

- To document data, users, procedures, and how they interact with one another
- As a system development tool, it provides
  - Copy files for consistent presentation of data
  - Integrating force in systems development
- As a data administration tool for the control and integrity of data
- As a planning tool to predict the impact of changes
- As an inventory of resources to identify where information is located

Advantages

Many advantages are derived from using the data dictionary.

- Organization of data
  - Sources and uses
  - Relationships
  - Physical characteristics
  - Identification of users
  - Definition of "where kept"
- Flexibility
  - Site-specific definitions
  - Reporting flexibility
  - Synonyms
- Control of data
  - Naming conventions
  - Standardized processing
  - Operations scheduling
  - Data security
- Integrity of data
  - Standardized definitions
  - Assigned responsibility for data items
  - Standardized validation rules
- Systems development tool
- Basis for inquiry and analysis

Users

People and data are an organization's greatest assets. The dictionary enhances the productivity levels of both people and data in the organization.

Systems Developers.   For systems developers, the existence of a data dictionary facilitates the systems development process. Where there are multiple project teams working from common data bases, a data dictionary serves the purpose of ensuring that data standards are communicated throughout the organization and that these standards are incorporated into the file structures and programs that are being developed. The dictionary is a focal point for documentation about the systems, programs, and data files; it is the base of information that is needed for future enhancements and maintenance to the systems.

Systems Analysts. For systems analysts, the dictionary provides application design tools that make the data descriptions in the dictionary available to the application design process. It provides comprehensive documentation and reporting facilities for documenting all the system components and analyzing the same. This ensures that orderly system changes take place by providing facilities that encourage a systematic approach to the design and implementation of applications modifications.

Application Programmers. For application programmers, the dictionary reduces the programming effort throughout a system's development by eliminating errors caused by invalid data definitions. The dictionary accommodates program changes by providing multiple versions of data descriptions, thus minimizing the impact of making program enhancements.

Data Base Administrators. For data base administrators, the dictionary is the focal point of data element definition and control. The DBA can achieve this definition and control by using the dictionary facilities. These facilities help the DBA to do two things: (1) define and categorize information required for effective data base management, and (2) reduce data redundancy (by recognizing synonyms, extracting aliases and descriptors, and analyzing relationships between data and program usage.) The dictionary can automatically generate file copybooks from the descriptions contained in the dictionary data base.

Operations Staff. For operations staff, the dictionary reduces production failures by maintaining strict version and status control over "production" entities in the dictionary, and also allows operations to enforce their set of standards through the dictionary facilities.

Managers. For managers, the dictionary instills confidence that system changes can be managed without affecting current production operations, and that dictionary data can only be modified by personnel with the appropriate level of security privileges.

End Users. For end users who want to see the information about what data are available in the "production" files and make decisions about how to proceed based on it, the dictionary serves as a reference to the data that are available to satisfy their computational tasks. Thus end users do not have to be bothered with the problems of dissimilar file structures and inconsistent naming conventions that may exist in the various systems that are operational in the data center; they would specify their data extraction needs using standard naming conventions, and let the dictionary provide the translation mechanism to extract the data from the production data bases in the data center. Then they can iteratively analyze the data and come out with reports that meet their needs. If end users are to get the answers they need quickly, flexible tools must exist that allow them to perform queries against the dictionary, and the data bases tied into it, in a transparent manner.

chapter 2

Information Management and the Data Dictionary

INTRODUCTION

This chapter traces the evolution of information management, examines current trends, and explores future directions. As the data dictionary is very much a part of this evolution, its role will be highlighted throughout.

Specifically, this chapter addresses the following issues. The first topic, the evolution of shared data files, discusses the reasons for sharing data files, the economies of doing so, and the advantages to be derived from it.

The next topic is the evolution of data sensitivity, that is, the link between program design and data design. The point is made that those programs that are designed in conjunction with a good data model are more maintainable than those that are put together in an ad hoc fashion. Since most MIS departments spend over 70 percent of their resources on program maintenance, the transition from an applications-based environment to a data-based environment would considerably reduce this maintenance burden.

The third topic brings us to the trend that has grown rapidly over the last two decades: the data base approach. This approach has been facilitated not only by the availability of technology for data sharing but also by the recognition that if MIS is to benefit the entire organization, there has to be a planned approach to implementing systems.

The approach that many organizations have adopted is the business systems planning method (BSP), pioneered by IBM®. This is the fourth topic discussed. Typical outputs of this method, including data models and migration plans, are shown, and the role that the dictionary can play in documenting the results from the BSP is indicated.

The fifth topic deals with the applications systems development process. The discussion centers around how the plans and the data base approach mentioned earlier, together with the dictionary, work to produce application systems that are more effective than those developed by older techniques without the benefit of a dictionary.

The sixth topic outlines the benefits to be gained from documentation that is stored in the dictionary during the systems development life cycle to the MIS operations department. Included are sections on scheduling, auditability, and data security.

Finally, the dictionary's role in end-user computing is outlined.

WHAT IS INFORMATION MANAGEMENT?

Information management is an umbrella term that covers the areas of information systems planning, data administration, systems development, operations, and some aspects of end-user computing. The task of information management is to manage the processing of information within an organization. As this chapter traces the evolution of information management from an applications/program-centered environment to a data/information-asset environment, we witness the growing need for data control and management. We will also see how that data control is provided by a data dictionary.

Growth of Information Management

Information management has been forced to grow in order to accommodate two trends: (1) the scope of information management has enlarged to include more and varied users, and (2) the number and variety of tasks being automated is rapidly increasing. These two trends have brought to the forefront a growing need: the need for data control and management.

Growing Scope. The scope of information management traditionally has included the systems and data bases supported by MIS departments. The activities in a typical MIS environment that fall within the scope of information management are business systems planning, systems development, data base administration, and computer operations.

Recently, however, the increasing role of end users in creating and using systems has enlarged the scope of information management to include these systems. This end-user activity must now be considered within the scope of information management because they use many of the same data items that exist in MIS-based files and data bases. They use these as a baseline and then add processing which enables them to do many more things with the data and thus come up with specialized reports and graphs, as well as data bases which they maintain. The reports and graphs are used in making decisions which in turn affect the mainstream business processes. This flow of information is shown in Figure 2–1. With this enlarging scope and varied users,

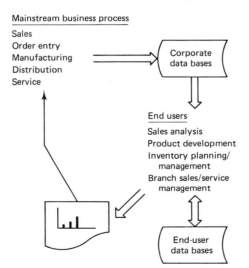

Mainstream business process

Sales
Order entry
Manufacturing
Distribution
Service

Corporate data bases

End users

Sales analysis
Product development
Inventory planning/
    management
Branch sales/service
    management

End-user data bases

Figure 2–1 Information flow between corporate data base and end-user data base.

"islands of automation" are built up that need to be linked to the mainstream business applications, to achieve synergy for the organization.

Growing Automation. In addition to the enlarged scope of information management, the pace of automation of many functions in today's businesses is increasing rapidly. In some cases, the procedures that were put in place to address an operational requirement included an automated system. A corollary to this is the fact that the subject of automation has crossed organizational boundaries and has redefined the scope of the business. In some cases, the decision to go into a particular mode of operation would depend on the availability of a system. For example, a company may choose to go into telephone support for answering customers' questions not only after ascertaining that adequate telephone facilities exist, but also after ensuring that a data base of technical symptom and solution information is available to respond to the customer as rapidly as possible.

Knowing that the forces of automation are necessary in various parts of the organization and that many of these automation projects are information driven, top management sooner or later comes to the conclusion that it would be better, from a business standpoint, to harness the forces of automation and manage projects from a strategic plan. Since data constitute the one thing that most of these automation projects share, data control and management becomes a critical issue.

EVOLUTION OF SHARED DATA FILES

Most MIS departments have evolved from a few application systems that serviced the accounting needs of the organization to serving the automation needs of a variety of users. Initially, MIS departments developed applications in response to user requests for automating certain aspects of their operations. The net result of this was that the systems and the underlying data structures did not conform to any well-laid-out architecture. Problems arose when systems had to talk to each other because the individual systems had been developed using different data element conventions. For example, Figure 2-2 shows two files that contain account number in a service organization: the general ledger file and the customer service file. In the general ledger file, the role of the account number would be to maintain the accuracy of accounting transactions. In the customer service file, the account number would be an alias for an organizational identifier under which service information could be logged. Although the name "account number" is the same and the values should be identical between the two files, the possibility exists that the account number could be set up differently in the customer file.

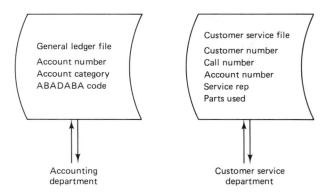

Figure 2-2   Files containing similar data elements.

Another important issue had to do with the concept of ownership of the data. It was assumed that the system that dealt with the data automatically owned the data. Thus, in many instances, the same data items would be duplicated in different systems with editing and validation rules that could vary within the organization. Then, when a user wanted a report based on data that went across system boundaries, the report contained data inconsistencies that had to be resolved. This led to a loss of credibility in the MIS data bases. The problem could have been avoided had the authoritative source of a data item been identified, and all other systems obtained that data item from a file that was maintained by this source. For example, in the example above, if the authoritative source for account number was defined as the accounting department, all the updates to that field in various files should be done through the accounting department. Thus the account number value in the customer service file could not be updated by the customer service department unless authorized to do so by the accounting department.

With the older concepts of system and file ownership, problems arose when a new person or group wanted to use those data in that file. This would have meant that the new user of that data item would have had to get the permission to use that data item from the authoritative source. To get around this organizational problem, data base administration functions were established whose role was to assume custody for all data and ensure that the proper data flows were taking place from one system to another in order to maintain data integrity. This had the additional benefit of systems sharing the data, thus reducing the development time.

EVOLUTION OF DATA SENSITIVITY

There is a change in the way business systems are being implemented and the recognition given to data design during the systems design activity. When systems are implemented, application generators based on an underlying data design are being used. Plans for the future are including the role of end-user computing, by shifting from what systems will do, to what data will be available.

The role and concerns of the systems designer began to shift in the early 1970s. The cause of the shift was the emergence of the view that the structure of a program design was largely determined by the data underlying the design. A sound data structure gives the program a good structure because this technique produced better systems based on maintenance experience with systems built before data design techniques were formalized as a method. Any programmer who has maintained a system developed by others can confirm that certain programs are often easier to maintain than others. It has been found that the easier-to-maintain programs typically followed the principle that the program structure resulted from the data structure. The implications that followed from this observation were that this was a formalization of what good designers do on an intuitive basis and that the technique was one that could be used in the future to produce other good designs.

If one agrees that data structure gives not only program structure, but can be used to define system structure, its implications are rather far-reaching. This suggests that not only do data structures tell what the program in a system should look like, but also what the system owning the program should look like and what its boundary to other systems should be. This observation has led to the emergence of a field alternatively called enterprise or systems architecture, information engineering, and strategic data planning.

All these disciplines have the same thread of defining a group of systems an organization should have based on an underlying data design which is developed for that organization. In terms of major steps, the following are typically defined:

1. *Establish organization data design.* The definition of the organization data design is based on an analysis of the external documents that flow through the organization. This technique of analysis is similar to the one described above but the analysis covers much more of the organization. The output is typically a rather large data model covering many applications. This data model is then used to define the application architecture. The definition is driven by a basic principle that data structure gives systems structure.

2. *Define application architecture.* If two applications have different underlying data designs, they are different systems. This means that the logic from one application can be reused in another application only if the underlying data structures are the same. Where identical data designs exist, both time and effort can be saved by identifying what the reusable components are and what applications would be appropriate to develop that use the reusable logic. Conversely, if one does not know the underlying data structure, the system structure is unknown. Although there are ways to circumvent this in that one can impose a system structure, the implication of this is that one also imposes a data structure and there is no guarantee that this data structure matches user requirements.

3. *Establish migration strategy.* A revision to the data model would appear to be necessary only when the organization undertakes a new business area. The application architecture that is derived from the data structure is where one would like to go. The reality of the situation is that typically this application architecture is ideal and that, in fact, one moves toward the ideal via a migration strategy. This migration strategy is a pragmatic document balancing such concerns as the status of present systems, the use of application software, and return on investment. Experience has indicated that the migration strategy is the key part of the organization architecture and the most demanding to develop.

DATA BASE APPROACH

Traditionally, application systems have typically been designed to satisfy specific, usually carefully defined output requirements (such as payroll, accounts payable, order entry, bill of materials, etc.). Each application was set up with its own input files with specific processing rules and generated its own set of data files. Hence the same data items resided in several files subject to different processing rules. This resulted in several versions of the same data, some of them inconsistent.

In addition, application systems have been developed for individual managers and departments, reflecting the organization structure and information requirements at a given point in time. They also reflected the individual styles and preferences of the managers and analysts who built them. Changes in organization, management philosophy, or style tend to have significant impact on application systems because they redefine information needs.

The data processing environment created by using the applications approach to developing computer systems results in data processing input, storage, and processing techniques geared to specific output needs. The applications approach implies that:

- Systems are built for individual managers, not for the company as a whole.
- Justifications for data processing services are based on cost trade-offs on an application-by-application basis rather than on company plans to improve overall efficiency or productivity.
- The data processing environment services managers who want computerization (i.e., it evolves along the path of least resistance subject to managers with budget dollars).
- The data processing department is viewed as a program development shop.

It is often easy to imagine that the data structure design for an application represents its ultimate content and usage. The analyst generally leaves spare characters (i.e., filler) in the record with the hope that these will accommodate the changes that will occur. Consequently, the analyst ties the data to a physical organization which is efficient for that particular structure. Time and again it has been proven wrong because the requirements changed in unforeseen ways. The data structures have to be modified, which in turn requires application programs to be rewritten and modified, which is an expensive process.

The data base approach, however, is characterized by the recognition by top levels of management that data are a corporate resource and must be subject to the same disciplines and controls as assets and labor. A data base is a repository of data, not information. Information can be generated from the stored data. A data base is the starting point from which information processes are constructed. The data base must provide sufficient breadth to permit an information system to weather the storms of change. The data which describe a company and its relationship to its environment would be independent of the organization of the company. The operational functions and the data necessary to support the operational functions are relatively stable. Only the information produced from the data base reflects the personality of management.

The data base approach has been facilitated by the advancement in file management technology. Concerns such as record locking, concurrent access control, handling of update conflicts, and transaction rollback and recovery, have been addressed by the file management system so that many different applications can access the same data base without fear of damaging the data integrity of the data.

The data base approach requires an architecture so the data bases will be able to serve a variety of applications through the use of common, shared data. Usually, this architecture consists of a systems-to-data flow diagram that maps the data bases and the various systems that need to access that data base, at a fairly high level. This architecture then becomes the target toward which data base access decisions are made as each application system comes up for implementation. Using common data implies that trade-offs must be made to ensure that performance requirements are met.

The data base environment that results from the adoption of the data base approach consists of the three structures:

1. *Data base input control systems.* The data base input control systems collect and manage input to data bases and ensure data quality and integrity. Input data validation against control or reference data files is an essential part of this function. The data base input control systems, once established, should not undergo many changes because they deal with relatively stable business functions.

2. *Data base output control systems.* The data base output control systems operate completely differently from the input control systems because they are subordinate to both organizational structure and management information requirements. In a properly developed data base, changes in output requirements should rarely cause changes in the data base input control system because the information required to satisfy 80 to 90 percent of management's decision-making needs is, in most companies, developed from combining, arranging, analyzing, sorting, and reporting a subset of between 400 and 800 basic data items.

3. *Data base storage and processing control systems.* The data base storage and processing control systems manage the operations (storage retrieval) within the data base and also include capabilities for backup, recovery, data availability, security, etc.

These three structures do not imply three sets of data bases; they represent three ways of structuring data bases. They may be optimized separately or together; the data base approach implies that these structures should be optimized together. This is where trade-offs occur. The data base and system designers must be aware of the variations in requirements as data are entered, processed, and output as information. The data base environment is the result of implementation of a data base plan that is in synchronization with the long-range needs of the business.

BUSINESS SYSTEMS PLANNING

Most of the systems that are developed within MIS are the systems that meet the needs of the operational level within the organization. For example, a service contract processing system would tend to emphasize the contract number and its attributes as central to the system, because the administrative aspect of the business is carried out based on contract number. These needs vary significantly from the type of information needed by the functional and general management levels within the organization. In many cases the data to support these different levels are aggregates or combinations of the data produced at the operational level. For example, the data required by the marketing department are generally based on aggregates of contracts based on customer type or equipment type. Figure 2–3 illustrates these data usage objectives.

Figure 2–3 Data usage objectives.

The operational level needs very specific information for daily activities. The management control level corresponds to the second line of management or higher, and is concerned with summary information, historical data, quarterly information, year-to-date data, and so on. Strategic planning is done at the upper levels of management and requires data to help with setting of long-range policy and company direction. When systems are usually developed without concern for overall requirements, it is difficult to share data for these multiple needs. To have a flexible information structure serve all system needs and levels of management, vertical and horizontal integration of data is necessary. Therefore, a process is necessary that serves to integrate the informational requirements into a cohesive framework. One example of such a process is the Business Systems Planning (BSP) process originated by IBM.

The BSP analysis requires that a company look at all its business needs. When these needs are identified as to specific information and system requirements, these requirements can be grouped into projects and the projects given priorities appropriate to the company's objectives. Implementation plans for these projects can then be developed. Analysis of business requirements produces an information architecture, which is a correspondence between classes of data and the business processes that use those data. Once the information requirements for a business are clear, applications can be developed that will properly support these requirements.

Thus BSP helps the company to clarify and understand all of its information requirements, current and future; understand the role of data processing support;

identify information structures and data models; establish priorities of implementation projects; and develop action plans for follow-on projects. BSP encompasses both a long-range plan for developing information systems, and a short-range plan for implementing a first system. The tasks involved in the BSP analysis include organizing, storing, manipulating, retrieving, and analyzing data.

Data Dictionary as a Base for Information Planning and Data Modeling

The part of the data dictionary that would be most useful for data modeling is the list of standard data item definitions that is maintained by the data base administrator. Additional entity types corresponding to logical groupings of data items, activities, processes, and functions can be created to assist in information planning and data modeling. The way in which these can be related in a typical data dictionary is shown in block diagram form in Figure 2–4.

For each function (i.e., production, marketing, etc.) a set of business process may be defined. Additionally, each business process has a set of specific business actions referred to as business activities which must be completed on a continuous basis in order to achieve the objectives of a process. Each of these activities require data entities in order to achieve the objectives of a process. Each of these activities requires data entities in order to be carried out successfully.

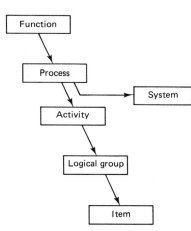

Figure 2–4 DD entities required to support information planning and data modeling. A *function* is the highest-level summary of action that must take place to perpetuate the business. A *process* is an ongoing set of related activities that support one of an organization's functions. An *activity* is a repetitive well-defined set of tasks or transactions usually completed according to a given schedule. A *logical group* of data items ties together the data that correspond to something that has separate and distinct existence.

Entity analysis is the process by which the data items can be grouped together to reflect the association (or strength of relationship) that exists between the data items. An assumption that is often made in entity analysis is that there is a natural hierarchy of relationships between data entities that can be identified.

Example

Business function:	Production
Business process:	Manufacturing product A
Activities:	Determine quantity
	Purchase raw materials
	Schedule production
	Determine product specifications
Entities:	Employee
	Supplier
	Inventory
	Contract
	Product

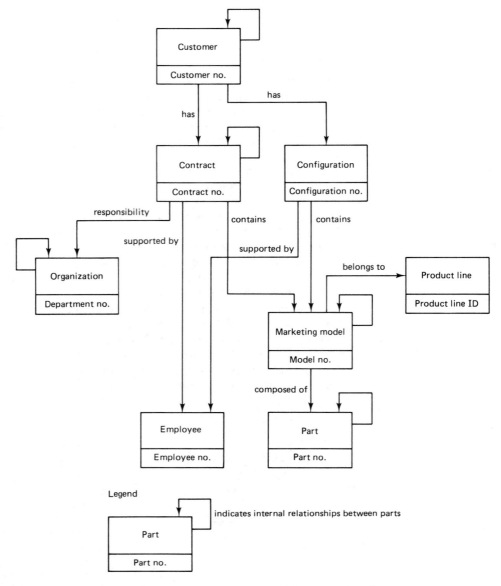

Figure 2-5 Data model for administrative data bases.

The end result of data modeling is to come up with the set of logical data structures needed to support the business requirements. The structures would be the basis on which the data base administrator will design and develop the actual data base definitions to meet the development schedule of different application systems. What the data model affords the DBA is an overall perspective and direction that would result in a stable set of data bases no matter which data structure or application was implemented first.

What is coming out of these systems architecture efforts, until recently, has been systems that tend to emphasize the data base orientation with coordinated use of shared data and planned redundancy of data when appropriate. More recently, with the emegence of the microcomputer, the efforts are beginning to emphasize the use of more distributed approaches with department machines to do local processing. The latter has occurred especially when the departments can be established to be autonomous in their actions. In this case since the processing on the department machines is based on the underlying data structure, it is feasible to define local data bases and initial communication requirements. This, in turn, can be used to do an initial sizing of the machine and communication approaches. From this, an economic assessment of the utility of the architecture can be established.

Examples of outputs from a typical BSP study are shown in Figures 2-5 through

Data Class	Customer	Product Line	Marketing Model
Responsible source	Credit department	Product marketing	Pricing, policies, and product marketing
Items	Number Name Addresses SIC Location code Tax jurisdiction D&B rating D&B number National account code Customer class Remit to code	Product line code Description Product line group Description	Number Description Rental prices Purchase price Maintenance price Transfer price License fees Extra use rate Sales availability Standard factory source Discount Retrofit charge Installation assistance fee Per student price Effective dates

Data Class	Order	Part
Responsible source	Sales/contract administrator	Producers and suppliers
Items	Order control number Agreement number Term Price protect period Rental escalation percentage Company sign date Customer sign date	Number Name Factory source Cost Tracking code Departure point Product class

Data Class	Employee	Organization
Responsible source	Personnel, personnel and commission administrators	Accounting
Items	Number Social security number Job code Status Hire date Job effective date Location Education level Job skills	Department number Name TWX code Distribution code

Figure 2-6 Data elements within data classes.

2-10. Figure 2-5 illustrates the data model. The data model represents hierarchical data relationships that occur in an organization structure or a bill of materials, as well as relationships between data that represent customer and contract. The main purpose behind the data model is to portray the important data interrelationships that exist in the business and need to be propagated throughout the systems and procedures that are implemented. The direction of the arrows between the data is significant; for example, the diagram indicates that a customer can have one or more contracts, whereas a contract can belong to only one customer.

Figure 2-6 represents the contents within the data classes in the data model discussed earlier. In addition to the listing of data items, a responsible source person and/or organization is identified. This is generally the department or function within the business that is held accountable for the creation of those data items in the business.

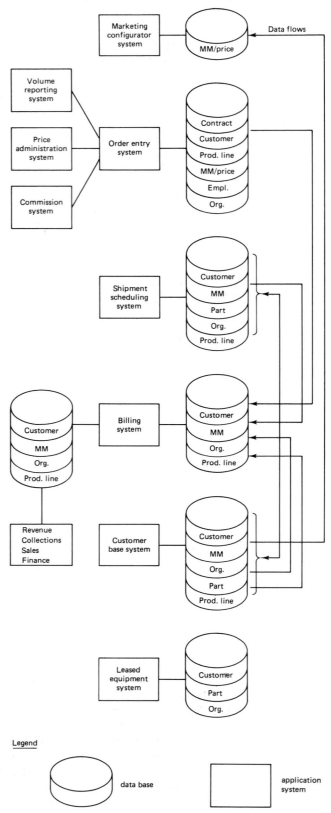

Figure 2-7   Migration strategy: I.

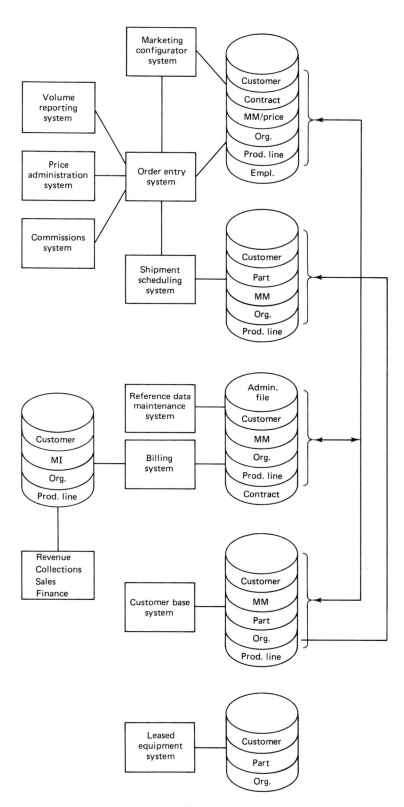

Figure 2–8 Migration strategy: II.

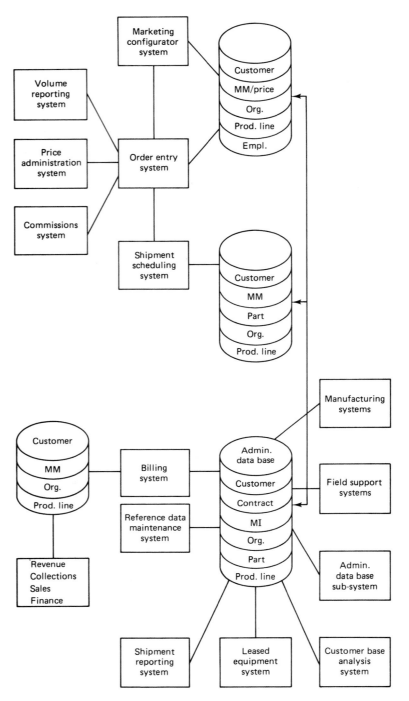

Figure 2-9 Migration strategy: III.

A migration strategy is depicted in the form of a series of system to data relationship charts. The first chart (Figure 2–7) represents the existing systems and data base environment. Note the occurrence of the same data in the application system data bases in the first chart. This indicates that there is considerable redundancy in the

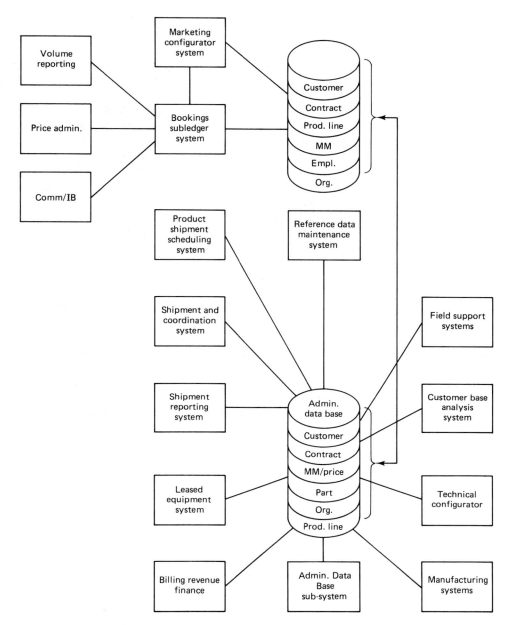

Figure 2–10 Migration strategy: IV.

current situation. The lines between data bases indicate the need for extra processing and controls that are needed to maintain consistency between the data bases.

The next three charts (Figures 2–8 through 2–10) depict the transition from a system environment consisting of independent data files to an integrated data base called "admin. file." Note that as more and more application systems are tied into one set of nonredundant data bases, a separate process for the maintenance of reference (or common) data needs to be established. In Figure 2–9, additional applications, such as producer shipment administration, can utilize the common data base instead of creating a new set of files.

SYSTEMS DEVELOPMENT, INFORMATION MANAGEMENT, AND THE DATA DICTIONARY

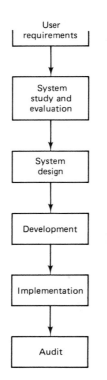

Figure 2–11 Phases of system development life cycle.

The development and operation of application systems in various aspects of the company's business is central to the process of information management, and the dictionary plays a key role in the systems development process, often referred to as the systems development life cycle (SDLC). Following is an outline of the SDLC process that highlights and identifies the role of the data base administrator (DBA), who usually provides the interface to the dictionary. System development can be divided into five main phases, with smaller divisions within each phase. On the following pages is a sample system development life cycle. Each phase and/or division contains details about who does the tasks, who participates, what resources are relied on, exactly what the tasks are, what the results will be, and the role of the data dictionary within this life cycle. The five main phases of the SDLC are: (1) system study and evaluation, (2) system design, (3) system development, (4) implementation, and (5) audit. Figure 2–11 shows the five phases in block diagram format.

1. System Study and Evaluation

The primary purpose of the system study and evaluation phase is to define the system from the business point of view and to have the system design approved by the relevant user organizations. The user of the system must be fully cognizant of the various features of the system and the implications of the system in the areas of user training, conversion to new procedures, and hardware and software requirements. In addition, this is the phase where a preliminary cut is taken at defining all the data items that the system will use, so that the DBA will begin to plan the logical structures and visualize the impact on existing files and data bases.

Scope Done by:

Analyst, user

Resource Documents:

System documentation
Project request
Existing documentation

Tasks:

Analyze needs and benefits.
Analyze current business practices.
Prepare proposed system overview, narratives, and diagrams.
Prepare cost/benefit analysis and evaluation.
Perform system evaluation.

Comment:

DBA consulted to determine impact of system on existing and proposed data bases. DBA notified of impact on other systems. DBA consulted to investigate similarities in utilization of data resources.

Outputs:

Finalized user-supplied requirements
Finalized project scope
Finalized information required
System performance criteria—ballpark (includes hardware proposal)
System overview—narrative and diagrams (conceptual design)

Sign-offs

System study and evaluation

Analyst has a written document defining the information the system should generate

Analyst creates a description of the proposed system and a schematic of the proposed system

Analyst creates a cost/benefit analysis for the proposed system, if required

User signs off and understands the system

2. System Design

The system design phase includes two activities: (a) data requirements and design and (b) program design. These two activities should proceed in close synchronization with each other, because changes in one could affect the other. For example, if a response-time requirement was set to close tolerances, an existing file may not be usable to get the desired response time. On the other hand, if the application requires that data be sourced from different parts of the organization, the time it would take to build these interfaces must be factored into the project schedule.

A. Data Requirements and Design

Done by:

Analyst, DBA

Resource Document:

System study, evaluation document

Tasks:

Define data flows.

Prepare data definitions for data dictionary.

Develop a list of the access paths needed.

Develop a generic diagram of new or revised data structure.

Review a data base design.

Develop a security plan.

Develop a backup and recovery plan.

Comment:

With the assistance of the data dictionary and the DBA, the programmer/analyst will develop a list of the data items. These data standard items and their narratives are added to the dictionary only after appropriate approvals have been obtained.

Outputs:

Preliminary file design

Logical data flow diagram

Standard data names

Understanding of information the system will use and generate

B. Program Design

Done by:

Analyst/programmer, user, DBA

Resource Documents:

Completed and approved system specifications

Programming standards

Finalized user-supplied requirements

Tasks:

Define input/output (screens, FDs, DB copybooks, files, etc.).

Prepare program narratives, specifications, and detailed test specifications.

Prepare development schedule and estimates.

Define user-prepared system acceptance criteria.

Outputs:

Program specifications—charts, narratives, etc.

Testing specifications

System acceptance criteria

3. Development

The purpose of the development phase is to build and test the components of the system as specified in the prior phases. Concurrent with the development should be the process of user training, building conversion interfaces and strategies, ensuring that the operations department is kept up to date about the new system and the additional processing loads being placed on existing files and machines. This will allow the operations department to schedule the impact of the new system and balance the load. The development phase consists of four parts: (a) data base preparation, (b) program preparation, (c) subsystem development, and (d) systems integration testing.

A. Data Base Preparation

Done by:

DBA, programmer/analyst

Resource Documents:

File design

Data base standards

Tasks:

Review data base design.

Analyze data items.

Finalize data base security/recovery.

Load/update data dictionary.

Create data base.

Test data base.

Create/alter copybooks, schema.

Outputs:

Finalized file design

Updated data dictionary

Test data base

Comment:

Any changes at this stage have to be approved by the managers concerned. Any new data items *must be completely entered* in the data dictionary.

B. Program Preparation

Done by:

Programmer/analyst

Resource Documents:

Program specifications
Testing specifications
Programming standards
Data base specifications

Tasks:

Prepare flowcharts.
Write code and incorporate data base error handling in *all* programs.
Prepare program test data.
Test program.

Outputs:

Error-free program
Program documentation
Dictionary updated with program narrative

C. Subsystem Development

Done by:

Programmer/analyst

Resource Documents:

System documentation
User-supplied requirements
Acceptance criteria
Operations standards

Tasks:

Prepare operations procedures.
Prepare subsystem test data.
Test subsystem.
Prepare user procedures.
Familiarize training staff.

Outputs:

Preliminary operations procedures
Preliminary user procedures
Error-free subsystems
Approved test results

D. Systems Integration Testing

Done by:

Programmer/analyst, DBA, operations

Resource Documents:

Preliminary operations and user procedures

System documentation
Preliminary implementation plan
Acceptance criteria

Tasks:

Perform system test.
Perform system review and acquire approval (includes standards).
Finalize operations and user procedures.
Start training users.
Finalize implementation plan.

Outputs:

Finalized operations and user procedures
Finalized implementation
Accepted system, including list of outstanding issues
Training material

4. Implementation

The implementation phase consists of two steps: (a) data base preparation and (b) beta or parallel test and implementation.

A. Data Base Preparation

Done by:

Programmer/analyst, DBA

Resource Documents:

Finalized implementation plan
Operations procedures
System specifications

Tasks:

Create data bases.
Expand existing data bases.
Load data bases.
Monitor performance.
Install data bases.
Perform capacity (load) tests.
Check data integrity.
Check security requirements.

Outputs:

Data bases are on appropriate machines.
Communication networks are in working condition.
System subsystem report is issued from data dictionary.

B. Beta or Parallel Test and Implementation

Done by:

Analyst, user, operations

Resource Documents:

Entire system documentation

Tasks:

Install system.

Train users.

Test system.

Review and approve results.

Implement.

Outputs:

Approval to implement

Completed system

Completed procedures

5. Audit

System Evaluation Done by:

Analyst, user

Resource Documents:

Entire system documentation

System processing results

Tasks:

Evaluate user satisfaction.

Evaluate performance.

Evaluate security.

Evaluate control.

Evaluate backup and recovery.

Outputs:

Evaluation report with recommendations

COMPUTER OPERATIONS ROLE WITHIN INFORMATION MANAGEMENT

Scheduling Resources for Computer Operations

The data dictionary assists with computer operations management because it provides a comprehensive view of the information map of the organization and gives a detailed operational view of the systems that are running in the various computers. User needs are communicated to the analysts and programming, then turned over to the operations staff to be processed according to cyclical schedules.

In an integrated data base environment, where many application systems may access the same data bases, the interdependencies between various procedures become quite complex. These interdependencies can be portrayed in the data dictionary and the information made available to the operations staff in an on-line mode. The uses of a data dictionary in a basic production environment are outlined below.

1. Recovery Procedures. The data dictionary is especially useful in planning a recovery from a condition not previously experienced or evaluated. It can also be helpful when establishing contingency procedures for recovery from any number of unusual failures, thus saving precious time when such a failure occurs. The data dictionary is a point of reference to operations personnel in the following DBMS-oriented procedures:

1. Taking a data base save or unload
2. Recording the log tape identification
3. Starting the TPMS system
4. Recovering the systems from various failures
5. Bringing the TPMS system down gracefully

2. Scheduling Normal Operations. The major objective of any operations facility is to meet the information requirements of the enterprise. Information about the different steps in a system, such as frequency, required time, and accuracy, is contained in the data dictionary. This information can then be used as a basis for scheduling systems and determining the impact of new systems on an existing schedule. In addition to information about a system's anticipated run times, input of actual run times into the data dictionary would complete the evaluation loop and enable the operations staff to monitor the performance of systems and machine configurations.

3. Resource Utilization. In general, most operations departments have to utilize scarce resources to provide a high level of service and to optimize the hardware and software available. This can be done better if the mix of jobs to be executed, and the processing resources the jobs will need, are identified. Processing resources include CPU, memory, I/O rates, tape media, disk media, hard-copy media, laser, microfiche, files, records, and data. Using information about the current environment, the operations and data base administration staffs will be able to reduce contention, route output correctly, assess the desirability of file reorganization and schedule such reorganization to maintain a smooth production environment.

Auditability Controls

In a transaction-oriented DBMS environment, the auditor faces the unique problem of having to assess the impact of each transaction on the data base itself. Specifically, the DD can provide complete and accurate information relating transaction programs to records and data items. Using the information above, the auditor can understand exactly how each transaction enters the data base and how it traverses from one record type to another. This allows proper evaluation of the degree to which controls are necessary during the transaction processing. The DD functions that assist the auditor are:

- Documentation of data and systems, including recovery procedures
- Audit trail from where-used information; insurance that the data can be traced backward and forward through the entire data base update or downdate functions
- Control through generation of file descriptions and the inherent facility for change control procedures
- Access control information that can be stored in the DD and actively used at program execution
- Usage statistics, including programs that can access the data base, response statistics, and size statistics, that can be used to control the data base

Data Security

The data dictionary is the centralized respository of information relating to the machines, systems, programs, and data files in the company. Within the data dictionary will exist the information about the sources and users of data at the data item level. This will be the basis on which users will be assigned access permissions to use the programs through which they can access the file and data. Thus the data dictionary serves as a source of verification of access at the data item level.

The data dictionary contains the relationships between the data item, file, program, and machine. The entities called *item, file, program,* and *machine* are relevant to the security program. The data dictionary must be fully populated for those data items for which a security program must be established. This means that if there is to be an assurance that a certain data item is to be protected, the existence of that data item in all the files must be identified and cataloged in the data dictionary. It is then possible to produce a list of all the files and thus the programs and machines at which access controls must be established. Thus it is possible to ensure that the appropriate levels of access controls are in place to provide a certain level of security assurance.

END-USER COMPUTING IMPETUS

As more and more computer applications are demanded by the organization, the MIS department has not been able to keep up with the task of providing these applications. Meanwhile, the improvements in the hardware and software tools have made it possible for nontechnical users to be trained successfully to process much of their information. Microcomputers allow users to set up their own stand-alone applications instead of waiting in the MIS queue. In many cases these applications are based on data extracted from production data files. Thus it is becoming apparent that company-wide projects are in the domain of the MIS department, whereas departmental or individual computing applications are becoming the responsibility of end users (Figure 2–12).

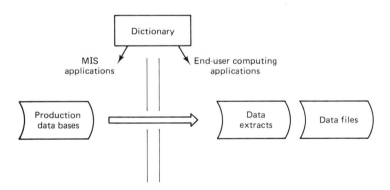

Figure 2–12 Dictionary role in end-user computing.

The result of this tremendous surge in popularity of end-user computing is that there is the potential for the creation of an increasing number of data files at the individual level and the departmental level. This is not necessarily bad provided that these files are used only within the department or for the individual. When the data are commonly used across many departments, and the reports from these files cross organizational boundaries, problems arise because of inconsistencies in the definition and usage of data.

As a starting point, the proper definition of the data that are provided the end user from the "production" data bases must have standard definitions that clearly specify the meaning, derivation, and use of the data item. In fact, if that definition is carried over onto the application development or application processing system that the end user is using, the end user will be spared the rather arduous task of having to redefine each of the data items to his or her individual development and processing workstation, and can, instead, spend time on solving the business problem at hand. This is where the dictionary, with its capability to link to application development systems on other machines, comes in.

chapter 3

Data Dictionary
Concepts

INTRODUCTION

This chapter begins by tracing the evolution of dictionaries from being appendages of DBMS systems to their larger role in supporting the MIS systems development, DBA, and operations functions. The dictionary's role as a repository of metadata, and as a tool in an information management environment, are treated as separate topics in this chapter, although the metadata comprise the basis on which the dictionary functions as a tool. A brief introduction to dictionary terminology, such as entity, attribute, and relationship, is given, to set the stage for explaining the ways in which metadata are organized in the dictionary. The nature of the metadata generation process is explained via an application example. Then, examples of other kinds of metadata, such as data standards, and the reports that can be obtained by organizing the metadata in certain ways are described.

The role of the dictionary as a tool is shown via its relationship to other components in a computer system. The inputs and outputs, as well as the relationships between these and components such as compilers, report generators, and file mechanisms are discussed. This leads to a discussion of active dictionaries and what makes one dictionary more active than others. In this context a discussion of the merits of active versus passive dictionaries is brought up. This leads to a discussion of fourth-generation language (4GL) technology and the use of the DD as a key component for controlling and documenting the 4GL application development process.

The final section of this chapter discusses the data dictionary in a distributed computing environment, and the issues that have to be addressed. This leads to the question of global dictionaries. With the increasing use of data dictionaries within 4GL software packages, there is a danger of proliferating several different types of dictionaries in the organization. A strategy to link these dictionaries within an overall framework is suggested.

EVOLUTION OF DICTIONARIES

The generic data dictionary evolved out of the growth in data-based systems in those data processing environments where several systems needed to access common files of data. As the complexity of these systems grew, it became clear that a mechanism was needed that would keep track of the data and the interactions between the programs and the data. Because of the number of programs that interacted with certain files, any change in the file structure could be made only after careful analysis of the impact on all the systems that used that file.

Since edit validation rules were coded by the application system programmer, it was possible that two programmers could have a different perception about the edit criteria and hence go about it in different ways. To prevent this situation from happening, edit validation criteria were included as part of the standard definition of the data item, so that different programs accessing the same data item would follow a consistent editing rule.

Generic data dictionaries were developed as an adjunct to data base management systems (DBMSs). These dictionaries addressed the issue of maintenance and generation of file structures, with less emphasis placed on the dictionary as a tool in the system development and maintenance process, let alone the use of the dictionary in the end-user computing environment.

Let's elaborate on the system development aspect first. As more and more business processes get automated over time, it is clear that the process of automation has followed the whims of individuals in the organization who wanted and could afford automated systems. Data bases were generally considered the preserve of the person sponsoring the particular project. As so often happens in such cases, data structures were subordinated to the application instead of being designed in conjunction with a longer-term perspective in mind. This led to inconsistencies and redundancies within the file structures of the organization, with the result that the integrity of the data was in question.

As the scope and level of the business expand, the application demands on the information system should be met without costly restructuring of the data base. This is possible only if the data structures have been planned in such a way that they can accommodate the changes in application requirements over time. Therefore, one of the key outputs from the planning process is a definition of the normalized data structures that would service the business need in the longer term.

The process of deriving these data structures has been dealt with in many books. However, whether one takes the top-down approach or the bottom-up approach, a starting point has to be established for the analysis and planning process.

Generally, most people feel more comfortable talking about the future in terms of the present; that is, they use the terminology that is in use currently. This imposes the need for a glossary of system and data definitions that are commonly accepted by both the user community and the MIS department; note that we used the words "commonly accepted" rather than "accurate"—what is important is that there be agreement on the name of a data item and its associated definition. Bear in mind that a particular standard data item name should be associated with only one definition.

The data dictionary is the logical place to store and maintain the standard data definitions. For the planner and systems architect, this information would be the building blocks on which models of logical groups of data items are combined. In building these models and gaining commitment to the models from users, the existence of common definitions across the entire model gives the users the confidence that they are dealing with the same basic concepts with which their counterparts in another group are dealing. This reduces the potential resistance of people who feel that contributing to a corporate-wide effort is like trying to deal with the Tower of Babel.

During the system development process, the role of the dictionary is easily identified. The dictionary is a resource of information about current systems and data bases that will assist the analyst and designer in ensuring that system projects are built on the foundation of existing systems, and integrate into an overall architecture, rather than exist in a world of their own. File definitions have to conform to dictionary conventions; this also applies to screens and reports.

During the system development process, much information is generated that could be of use to future development activity. The dictionary is a good place to store these vital bits and pieces of information that the analyst gathers and may even consider trivial. Thus the dictionary is expanded to include system and subsystem narratives that are continuously updated during the system development process. Discretion needs to be used in determining the amount of narrative that should be included in the dictionary; this should be based on three factors:

1. Weigh the usefulness of the information to future users and MIS personnel.
2. Consider the amount of material that can be kept up to date and with relative ease.
3. Enter summaries of documents rather than entire texts of material so as to optimize the use of disk space. Descriptions should be ample but not lengthy; for example, 5 to 20 lines for an item, 10 to 50 lines for a program, and 25 to 50 lines for a system are recommended for typical situations.

The dictionary's use during the system operation and maintenance phases have not been seriously dealt with in the literature; this may be due to the fact that dictionaries are thought of in terms of assisting only in the system design and development phases. Most MIS departments spend the major portion of their time on maintenance and enhancements of current systems. The dictionary is easily justified as a tool that reduces the maintenance burden if it is viewed and used as a repository of up-to-date information about the system. The person doing the maintenance work would use the information about the system/program/data relationships that are stored in the dictionary, as well as operational data pertaining to recovery procedures, to identify and resolve a problem.

A major problem with implementing dictionaries is that for a dictionary to be viewed as useful, it must initially be populated with accurate data and then kept up to date with new information. Unless all the current systems are put into the dictionary, systems developers will not realize one of the major features of the dictionary, namely, the capability to do where-used analysis. Where-used analysis refers to the answering of such questions as "What programs use this data item?" or, alternatively, "What are the common data items used by two or more systems?" This permits the analyst to assess the impact of changing the size of a data item on all the programs and systems affected by that data item.

A feature of the MIS environment that has been changing over the years is that they utilize hardware and software from multiple vendors. A multitude of file structures are in use. The dictionary is able to handle structures that occur in the mainframe machines as well as those that occur in the minicomputers and microprocessors. The dictionary that can handle multiple structures and can adapt to new structures will be in demand because it will bridge the technical gaps between different vendors and allow the MIS manager the flexibility to specify equipment from different vendors.

The commitment to an information management environment requires the dedication of considerable resources to populate and maintain the dictionary, and it is natural that users would expect the dictionary to handle newer technologies without major efforts on the part of the users. Therefore, one of the criteria for selection of the dictionary must be whether it will interface with other technology-based dictionaries.

METADATA

Metadata Terminology

The information that goes into the dictionary is divided into broad categories to facilitate the storage and retrieval of the information. Examples of broad categories are programs, data items, records, files, and so on. These broad categories are referred to as entities.

Entities are recorded into the dictionary by means of a key, so that they can be directly accessed using that key. There are other names and aliases by which that entity may be known. These are referred to as access keys, because they are alternative methods of accessing the entity, and they provide a means of collecting entities together that happen to have a common access key.

Several descriptive as well as identifying pieces of information are connected with an entity. Textual narrative as well as graphics are used to describe the entity; edit rules for a data item entity consist of lines of program code; legitimate values for a data item would be specified as a table of values. The above are instances of descriptors that are called attributes of an entity.

Entities are related to other entities in the real world; these relationships are portrayed in the dictionary in terms of cross-references or relationships. It is also possible to describe the type of relationship that exists between these entities so that reports from the dictionary are more readable. For example, it is easier to read "Contract maintenance program 'produces' customer edit report" than "Contract maintenance program 'is related to' customer edit report."

Metadata Example

The dictionary contains different kinds of information about data, and this was referred to as the metadata. We will explain the creation, update, and use of the metadata via an example of the use to which the metadata are put. We start with data item definition. Let's say that the manager of the contracts administration department is interested in doing an analysis of the contract revenue by type of customer in a contractual service type of business. The following may be data items in which the manager is interested:

- *Contract number:* the number of the contract that was assigned the customer. This data item will be six characters long, the first character always being alphabetic and the other five being numeric. The data item will be created by the contracts administration.
- *Customer type:* the type of customer according to the following category:

  AC commercial
  AG government
  AE education

- *Contract revenue:* the amount in dollars per month of payments made by the customer for contractual service.
- *Customer name:* the name of a customer, up to 15 characters long.

In the example above, the manager is faced with the fact that he or she can only report by the customer classification that is available in the data file above. However, if the manager wanted data on customers by some other classification, such as amount of sales for that customer in millions of dollars, that would be a different criterion.

Once the manager has defined the data items that are of interest, the next step is to group these together in a logical fashion by defining a record. A record could be thought of as a grouping of data items that tie together based on a single key.

In the example above we could create a record called "contract revenue record" which would consist of four data items: contract number (key), customer type, contract revenue, and customer name. The contract revenue record may be defined as a record that contains information about the type of customer and that customer's contract revenue based on contract number.

Most major file management systems work on the concept of groupings of data items. There may be hundreds of contracts that would have to be held for further analysis. The record occurrences are generally held in files. Thus we could define a file for these data and call it "contract revenue file." Its definition would run as follows: The "contract revenue file" contains the "contract revenue records." Further details about the file may include the fact that it is organized in a sequential format; that is, one record follows the other. An example of actual data is shown in tabular format in Figure 3–1. Thus the data values can be understood completely if the definitions of the file, record, and data item were documented in the dictionary. The description of the data element layout is often called a format. A format for the record in Figure 3–1 is shown in Figure 3–2.

In addition to defining the data items and grouping them together, let's say that the manager wrote a sort program to produce a report that consisted of total revenues by customer type. Then there would be two more things that could be entered into the dictionary: the description of the sort program, and the description of the report. The sort program, whose name could be "contracts revenue analysis program," could have the following definition: This program sorts the data in the contracts revenue file by customer type and calculates the subtotals for each revenue category.

The program listing shown in Figure 3–3 comprises the programs that acted on the data file. The report called "contract revenue by customer type" could read: "This report is a report of the revenue by customer type and is produced on demand

Record	Contract	Type	Revenue	Customer name
1	A51245	AG	543.00	Contra Costa
2	A34122	AC	765.00	Sperry Corp
3	A23423	AC	345.00	U.S. Steel
4	A33452	AC	345.00	Texas Instr
5	A23345	AC	367.00	Delta Airl
6	A33455	AG	236.00	Comm Mass
7	A23365	AE	543.00	Wayland Sch
8	A33467	AE	533.00	Norfolk Cnty

Figure 3–1 Example of data values in contract file.

```
start_format      con_rev_rpt
contract number   1        8
customer type     9        16
contract revenue           17       22
customer name     25       37
end_format
```

Figure 3–2 Format description for contract file.

```
sort/o/c=con_rev_pgm

CON_REV_PGM
input file is "contract_revenue_file".
output report is "contract_rpt", rformat is "con_rev_rpt"
from file "con_rev.rforms".
key 9/10.
pad to 80 characters with " ".
replace tabs in 1/last with " ".
sort.
end.

CON_REV.RFORMS
start_report      con_rev_rpt
qformat  con_rev_rpt
lin/pg   54
col/lin  80
header   4      c              "TYLER SERVICE COMPANY"
header   6      c              "Contract Revenue Report"
header   6      66             DATE
header   7      36             PAGE
header   9      8              "Customer"
header   9      24             "Contract Number"
header   9      46             "Contract Revenue per month"
break    customer type         pre_break_space
break    customer type         post_break_space
break    customer type         post_break_space
detail   1      6              customer name
detail   1      26             contract number
detail   1      47             contract revenue
break    customer type         4        "Contract Revenue Subtotal
for"
break    customer type         38       customer type
break    customer type         47 .     "="
break    customer type         52       total (contract revenue)
total    1      8              "Contract Revenue Total "
total    1      47             "="
total    1      52             total (contract revenue)
end_report
```

Figure 3–3   Contract revenue analysis program listing.

```
                        TYLER SERVICE COMPANY

                      Contract Revenue Report            05/11/86
                            PAGE    1


         Customer            Contract Number       Contract Revenue per month

         Delta Airl          A23345                367.00
         Sperry Corp         A34122                765.00
         U.S. Steel          A23423                345.00
         Texas Instr         A33452                345.00
         Contract Revenue Subtotal for        AC         =         1822.00

         Norfolk Cnty        A33467                533.00
         Wayland Sch         A23365                543.00
         Contract Revenue Subtotal for        AE         =         1076.00

         Contra Costa        A51245                543.00
         Comm Mass           A33455                236.00
         Contract Revenue Subtotal for        AG         =          779.00


         Contract Revenue Total                          =         3677.00
```

Figure 3–4   Contract revenue report.

by executing the contracts revenue analysis program." A sample page from this report is shown in Figure 3–4.

Entity Relationships

Now that we have developed information about several metadata entities, such as file, program, and report, it is possible to portray some relationships between these. The use for the relationships is twofold:

1. It makes it possible to query the dictionary in several different ways and obtain all related information about an entity quickly.
2. If one of the entities were to change, it would be possible to identify quickly all related entities that would be affected, so that changes could be made consistently.

Figures 3–5 and 3–6 show how the metadata entities can be linked together to provide meaningful information in a typical dictionary.

Relationship Notation. If we wrote on paper the information about the data items, records, files, programs, reports, and so on, and then continued to collect and store this type of information, we would indeed have a crude dictionary. However, to analyze this information, we would have to look through a lot of informa-

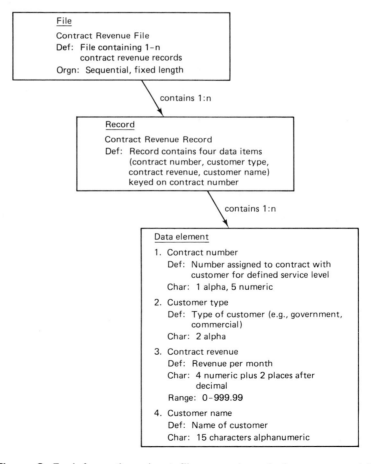

Figure 3–5 Information about file, record, and element stored in dictionary.

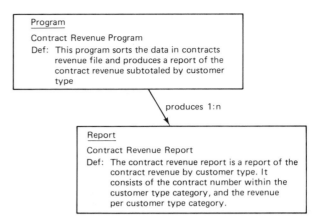

Figure 3–6 Information about program and report stored in dictionary.

tion, which would be very time consuming. If these pieces of data were to be organized and stored so that they could be retrieved easily, we would have the makings of a modern-day dictionary.

In the description of the file we put in the name of the record, and in the description of the report we stated which program produced that report. If we created the dictionary with the capability of storing a pointer from one piece of data to another, we do not have to store the data in the description but could store the data outside the description, such analysis would be easier to do. As more and more data were put into the dictionary, the cross-references or pointers would become important in their own right in quickly answering "what-if" questions.

From our example, some relationships are obvious. The data items Contract Number, Customer Type, Contract Revenue, and Customer are part of the contract revenue record. Conversely, the contract revenue record entity can be thought of as owning the individual data items. Therefore, a cross-reference between the record entity and the data item entities seem appropriate. It is possible that the data item Contract Number could also exist in a different record in a different file. Thus, using the dictionary, it would be possible to answer easily the question "List the records in which Contract Number exists" This sort of question could arise in a situation where a decision has to be made to increase the size of the contract number item. Using a similar logic, the program entity is related to the report entity in a parent–child relationship (i.e., the program produces the report).

One other relationship that is worth considering is the relationship between program and record. This relationship would be useful in answering the what-if question that was asked earlier: List all the programs that would be affected by a change in the contract number item. This gives an idea of the extent of changes to programs caused by changes in a data item. These relationships are shown in diagrammatic form in Figure 3–7.

In order to give you another way to visualize the relationships stored in the dictionary, think of two sets of card indexes that contain information about entities

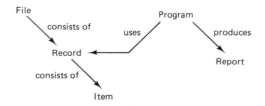

Figure 3–7 Entity relationships for example.

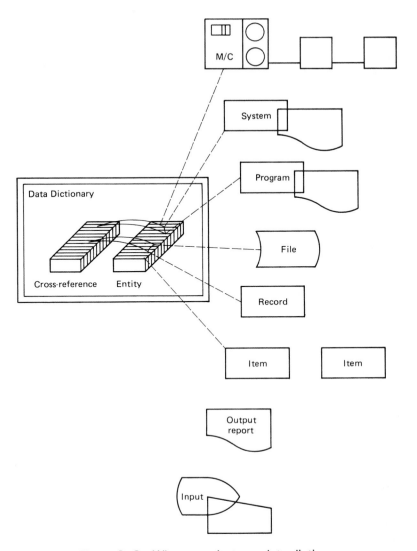

Figure 3-8 What constitutes a data dictionary.

(called ''entity''), and cross-references between entities (called ''cross-references'').
The entity card index contains information about entities, whereas the cross-reference
card index contains information about the contents of the entity card index. This
is illustrated in Figure 3-8.

Entity Reporting

If the data were to be organized in a way that permits flexibility in reporting, there
must be flexibility in the organization of the dictionary itself. From this it follows
that any combination of entities and the cross-references between them ought to be
supported by the dictionary in order to satisfy user needs. An example of a set of
entities from a customer dispatch system is shown in Figures 3-9 through 3-12. The
structure of this report is as follows:

```
Central Dispatch System              (system entity)
   CDS_WEEKLY_ACTIVITY.CLI           (job entity)
      CDS0802P.CO                    (program entity)
         CDS0802.R6                  (report entity)
```
Figure 3-13 is a page from the actual report CDS0806.R1.

DATE: 7/17/88   DATA DICTIONARY SYSTEM   PAGE: 1
                                 SYSTEM/SUBSYSTEM REPORT

CDS (SYSTEM)

NARRATIVE

CDS stands for Central Dispatch System. This system was designed to support field personnel in their daily service activities.
The system provides centralized and consistent processing of customer service requests which increases service efficiency and customer satisfaction. It also includes monitoring and reporting capabilities which provides management with better planning and assessment tools.

Field activity collection was added to enable field management to collect more accurate and timely data on field service activity. Therefore, enhancing reporting capabilities.

Keys

ALIAS	: CENTRAL DISPATCH SYSTEM
	: DISPATCH SYSTEM
KEYWORD IN CONTEXT (KWIC)	: DISPATCH
	: SYSTEM
	: CENTRAL

Figure 3–9

DATE: 7/17/88   DICTIONARY SYSTEM   PAGE: 2
                                 SYSTEM/SUBSYSTEM REPORT

CDS_WEEKLY_ACTIVITY. CLI (JOB/MACRO)

NARRATIVE

THIS MACRO BATCHES THE PROGRAM CDS0802P – WHICH CREATES THE WEEKLY ACTIVITY (WAS) REPORTS.

Keys

ALIAS	: CDS_WEEKLY_ACTIVITY. CLI
KEYWORD IN CONTEXT (KWIC)	: CDS
	: WEEKLY
	: CDS0802P
	: WAS

Figure 3–10

DATE: 7/17/88   DICTIONARY SYSTEM   PAGE: 3
                                 SYSTEM/SUBSYSTEM REPORT

CDS0802P.CO (PROGRAM)

NARRATIVE

CDS0802P IS CALLED FROM CDS_WEEKLY_ACTIVITY.CLI. THIS IS A WEEKLY JOB WHICH CREATES THE WEEKLY ACTIVITY SUMMARY (WAS) REPORTS. THESE REPORTS CONTAIN ALL THE CALL ACTIVITY INFORMATION THAT TOOK PLACE THE PREVIOUS WEEK.
SIX REPORTS ARE CREATED. CDS0802.R6 – ACTIVITY BY AREA. CDS0802.R5 – ACTIVITY BY REGION. CDS0802.R4 – ACTIVITY BY BRANCH. CDS0802.R3 – ACTIVITY BY OFFICE.
CDS0802.R2 – ACTIVITY BY TEAM. CDS0802.R1 – ACTIVITY BY F.E.

Keys

ALIAS	: CDS0802P.CO
KEYWORD IN CONTEXT (KWIC)	: CDS
	: WEEKLY ACTIVITY REPORT
	: CDS0802

Figure 3–11

DATE: 7/17/88   DICTIONARY SYSTEM   PAGE: 4

SYSTEM/SUBSYSTEM REPORT

CDS0802.R1 (REPORT)

NARRATIVE

WEEKLY ACTIVITY SUMMARY REPORT: Provides Branch, Region and Area Managers with information to analyze the performance of their areas of responsibility during the preceeding week.

Calls on a system are as follows: Beginning Calls: Calls still open from previous week
New Calls Requested: Calls received from beginning of week to end
Calls Closed: Calls closed from beginning of week to end
Ending Calls: Calls still open as of week ending date

Keys
ALIAS   : CDS0802.R1
KEYWORD IN CONTEXT (KWIC)   : CDS
                                       : CDS0802.R1
                                       : WEEKLY
                                       : SUMMARY
                                       : REPORT

Figure 3–12

RPT#: CDS0806.R1   CENTRAL DISPATCH SYSTEM   11/10/88   08:38
NAME: WEEKLY ACTIVITY SUMMARY   4888-2141-3052   PAGE: 7
      WEEK BEGINNING 10/17/   WEEK ENDING 10/23

32252   PAUL BANKER

CALL ACTIVITY	TOTAL	IMMEDIATE	DEFERRED	SCHEDULED (PM)	SCHEDULED (OTHER)
BEGINNING CALLS	3	0	0	3	0
NEW CALLS RECEIVED	6	6	0	0	0
FS INITIATED CALLS	0	0	0	0	0
CLOSED CALLS					
CANCELED	0	0	0	0	0
PHONE FIX	0	0	0	0	0
SITE FIX	8	5	0	3	0
ENDING CALLS	1	1	0	0	0
FOLLOW-UP CALLS (CB)	0	0	0	0	0
RESPONSE TIME		1.4	0.0	6.4	0.0
(SITE FIX ONLY)		0.0	0.0	0.0	0.0
CONTRACT CALLS	8				
T&M CALLS	0				
CALLS WITH NO OS TIME	1				

WORK LOAD/PRODUCTIVITY   TERRITORY MANAGEMENT

(USEFUL ONLY FOR CURRENT WEEK)

NUMBER CONTRACT CUSTOMERS	16	TOTAL CALLS IN TERRITORY	8
NUMBER T&M CUSTOMERS	1	CLOSED OUTSIDE TERRITORY	0
AVAILABLE DAYS	1.0	CLOSED BY ASSIGNED FE	7
CLOSED CALLS/AVAILABLE DAYS	8.0	CLOSED BY OTHER FE	1

ALERT STATUS

PAGE ALERTS	0	ACTIVE ALERTS LEVELS 4	1
RESPONSE ALERTS	0	ACTIVE ALERTS LEVELS 3	0
WAITING PARTS ALERT – 3	0	ACTIVE ALERTS LEVELS 2	0
WAITING PARTS ALERT – 2	0	ACTIVE ALERTS LEVELS 1	0
WAITING PARTS ALERT – 1	0		

Figure 3–13   Sample page from the report CDS0806.R1.

Data Elements

Figures 3–14 and 3–15 contain information about a data item that is stored in a typical dictionary. While browsing through these, note the different kinds of descriptive information that can be stored on a data item, and try to mentally formulate queries against a set of these data items via the descriptors.

Components of Elements. In these examples of data items, there was a lot of specific information pertaining to the actual use of the data item in various files and application systems, and the source of the data item. This kind of information makes the dictionary very useful to the person who may be familiar with one application and now can get a broader picture of the source and use of the data item. One of the questions that the dictionary administrator would have to face is: How much information is enough? After all, the information may have to be pieced together from many different sources, and this takes a lot of time and effort. But once the process gets going, it is not as difficult as it seems. If the dictionary has an entry screen that has been tailored to collecting this information, the end users would be able to fill in most of this information, and the project manager would have to go to the MIS department only for system-related information.

General Ledger Account Number

Description

The general ledger account number is a composite number, containing the ledger designation, ledger account number, sub-account number, and a department or sub-sub-account number.

Applications Affected

Factory accounting systems
Personnel accounting systems
General accounting systems
Accounts payable

Data Format

The general ledger account number consists of a 14-character alphanumeric field; described as follows:

Ledger number	2N
General ledger account number	4N*
Sub-account number	4AN
Department number or sub-sub-account number	4AN

*First character must be numeric; last three may be alphanumeric.

COBOL Name

GEN-LED-ACCT-NO

Data Origination and Change

Accounting operations staff is responsible for this data item.

Data Hierarchy Requirement

Control File

Chart of accounts

Reference Documentation

None

Figure 3–14 General ledger account number data item.

Dun's Number

Description

The Dun's number is a unique number assigned to a business entity by
Dun & Bradstreet. This number is a key field in Dun & Bradstreet reports.

Applications Affected

Order entry
Accounts payable
Accounts receivable

Data Format

The Dun's number consists of a nine-character numeric field. On the
Dun & Bradstreet reports it is expressed as XX-XXX-XXXX; but the
hyphens will not be carried in data files.

COBOL Name

DUNS-NUMBER

Data Origination and Change

The data management organization that is responsible for the initial loading
of customer data will enter the number into the control file. The Dun &
Bradstreet directory is the official source.

Data Hierachy Requirement

This number is a part of the basic customer data and will be maintained in
the customer record. It may also be a part of the vendor record, if deemed
necessary.

Control File

The control file for this data item is the administrative data files (ADF).

Reference Documentation

Dun & Bradstreet directory.

Figure 3–15 Dun's number data item.

In Figure 3–16 we have taken the information about the Dun's number that
was presented earlier and have broken it up into its components, namely the alternative names, such as aliases, access keys, and keywords in context (KWICs), the
different attributes that were described, and the relationships indicated by different
systems and files. In Figure 3–17 a data-entry screen on a dictionary is shown by
which this information would be entered into the dictionary system.

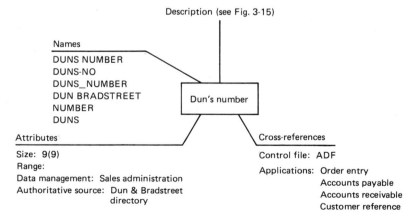

Figure 3–16 Components of a data item in the dictionary.

```
                        DD/DS STORE ITEM SCREEN

        Name: DUNS NUMBER     Version: 01      Data Std: Y

        Cobol Name: DUNS-NO; PL1 Name: DUNS_NO; Alias: CUST-REF

        Keywords: DUNS , NUMBER

        Size: 9(9);     Signed: N;       Alignment: Aligned;

        Code set: ASCII;  Data type: Fixed binary;

        Usage is: DISPLAY;

        Report heading: Dun's No.

        Data Mgmt: Sales admin;  Auth. Source: Dun & Bradstreet

        XREFS:
          Control File: ADF
```

Figure 3-17   Data item store entry screen.

Index Reports

Reports obtained by going through an index are useful outputs from a dictionary. This is one way to identify groupings of data items that are of interest. Figures 3–18 and 3–19 are examples of indexed reports. Note that the data items originally contained this key as part of the information entered into the dictionary.

<u>INDEX BY OWNER</u>

MANUFACTURING MATERIALS (MTLS)

FORECAST-PAST-DUE-MAIN-INDIC	ITEM
FORECAST-TYPE	ITEM
FORECAST-TYPE-OFFSET	ITEM
GAIN/LOSS-QUANTITY	ITEM
IN-TRANSIT-LEAD-TIME	ITEM
IN-TRANSIT-MANIFEST-NUMBER	ITEM
IN-TRANSIT-ORDER-TYPE	ITEM
ISSUED-DATE	ITEM
ISSUED-QUANTITY	ITEM
KIT-CODE	ITEM
LINE-NUMBER	ITEM
LOCALLY-MANUFACTURED-PART-NUMBER	ITEM
LOT-NUMBER	ITEM
LOT-STATUS-CODE	ITEM
MANUFACTURED-PART-NUMBER	ITEM
MARKETING-HOLD-SELECTOR	ITEM
NO-PRINT-STATUS-SELECTOR	ITEM
ORDER-NUMBER	ITEM
ORDER-STATUS-CODE	ITEM
ORDER-TRANSFERRED-QUANTITY	ITEM
PART-EXTENDED-QUANTITY-REQUIRED	ITEM

Figure 3-18   Index by owner (manufacturing) report.

INDEX BY OWNER

MARKETING (MKT)

8 ENTRIES QUALIFY

CORP-SALES-ORDER-MARKETING-HLD-IND	ITEM
CUSTOMER-CONTRACT-NUMBER	ITEM
CUSTOMER-NAME	ITEM
EARLIEST-POSSIBLE-DELIVERY-DATE	ITEM
SALES-ORDER-ITEM-QUANTITY	ITEM
SALES-ORDER-RELEASE-NUMBER	ITEM
SHIPPING-ORDER-VALUE	ITEM

Figure 3-19 Index by owner (marketing) report.

Other Metadata

Although the data dictionary is a repository of information about data items, it is also used to store information about other entities, such as systems, programs, records, machines, users, sources, and their interrelationships. Specifically, the data dictionary contains:

- Edit and validation criteria for data items
- File definitions
- Cross-references between programs and data items and files
- Summary information regarding systems, subsystems, jobs, and programs
- Responsibility for data sourcing and usage
- Operations data related to scheduling

Examples of metadata that are handled by IBM's DB/DC dictionary are shown in Figure 3-20. "Element" and "item" are synonymous.

DATA DICTIONARY ROLE AS A TOOL

The role of the dictionary as a tool is explored in this section of the chapter. As a tool the dictionary utilizes the metadata to direct and control other processing activities in the computer system. We have already discussed the evolution of the metadata to support the system development life-cycle activities. In a similar fashion, the uses of the dictionary have evolved over time into a more powerful and useful tool set.

Data Dictionary Role within System Components

Where does the data dictionary fit within the various components of a system (i.e., hardware, software, procedures, etc.)? The different components of a system are the operating system, the file handlers, the system development technique/process, source libraries that contain the procedures and programs, DBMS, and data dictionary, as shown in Figure 3-21.

The distribution of responsibility for data-oriented activity between these components is a function of the flexibility needed. For example, the operating system and file handlers have standard functions and well-defined interfaces with which communication can be established. DBMS systems have flexibility built into them to accommodate the expansion of the data base without substantial rework. Data dictionaries, on the other hand, need to be responsive to the evolution of information management within the entire organization.

CATEGORY

Name
Attributes
Description
Relationships
Relationship data

RELTYPE

Name
Attributes
Description
Relationships
Relationship data

ATTRTYPE

Name
Attributes
Description
Relationships
Relationship data

TRANSACTION

Name
Attributes
Type
Code
Description
Relationships

PSB

Name
Attributes
Language
DL/1 parameters
Description
Relationships

SYSDEF

Name
Description
Relationship data
Type of scheduling

SYSTEM

Name
Description
Relationships

JOB

Name
Description
Relationships

PROGRAM

Name
Attributes
Language
Type
Size
Description
Relationships

MODULE

Name
Description
Relationships

DDUSER

Name
Attributes
Description

PCB

Name
Attributes
Key length
Type
Description
Relationships
Relationship data
Sensitive segment structure
Processing options

ELEMENT
(field)

Name
Attributes
Length
Type
COBOL attributes
PL/1 attributes
Inquiry attributes
Effective date
Description
Relationships
Relationship data
Start position within segment
Contained in another field

SEGMENT
(record)

Name
Attributes
Length (fixed or variable)
PL/1 alignment
Effective date
Description
Relationships
Relationship data
Level
Rules for insert, delete, and replace

DATA BASE
(data set)

Name
Attributes
Block sizes
Access methods
Names of data definition statements
Name of user-supplied randomizer
Name of direct access anchor points
Indicators for data set groups
Description
Relationships
Relationship data
Parent-child relationships
Hierarchical structure of segments

Figure 3–20 Metadata handled by IBM's DB/DC dictionary.

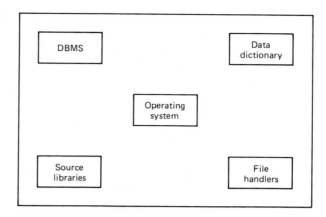

Figure 3-21 Dictionary position within operating components of a computer system.

Therefore, considerable flexibility has to exist in the dictionary. Some of this flexibility is obtained through the "extensibility" feature, which was discussed earlier. Other forms of flexibility that will be seen in the tools side include the ability to translate from one file format to another and to adapt to different programming languages and interfaces, and the ability to talk to different data dictionaries.

Active versus Passive Dictionaries

Dictionaries are often classified as being either "active" or "passive," depending on whether the dictionary and other system components are integrated together and operate in synchronization.

In a perfectly "active" dictionary, every request for data would be addressed to the dictionary, which would then be the arbiter of how the data are cataloged, where they are located, who has access to them, their value transformations, edit validation, presentation characteristics, and so on, and the dictionary would then direct the DBMS, file handlers, and operating system to obtain the data item and apply the various operations on the item before final presentation to the user. Such "active" or "run-time" dictionaries suffer certain practical performance problems because of the amount of activity that would have to be coordinated through the dictionary.

When such a system is designed for practical use, the amount of flexibility in the use of the dictionary by other applications, such as data planning and modeling, are limited since the dictionary is optimized toward production performance. Because of the physical size limitations that the designers have to live with in order to increase performance, the amount of free-form data that can be entered, and the amount of extensibility, are also restricted.

"Passive" dictionaries, on the other hand, do not have direct tie-ins to the operating system. They are like application systems that provide generic features for the use of data administration, but require the user to bridge the gap between information in the dictionary and machine utilization. This can be done via user procedures or user-developed programs.

The dictionaries that have been designed to work with DBMS systems by the computer vendors generate data file definitions that can be automatically included in the program during the compile step; some of the more recent fourth-generation language (4GL) products include run-time features. However, most dictionary products are neither purely active nor purely passive—they are somewhere in between.

As mentioned earlier, it would be advantageous to have a dictionary that is more active; however, active dictionaries require enormous amounts of processing power and therefore are not as flexible to organizational and implementation needs as a more passive dictionary would be. An example would be the case where the dictionary is used at the compile stage only as opposed to the run-time stage. The compiler link to the dictionary ensures that the programs contain the correct file descriptions. A run-time dictionary would also ensure that the version of the data base corresponds to the version described in the dictionary, before the program could access the file.

Another aspect of flexibility has to do with the ability to introduce dictionary utilization within the organization on a gradual basis. The dictionary project manager may put into effect a policy which states that all new systems will compile data definitions directly from the dictionary, whereas older systems would be exempted from this requirement. With a dictionary that is more flexible, this can be achieved procedurally. If the implementation of the dictionary requires that all systems, whether new or old, have to be compiled from the dictionary, that puts a restriction on the project manager to convert all the old systems to dictionary format before implementing the policy.

In considering active dictionaries, one aspect that is an overriding concern is the performance aspect. Vendors' claims about their products should be checked out under full-load conditions, that is, where the dictionary is fully loaded with all kinds of entity information and relationships, and the data bases are fairly large and are typical of the stable size of the base over its operating life.

Fourth-Generation Languages

Fourth-generation languages (4GLs) are an outgrowth of the need to make applications development and maintenance easier. Some of the benefits of 4GLs are:

- The user of the 4GL development facility does not have to be concerned with technical details of file structures.
- The user can specify the data requirements in simple menu-driven screens into a dictionary which will transform these into a physical file structure.
- The user specifies the procedures in a natural language or via menu-driven screens.
- Changes can be made to either data or procedure definitions, and these will be applied to the application in transparent ways.

The dictionary plays an active role in 4GLs. The ability to maintain data about different entities and the ability to build change control procedures around these data is what makes it valuable to the 4GL. The dictionary also maintains the relationships between the procedures and the data, so that a change in either can trigger the appropriate adjustments to the affected entities.

Prototyping

Another process that is taking place with the advent of fourth-generation language tools is the process of prototyping. Prototyping refers to the process of modeling an application on a small-scale basis and making quick changes to it based on input from the users. This not only helps speed up the design process by giving the user a preview of what to expect when the system is finally completed, but also gains the user's commitment to the final product because the user can have input during the development process.

The prototyping tools allow the application to be created and turned around more quickly than with the conventional systems development life cycle. An important part of these prototyping applications is their reliance on a dictionary. The dictionary contains not only the data definitions pertinent to the application, but also a model of the data and the ways in which the data will be processed. A feature of these prototyping tools is that the results of the session which are stored in the dictionary can be used to develop a full-scale application for a production environment to be run on a regularly scheduled basis.

Depending on the volume of data processed, and the transaction loads and other operational criteria, it may be necessary to rewrite the application utilizing a data base management system (DBMS), a transaction processor, and a different host language interface. The application would have to be interfaced to existing files utilizing different file handlers on different machines. All of these requirements imply that the application that was prototyped would have to be redone using different data structures and different programming constructs. This process of mapping the prototyped data structure to existing file structures is facilitated by the data dictionary, because the data dictionary possesses information about the existing file structures. In addition to the data structure mapping, the procedures developed as part of the prototyped system will have to be translated into programming languages that run on the host machine.

Dictionary Inputs and Outputs

What are some of the inputs to and outputs from the data dictionary? Figure 3–22 shows a few of these, including standards, file definitions, system/program descriptions, and cross-references as inputs, and file layouts, where-used reports, and copy code (include files) as outputs.

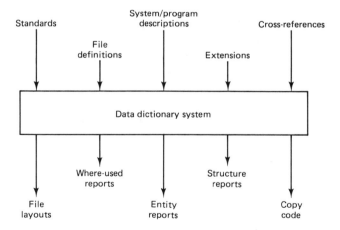

Figure 3–22 Inputs and outputs from dictionary.

Typical Dictionary Facilities

Figure 3–23 illustrates the typical dictionary facilities through which information is input to the dictionary and output from the dictionary. This should give an indication to the reader of the ability of the dictionary to accept data from human as well as machine sources and make it available in the appropriate format to compilers, 4GLs, run-time interfaces, and other system-level components.

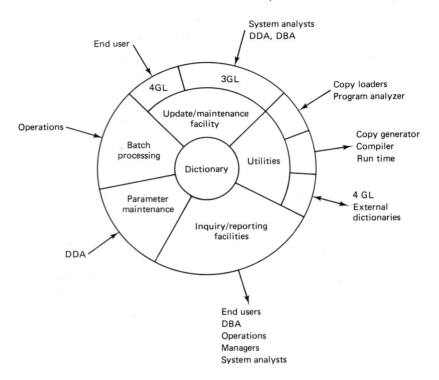

Figure 3-23 Use of typical dictionary facilities.

DISTRIBUTED DICTIONARY

With the growth of information processing and the use of 4GLs and development of distributed applications, the need to coordinate the information contained in several dictionary-based systems arises. Facilities that can extract a portion of the dictionary into a format that can then be loaded into another dictionary is part of a distributed dictionary scenario. The concept of "source" dictionary and "receiving" dictionary will need to be established, in addition to the type and direction of data transfer.

For example, standard data definitions may be downloaded from a central location to a remote location for use by personnel at that location. The extracted data have to be understood, edited, and previewed at the receiving location, prior to loading that dictionary.

In some cases, the remote installation of a dictionary might call for the loading of different types of information. The flow of information from the "receiving" dictionary to the "source" dictionary also has to be considered. A system developed at a remote site will have entities that need to be transferred to the central location. There will be several different kinds of entities, and the integrity of the relationships between these entities must be maintained during the transfer. An important application occurs when different parts of a project are done at different locations. During the project, certain common standards have to be enforced; after the project, the separately developed pieces have to be merged, with the aid of the dictionary.

The transfer of a specific structure from one dictionary to another must be done with caution because of the danger of overlaying existing entities or creating unnecessary new ones in the receiving dictionary. Thus any new structure that has to be incorporated into an existing dictionary must be previewed and edited to ensure that the integrity of existing entities and their interrelationships is protected.

Issues

There are technical and control issues facing the implementer of a distributed dictionary. The key is to maintain the currency of the dictionary contents while providing a two-way flow of information between the central dictionary and other installations. Described below are some suggested techniques and their drawbacks:

1. Distribute the updated central dictionary.
   a. Extract new data from a central file based on activity date and process these new data against the "receiving" dictionary. The major problem is the handling of deletes since the previous update.
   b. Process log files against local versions of the dictionary. Since both dictionaries are being updated with different types of information, the feasibility of doing this while maintaining data integrity is in question.
   c. Maintain parallel systems at each site; one system will be used for local development and feeding to the central system, while the other will be a read-only copy of the central file.

2. Maintain the currency of the data in the dictionary at the local sites and the handling of deletes and/or obsolescence.
   a. Run a comparison of dictionaries to handle all changes. This would be a slow and expensive process.
   b. Set delayed delete to be handled automatically in the local system. Timing has to be coordinated carefully, and visibility to deletes has a short window.
   c. Use the obsolete status indicator in conjunction with a deferred delete date to handle deletes. This would also handle the problems of phasing out systems as they are replaced.

3. Maintain the data standards. Include accepting new standards proposed by remote locations and the resolution of the discrepancies in definition.
   a. This can be handled by instituting a request procedure for additional data standards.
   b. This can be handled as part of the local data that are transmitted to the central site.
   c. A formal review process before the item can be assigned by the local site can be set up, but would require a longer time frame.

4. The portion of the central dictionary that should be available to the local site needs to be defined. It could be the entire dictionary, or it could be the local systems information, relevant corporate systems, and all data standards. Depending on what is decided, the strategy to keep all the entities and their relationships refreshed on a periodic basis has to be defined and implemented.

5. The enforcement of naming conventions across several sites, and how discrepancies are to be handled are important elements that must be addressed as part of the implementation strategy for the central dictionary initially, and then resolved for the problems between the central dictionary and the remote dictionaries.

GLOBAL DICTIONARY

Most large and small companies will require information management functions to manage and derive the most benefit for the business from the data asset and to remain competitive. The first task in getting to an information management environment is the population of the data dictionary with the definitions of the data items in use within the business. Although this may imply the existence of a single data dictionary for the enterprise, and in most cases this will be true, the dictionary will contain the definitions that are common within a corporate or organizational culture.

In the case of conglomerates, several corporate cultures may be represented within the businesses based on the fact that the businesses may be different. Thus in a conglomerate that has a food business and a travel business, these businesses may be so far apart in terms of the commonality of definitions that the best thing to do would be to have separate dictionaries for each. A distinct business can be serviced from one data dictionary, often referred to as a global data dictionary. This is the repository of the data definitions, data models, and data standards that management wishes to propagate throughout the business.

In a large data processing environment where several machines are in use and where different software systems need to be integrated, the role of a global data dictionary contains the results of the modeling process as applied to the business as well as the data flows. This consists of the normalized data structures as well as the business entities and information flows that are desired in the business.

Each individual application has to be consistent with the global data and business models. To accomplish this, a procedure to communicate with the global dictionary must be set up. The problems that have to be overcome are not only the technical ones indicated in the preceding section on the distributed dictionary, but also the organizational issues of authority and jurisdiction.

Tools that perform data modeling or prototyping will have to be tied into the global data dictionary for the validation that is required to maintain the consistency. The well-populated global dictionary will serve as the reference point for the development and implementation of all information processes for the business, no matter where the physical locations of the processing are located.

chapter 4

Organizational Implications

INTRODUCTION

This chapter deals with the organizational structure and attitude that must be in place for a data dictionary to be successful. The first part of this chapter deals with management commitment to the project. Then the discussion is directed to the functions that have to exist in the organization for the data dictionary to be implemented. The next section deals with the environment that has to exist. The chapter ends with a description of the organization that is recommended for the implementation of data dictionary to succeed.

MANAGEMENT COMMITMENT

Management commitment to dictionary implementation is absolutely crucial. This commitment has to be given over an extended period without expecting immediate payoffs. Depending on the staffing of the data dictionary administration function, payoffs could be visible within one to two years.

Management support could be exhibited through the following activities:

- Involvement and support of the corporate information systems planning process.
- Support of a methodology for the design and development of information systems. Most methodologies or systems development life cycles (SDLCs) require extensive use of a dictionary. The data dictionary administration function must have the authority to establish and enforce the naming conventions and other policies needed to manage the data resource. The use of the dictionary in the development process must be made mandatory.
- Support of standards and disciplines for program development and maintenance is extremely important because this provides the foundation for effective application management. This includes the procedures for control of changes to programs and subsystems, and the use of the dictionary to document and ad-

minister the changes that are made through the use of the version control facility of the data dictionary.

- Support of the dictionary as the only source for data definitions in the entire organization. As a corollary to this, management should not accept documentation about data items that are not directly sourced from the dictionary.

Selling Senior Management

To sell the senior management within the company is no easy task; however, it is made simpler by the very fact that there exists a backlog of pent-up demand for applications in any MIS shop. Many of these demands use data that are in use by some other department, but the file structures, and access techniques may not suit the new application request. Thus a lot of time and effort is spent in duplicating efforts to create new files out of existing data. With each new file comes extra programming and operational effort to ensure that the data are consistent. It can be demonstrated that if the files and data bases were the responsibility of a single function, that function could have designed the files with multiple access paths and uses in mind, and thus different applications could share the files, which would help reduce the application backlog and improve the organization's productivity.

Responding to the requirements of more new applications to use shared data (or data carefully controlled across application systems or data centers), along with on-line data access and update, creates an increasingly complex environment where the data usage for various systems must be carefully analyzed, coordinated, and controlled. As an organization develops more systems and provides more support to higher levels of management for control and strategic planning, the integration of systems and data becomes necessary, and increased levels of shared data, resource management, and data administration become necessities.

Another problem that many MIS units have is that they are working at a furious pace to satisfy user demands for systems and an inventory of what data are in existence is not available in a central location or in an easy-to-obtain manner. This frustrates users when they realize the amount of effort one has to go through, and the staff work involved to obtain information needed to run the business. This is where the simple application of data and data base administration techniques could make this information available to end users from a central location.

In order for the foundation to be laid for the establishment of data and data base administration functions, communication between company management and MIS should be improved by establishing a common understanding of business strategic plans so that MIS and company management can develop and implement tactical system plans and data plans. What this means is that in addition to selling the need for systems plans, senior management must be sold on the need for the creation of a data plan that underlies system development activity for several years into the future.

In companies where end-user computing efforts have expanded because of the user's willingness and familiarity with end-user tools to perform the processing themselves, the argument that can be used to support data and data base administration activities is the fact that end users need data from data bases that are controlled and validated in order to come up with meaningful results. If they did not have confidence in the data they were using, their analyses would be subject to doubt, and worse, loss of credibility. Therefore, the end users who perform end-user computing would be natural allies of the person trying to sell the concept of data and data base administration.

To summarize, tangible and intangible benefits must be presented to senior management in a succinct manner. Some traditional benefits of data base management are:

- More data sharing because the data structures are based on the organization's definition of data, not a specific system

- More consistent information because of standard terminology and definitions
- Increased knowledge of data availability because of a centralized mechanized inventory of information about data
- Better systems planning as the approach fosters the integration of systems functions based on the commonality of data
- Reduced costs by minimizing data analysis efforts, by providing initial physical structures much earlier in the development cycle; and by reducing maintenance efforts with more common input/update processing

Other kinds of business benefits that should be cited are:

- Aiding the company in reaching its goals and objectives by improving management's ability to obtain required information by making data available and timely. This increases management's ability to make knowledgeable decisions.
- Establishing plans that tie data planning and systems development with business requirements. This provides management with the data that they require within the appropriate time frame.

PREREQUISITES

In order to have a successful implementation of a data dictionary, a data administration and a data base administration function must be explicitly recognized and operational within the organization. Typically, these functions will be within the MIS department, reporting to the director or manager of MIS for the corporation. Although the establishment of data and data base administration functions are treated more fully in other books, a few points will be made here about their role.

Data Administration

The data administration function must encompass all the technical and management activities required for organizing, maintaining, and directing the data base environment. The objectives of data administration are:

- To optimize the use of data in a shared data base environment. This is done through the design and management of DBMS-controlled data, by defining, organizing, documenting, and protecting the data base and by providing the technical DBMS support to the applications development staff.
- To implement a systematic methodology for the centralized management and control of data resources. This is done through the development of policies and procedures for the control of the total data resource, including research, communications and training, and the formulation of the procedures for the definition, utilization, and protection of the data.
- To balance conflicting objectives with respect to the organization's mission and the overall economy of data handling. This is done through the awareness of business direction and priorities, and the role that the appropriate application of data standards and procedures would have in different application areas within the business.

The functions of data administration are

- To maintain the data dictionary, standardize data-naming conventions, and maintain data definitions. The objective here is to develop policies, procedures, standards, and controls that are necessary for the development, maintenance, and operation of data base systems. The data administration function must have the authority to enforce the data standards.

- To plan the data bases, provide the data models that are the results of business systems planning and data requirements planning. The objective here is to provide the systems development and data base administration groups the window into the future business strategies as seen from a data point of view.

- To design data base structures to support the varying needs of different applications: schema, subschema, transaction definition, backup, and recovery procedures. It is the data base design that provides the foundation for the integration of the corporate data resources residing in the computers. Thus data base administration is charged with designing an overall data base structure that is stable in the long term but meets the needs of the component systems in the short term.

- To create data base procedures, documentation, and standards, including I/O handlers, error handling, and special recovery procedures. Since several users are utilizing the data base concurrently, it is extremely important that recoverability is built into the design and operation of the system so that users do not inadvertently cause harm to each other.

- To provide assistance to all users of the data base: programmers, analysts, and end users.

- To maintain data base integrity and availability via implementation of adequate backup and recovery techniques, ensuring that the on-line and query processors function properly, and secure access through the provision of concurrent access controls. The fact that on-line availability has become a critical issue means that the performance of the data base must be monitored continuously, and measures taken to improve the efficiency of the data base.

SYSTEM/DATA ENVIRONMENT ASSESSMENT

In making decisions as to where and how to implement the dictionary, an assessment of the systems and data files in the MIS environment will be worthwhile to undertake. The complexity of the business that the dictionary supports, as reflected in the number of functions and the data items that are in use by the business, is proportional to the benefit that can be derived from implementing a dictionary system. This is because the different functions need to use the dictionary as a communications vehicle about the terminology that exists in different parts of the company, and encourage the cross-flow of data and information between these parts.

In most cases, other than in a brand new MIS setup, the dictionary will have to be retrofitted onto an existing set of programs and data files. If the sheer number of programs and files are large, the dictionary will play a role in reducing the complexity level by providing documentation and procedural control. The complexity of an MIS department with large amounts of systems and complex data interactions tends to deteriorate with the addition of new ones because it is easier to create new data items and the procedures associated with updates to these items than to see if any existing files or procedures could be used. Thus the value of a dictionary which records existing data items and procedures can save the organization considerable development time and effort.

Another dimension of complexity that should be examined is the operational environment, that is, the number of physically separate machines that do the processing, the amount of telecommunication linkages, as well as local networking between machines. As the number of machines increases, the effort required to keep the versions of programs and data in synchronization increases in a geometric fashion.

The overall maturity of the MIS organization is another variable that will have an impact on the value and ease of implementation of the dictionary. The maturity is a reflection of the level to which standards and naming conventions have been consistently applied during the system development life cycle. If standards are already in place, the dictionary can be quickly populated without going through lengthy conflict resolution processes, thus making the dictionary usable within a shorter time frame.

The degree to which data are shared in the MIS environment will have an impact on the usefulness of the dictionary. If there is heavy sharing or movement toward use of nonredundant file structures, then a dictionary that provides a map of the where-used information is invaluable to the design and development as well as the operations staff. It would be of critical importance to know the impact that changes in one part of a complex system will have on other parts of the system. If this information were not tracked via a dictionary system, this could result in production failures and unanticipated costs of development and maintenance.

If there is a high degree of turnover in personnel that develop and maintain systems, a dictionary would be seen as of value in retaining information within the organization that would normally be lost to the enterprise with the loss of the individual. Also the dictionary would reduce the learning curve for new employees.

USER IMPACT

The implementation of the data dictionary system has to be planned with full knowledge of its impact on the various user communities. The implementation of the procedures around the dictionary could change the existing ways of doing things. For example, if project teams within an MIS department are used to setting up their own file structures without central control, there may be resistance to the idea of procedures for ensuring that file structures follow standard conventions. This may be due to the fact that these procedures introduce a delay factor into the project schedule. Implementation of dictionary procedures do require extra time up front in the system development process, and this should be incorporated into the schedule for the project.

The dictionary will perform a major role in the standardization of data items and will enable different groups in the organization to communicate with each other using commonly accepted terminology. This implies that all authorized users on the system will be able to view information about all the data items in the organization. In addition, users will be able to request data extracts through the dictionary without regard to which data base the data are actually stored in. This may cause some concern to those who view as their own the data in a particular data base. It must be made clear at a very early stage that the data belongs to the organization as a whole, with responsibility for the maintenance of the data items allocated to different subunits.

Within the MIS department, the implementation of the dictionary will require an aggressive and skilled data dictionary administration function capable of educating the staff and responding rapidly to their needs. This function must have the full cooperation of the managers in the development and operations areas. To prove the merits of the new services provided by the dictionary, managers will have to commit resources to load the dictionary with the current system information. During this phase, the procedures must be in place to update the dictionary.

This process will help to ensure that the dictionary is continuously being used by all the staff members. The update to the dictionary can be restricted to a few people, to monitor the quality of the information going into the dictionary; this leaves the vast majority of the staff unfamiliar with the dictionary. From an administrative point of view, a strong level of understanding and support for the dictionary is crucial to its success; hence as many persons should participate in its loading and maintenance as can reasonably be accommodated by the system, even if it means sacrificing some quality initially.

ORGANIZATIONAL PLACEMENT

There are two aspects to dictionary implementation: The first aspect is to promote it as a concept and establish it within the organization so that it becomes part and parcel of the organization's way of life. The second aspect comes into play after the dictionary has been implemented and needs to be administered on a more or less routine basis. The first aspect requires that the organization be a change agent; the second aspect is well suited to any function that carries out administration functions.

The traditional structure of the data dictionary function as part of data administration is shown in Figure 4–1. This kind of organization works well in an organization after the dictionary has been implemented and has been instituted as part of the system development life cycle. However, the initial stages of dictionary implementation require an aggressive project team with the authority to mediate conflicts and get consensus among different groups. Two alternative organizational placements are recommended when organizing the project. Figures 4–2 and 4–3 show the organizational structures. Note that in Figure 4–2 the dictionary project manager is

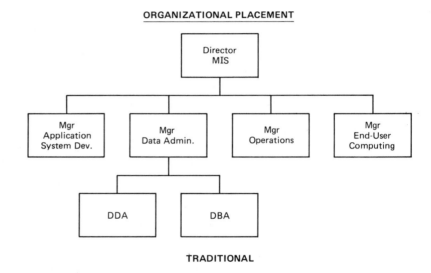

Figure 4–1 Traditional organization.

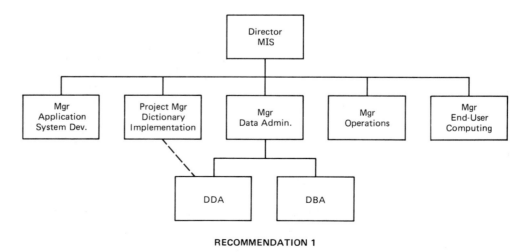

Figure 4–2 Dictionary organization within MIS.

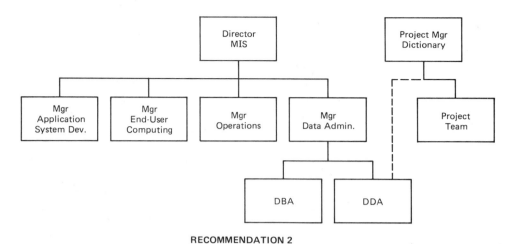

RECOMMENDATION 2

Figure 4-3 Dictionary organization outside MIS.

part of the MIS organization but reports at the same level as other functional managers within MIS. In Figure 4–3, recognition is given to the role that end-user departments play in populating the dictionary and insisting on the dictionary's use in the system development process. In this organization structure, the dictionary project manager reports to a functional department other than MIS, but has a dotted-line relationship with the DDA function within MIS. Once the project has been implemented, the responsibility will revert to the traditional data administration function within MIS.

Another variation on this theme is to have a senior staff person be the project manager and have a team of representatives from the various mainstream functions report to this person for a fixed period of time until the project is accomplished. The project manager should be given a fixed charter and a clear indication of the results expected and the time frame. A sample set of expectations may be as follows:

1. Define dictionary requirements.
2. Select dictionary system.
3. Define dictionary procedures.
4. Populate dictionary standards.
5. Incorporate into end-user computing procedures.
6. Incorporate into systems development life cycle.

THE DICTIONARY AS A STANDARD

Invariably, the subject of standards comes up whenever "data dictionary" is mentioned. In an MIS environment where standards are being developed for systems development, data base administration, and computer operations, it is extremely important to include dictionary procedures as part of the standards of the MIS installation. It would be wise for the dictionary project manager to be a part of the team that develops the standard; if the standard can be developed around the strengths and weaknesses of the dictionary, the task of implementation of the standard will be that much easier. It would be a lot more difficult to fit the dictionary to the standards and procedures that are already in place if they do not include dictionary updates; on the other hand, it would be easier to sell the dictionary if the update procedures for a dictionary have been thought through during the development of standards.

Thus, commitment to a set of standards and procedures for systems development, data base administration, and operations is a must for the dictionary to survive the initial reactions to the implementation of any new set of procedures. This commitment should be tied to the performance review of individuals and managers in the MIS environment.

Additionally, the documentation produced from the dictionary should be used as proof of the following of standards. The credence given to the output from the dictionary will be symbolic of the levels of commitment given to the implementation of the dictionary by senior management. Without this, the pace of dictionary implementation will falter because in the effort to get projects done, ways will be found to bypass dictionary standards.

In order to propagate the expectations of the dictionary to the various user groups, a significant training program should be undertaken. The training program should include the generic dictionary concepts with an additional amount of time dedicated to procedures that are specific to a user group, such as operations and applications development. Solid examples of what kinds of output are supported by the dictionary should be provided to give users a feeling as to its value; otherwise, different users may follow the procedures but come up with totally different results. One important aspect of the dictionary is its use in promoting consistent quality of documentation and communication.

DATA DICTIONARY ADMINISTRATION

It is important that adequate staff be assigned to administration of the dictionary. There are three functions that need to be performed:

1. Identify the installation parameters of the dictionary, including entity analysis, needs identification, procedures development, and communication of the information to the users. Another responsibility is the planning of the stages of implementation and getting the necessary support from different parts of the organization. This is essentially a project manager or leader position.

2. Collect and update the information for the dictionary, ensuring that the stored information is formatted according to departmental standards. In this role the person will act as the primary interface to systems development, operations, data base administrators, and end users, for all matters concerning the dictionary. This is more of an administrative role and is a focal point for all day-to-day inquiries concerning the dictionary.

3. To provide the data dictionary administrator with appropriate information, time must be allocated to this effort by the managers of the various groups, such as data base administration, systems development, operations, and their staff. Since this task is not trivial to the implementation of the dictionary and can easily be ignored in the daily routines, this activity must be planned for with a high-priority level assigned to it.

Role of the Data Dictionary Administrator

Overall, the major function of the data dictionary administrator is to manage and control access to the dictionary once the dictionary has been installed. This includes such functions as developing, implementing, and maintaining methods and procedures related to the dictionary. This function requires individuals with strong communication skills as well as technical knowledge of how the dictionary works. The data dictionary administrator will play a key role in training the users of the dictionary, and will develop and maintain the dictionary standards and guidelines. Thus the DD Administrator plays the role of guardian of the data in the dictionary, and the position should reflect the critical importance of this activity. Although the administration function could be done by one person, management must make a determination of the skills required and the skills available within the organization before staffing this function. It will become apparent from reading the rest of this book that the initial setting up of the dictionary will require a certain set of organizational and technical skills, but are quite different once the dictionary procedures are routinized. Thus the dictionary implementation can be thought of as a two-step process when planning staffing requirements.

The project manager of dictionary implementation should first be hired as part of this function. This person would be a senior individual within the organization with the experience and expertise to implement company-wide projects. Working for the project manager would be other individuals who would complement the technical aspects of the dictionary and assist in the actual population of the dictionary. At the end of this section you will find sample job descriptions that can be referred to in choosing for these positions. Staff choices are critical because this will be the first staff and also because resistance will be encountered to implementation of new procedures.

The data dictionary functions (referred to as DDA or administrator) are a group of activities explaining how to set up the data dictionary system (DDS), how to customize it to the user site, and how to use it on an ongoing basis. The initial setting of the parameters to those recommended by the vendor of the data dictionary system should be sufficient to set up the dictionary. (The types of parameters that need to be set up is explained later in this book.) The DDA must also have the ability to add information tailoring the operation of the dictionary to his or her unique operating environment. Given below are some of the activities that need to be performed on the dictionary system in order to utilize it.

- The DDA enters the name of the installation in the control region. This is the name that will print on report headings.
- The DDA specifies any additional type codes and names additional classes of entities, attributes, and access keys that are permitted in the data dictionary. The DDA defines the type codes and corresponding names using the type code definition screen. Note that the standard default set of type codes provided with the dictionary cannot be modified. A typical dictionary may have certain rules for the assignment of new type codes. Parameters have to be entered into the dictionary for:
  — The entities that will be supported by the dictionary system
  — The access keys that will be allowed for the different entities
  — The attributes that will be supported for each entity
- When the additional classes of entities, attributes, and access keys have been defined, the DDA defines the relationships that will be permitted in the data dictionary. A relationship can be defined *only* between those entities or entities and attributes that have already been stored in the data dictionary. The relationship between two entities may consist of a four-digit field where the first two digits represent the superior entity type. With a relationship between an entity and an attribute, the first two characters always represent the entity type and the last two characters represent the type code of the attribute.
- To be a valid user of the data dictionary system, you must have a valid username and password assigned by the DDA, through the Username/Password screen. The DDA assigns global permissions to usernames permitted to access the dictionary based on the username/password combination; that is, each username is given specific permission to create, write, or read certain classes of data at the global level.

SAMPLE POSITION DESCRIPTIONS

Data Dictionary Project Manager

Job Summary. Applies previous managerial and work experience to implementing the data dictionary by planning, coordinating, and administering personnel and capital resources. Manages a single large project in the control and implementation of all aspects of the system (i.e., budgetary responsibility, labor utilization, technical performance, user interface, and installation and operational issues).

Principal Tasks

1. Develops the goals of the project and sets the overall tone and direction for the project.
2. Meets with users to analyze dictionary requirements; also, provides recommendations and develops system specifications.
3. Develops proposal for implementing the dictionary project and gets management and user approval.
4. Manages a group of analysts assigned to the project so as to meet project milestones and assure compliance with system specifications.
5. Arranges to procure a dictionary system based on analysis of dictionary functions required, and features available in packages available in the marketplace.
6. Provides total project effort estimate, establishes internal procedures for monitoring project status, and makes periodic presentations to management on project status.
7. After the dictionary is operational and the procedures entrenched within the organization, control of the system is transferred to the data dictionary administrator.

Education Required. B.S. degree in technical area. Experience in implementing large projects in medium-sized to large company could substitute for degree required.

Experience Required. Minimum of six years' experience in implementing projects with a major portion in the implementation of computer systems projects. Experience in working in heavy-user-contact position.

Human Relations/Communications. Requries outstanding communication skills necessary for interface with senior management, users, and subordinates.

Complexity (Decision Making/Problem Solving). Has to plan and implement a project that would have a long-term impact on the information management activities within the company. Has to understand the implications of complex software systems on the information processing activities within the organization and be able to communicate the same in nontechnical terms. May continue to function as a major direct contributor to project work while carrying out project management activities.

Manager of Data/Data Base Administration

Job Summary. Manager of data/data base administration manages the creation and revision of the information plan and models and the development of data structures necessary to conduct business. Responsible for developing and getting approval for the information plan which describes and relates all business systems and the development and coordination of the data structures necessary to support those systems. Responsible for establishing and enforcing policies and procedures related to the data base, including data security and integrity controls, data dictionary, and data base support tools.

Principal Tasks.   Functions as both a manager and a highly skilled technical expert.

As a Manager

1. Develops and changes the information plan and models consistent with the needs/direction of the business as determined by the senior staff and directors.
2. Coordinates the creation and implementation of the information plans and models within the company.
3. Selects appropriate data base structure(s) for the company based on staff recommendations.
4. Approves tools and techniques used to cause input/output to the data base.
5. Approves the addition/expansion of the data base necessitated by business change or business growth.
6. Advises director on impact of change and alternative actions.
7. Manages a technical staff preparing or implementing the aforementioned.

As an Individual Contributor

1. Evaluates effectiveness of the data base(s).
2. Evaluates new data base methodologies or implementations.
3. Advises manager on same.

Education Required.   B.S. in technical discipline or equivalent experience.

Experience Required.   Seven to nine years' experience in systems use, design, development, and management, with at least one to three years in a data base administration capacity. Supervisory experience required. Requires technical expertise and business acumen.

Human Relations/Communications.   Must have good communication skills, as contact with various levels of management will be required. Strong human relations skill required in motivating qualified technical staff.

Complexity (Decision Making/Problem Solving).   Requires an incumbent with a broad understanding of business. Requires excellent applicable technical experience in a large data base and transaction processing environment. Requires the ability to make accurate technical evaluations and design decisions and the ability to attract, motivate, and retain qualified personnel. Requiring the ability to conceptualize and approve plans in the systems and data base area that will have a three- to eight-year life cycle and will consume several (100 to 200) person-years of effort.

Data Base Administrator

Job Summary.   Without appreciable direction, participates in the physical design and creation of the physical data structures and is responsible for their integrity and efficiency. Coordinates data base design and development activities among application programmers, system designers, systems programmers, and data center operations. Is conversant with data structures, communications systems characteristics and protocols, and has a working knowledge of related tools and techniques. Should be able to evaluate technical trade-offs for a particular environment and present such to management. Provides technical data base training and support to MIS staff.

Principal Tasks

Data Base Design/Redesign

1. Evaluates application technical needs; selects appropriate DBMS software.
2. Designs and develops storage structures, mapping and search strategies, and access methods.
3. Designs and develops support software for creating, maintaining, and reorganizing the data base.
4. Carries out redesign and restructuring activities as needed.
5. Proposes technical standards, design rules, and conventions for data bases.
6. Identifies and implements software tools to aid in data access.

Data Base Creation

1. Specifies, designs, and develops data extract and load software.
2. Performs data base loading, testing, and validation.
3. Implements data definitions.
4. Implements and maintains data dictionary/directory and other data base support software.

Data Base Security/Integrity

1. Installs and maintains tools needed to guard against unauthorized access to the data base and unauthorized update, copying, removal, or destruction of any part of the data base.
2. Installs and maintains tools needed to ensure the correctness and accuracy of the data.

Data Base Performance Monitoring and Evaluation

1. Reviews, tests, and evaluates the performance of activity against physical data structures.
2. Initiates system improvements when indicated.
3. Assesses the impact of change.
4. Maintains awareness of the state of the art.
5. Recommends data base redefinition, redesign, and restructuring when indicated.
6. Implements restart, recovery, and backup procedures.

Selection and Procurement

1. Evaluates, recommends, installs, and supports appropriate hardware and software related to data base administration and distributed data base/data processing.

Education Required.   Bachelor's degree or equivalent education and training normally associated with a bachelor's degree. Equivalent direct work experience or additional industry training in data base and data communications systems may be substituted.

Experience Required.   Six to nine years of related experience, including three years as a systems programmer or programmer analyst.

Human Relations/Communications.   Must be able to explain technical concepts to multiple levels of management. Must have a cooperative, positive attitude and be able to communicate effectively both orally and in writing.

Complexity (Decision Making/Problem Solving). Requires the highest technical, analytical, and design capabilities. Requires the intelligence, analytical ability, and maturity to make the technical decisions critical to successful development and operation of application systems. Requires the experience and state-of-the-art knowledge in both hardware and software to determine appropriate optimum configurations.

Data Dictionary Administrator I

Job Summary. The data dictionary administrator I (DDA I) administers the data dictionary for the entire company. The DDA I ensures that the data dictionary is functioning by generating accurate copybooks, analyzing programs for conformity to standards, and monitoring file space and access controls in conjunction with meeting the data needs of the company.

Principal Tasks

1. Enters accurate data into the data dictionary by collecting information about existing systems, programs, files, and operational procedures. Also collects documentation generated from the system development phases, and provides synopses and updates, and creates the cross-references to the data files in the dictionary.
2. Generates *copybooks* for systems development staff and ad hoc use and ensuring use of appropriate copybooks in programs through use of the program analyzer.
3. Monitors the growth of production files, analyzing disk space availability. Identifying potential problems, and planning for expansion and problem resolution in conjunction with the manager of DA/DBA.
4. Assigns and monitors access controls on all files in the MIS data center. The data dictionary will be the key point of reference in assignment of permissions to view or update files at the data item level by all users.

Education Required. Associate's degree or equivalent. The ability to grasp basic technology concepts and work with computer-based tools is important.

Experience Required. Experience with computer-based systems in either an operating role or programming role would be desirable.

Human Relations/Communications. Although a majority of the tasks require individual contributor skills, the ability to interface with individuals in the systems development organization and end users.

Complexity (Decision Making/Problem Solving). The person must know when to seek expertise (both inside and outside the department) in order to reconcile conflicting definitions in the dictionary. Must also possess tact in handling multiple task situations.

chapter 5

Entity Model

The information that goes into the dictionary is divided into broad categories to facilitate the storage and retrieval of the information. Examples of such broad categories that have already been mentioned include programs, data items, records, and files. These broad categories are referred to as entities.

An entity is a person, place, thing, concept, or event about which data may be recorded. Thus an actual occurrence of a record called the contract revenue record would fall under the "record" entity. Another record, such as the dispatch control record, would also fall under this category. Thus one could go to the dictionary and ask for a listing of all the information under the "record" entity, and that request would result in a listing of the descriptions of the contract revenue record and the dispatch control record, if those were the only ones stored in the dictionary.

In most dictionaries it becomes tedious to refer to a "record" entity or a "file" entity in all references to the occurrences. Therefore, a shorthand method of classifying entities is used. This may consist of a two-digit classification scheme, with "record" being assigned the number "03" and "file" being assigned the number "05." These numbers are referred to as entity type codes. Thus the dispatch control record would be stored under entity type code "03," whereas the dispatch control file would be stored under entity type code "05."

But not all entity categories are self-evident. You may ask, "How do I identify entity categories specific to my organization? Their relationships to each other? Their characteristics (i.e., attributes)? How do I develop ways for users to access all of this information (access keys)?"

The remainder of this chapter addresses all of these questions. By proceeding through six steps, you will see how to develop the entity model for information management within your organization. The six steps are:

1. Develop objectives by collecting information.
   a. Define functions and subfunctions within information management.

b. Create information flow diagrams.

c. Define metadata required to support information flow diagrams.

2. Identify entity categories and relationships.

3. Identify relationship notation.

4. Develop entity attributes.

5. Develop entity access keys.

6. Develop the entity model diagram.

As discussed above, the information in the data dictionary system is grouped into entity categories. Each entity category is identified by a code. The entity categories that are normally defined in any dictionary come about as a need for their use in the organization exists or is seen to exist. How does one go about identifying the entity categories? In the data processing environment, certain categories are self-evident. Computer programs can be put into a category called "program," regardless of whether they are written in COBOL or FORTRAN or assembler. Another entity category is "item," representing data items. This category includes the standard data items that would be maintained by the dictionary administrator in conjunction with end users, as well as the data items that are part of file definitions.

Thus dictionaries have standard entity categories that are defined to support data base administration. However, to plan a useful data dictionary, the data administrator must have a clear understanding of all the objectives to be met by the data dictionary system. In addition to standard entity categories, the dictionary administrator has the ability to define entity categories that are specifically related to the needs of the organization. The specific objectives of the dictionary must be well defined and publicized. Starting with the data base administration responsibility for cataloging the data resource within the organization, it is thus possible to expand the role to other functions within the MIS department (e.g., to allow analysts to automate documentation during the design of new systems).

STEPS TO DETERMINE AN ENTITY MODEL

1. Develop Objectives

In order to determine the uses of the data dictionary system in other departments or contexts, such as end-user computing, the DD project manager must interview the management and the prospective users on their expectations from the dictionary. The expectations of individual users will overlap, and there may exist interdependencies about which they may be unaware. For example, if the end-user computing user wishes to use the dictionary to inquire about what data exist in the organization, he or she may not be aware that an effort has to be started to populate the dictionary with that information. The DD project manager has to take this expectation and define its impact on other activities that need to go on concurrently or as prerequisites.

The DD project manager's objectives for the dictionary will include the user's expectations but will include other things that need to be done to meet user expectations. The list of objectives should be detailed enough to permit a first cut of the categories to be obtained. It is not necessary to have detailed report specifications at this time. Since the dictionary is flexible, many different report formats can be generated as long as the basic data can be stored. A sample of an objectives statement is given in Figure 5–1.

The last step in generating the statement of objectives is to publish the final document. In addition to providing the DD project manager with a basis for future planning, evaluation, and implementation of the data dictionary system, a written statement of objectives provides dictionary users with a general description of the types of information they can expect to find in the data dictionary.

Data Dictionary
for
NSC Corporation

General Objective:

To provide a central location for information about
data.

Specific Objectives:

To provide information about the following kinds of
data:
    Data residing on data bases
    Data residing on non-data base files
    Data residing in manual media (handwritten
      reports)

To provide information about the following aspects
of data and data usage:
    Physical characteristics of data
    Logical groups and relationships between data
    Sources and users of data
    Functions performed on the data

To provide information to be used by people in the
following areas:
    Data base administration
    Systems design and development
    Computer operations
    Systems architecture and planning
    Documentation and support
    Auditing
    End-user computing users

Figure 5-1 Sample objectives statement
for data dictionary.

Entity Model. From the statement of objectives, and based on follow-up interviews with the users, an entity model can be created that is representative of the kinds of data that will be stored in the dictionary and the kinds of attributes, access keys, and relationships between entities that will be maintained in the dictionary. During the interviews, there may be difficulties in getting answers from users because they may not have any idea of what the dictionary is supposed to provide. It may be helpful to show the users sample reports from any published dictionary specification as a starting point.

As the dictionary usage becomes more widespread, and reports based on the information in the dictionary become available, users can visualize their needs by looking at existing reports. After conducting the interviews, the DD project manager sorts the user's requests into two types: those that are within the scope of the objectives statement and those that are not. Requests that cannot be handled immediately should be reviewed to make sure that their implementation at a later date is not precluded by the entity model that is defined. By using an example, we will show a systematic approach to the collection of data to support the derivation of the entity model.

Functions and Subfunctions: The first step is to define the functions that are related to the process of information management in the enterprise. The functions can be arranged in a hierarchical sequence, as shown in Figure 5-2. Once the functions are identified, the flows of information needed to perform the functions can be identified. Note that the functions in Figure 5-2 are not representative of any implied organization structures. An interview should be held with the persons responsible for fulfilling the information management function within the enterprise to get that person's concurrence with the functional model. Each of the subfunctions should be described in relative detail so that there is no confusion as to the meaning and definition of the subfunctions. For example, definition of the subfunction called "Maintain Data Bases": The process of monitoring the data bases to ensure that

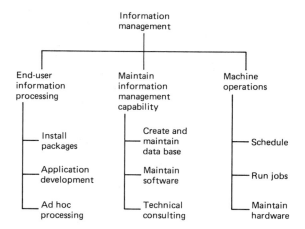

Figure 5-2 Functions related to information management.

the data bases are operable. This includes, but is not limited to, access controls, space, backup, recovery, restart, reorganization, and data item integrity.

Information Flow Diagrams: The information flow diagram consists of a subfunction description, role statement, and a diagram indicating information flows. Figure 5-3 is an information flow diagram for the Maintain Data Bases subfunction. Note that the data stores do not imply separate physical files; the idea is to represent the information that is required without regard to individual data items. As the information flow diagram gets better refined, the actual groupings of data items will fall in place.

Figures 5-4 through 5-6 are examples of information flow diagrams for some of the other subfunctions. Figure 5-4 represents an information flow diagram for ad hoc processing requests from end users. Figure 5-5 represents the information flow diagram for application system development. It indicates that organized libraries of utilities and relational models are available for use by the application development function. Figure 5-6 shows the information flow diagram for machine operations. The information flow diagrams for the functions reveal that there are common data stores that are used. The diagrams must be reviewed by the appropriate users to ensure their accuracy, and final sign-offs obtained, before proceeding further.

Subfunction: Maintain Data Bases

Role: Includes the monitoring of the data bases; the management of disk space; control and evolution of data base definitions; security, backup, and recovery of data bases.

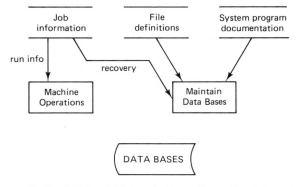

Figure 5-3 IFD for "Maintain Data Bases" subfunction.

Subfunction: Ad Hoc Processing

Role: Provision of reports to end users from strips of
"production" data bases; software technical assistance;
access to data bases.

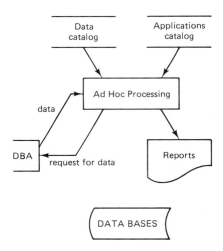

Figure 5-4 IFD for "Ad hoc Processing"
subfunction.

Subfunction: Application Development

Role: To analyze information requirements; design
and develop application system to user approval; and
implement the system consistent with data base and
operational standards.

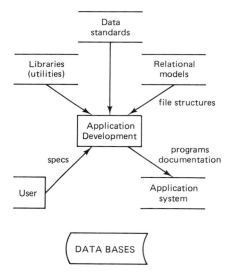

Figure 5-5 IFD for "Applications Development" subfunction.

2. Identify Entity Categories and Relationships

Once the users have signed-off on the diagrams, the next step is to identify the entity
categories and their interrelationships that would be necessary in order to perform
the functions. This is similar to the process of normalization with an additional twist—
since dictionaries offer considerable flexibility in organizing the entities into a model,
it is of the utmost importance that the appropriate trade-offs are made in choosing
the proper entities and the interrelationships.

From looking at the information flow diagrams it is apparent that data standard items must be one category. In addition, the regular data items that are defined
as part of a file can also fall under the generic entity category of data item. Systems,

Subfunction: Machine Operations

Role: To maintain the computer facility and network; to run jobs to a schedule; to maintain and evolve resources to meet ongoing and future needs.

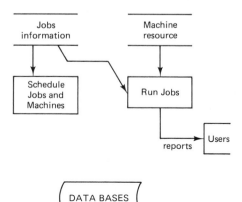

Figure 5-6 IFD for "Machine Operations" subfunction.

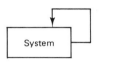

Figure 5-7 "System" entity category.

programs, and jobs are other entity categories that need to exist as separate categories. However, the definition of subsystems or subprograms as separate entity categories is questionable. That is because a subsystem is the same kind of entity as a system, only that it is a smaller piece of a system, defined so as to make the implementation of a project more feasible. Therefore, it would make sense to make systems and subsystems part of the "system" entity category. In order to represent the fact that subsystems will be subordinate to system entity occurrences in the data dictionary, the notation shown in Figure 5-7 can be used. The notation means that occurrences of the generic entity called "system" can be related to other occurrences in a hierarchical fashion. An example of the central dispatch system is shown in Figure 5-8

Figure 5-8 Illustration of notation.

to illustrate the notation. Note that CDS01, CDS02, CDS03, and so on, are subsystems subordinate to System. Each of these subsystems performs certain functions through the execution of job macros and programs. In some cases the job macros execute the programs; and in other cases, where the programs are interactive, they are executed directly by the user. For example, if programs called CDS0201 and CDS0202 were to be executed from a macro called CDS0201.CLI and another program called CDS0205 was to be executed directly by the user, these could be represented as shown in the hierarchy chart in Figure 5-9.

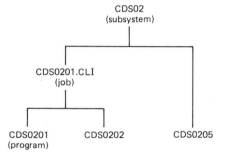

Figure 5-9 System hierarchy example.

Since there is a distinct difference between jobs and programs in the MIS operational environment, these can be put into two distinct entity categories and the entity model diagram can be redrawn to include the two entity categories and their interrelationships, shown in Figure 5–10. This entity model can accommodate the structuring of jobs within systems and subsystems, programs within jobs and subsystems, jobs within jobs, and programs within programs. The lines between the boxes and the arrows indicate the direction in which the entities will be stored (i.e., the superior-to-subordinate relationship). It does not mean to imply a restriction on the number of subordinates that a superior entity can have, or vice versa. The notation to the left of the line indicates the nature of the relationship in the direction of the arrow, whereas the notation to the right of the line indicates the nature of the relationship in the reverse direction. For instance, the relationship between the "system" and "program" entities should be read thus:

> System contains programs;
> Programs [are] within a system.

As the entity model is being developed, it is important to keep asking about potential reports that would be required from the model, because the paths in the entity model will be the basis on which reports are produced automatically by the system. For example, a person needing information about a program would also like to know about the job that drives the program and the subsystem of which the job is part. A person needing information about a file would need information about the records and data items that are part of the file as well as the programs that use that file.

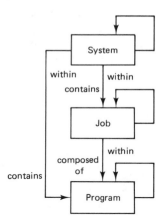

Figure 5–10 Example of entity model covering system, job, program.

3. Develop Relationship Notation

There could be many possible relationships between different entities. These have to be specified on the entity model diagram and the dictionary for the following reasons:

- Persons reading the entity model diagram will find it easier to understand the relationships.
- Reports from the dictionary will be easier to read if the nature of the relationship were identified.
- Information about the nature of the relationship can be stored and retrieved to facilitate machine interfaces.

For example, the relationship between the entities called "system" and "program" could be notated to produce the text "system *contains* program" and/or "programs *within* system." The information about the relationship that has to be portrayed on the entity diagram is the word "contains" for the relationship where "system" is the subject, and the word "within" for the case where the program is the subject. These notations are rules that the dictionary follows in presenting data to the user, whether it be in graphic form or text form.

4. Develop Attributes

Attributes are characteristics of an entity; they are often referred to as descriptors. The major difference between an attribute and narrative is the length of the description and the usage. Attributes are generally short and have a specific format; narratives can be any length and the format is left up to the user who enters the narrative. There is also a difference in the usage of attributes and narrative; attributes are used by machine interfaces to the dictionary, whereas narratives are generally used by humans to aid and enhance the understanding of the entity. Therefore, attributes have to be entered in precisely the way in which the machine expects it.

Once the major entities have been developed, the attributes for each entity must be developed. The attributes for each entity category must be developed to provide adequate input to the functions that will use them. In the case of entities that are required for machine interfaces such as copybooks or include files, the attributes have to follow the conventions of the receiving compiler. For instance, the Select clause for a file definition has to have an Assign statement and an Access Mode statement associated with it. Thus the Select, Assign, and Access Mode could be attributes of the file entity. The storing of these attributes has to follow the conventions of the COBOL compiler that is being used in the site. Attributes such as the origin of a data item, or the authoritative file where it can be found, are instances of attributes that need to be present in a specific format, and can be entered by the user from a screen.

Attribute as a Pointer. Bear in mind that an attribute could be used to contain a pointer or an address to another entity in the data dictionary, a file in the dictionary structure, or another physical object. This use of the attribute is beneficial for those applications that have to extract the pointer or address of that entity from the dictionary and then have to go to the address in a mechanical manner to operate on whatever exists at that address. The value of the attribute must thus be machine readable. For example, if the dictionary were to be used to point to a filename for a "copybook" entity, the full pathname from the root directory must be stored as the value of the attribute in order for the machine to decode the value and go to the filename in the directory in which it is located.

Attributes must be chosen with precision in mind, and the rules for entering the values must be specific in order to take advantage of mechanical interfaces to the dictionary. The vendor of the dictionary product will create the attributes for those interfaces that come with the package. These attributes cannot be modified. However, it is possible to add other attributes.

Attributes should be developed with a view to meeting the current and proposed reporting needs. Examples of reporting needs include reports on the programs developed by a certain author, person responsible for a set of data items, and sizes of certain groups of items.

5. Develop Access Keys

Access keys to the entities in the dictionary have to be defined with the end user in mind, because it is the end user who with very little knowledge of the contents of the data dictionary must be able to locate an entity by the terms most familiar to him/her. This means that the selection of access keys must be done with an idea of the most likely access paths to an entity occurrence. There are certain standard types of keys that are prevalent in the industry: enterprise names, aliases, and keywords in context (KWICs). You can develop other kinds of keys that will be useful in your organization. Both standard and customized keys will be discussed.

Enterprise name refers to the name by which an entity is generally known in the company or business enterprise. For example, the enterprise name for referring to customer identification could be "customer number" in some companies and "account number" in other companies. The data dictionary administrator must decide whether the enterprise name access key is also the standard name for the entity. In some installations, if the preponderance of usage against the dictionary is by systems development staff, the entity name could be the COBOL mnemonic that is used. For example, the entity called CUSTOMER NAME may be known by everybody as ACCOUNT NAME. It is recommended that only the commonly accepted name be stored as an enterprise name.

Aliases, as the term suggests, are alternate names given to the same entity. Aliases would generally be developed for those cases where the same entity could be referred to by different names by different categories of staff. In one such case, the COBOL mnemonic used by the systems developmment staff would be an alias to the entity. Note that there is another use for the alias key. If different entity occurrences having the same alias need to be tied together, it would be possible to do so utilizing the capabilities of the dictionary. For example, a rule that might be enforced in an installation might have the programmer put the standard COBOL name as an alias to the entity name, which consists of the standard name prefixed by a number. In such an installation, the entity called I023-CUST-NO would have an alias called CUST-NO.

Conversely, the standard COBOL abbreviation could be stored as an alternate key for an entity. For example, the entity called R052-CUST-NAME would have the COBOL mnemonic CUST-NAME stored as an alternate key. This facilitates the retrieval of all entities that have CUST-NAME as part of a record description, making it possible to locate the various occurrences of CUST-NAME within the organization data resources.

Another example of alternate key use is in cases where CUSTOMER NAME may be referred to as PROSPECT NAME by the salespeople and ACCOUNT NAME by the service people within the company. Hence PROSPECT NAME and ACCOUNT NAME are alternate keys for CUSTOMER NAME.

A recommended strategy is to use access keys in conjunction with a naming convention to tie together similar items that exist in several files within the MIS environment. For example, a standard COBOL name can have an access key that has the same name as the standard COBOL name. Note this example:

An entity called CUSTOMER NAME is defined as a standard. It has a COBOL name standard called CUST-NAME. Assume there is an element in a file that represents customer name; the element is called I041-CUST-NAME, following a particular naming convention. This element should have as its alternate key name "CUST-NAME." Figure 5–11 illustrates the resulting set of keys connected to the entity names. All elements with CUST-NAME as part of the entity name have the alternate key

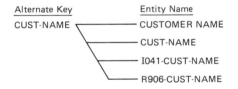

Figure 5–11 Relationships between alternate key and entity names.

"CUST-NAME" designated. Therefore, if you specify the alternate key "CUST-NAME," you receive a list of all the entities, within all the files, which have that name embedded in the COBOL name of the items.

Keywords in context (KWICs) represent keywords within the context of the entity name that can be used to access the entity. In the entity called "CUSTOMER ACCOUNT NUMBER" the keywords in context are CUSTOMER, ACCOUNT, and NUMBER. Selection of appropriate keywords should be done with an idea of the kinds of access words that could be used to access that entity. Trivial words or words that are not central to the entity or its context should not be stored as keywords.

Other Keys. Access keys other than alternate names may be used to tie entities together for various purposes. One of the significant access keys is Responsibility. This key represents the job, position, organization, or individual responsible for the support of the logical components represented by the entity. Authoritative Source represents the source of a data item. Data Management Function represents the intermediate or secondary function within the organization that acts as a funnel of data into the mechanized systems. Distribution indicates the users of entities, such as reports, data items, and programs.

When using these access keys, the administrator should be aware of the types of questions that can be answered by keeping the dictionary up to date. Questions such as "What reports are used by the different groups within the company?" can be answered by going to the access key value (in this case, Distribution) and tracing all the entities to which that key is connected.

Definer is a key that can be used to identify the person or department that provided the narrative for any entity in the data dictionary. In large organizations, it is especially important to be able to assign responsibility for developing the narrative for standard data items to the end user who is closest to the data item. This also provides an additional vehicle for communication of data definitions that can be used by all end users.

Category is another key that allows the grouping of standard entities into exclusive groups. An example of the values of the category key is given below.

The categories listed in Figure 5–12 are intended to provide an exclusive and exhaustive partitioning of all the data items entered into the data dictionary. The reason for exhaustive identification of standard entities through the various keys is to enable end users and system developers to identify the data resource in unambiguous terms. The fundamental premise is that a definition of an entity should have a unique title and thereby a unique tag. This tag is extremely important because the tag provides the means by which the data in the mechanized system can be stored and accessed. Once the entities, their attributes, and the access keys are defined, the next step is to develop the procedures that describe the persons and the circumstances under which the entities are created and modified.

6. Develop the Entity Model Diagram

The data dictionary system is designed on the premise that the user requires different kinds of entities. The user specifies entities and their potential interrelationships in block diagram form. This diagram represents the model on which the users will store data in the dictionary system.

The model must represent the entities and interrelationships that will be useful to the organization in fulfilling its functions. Initially, the DD project manager must create a list of entity classes in which the organization is interested. When defining an entity class, also define the entity types comprising the class. The entities (types)

Category	Definition	Examples
Name	Alphabetic characters that identify specific entities.	Customer name Employee name
Number	Alphanumeric characters that identify specific entities.	Part number PO number
Code	Characters that identify classifications or conditions of entities.	Alert status Type code End of file Change flag
Quantity	The number (including fractions) of anything except currency.	Record count Quantity ordered
Currency	Monetary amounts.	Unit price Total billed
Time	Temporal duration, interval, or occurrence.	Ship date Arrival time
Relation	A logical, mathematical, or natural association between one or more things.	Average downtime Percent failure
Location	The place or site where something is located.	Customer address Mail stop
Quality	An attribute of an entity; a property of a thing.	Color Size
Text	Data having relatively undefined (i.e., free-form) content.	Description Instructions

Figure 5-12 Data item categories.

defined as part of one entity class must be clearly different from the entities in another class, so that you can distinguish between classes. For example, the entities called "system" and "subsystem" have enough similarities that they can be put into one entity class called "system." In a similar fashion, rather than have several entity classes for report, voucher, check, microfiche, and so on, these can be categorized into one entity class called "output." Figure 5-13 shows entity classes and the kinds of "things" included within each class.

Entity Relationships.   Once the entity classes have been identified, the permissible relationships between the entity classes must be specified. Two types of relationships can be depicted: (1) intra-entity relationships and (2) inter-entity relationships.

An intra-entity relationship indicates that different occurrences of the same entity can be related among themselves. The notational representation for an entity that

Entity Class	Includes
1. Organization	Company, division, department
2. Manager	President, vice-president, director, manager, supervisor
3. System	Project, system, subsystem
4. Program	Job step, activity, utility, program
5. Output	Report, check, invoice, microfiche
6. Input	Form, screen, OCR cards

Figure 5-13 What an entity class includes.

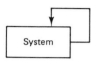

Figure 5–14 Intra-entity relationship.

possesses an intra-entity relationship is shown in Figure 5-14. Specifically, within the notational scheme described above we could relate different instances of the generic entity called "system," which includes project, system, and subsystem. Figure 5-15 shows the hierarchy of entity occurrences and their relationships which can be portrayed within an intra-entity relationship.

An inter-entity relationship indicates that several occurrences of a subordinate entity can be related to a superior entity. The notational representation of entities

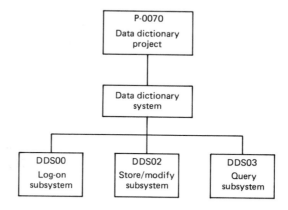

Figure 5–15 Example of intra-entity relationship.

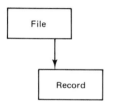

Figure 5–16 Inter-entity relationship.

that possess an inter-entity relationship is shown in Figure 5-16. Specifically within the foregoing notational scheme, we could relate several occurrences of a subordinate entity (e.g., records) to one occurrence of a superior entity (e.g., file). Figure 5-17 shows the occurrences of superior and subordinate entities and their interrelationships that can be portrayed in an inter-entity relationship.

The entity classes are shown in boxes drawn in a model diagram. The relationships are then drawn between the boxes and within the boxes. When developing the model diagram, note the reporting function that is inherent in the dictionary system. The objective of storing entities and relationships between entities is to generate reports depicting these relationships in a logical or hierarchical sequence. For example, a report

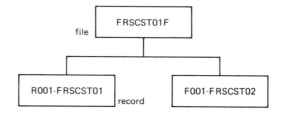

Figure 5–17 Example of inter-entity relationship.

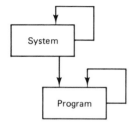

Figure 5–18 Model diagram relating system to program.

depicting the programs within subsystems within a system may be necessary. The model diagram shown in Figure 5-18 allows this.

To enable you to gain an understanding of the practical application of entity models, examples of entity diagrams from the IBM DB/DC dictionary, Cullinet's IDMS integrated data dictionary, and the author's model are shown in the next few pages. IBM's DB/DC dictionary model is shown in Figure 5-19. Most of the entity categories are self-explanatory. The entities PSB (program structure block), PCB (program control block), and Segment (equivalent to record) are related to IBM's information management system (IMS) data base product. Copy library members such as source definitions can be stored under the Module entity. Cullinet's IDMS integrated data dictionary model is composed of basic, teleprocessing, and special en-

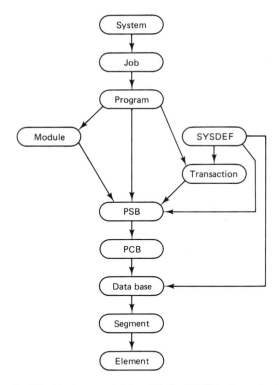

Figure 5-19 Entity model for IBM's DB/DC data dictionary.

tities shown in Figure 5-20. Figures 5-21 and 5-22 illustrate the entity model for the basic entities and teleprocessing entities. When looking at the teleprocessing model, note that there are linkages to entities such as programs, systems, users, and records, which occur in the basic entity model. The entity model developed by the author is shown in Figure 5-23. The model includes entities for data base administration, systems development, and computer operations.

Basic entities	Users
	Systems
	Files
	Elements
	Records (reports, transactions)
	Programs
	Entry points
	Modules (QFILES)
Teleprocessing entities	Messages
	Panels (screens)
	Maps
	Tasks
	Queues
	Destinations
	Lines
	Physical terminals
	Logical terminals
	Tables
Special entities	Classes
	Attributes
	User-defined
	Load modules

Figure 5-20 Table listing IDD entity types.

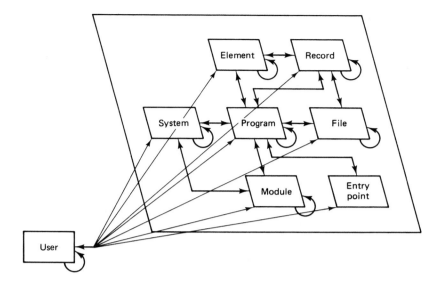

Figure 5-21   Basic IDD entity model.

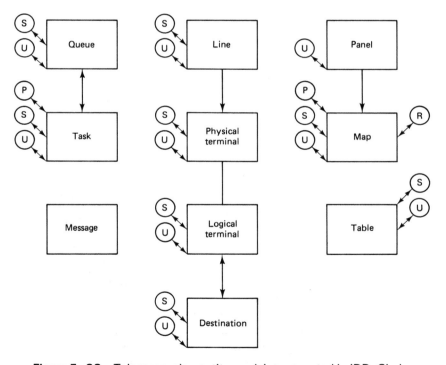

Figure 5-22   Teleprocessing entity model represented in IDD. Circles containing the letter P.S.U. or R indicate relationships with programs, systems, users, or records, respectively.

CODING SCHEME

The following section goes into further details of how the coding schemes within a typical dictionary are organized. The objective is to give the reader an understanding of the functions that have to be built into the dictionary for the user to be able to customize it and make it suitable for implementing in his/her environment.

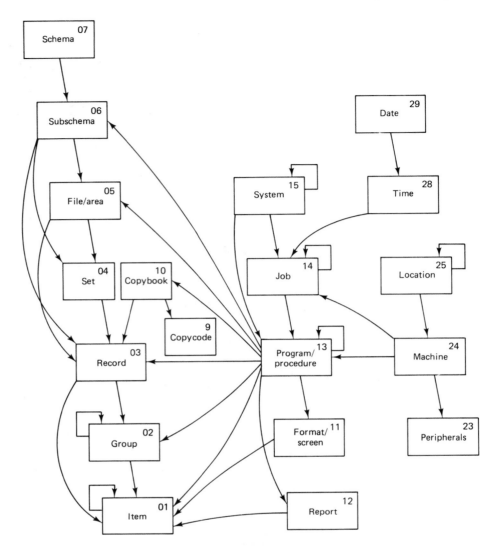

Figure 5-23 Author's entity model diagram representing relationships among data, system, machine, and time variables.

The data dictionary system is driven by parameters which are stored in the control region. These parameters consist of the entities and the relationships between them. The administrator establishes valid attribute classes, access keys, and entity-to-attribute combinations. The user, however, assigns the actual characteristics to the attributes. For example, the administrator establishes the entity "program" and the attribute "author" and permits a relationship between the two. The user assigns an actual name to "author."

All dictionary programs and procedures refer to the control tables before entities, access keys, attributes, or relationships can be stored in the dictionary. Therefore, it is extremely important that all relevant control information be stored accurately in the dictionary.

Figure 5-24 contains a list of entities and their associated type codes that were developed from the author's entity model shown in Figure 5-23. In the author's data dictionary system, to store the entity descriptions in the control table region, you would use the following procedure:

Entity	Type Code
Item	01
Group	02
Record	03
Set	04
File/area	05
Subschema	06
Schema	07
Copycode	09
Copybook	10
Format/screen	11
Report	12
Program/step	13
Job/procedure	14
System	15
Peripherals	23
Machine	24
Location	25
Time	28
Date	29

Figure 5–24 List of entities for author's entity model.

1. Log-on to DDS.
2. Select the Access Control function on the menu screen.
3. Select the Attribute/Access Key/Entity function on the control screen.
4. Enter ''ED'' for control code. Enter ''01'' for control type and ''Item'' for description. Then press the Add function key to store the ''01'' type code.
5. Repeat the process for the other entity codes.
6. To delete an entity code, follow steps 1 through 4 and press the Delete function key (instead of the Add function key in step 4).

Relationships between entities that constitute the model can be stored as four-digit codes. The first two digits represent the superior entity and the last two digits represent the subordinate entity. When there is a relationship of an occurrence of an entity to another occurrence of the same entity (intra-entity relationship), the first and second sets of digits are identical. This is shown in Figure 5–25. When there is an inter-entity relationship that has to be described in the dictionary, the superior entity's code is followed by the subordinate entity's code. This is shown in Figure 5–26.

Relationships constituting the model could be entered into the dictionary by the administrator, using the following procedure:

1. Log-on to DDS.
2. Select the Access Control function on the menu screen.
3. Select the Allowable Relationships function on the control menu.
4. Enter the relationship on the screen and press the Add function key.
5. Repeat this process until all the entity-to-entity relationships are stored.

Relationship Notation

Relationship notations are entered into the dictionary through the use of codes to designate which notations go with which relationships. The system will ask the DDA to enter the relationship notations for relationships at the time the relationship is stored.

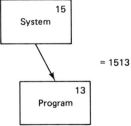

Figure 5–25 Coding for an intra-entity model.

Figure 5–26 Coding for an inter-entity model.

Attributes

The DD administrator first defines all the attribute classes that will be allowed in the dictionary system. An attribute is a property or characteristic of an entity (e.g., the color of a chair is an attribute of the chair). Level, picture clause, usage, and so on, are attributes of an item. Attribute classes that have already been entered into the dictionary can be used and additional attributes can be defined by the administrator. Each attribute has a two-character type code associated with it. The first character must be numeric (1–9) and the second character must be alphabetic (A–Z). The attributes and their type codes that were entered are shown in Figure 5–27.

1A	LEVEL
1B	REDEFINES
1C	OCCURS
1D	PICTURE
1E	USAGE
1F	SIGN
1G	SYNCHRONIZED
1H	JUSTIFIED
1J	VALUE
1K	RENAMES
1L	RANGE
1M	RECORD NAME
1N	EST. NUMBER
1P	TITLE
4A	SCHEMA NAME
4B	SCHEMA CREATE
4C	SCHEMA CHANGE
4L	DBMS-STATUS
4M	SUBSCHEMA
4N	WITHIN
4P	SET NAME
4Q	ALLOWS
4R	OWNER
4S	MEMBER
4T	INSERTION
4U	RETENTION
4V	ORDER
4W	SET KEY
4X	SET DUPLICATE
4Y	MEMBER LIMIT
4Z	OWNER MEMBER RATIO
5A	SELECT
5C	ASSIGN
5D	RESERVE
5E	ORGANIZATION
5F	ACCESS MODE
5G	FILE STATUS
5H	INFOS STATUS
5I	PARITY
5J	INDEX SIZE
5K	DATA SIZE
5L	TEMPORARY
5M	MANAGEMENT
5N	ROOT MERIT
5P	RECORD KEY
5Q	KEY ITEM
5R	ALLOW SUBINDEX
5S	COMPRESSION
5T	FD
5U	BLOCKSIZE
5W	RECORDING MODE
5X	LABEL
5Y	VALUE OWNER
5Z	EXPIRATION
6A	SEQUENCE
6B	GENERATION
6C	ACCESSIBILITY
6D	OFFSET
6E	VOLUME STATUS
6F	USER VOLUME
6G	USER HEADER
6H	USER TRAILER

Figure 5–27 Attributes and type codes in author's model.

6I	DATA RECORD
6J	LINAGE
6K	CODE SET
6L	FEEDBACK
6M	PAD
6N	INDEX NODE
6P	MERIT
6Q	PARTIAL
7A	USER MANAGER
7B	USER COORDINATOR
7C	SYSTEMS ANALYST
7D	PROJECT MANAGER
7E	PROJECT NUMBER
7F	PRIORITY
7G	EST. MAN WEEKS
7H	DOCUMENT ID
7J	FORM
7K	OUTPUT FREQUENCY
7L	OUTPUT VOLUME
7M	OUTPUT MEDIA
7R	MEDIUM
7S	INPUT FREQUENCY
7T	PROCESSING TIME
8A	AUTHOR
8B	LANGUAGE
8C	LINES OF CODE
8D	MEMORY
8E	SCHEDULE DAY
8F	SCHEDULE FREQUENCY
8G	SOURCE PATH NAME
8H	OBJECT PATH NAME
8I	TAPE DRIVES
8J	OPERATING SYSTEM
8K	OPERATING SYSTEM VERSION
8L	COBOL VERSION
8M	DISKS
8N	COPY BOOK
9P	CALL FORMAT

Figure 5-27   Continued

You would use the following procedure to enter the allowable attributes and their type codes into the dictionary.

1. Log-on to DDS.
2. Select the Access Control function on the menu screen.
3. Select the Attribute/Access/Key/Entity function on the control screen.
4. Enter "AD" for control code. Enter "1A" for control type and "Level" for description. Then press the Add function key.
5. Repeat the process for the other attributes.
6. To delete an attribute code, follow steps 1 through 4 and press the Delete function key (instead of the add function key in step 4).

When the entire list of attributes has been entered into the dictionary, the entity-to-attribute relationships must be entered; that is, the administrator defines the attributes that can be entered for a particular entity. You are limited to storing only those attributes for an entity that have been defined by the administrator. The list of entities and the attributes allowed for each are shown in Figure 5-28.

Access Keys

An entity may be one way of identifying an occurrence of an entity. However, for query purposes, it may be useful to determine other names by which the entity may be known or accessed. The dictionary system can accommodate several types of access keys. Examples of some standard types of access keys that have been entered

Entity	Attribute	Relation
Item	Level	011A
	Redefines	011B
	Occurs	011C
	Picture	011D
	Usage	011E
	Sign	011F
	Synchronized	011G
	Justified	011H
	Blank Zero	011I
	Value	011J
	Renames	011K
	Ranges	011L
	Title	011P
	Allows	014Q
Group	Level	021A
	Redefines	021B
	Occurs	021C
	Picture	021D
	Usage	021E
	Sign	021F
	Synchronized	021G
	Justified	021H
	Blank Zero	021I
	Value	021J
	Renames	021K
	Title	021P
Record	Level	031A
	Redefines	031B
	Renames	031K
	Record Name	031M
	Allows	034Q
	Order	035V
Set	DBMS-STATUS	044L
	Set Name	044P
	Allows	044R
	Member	044S
	Insertion	044T
	Retention	044U
	Order	044V
	Set Key	044W
	Set Duplicate	044X
	Member Limit	044Y
	Owner Member	044Z
	Key Item	045Q
File/Area	Title	051P
	Select	055A
	Assign	055C
	Reserve	055D
	Organization	055E
	File Status	055G
	Infos Status	055H
	Parity	055I
	Index Size	055J
	Data Size	055K
	Temporary	055L
	Management	055M
	Root Merit	055N
	Record Key	055P
	Key Item	055Q
	Allow Subindex	055R
	Compression	055S
	FD	055T
	Blocksize	055U
	Recordsize	055V
	Recording Mode	055W
	Label	055X
	Value Owner	055Y
	Expiration	055Z
	Sequence	056A
	Generation	056B
	Accessibility	056C
	Offset	056D
	Volume Status	056E

Figure 5–28 Entity to attribute relationships in author's model.

Entity	Attribute	Relation
	User Volume	056F
	User Header	056G
	User Trailer	056H
	Data Record	056I
	Linage	056J
	Code Set	056K
	Feedback	056L
	Pad	056M
	Index Node	056N
	Merit	056P
	Partial	056Q
Subschema	Subschema	064M
	Within	064N
	Allows	064Q
Schema	Schema Name	074A
	Schema Create	074B
	Schema Change	074C
Format/Screen (Input)	Medium	117R
	Input Frequency	117S
	Processing Time	117T
	Form	127J
	Output Frequency	127K
	Output Volume	127L
	Output Media	127M
Program/Step	Title	131P
	Author	128A
	Language	138B
	Lines of Code	138C
	Memory	138D
	Source Path Name	138G
	Object Path Name	138H
	Tape Drives	138I
	Copy Book	138N
	Call Format	138P
Job/Procedure	Schedule Day	148E
	Schedule Freq.	148F
System	User Manager	157A
	User Coordinator	157B
	Systems Analyst	157C
	Project Manager	157D
	Project Number	157E
	Priority	157F
	Est. Man Weeks	157G
	Document I.D.	157H
Machine	Memory	248D
	Tape Drives	248I
	Operating Sys	248J
	Operating System	248K
	Cobol Version	248L
	Disks	248M

Figure 5–28 Continued

into the control table region of the data dictionary are shown in Figure 5–29. The access key code is a two-character field: the first character is alphabetic and the second character is numeric. Use the following procedure to enter additional access key types.

1. Log-on to DDS.
2. Select the Access Control function on the menu screen.
3. Select the Attribute/Access Key/Entity function on the DD Control screen.
4. Enter "KD" for control code. Enter the appropriate type code (e.g., "B7") and the corresponding description, and press the Add function key.
5. Repeat step 4 to enter additional access key types. To delete an access key type, enter the pertinent information about the key type and press the Delete function key.

Enterprise	A1
Alternate Key/Alias	A2
Keyword in Context (KWIC)	A3
Keyword out of Context (KWOC)	A4
Definer	A5
Author	A6
Category	B1
Authoritative Source	B2
Data Management Function	B3
Business Process	B4
Distribution	B5
Responsibility	B6

Figure 5–29 Access keys and codes.

When the administrator has entered the valid access key types, you can create entities and store as many access keys for an entity as may be necessary. Since the system does not impose any restrictions on the number or types of access key that can be stored for an entity, it is important that the DD project manager define the conventions that should be used.

chapter 6

Entity Naming Standards

IMPORTANT OF STANDARDS

IMPORTANCE OF STANDARDS

Standardization helps to simplify the tasks of anyone concerned with understanding and communicating with others and with the systems. By proper use of naming conventions, documentation standards, program source and copy file library procedures, it should be possible for MIS staff to pick up other people's work and understand what they are doing with their systems, programs, files, and so on. From the user perspective, the use of naming conventions in the dictionary will make it easier for users to locate information, understand the meaning of this information, and to use the data dictionary in their day-to-day working environment.

One of the major problems that will confront the dictionary project manager is the multitude of naming conventions that have cropped up over time in the systems in MIS. It is a rare MIS environment that has a single naming convention throughout all its systems and data bases. This is because of the way in which systems were built and the ease with which programmer/analysts have been able to put their own personal stamp on naming different objects. This is not something that happened by design, but more because programmers have thought of themselves as creative individuals, and one area where their creativity could bear a personal stamp is in the naming of data items.

The issue of naming conventions comes loaded with emotional overtones. People who are used to one naming convention are loath to change to somebody else's naming convention for the "greater" good; thus we have a major political task on our hands. An argument that is often used by programmers is that as long as interfaces are developed around a data base that provide a unified view, it is not necessary to conform to a single standard. An example of this is when one application group may decide to expand a customer number from 7 bytes to 8 bytes, assuming that by doing so it can satisfy the local need as well as accommodate the information from different systems using the 7-byte convention. There is a fallacy in this approach. If every application group were to develop a different convention that met the local site's needs, integration of these differences later would cause enormous difficulties.

If there is inconsistency between the size of items between various data bases, it would be difficult for different applications to transfer that data item without the requirement for conversion routines. Not only is it important to keep to the same standard across all application systems for the sake of maintainability of the data bases, but also to ensure that people and systems can communicate with each other in a consistent fashion. The objective with any standard is to give persons working on projects related to the data base a warm and comfortable feeling that certain ground rules will not be changed without major thought and consideration. The standard will also make it possible to develop programs against the same date base concurrently.

One of the arguments that is often encountered from programmer/analysts who have to contend with changes in the size of data items is to make the data items' size as large as is practical so that changes do not have to be made at a later date. For example, if the customer name field size needed to be expanded from 30 to 35 characters, these persons would argue that it should be expanded to 40 characters, once and for all time. However, depending on the file management system and report writing systems being used, this practice may have untoward ramifications on disk space utilization and report layouts. In the case of disk space, every customer record would have to carry five extra characters; in the case of reports, space would have to be allocated for the extra characters and the report layout may become too cumbersome.

It is important to take into account future expansion possibilities as far as any identifying number such as customer number is concerned. However, in one case where the customer field size was expanded from 5 bytes to 7 bytes, the argument was made to expand it to 8 bytes as a safety precaution. Since the future cannot be predicted, the question that comes to mind is: "Why choose 8 bytes, as opposed to say 10 or even 12 bytes, since the larger the size of the field, the greater the safety factor?" With 7 alphanumeric bytes, it seems sufficient for future expansion (possibility of 34 billion combinations), as opposed to 5 numeric bytes, which would have allowed for only 99,999 customers! There does not appear to be that much difference between 7 bytes and 8 bytes, except that there is a fairly large investment in 7 bytes in the programs and files that would need to be changed, whereas there is not a similar stake in an 8-byte field.

An argument that is often brought up has to do with the technological advantages of schemas and subschemas, where the subschema veiw of the data base can be different from the schema view, and the data base management system (DBMS) will make the differences transparent to the user. Thus the data base can have a physical size of 8 bytes but a logical (or subschema) view of 7 bytes. The argument seems to be based on the logic that as long as what the person is doing can accommodate the information from other systems and not do any harm to someone else, it will not make any difference! This argument can boomerang because the next programmer/analyst can come along and using the same logic, make the customer number field 9 bytes long. This situation only leads to more problems for the organization in the long run.

It cannot be emphasized enough that all the arguments to have different standards to suit a local situation must be treated as an exceptional situation that must be reviewed for overall impact. That is not to say that there will not be any exceptions. Changes created in one data item will have repercussions on many data bases and programs, as well as extract files and end-user computing users, which could result in a lot of confusion and frustration. The efforts that are made to put forward a single consistent view of a data item into the data dictionary will have been in vain.

The role of a standard, whether it is a naming convention, a procedure, or a field size is not only to ensure that people and systems can communicate with each other in a consistent fashion, but to give different programmer/analysts from different parts of the organization working on a common system the feeling that certain ground rules are there that will not be changed without major thought and consideration. This is where a listing from the dictionary specifying all the impact of changing the name or size of a data item can come in handy in convincing the recalcitrant programmer/analyst or project leader.

In addition to the complications arising from inconsistent naming conventions, the use of a mechanized dictionary system imposes its own set of restrictions that have to be accommodated. Thus the DD project manager is faced not only with the task of reconciling existing naming conventions, but with coming up with something that can be used with the dictionary system. The best advice that can be given is to try to come up with a naming convention that causes as little upheaval to the organization as possible. One other twist to this is the implementation strategy for the dictionary—if it is decided to implement an existing system into the dictionary, it may be beneficial to be flexible in the approach to a naming convention. Some exceptions to the naming convention can be made to demonstrate a result that will help sell the dictionary to other prospective users. In all other cases, no compromise to the naming convention should be allowed.

STRUCTURED APPROACH TO NAMING STANDARDS

What is needed is a structured approach to describe data characteristics that will make it possible for a requester to find information in the dictionary when only a general description of the item is known. For example, a system analyst may need to know whether a data item already exists or is being defined for the first time. If it already exists and has been defined in the dictionary, the analyst will have to consider present users of the item and choose between the existing description or allowing a different description to coexist in the dictionary. An occasional user may want to know if some data item is part of the organization's data bases, if it really represents what is needed, and if so, what name it is stored under. For example, the documentation about a data item could contain information such as:

- Its meaning
- Its standard name for program use
- Who has responsibility for specifications, definition, etc.
- Its characteristics (size, type, etc.)
- How it is obtained (source document, computation, algorithm, etc.)

The name given to an entity within the dictionary is the key or handle by which it will be primarily referenced in the screens and reports of the dictionary system. Thus a lot of thought has to be given to coming up with appropriate names. Also, remember that the names that are entered in the dictionary are the ones that will be used and propagated throughout the systems that are developed in MIS and in the end-user computing environment. One of the major reasons for having a consistent naming convention is that independently developed systems should use the same name to reference the same entity. If different names are allowed, multiple systems may be duplicating data. The resultant data redundancy poses problems of both nonparallel update and poor usage of physical storage space. When naming conventions are used, the data administrator can recognize nonstandard names readily.

Other names, such as aliases and access keys, can also be used to link to the primary name. Where the primary name of an entity should be unique, the aliases and access keys can point to several primary entities. The user should be able to reference a primary name with the full confidence that it is unique and possesses a singular meaning or definition that is different from other entities. Access keys, on the other hand, are used to locate a primary entity; thus they are useful in a search process, and their creation should be based on the assumption that the user needs the access keys to help narrow down the search for the primary entity. For example, if the primary entity name is CUSTOMER NAME, and it has keys such as CUSTOMER, NAME, NAME OF CUSTOMER, CUSTOMER ID, and CUST-NAME, then a user who wishes to browse through the dictionary and enters the key word CUSTOMER would be presented with several alternative primary entity names to choose from, such as CUSTOMER ADDRESS, CUSTOMER NAME, and CUSTOMER TYPE, and could then make the appropriate choices.

The dictionary provides other kinds of access keys to suit the needs of users. Such access methods as keyword in context (KWIC), enterprise name, and category permit entity identification schemes that allow for greater flexibility in using the dictionary for the end user who may not be familiar with the terminology or acronyms prevalent within the various groups within the organization. Rules and procedures for the creation of different alternate keys must be defined by the data dictionary administrator, so that consistent naming conventions are followed.

The data dictionary is commonly used as a store for the definitions of logical data items as well as their physical representation on computer files. Every data item in the files is stored as a separate occurrence of an entity in the data dictionary. Hence every data item must have a unique name in the dictionary. This can be achieved only through the consistent application of a naming convention. In most installations, a prefix to the standard name of the data item is used to uniquely reference that data item in the program. As an example:

If the standard mnemonic for customer number is CUST-NO, its usage in various files could be I065-CUST-NO, D128-CUST-NO, I129-CUST-NO, and so on, where the I065, D128, and I129 are prefixes to the standard name. The alternate key or alias for each of these items could be the same as the standard mnemonic (i.e., CUST-NO). Thus we would have the links shown in Figure 6–1. Thus a query through the

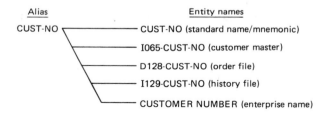

Figure 6–1 Entity names and alias.

alias key of CUST-NO will display all the entity names shown. Incidentally, this provides one way of doing a where-used analysis if there is a need to find out the physical occurrences of customer number in the organization's data base of information.

ENTITY IDENTIFICATION

The primary entity is the key by which that entity is known. In the case of a report entity, the primary name could reflect the fact that only one occurrence of the entity needs to be stored. However, in the case of a program, there may be the need to store multiple occurrences of the same entity. For example, a program could be under development and a description of the program is stored in the dictionary. Then when the program is implemented and put into "production," that occurrence of the program entity in the dictionary needs to be preserved intact so that the operations personnel can view it.

Until now we have had only one occurrence of the program entity stored in the dictionary. As happens in most MIS departments, the users of the system require some enhancements to the program. To assure that the information about the program as it is enhanced is entered into the dictionary, another occurrence of the entity has to be created, so that the contents of the "production" version are kept intact. Thus we now have two occurrences stored in the dictionary, a "production" occurrence and a "development" occurrence. This is shown in Figure 6–2.

In a typical dictionary, these occurrences are differentiated by a "status" indicator, with a "P" code to represent production and a "D" code to represent development. Other status codes, such as "T" for test, "O" for obsolete, and "I" for inactive, are to be found in most dictionaries. The status code serves a dual purpose: It facilitates the transition from development to test to production to obsolete for a single occurrence in the dictionary, thus allowing a change control function to be incorporated; it also allows for the existence of multiple occurrences of the entity, thus allowing for the update protection of the "production" occurence.

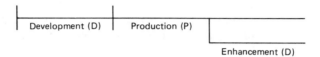

Figure 6–2 Entity occurrences.

The dictionary serves as a focal point for conflict resolution with respect to data definitions. For example, there may two groups that claim to have the "correct" definition for an entity called "part." But we have stated that in the dictionary there should only be one definition for one entity with a primary name. To facilitate the conflict resolution process, it is important that the different versions of an entity be stored in the dictionary. That way, all parties will have a chance to be recognized and heard as far as the dictionary facility is concerned. Thus multiple occurrences of the same entity can be stored using version numbers. Generally, version numbers start with 1 and go up to 99.

In many system design situations, several versions of an entity may be defined; ultimately, one of these versions may be selected as the final version. It may also be necessary to exert version control in a project management situation, where several entities possessing the same version number may need to be tied together. For any entity that is created, a default version number of 01 is set by the system unless the user specifically enters a different version number.

An entity must be identifiable by an identifier; that is, it must have a unique handle or key by which it can be stored in electronic media and retrieved in a short amount of time. The entity name alone is not a suitable unique identifier, because there may be situations where the name of two different kinds of entities may be the same. For instance, there may exist a file called "CUSTOMER" and a record called "CUSTOMER." Therefore, a differentiating factor must be brought in to uniquely identify an entity occurrence within an entity class. Since each class has a unique type code, the type code can be added to the entity name to uniquely identify each occurrence.

In the data dictionary system, each class of entities is assigned a type code. To identify a record called "CUSTOMER," you would have to specify an entity type of "record" and an entity name of "CUSTOMER." It is not necessary to carry the entity type within the name of the entity.

EXAMPLE OF ENTITY IDENTIFICATION

The key by which an entity occurrence is stored in the author's data dictionary system is a combination of the following fields:

Entity name	Up to 30 characers
Entity type code	2 characters
Entity status	1 character
Entity version	2 characters
Entity qualifier	2 characters
Entity node	2 characters

Thus any combination of the above automatically results in the creation of a new entity occurrence in the dictionary.

Type Code

The entity identification process starts with what type code the entity belongs to (e.g., data item, program, report, input, etc.). Each of these entity classes has a unique two-digit identifier that is assigned by the data dictionary administrator. The following type codes have already been defined for the data dictionary system.

Type	Entity Class
01	Item
02	Group
03	Record
04	Set
05	File/area
06	Subschema
07	Schema
10	Copybook
11	Format/screen
12	Report
13	Program/step
14	Job/proc
15	System
23	Peripherals
24	Machine
25	Location
28	Time
29	Date
31	Logical group
32	Activity
33	Process
34	Function
35	Subject data base

Additional entity classes may be defined by the data dictionary administrator to meet the needs of the installation via the extensibility feature.

Status

Status is a one-character field that represents the status of the entity that is in the data dictionary. The status field would be used, for example, in the system development process where a program is first in development status, then goes through testing, and then goes into production. As the program goes through these stages, only the status field needs to be changed for the program entity. The status field can have the following values:

Production   P
Future   F
Test   T
Inactive   I
Development   D

By default, the system sets the status field to a space. Rules must be established and enforced to ensure that the status fields change when the status of the project changes.

Version

Version is a two-digit numeric field that represents the version number of the entity. In the situation with evolution and enhancement of systems, multiple versions of entities are needed to reflect the fact that multiple versions are being supported at different sites in a "production" mode.

Qualifier

There are several situations in which the use of a qualifier is beneficial. In installations that use a CODASYL-type data base management system, the subschema definitions of records and items are generally the same as the schema definitions of records and items. In the dictionary, the entity type code for a schema record is the same as that for a subschema record or any record; the same applies to items. Therefore, the combination of record or item name and the corresponding entity type codes does not result in uniqueness of definition across a schema and one or more subschemas. The only way to ensure uniqueness is to use an additional field—the qualifier. The qualifier can have a value that is unique for each schema and subschema being defined. To avoid duplicate names, a qualifier is used. The qualifier is a two-character field designed to eliminate these problems. The user ensures the unique identity of any entity by using the entity name in conjunction with the entity type and qualifier.

Use of the qualifier is also beneficial in cases where a number of duplicate names are already in existence and must be entered into the dictionary. Suitable qualifiers can be specified, enabling the entities to be stored in the dictionary without any conflicts. Note, however, that when any operation is being performed on an entity with a qualifier, that qualifier becomes a part of the identifying key and must be specified. To summarize, the uniqueness of an entity is ensured by the combination of entity name, entity type code, and the qualifier. The default value of the qualifier is spaces. Qualifier values are set at the discretion of the user. It is recommended that rules be set within the installation as to when the qualifier should be used.

An example of the use of a qualifier would be to identify the standard elements used in the company to the users of the dictionary. The qualifier "DS," which indicates "data standard," would convey a specific meaning to the programmer/ analysts who would be using the dictionary during the system definition phase. Procedurally, the system analyst could enter a definition of a new item directly into the dictionary during the system definition phase. Procedurally, the system analyst could enter a definition of a new item directly into the dictionary without a qualifier. When the definition of the item is approved as a standard, then—and *only* at that time—is the qualifier entered into the dictionary.

Node

In data processing installations which have several mainframes or minicomputers, copies of the same program may run in several machines that are located physically apart. Or data may be stored in data bases in remote locations in a network of computer systems. Therefore, it is important that the data base administrator or the network administrator know the entities that belong to or are operational on a particular system within the network (or collection of computers, if networking is not in place).

Before using the two-character node field, the data dictionary administrator should be aware of the physical configuration of computers in the data processing installation and should establish a naming convention to identify each computer system. A node is defined as a machine configuration that includes a central processing unit (CPU), memory, and associated peripherals such as disk storage and communications interfaces. An example of a convention for naming nodes would be to start with "H0" for the main system and then "H1," "H2," and so on. If the user does not specify a value for the node field, the DDS sets the node to spaces.

The major reason for creating the node field is to account for the movement of data processing functions into what is commonly referred to as the "distributed data processing environment." This umbrella concept includes several dictionary functions. One such function illustrates the use of the dictionary as a directory. That is, if the data resources are located in different computers, you should be able to identify the location of these data items and retrieve them with the assistance of the data dictionary. Until the directory functions are fully established and well defined, it is recommended that the node field be set to spaces (the default value) as a standard practice.

GENERIC VERSUS SPECIFIC NAMES

Entity naming standards usually exist in the MIS environment; the extent to which they are consistently followed could vary depending on the enforcement of the standards. What normally exists is a combination of naming conventions that people get used to. Over time, the same entity is called by different names by different groups within MIS. To reconcile these differing naming conventions requires a strong and aggressive data administration group.

The data dictionary allows one name to be associated with an entity occurrence. This is the entity's primary name by which it is accessed in the dictionary. A given file, record, program, or data item can carry multiple names in the dictionary as secondary names or aliases. The alias is an alternate key by which the entity can be searched for. Note that two entities could have the same secondary name, whereas each would have a unique primary name. This allows different groups access to the standard entity through the use of synonyms with which they are familiar. In the course of time, use of the primary names will become prevalent throughout the organization. For example, customers may be referred to as 'prospects" by the salespeople but as "accounts" by the headquarters staff. Therefore, the primary name of "customer" with aliases of "account" and "prospect" would satisfy the needs of all groups.

An important aspect of creating names for data items is how specific the name should be. A definition of a data item that is too general will ultimately cause a conflict with another definition for a different data item because the primary names may turn out to be the same. To avoid this situation, it is wise to insist on definitions that are as detailed and specific as possible. For example, look at the titles and the respective abbreviations in Figure 6–3. The objective of the example is to illustrate the point that the naming standard goes beyond just obtaining unique primary names; in fact, the name should be derived with the full knowledge of other primary names

Quantity of parts	QTY-PART
Qty. of parts shipped	QTY-PART-SHIP
Qty. of parts received	QTY-PART-RECD
Qty. parts ship field	QTY-PART-SHIP-FLD
Qty. parts ship warehouse	QTY-PART-SHIP-WHSE
Qty. parts ship field period 1	QTY-PART-SHIP-FLD-P1
Qty. parts ship field period 2	QTY-PART-SHIP-FLD-P2

Figure 6-3 Example of abbreviations.

in the environment, so that the dictionary is a credible source of reference for all users. As the primary name list expands, it should be examined continuously to ferret out inconsistencies that could affect the credibility of the dictionary. This means that there should only be one primary name per definition, and that name should be as specific as possible.

Domain Concept

In this context, a useful perspective is the domain concept. The domain refers to the underlying type of data item that is sought to be standardized. Thus, if the quantity field in all systems is defined as an 8-byte numeric field, the variations of the quantity field by part within field are individual data items over the domain "quantity." Thus the reasoning goes that the edit and validation criteria for the domain need to be developed only once, and all variations are covered by that domain. Thus, in defining the more "specific" instance of the data item (i.e., QTY-PART-SHIP), quantity does not have to be defined more than once, and that will apply to all specific data items where quantity values are required.

OBSTACLES IN INSTITUTING NAMING CONVENTIONS

The rules regarding the derivation of entity names should be published for the benefit of all users. It is important that these rules be applied as consistently as possible so that users do not feel that names have been derived in an arbitrary manner. It has been the experience of many DBAs that instituting a naming convention in a department where several different standards have been followed is a trying one. There are several reasons for this.

Many data processing persons get comfortable using certain mnemonics for identifying data items in their programs and documentation, as well as in verbal discussions. These people have implicitly mapped a certain translation in their minds so that it becomes a habitual association. To change this habit and to ask a person to learn a new habit will elicit a certain reluctance on the part of individuals, and the dictionary administrator must be prepared to handle this.

Depending on how specific one gets in defining the data item, another definition may come along that is more specific than the previous one. If so, to maintain the integrity of the data item convention, it becomes necessary to rename the former item in order to accommodate the new item. Since all data items are not known ahead of time, it is impossible to prevent this situation from occurring.

As the scope of data administration expands, it is possible that organizational changes would have an impact on the naming standard. If a system that was developed in another organization is transferred to the jurisdiction of the data administration function, there may be a spillover impact from the differences between the different systems.

If the scope of responsibility of the systems organization changes from a national charter to an international charter, the need to incorporate global processing rules would force changes to the data item standard.

If there are changes in the edit rule for a data item based on the needs of a system, this may require the creation of a new name for that data item to differentiate it from the item that has a different edit rule.

However farsighted the administrator is in assigning a byte-size to a data item, it often happens that the original assumptions change. It is important to trade-off the immediate requirements with future requirements. Note that if the size of a data item is too large, it forces unnecessary burdens on the data entry operator to key in extra characters, forces changes in screen and record layouts, and so on.

Whether an item is defined as alphanumeric or numeric was decided based on the automatic edit features of the hardware and operating system. Since machines have become more powerful and can handle many more instructions in a program because of virtual processing and expanded memory size, it is not necessary to be totally restricted by the hardware edit criteria. It may be preferable to let the item be flexible to accept alphanumeric characters, but have edits in place to control the quality of the data that go into the data file.

SAMPLE NAMING CONVENTIONS

Although the issues listed above may appear to inhibit the development of adequate naming schemes for data items, most organizations do have naming conventions that are a combination of systematic rules, home-grown conventions, and site-specific nomenclature. IBM has developed a technique for deriving names that is referred to as the "OF" convention. Following this is a naming convention developed by the author for use in a minicomputer installation. The third example is taken from Cullinet's integrated data dictionary (IDD) user's guide. These descriptions are given with the intention of giving the reader some references to use in developing a naming scheme.

IBM'S "OF" CONVENTION*

Developing Designator Statements for Dictionary Entities

In most cases, a Dictionary user who is able to describe the data definition needed but has no other information to identify the machine readable COBOL, PL/I or Assembler name cannot retrieve the definition. By developing a descriptive designator of 40–80 characters and storing this information in the text (40 characters) or user segments (80 characters), a user could easily obtain the needed definition. The definition could be retrieved using SCAN or the report functions.

The following discussion is a technique that could be used to develop satisfactory designators. In addition, once these designator statements have been defined, it would be a logical next step to develop a keyword look-up capability.

Designator Statement

Identification and retrieval of DB/DC Data Dictionary information are essential requirements for computer manipulation of and human interaction with the Dictionary. Each element must have two types of unique identifiers—a Label (for the computer) and a Designator (for the human).

A Label is created by the analyst or data base administrator when the data item is specified. Labels and their definitions are organized into the Dictionary by entity type. Consequently, if the Label of a data item and entity type are both known to

*Pages 98-104 are reprinted by permission of IBM Corporation.

a user, retrieval of the definition of the data item is simple. However, if this information is not known, the data item would be impossible to retrieve.

The designator statement facilitates retrieval (using the Dictionary SCAN and REPORT commands) of the data item definition being sought by a user who is able to describe the item, but does not know it by any machine readable names. At data specification time, the data analyst chooses and organizes a series of key words to describe the data item being built in the Dictionary. The organization of these key words determines the Designator.

1. Structure. A Designator statement consists of, from left to right:

Class Word/Connector/Prime Word/Connector
/First Modifier/Connector. . ./Final Modifier

Each of these terms must be highly derivable, easily understood to insure effective usage, and arranged in a specific sequence. The organization of a Designator requires placement of the general term first, followed by the next general term, etc., until terminated by the least general or most specific term.

For example, consider the phrase "Abbreviated customer name." The most general term is "Name: since it can distinguish any person or thing. Ask the question, Name of what?"—obviously the answer must be "Name of customer?". The next question is, "What about the name of customer?". It is abbreviated. Therefore, to be organized in the proper Designator sequence, these three key words must be written, "Name, customer, abbreviated:. However, since this organization is not particularly readable in this form, several connectors are inserted to complete the Designator.

NAME (of) CUSTOMER (which is) ABBREVIATED

2. Connectors. These are six connectors (see Figure 6–4) which may be used to structure Designators to make them readable. The six connectors used are:

1. Of
2. Which is/are
3. The hyphen
4. Or
5. And
6. By, per, within

Since the preposition "of" is used most often in Designator structuring, the syntax of the Designator is called the "OF Language." The syntax of the "OF Language" does not provide for action or elaborate verbal structure, but simply names and qualifies nouns, adjectives, and their respective connectors.

Compound words should only be used when it is meaningful to do so. The guide to follow in using compound words for the Designator is to consider current usage. If you were seeking specific data, would you think of it in terms of a compound word? However, it is wise to avoid a cumbersome string of compound words. Refer to Figure 6–4 for examples of usage of connector symbols.

3. Class Words. The words that constitute the Designator are selected to provide maximum understanding of the data. To create meaningful Designators, the first word of the Designator Statement represents the class of the specified data. The Class

Symbol	Definition	Convention	Example
b	A blank space between terms designates "of" and is machine printed as "OF".	Blanks following the final term of the Designator, and single blanks on either side of another connector symbol will be recognized as blanks, not as "OF". Multiple blanks between terms will be recognized as a single "CF". (The graphic b is the symbol for a blank.)	Both bNAMEbCUSTOMER and NAMEbbCUSTOMER are recognized as NAME (of) CUSTOMER
*	An asterisk designates "which is/are" depending on the presence or absence of the letter "s" just prior to the asterisk.	None	1. NAMEbCUSTOMER* ABBREVIATED is recognized as NAME (of) CUSTOMER (which is) ABBREVIATED 2. NAMEbCUSTOMERS* ABBREVIATED is recognized as NAME (of) CUSTOMERS (which are) ABBREVIATED
-	A hyphen causes two or more words to become a single word, compound word, or phrase.	None	MAN-NUMBER
|	The perpendicular line designates "or".	None	COLORbMACHINE* RED|BLUE is recognized as COLOR (of) MACHINE (which is) RED (or) BLUE
&	The ampersand designates "and".	None	PRODUCTbWTC&DPC is recognized as PRODUCT (of) WTC (and) DPD
/	Slash between terms designates "by", "per", or "within".	None	AMOUNT DOLLARS YEAR-TO-DATE/ PROJECT is recognized as AMOUNT (of) DOLLARS* YEAR-TO-DATE (by) PROJECT

Figure 6-4 "OF" Language connector symbols.

Word identifies the general use of the data and a reference is provided in Figure 6-5. Eleven Class Words are provided for appropriate handling.

The *Prime* and *Modifier Words* are further modifying terms which insure the uniqueness of the Designator.

- *Prime word.* A given Designator's Prime Word is that single or compound (hyphenated) word which is modified or qualified by all other words. It is the most general term of those used to describe an item. An example which shows the use of the Prime Word is:

CLASS	con	PRIME
CODE	(of)	MACHINE

Symbol	Class Word	Definition	Example
N	NAME	Alphabetic data that identify specific entities	CUSTOMER NAME SUPPLIER NAME
#	NUMBER	Alphanumeric data that identify specific entities	PURCHASE ORDER NUMBER PART NUMBER
C	CODE	Data that identify classifications of entities	STATUS OF SHIPMENT CODE; UNIT OF MEASURE CODE
Q	COUNT (QUANTITY)	The number of quantity (including fractions) of anything except monetary amounts	QUANTITY ORDERED QUANTITY RECEIVED
$	AMOUNT (CURRENCY)	The quantity of monetary amounts	UNIT PRICE AMOUNT PAID
D	DATE	Actual calendar date	DATE ORDER PLACED PROMISED DELIVERY DATE
T	TEXT	Data having relatively undefined content	ITEM DESCRIPTION SHIPPING INSTRUCTIONS
F	FLAG	A code expressed as a bit and limited to two conditions	DELETED RECORD FLAG
X	CONTROL	Information used for control of other information during processing	CARD CODE TRANSACTION CODE
K	CONSTANT	Data that do not change value from one transaction to another	COLUMN HEADINGS PRINT MASKS
%	PERCENT	Ratios between other data values from one transaction to another	PERCENT OF SHIPMENTS ON TIME, PERCENT OF SHIPMENTS LATE

Figure 6–5 "OF" Language Class words.

- *Modifier word.* The Modifier Word is a single or compound (hyphenated) word which modifies or qualifies a Prime Word, a Modifier Word, or a combination of Prime and Modifier Words. It differs from the Prime Word in that it is more specific. An example showing the use of the Modifer Word is:

CLASS	con	PRIME	con	MODIFIER
CODE	(of)	MACHINE	(of)	IBM

4. Building a Designator. This example designates the reimbursable expense incurred by a Service Engineer to make a service call. Since the data is a quantity of dollars, the Class Word is Amount. This Designator might be written as follows:

AMOUNT (of) EXPENSE (of) CALL (which is) SERVICE

It is important to note the following:

1. Abbreviations or mnemonics should not be used to build Designators unless the builder is highly certain that a user with little prior knowledge of the data will correctly interpret the intended meaning.

2. The Designator example above identifies the data as a service call expense, but does not define which component. Designated thus, the data could be interpreted as time and material expense to the company for the service call. Ask the question, "What about the amount of expense which is service?" The answer is, "It is reimbursable." More explicitly structured then, the Designator may be written as follows:

AMOUNT (of) EXPENSE (of) CALL (which is) SERVICE
(and which is) REIMBURSABLE

5. Suggested Practices. Several suggested practices in using the connector "which is" are listed.

1. The connector "which is," denoted by an Asterisk, need not always appear in a Designator Statement. For example, a Designator Statement may be written as:

NAME (of) CUSTOMER

as opposed to

NAME (which is) CUSTOMER

or

CODE (which is) LOCATION (and) DIVISION

as opposed to

CODE (which is) LOCATION (and which is) DIVISION

2. When the connector "which is" is used in a Designator, it should be placed immediately following the word being modified. For example:

AMOUNT (of) EXPENSE (which is) CUSTOMER-SERVICE

In this example, Customer-Service modifies Expense and is placed immediately after it.

3. There is a use of the connector "which is" that is acceptable even though the connector and the Modifier Word do not immediately follow the word being modified.

NAME (of) MACHINE (which is) SERIAL-NUMBER

In this example, Serial-Number does not modify Machine. The connector "which is" is used to form a sentence-like structure.

4. When there is repeated use of the connector "which is" in a Designator, it is suggested that the two connectors "and which is" should be used following the first occurrence of the connector "which is"

AMOUNT (of) EXPENSE (of) CALL (which is)
SERVICE (and which is) SERVICE-ENGINEER

6. Summary. The uniqueness and comprehensiveness of a Designator Statement are its most important attributes. It should clearly convey the content of the data being described. An effective Designator provides for a highly probable retrieval by an inquirer seeking the data item. The best approach to creating an effective statement is to structure it from the perspective of an inquirer. Wherever possible, the descriptors should be closely related to the COBOL or PL/1 machine readable name assigned. This can be accomplished by using the class word abbreviation (one character) and abbreviating the modifier words. It would also be more effective if a standard set of abbreviations were used. A secretary's handbook of abbreviations could facilitate this process.

Now that we have learned how to develop a keyword designator statement, let's examine a couple of examples where a machine-readable derivative is developed from a designator statement.

As stated before, there are few DP organizations that will throw out their current standards for the approach just discussed. However, parts of this approach will have very little impact on current standards. For example, the designator statement itself will be placed in the dictionary's description or user data segments not affecting naming conventions or application programs. In addition, a number of users have elected to use the class identifier as the first character of their high-level-language names (i.e., COBOL and PL/1). In addition, many have also developed a glossary of terms and their abbreviations. These partial uses of this approach have greatly improved communication among users, and at the same time reduced redundancy.

Building a Designator and Its Machine-Readable Derivative

Example 1: Abbreviated customer name:

1. Class and most general term is: Name
2. Answer to question "Name of what?" is: Customer
3. Answer to question "What about the name of customer?" is: Abbreviated

Therefore, the language descriptor is

"NAME OF CUSTOMER WHICH IS ABBREVIATED"

or

"N CUSTOMER*ABBREVIATED"

or

"N CUST*ABBR"

The machine-readable derivative would be

"N-CUST-ABBR" — COBOL

or

"N__CUST__ABBR" — PL/1

Example 2. Maximum salary:

1. Class and most general would be: Amount
2. Answer to question "Amount of what?" is: Salary
3. Answer to question "What about amount of salary?" It is: Maximum

Therefore, the OF language descriptor is

"AMOUNT OF SALARY WHICH IS MAXIMUM"

or

"$ SALARY*MAXIMUM"

or

"$ SAL*MAX"

The machine-readable derivative is

$$\text{``$-SAL-MAX''} \quad - \quad \text{COBOL}$$

or

$$\text{``$\_\_SAL\_\_MAX''} \quad - \quad \text{PL/1}$$

Dictionary users who have elected to use the "OF language" approach or part of it have, in some cases, maintained a division or department code prefix on both the designator statement and the machine-readable derivative. This is fine if it makes it easier for the user to use. A word of caution here is that this prefix may have a negative psychological effect on the data administrator's effort to describe data as a resource owned by the corporation rather than the traditional concept of data ownership by department, division, and so on.

Keywords may not be practical in certain situations. A DL/I data base name can only have an eight-character assembler name and is not referenced by name in application programs. In addition, it is difficult to use the OF language or any other structured global name creation method to uniquely define a data base because many different types of data may be contained in it. In general, those entities that only require an assembler name and are for the most part created and used only by the data or data base administrator need not have a KWD. On the other hand, these entities may have a designator statement which, although not exactly recreatable in all cases, will still provide an abstract of the complete definition and be useful on reports and could be used in a keyword-in-context scheme.

Dictionary Keyword Index Technique

The following discussion explains a keyword indexing approach that may be utilized by a dictionary user to derive a keyword-in-context capability. It should be obvious to most everyone that a designator statement, which provides both a classification and keywords, is ready-made for KWIC reporting.

The DB/DC data dictionary provides an effective method for indexing entities on keywords that make up their definition. This is particularly the case if the entities are defined with a designator statement (e.g., OF language designator) stored in the text or user segments.

The keyword index is developed by selecting an entity type from the system data base (such as the Module entity) in which to store user-defined keywords. These keyword entities are related to any other entity containing the keyword in its designator statement. A report of the keyword entity (e.g., CUSTOMER) would indicate which entities contain that keyword in their definition.

The keywords and their relationship to entities containing the keyword in their designator statement may be set up using the dictionary commands or displays; however, it may be desirable to have these keywords and their relationships automatically created and maintained. This could be accomplished with a user program that searches the data bases on a regular schedule establishing and/or maintaining the index entries.

AUTHOR'S NAMING CONVENTION

A naming convention that was developed by the author for a minicomputer installation is given below. Compromises have to be made to accommodate the practical needs of various groups. Note that different entity types, such as system, program, and report, are dealt with in this naming convention.

To ensure that each entity in the data dictionary is unique, it is necessary to adhere to a fixed set of naming conventions. The naming conventions described in this section are those established by the MIS department of the corporation and specified in the corporation's standards manual. Entities defined for use in the data dictionary *must* be named in accordance with definitive naming conventions in order to maintain system integrity. Before following the conventions set up for each entity type, note these general naming rules.

1. Make the entity name as meaningful as possible. CUST NAME is preferable to either NAME CUST or NM CST.
2. Drop all prepositions from the title.
3. Drop all function words ("and," "the," etc.) from the title.
4. Do not use characters that are not legal within the entity type you are creating an entity name for.
5. Use the mnemonic form of the word when possible. A mnemonic is formed by dropping the vowels from the word. Exceptions to this rule are:
   - Do not drop the first letter if it is a vowel.
   - Do not drop vowels if it makes the mnemonic unintelligible—*tlphn* for telephone, for example.
   - Drop only one of the letters in the case of double vowels or consonants.
   - If a nonmnemonic abbreviation is more meaningful than the mnemonic, use it (e.g., *cust* rather than *cstmr* and *no* rather than *nmbr*).
   - If the word is short enough to be used in full, do so. *Part* is preferable to *prt*.

Specific naming conventions for each entity type follow.

System Name: A system is identified by a descriptive name, a COBOL name, and an acronym. The COBOL name can be up to 30 characters long and should be a combination of meaningful abbreviations or mnemonics separated by hyphens. The COBOL name can be composed from the characters A–Z, 0–9, and the hyphen (-). The system acronym can be up to six alpha characters long and is used in the naming of subsystems, programs, jobs, data files, and so on.

Examples

Description:	Central dispatch system
COBOL name:	CENTRAL-DISPATCH-SYSTEM
Acronym:	CDS

Description:	Data dictionary system
COBOL name:	DATA-DICTIONARY-SYSTEM
Acronym:	DDS

Subsystem Name: A subsystem is identified by a descriptive name, a COBOL name, and an acronym. The subsystem acronym consists of the system acronym followed by two digits (00–99). The format for the subsystem acronym is

```
        NNNNNNSS
where   NNNNNN      = system acronym (see System Name)
        SS          = subsystem number within the system
```

Job/Procedure Name: A job is a collection of programs that are executed in "batch" mode in a sequential manner, or in "transaction" (interactive) mode at random times. A procedure is a collection of activities or steps that may be performed in a manual or mechanical mode. The analyst assigns meaningful mnemonics that identify the purpose of the job or procedure within a system or subsystem, using job or procedure names that are unique within the system. The format for the job/procedure name is

```
NNNNNNSS.XXXXXX
```
where   NNNNNN   = system acronym (*see* System Name)
    SS   = subsystem number (optional)
    .   = literal "." (period)
    XXXXXX   = mnemonic (up to six characters long)

Note that the total number of characters that an operator must key in must not exceed 15 characters. Thus in some cases, if the system acronym is less than six characters, the additional characters can be used in the mnemonic provided that the total number of characters does not exceed 15. Also note that switches should be to the default value under normal operational conditions. Operators should have to key in switch values only when the norm is being overridden.

Program Name: The format for the program name is

```
NNNNNSSPP.XXX
```
where   NNNNN   = system acronym (*see* System Name)
    SS   = subsystem the program supports
    PP   = program number within the subsystem
    .   = literal "." (period)
    XXX   = extension identifying the program source file:
        CB for COBOL source file;
        Sn for sort command file, where n is a digit
         from 0 through 9;
        CLI for a macro command file

Examples

```
CDS0611.CB
CDS1205.S2
CDS0113.CLI
```

 Data Filenames: There are six types of data files: reference, work, data, transaction, report, and audit. *Reference files* are generally global to the corporation and/or the system. The format for reference filenames is

```
NNNNNNNNTT
```
where NNNNNNNN = meaningful name, abbreviation, or mnemonic up to eight
         characters long, composed from the characters A–Z and 0–9
    TT   = Two alpha characters indicating the file type:
        S   Sequential
        N   Relative
        I   Indexed
        DB   DBMS

Work files are temporary files used to pass information from one processing step to another. These files are often deleted after each processing step is completed. The format for work filenames is:

```
NNNNNNNNNNT.W#
```
where   NNNNNNNNNN = name of the program that generated the file
     T   = file type (*see* Reference Filename)
     .   = literal "." (period)

| W | = literal "W" |
| # | = digit (0–9) used for further qualification |

Example

CDS0602S.W1

Data files are the end result of one or more processing steps. These files usually are not deleted until passed on to the user and/or stored in the data library. The format for data filenames is:

NNNNNNNNNNT.##

where	NNNNNNNNNN	= name of the program that generated the file
	T	= file type (*see* Reference Filenames)
	.	= literal "." (period)
	##	= digits (01-99) used for further qualification

Example

CDS0602S.01

Transaction files contain transactions generated for input to business application or data base recovery procedures. The format for transaction filenames is

NNNNNNNNNNT.T#

where	NNNNNNNNNN	= name of the program that generated the file
	T	= file type (*see* Reference Filename)
	.	= literal "." (period)
	T	= literal "T"
	#	= digit (0–9) used for further qualification

Report files are similar to data files with the exception that they are formatted for printing. The format for report filenames is

NNNNNNNNNNT.R#

where	NNNNNNNNNN	= name of the program that generated the file
	T	= file type (*see* Reference Filename)
	.	= literal "." (period)
	R	= literal "R"
	#	= digit (0–9) used for further qualification

Example

CDS0602S.R1

Audit files are used when a program is required to supply certain statistics about its performance, such as run time, records processed, check values, and so on. The format for audit filenames is

NNNNNNNNNNT.A#

where	NNNNNNNNNN	= name of the program that generated the file
	T	= file type (*see* Reference Filename)
	.	= literal "." (period)
	A	= literal "A"
	#	= digit (0–9) used for further qualification

Example

CDS0602S.A1

Record Definition: When defining a record, both the record and the items within it *must* be named. The record may exist in the FD entry, working storage, or screen section. The format for record names is

MIII-NNNNNN

where M   = literal "R" for FD record name; literal "W" for a working storage record; or literal "F" for a screen format record

III   = record identifier ranging from 001 through ZZZ

-          = literal "-" (hyphen)

NNNNNN = name of the record, up to 25 characters long; should be a meaningful abbreviation or mnemonic composed from A–Z, 0–9, and the hyphen ("-")

NOTE: The record identifier "III" will be assigned by the data base administrator to ensure unique record identifiers across all systems.

Examples:

Record definition for an FD record entry:

```
01 R001-CUST-ORDER-REC.
    05 I001-CUST-NO              PIC 9(6).
    05 I001-CUST-ADDR           PIC X(125)
    05 I001-ORDER-SHIP-DT       PIC 9(6)
```

Record definition for a working storage entry:

```
01 W001-CUST-ORDER-REC.
    05 W001-CUST-NO             PIC 9(6)
    05 W001-CUST-ADDR          PIC X(125)
    05 W001-ORDER-SHIP-DT      PIC 9(6)
```

Record definition for a screen format entry:

```
01 F001-CUST-ORDER
    05 F001-CUST-NO             PIC 9(6)
    05 F001-CUST-ADDR          PIC X(125)
    05 F001-ORD-SHIP-DT        PIC 9(6)
```

Data Item Names: The format for item names is

TIII-NNNNNNNN

where   T   = S if the item record is in a sequential file;
N if the item record is in a CS indexed file;
I if the item record is in an Infos file;
(Schema Area ID) if the item record is in a DBMS file;
W if the item record is part of a working storage record;
F if the item record is part of a screen format record

III   = item record identifier

-          = literal "-" (hyphen)

NNNNNNNN = name of the item, up to 25 characters long; should be a meaningful abbreviation or mnemonic that can be composed from the characters A–Z, 0–9, and hyphen ("-")

Copybook Filenames: Copybooks contain file, record, and procedure information. The format for *file copybook* names is

(FILENAME)S.CC	Select Copybook
(FILENAME)F.CC	FD Copybook
(FILENAME)W.CC	Working Storage Copybook
(FILENAME)D.CC	Declaratives Copybook

where (FILENAME) = name of the file described by the copybook

S.CC = literal "S.CC"

F.CC = literal "F.CC"

W.CC = literal "W.CC"

D.CC = literal "D.CC"

Examples

```
CUSTOMERS.CC
CUSTOMERF.CC
CUSTOMERW.CC
CUSTOMERD.CC
```

The format for *record copybook* names is

RIIIF.CC   01 Record definition to be used with the file's FD copybook;
RIIIW.CC   01 Record definition to be used in working storage

where RIII = (*See* Record Name)
F.CC = literal "F.CC"
W.CC = literal "W.CC"

Examples

```
R001F.CC
R001W.CC
```

Input Description Names: Inputs are defined as forms, screens, or documents that are input to a program or activity step. The format for input description names is

NNNNSS.XXX...X

where NNNN = system acronym (*see* System Name)
SS = subsystem number (optional)
. = literal "." (period)
XXX...X = meaningful mnemonic or abbreviation up to 22 characters long (should be unique within the system)

Example

```
DDS.DDS-11-FORM
```

Output Description Names: Outputs are the result of the application processing steps by programs or activity steps. Examples of outputs are reports, screens, microfiche, forms, and so on. The format for output definition names is

NNNNNSS.XXX...X

where NNNNN = system acronym
SS = subsystem number (optional)
. = literal "." (period)
XXX...X = meaningful mnemonic or abbreviation up to 22 characters long (should be unique with the system)

CULLINET SAMPLE NAMING CONVENTION*

To determine a set of naming conventions that will accommodate the need for meaningful names for reporting purposes as well as meeting the needs of the system development and operations areas, such as programming language and JCL restrictions, each entity type is considered separately. The conventions selected are discussed below.

Users. The user name consists of the user's initials for individuals or the department or division number or departments or divisions represented by user occurrences. The user's (individual, department, or division) full name is also documented in the data dictionary.

Systems. The system name is a descriptive, meaningful name, such as Order Entry. To accommodate operational considerations for derivation of other entity names, each system is assigned a system code. The system code is not meaningful; it consists of the letter S (for System) followed by a sequentially assigned, 3-digit system number (e.g., S001). The system code is documented in the data dictionary.

Files. The file name is a descriptive, meaningful name, such as Order Transactions. To accommodate operational considerations for file names, each file is assigned an external name for each participation in a file/program relationship. The external name consists of the system code of the system to which the program belongs, followed by the letter F (for File), followed by a 2-digit, sequentially assigned file number. File numbers are not duplicated within a system. For example, if the Order Entry system code is S001 and a program within this system uses the Order Transactions file, the external name for Order Transactions within this relationship is S001F01.

Records. The record name is a descriptive, meaningful name. The application users agreed to the use of hyphens rather than spaces to separate words within the record names.

Elements. (Author's note: Elements are the same as items in the other naming conventions)The element name is derived to satisfy the company's primary programming language, COBOL. These names consist of concatenated qualifiers separated by hyphens. The last qualifier must indicate the type of element being defined and must be selected from a table of acceptable last qualifiers. This table is subject to change, as elements that do not fit into any table category are defined. The current version of this table is shown in Figure 6-6.

- *Elements.* Meaningful names for elements will be accommodated by the DDDL ELEMENT DESCRIPTION clause of the ELEMENT statement that was previously selected for use. The standard Element Description report provides a list of elements arranged alphabetically by element description.
- *Records.* Record names will be accommodated by the DDDL NAME IS clause of the RECORD statement that was previously selected for use.
- *Modules.* Meaningful names for modules will be accommodated by the DDDL DESCRIPTION option of the MODULE statement.
- *Programs.* Meaningful names will be accommodated by the DDDL DESCRIPTION option of the PROGRAM statement.

(*Pages 110-113 are reprinted courtesy of Cullinet Software Inc.)

If the Element Is:	The Last Qualifier of the Element Name Must Be:
A name	NAME
A mailing address	ADDR
A date	DATE
A time of day	TIME
A dollar (or other currency) amount	AMT
A nonmonetary numeric quantity	QTY
A description	DESC
A numeric value arrived at by counting the number of any commodity	COUNT
A numeric value expressed as a percentage	PCT
An identifying number	NBR
An indicator capable of having only one of two values (e.g., on or off, yes or no, 0 or 1)	IND
An indicator capable of having a range of more than two values (e.g., low, medium, high)	CODE
A group element used as a key field	KEY
A group element defined for ease in programming	GRP

Figure 6-6   Qualifier words.

Reconciliation of Naming Conventions.

Establishment of naming conventions creates another consideration: how existing entities will be handled (particularly elements) when the entities do not have names that coincide with the new naming conventions. Elements that participate in only non-IDMS records can be added to the data dictionary. However, elements that reside in IDMS records are already represented in the data dictionary, having been added by the IDMS schema compiler. Some of these IDMS elements have standard names; most do not.

Documenting IDMS elements that have standard names requires addition of documentational information (e.g., element descriptions, related users). Documenting IDMS elements that do not have standard names can be handled in one of two ways: by creating synonyms for the existing elements or by adding separate element occurrences with standard names. Before considering these two methods individually, you have to consider the data processing growth plan, which accommodates eventual changes to the application programs to reflect the new element naming conventions. Therefore, you may require the ability to remove the nonstandard names without affecting the new element names: any relationship between an old entity name and a new one must be easily dissolvable. Consideration of synonyms versus separate elements follows:

- Using element synonyms provides the ability to have both the standard and nonstandard names of an element in a single occurrence in the data dictionary. The new names would be synonyms of the existing primary names that were added by the IDMS schema compiler. New programs could reference the synonyms, and existing programs could continue to reference the primary names. However, since the old names could not be deleted without also removing the new (synonym) names, the use of synonyms is not aceptable in this case.

- Using separate elements allows the new name to be entered as a primary name. Use of the SAME AS clause of the DDDL ADD ELEMENT statement captures existing information about the old elements, but it does not create the desired relationships between the old and the new element names, and thus creates unrelated, redundant entries in the data dictionary.

The only exception to the rules for determining last qualifiers is an element defined as a COBOL CONDITION-NAME. Condition names indicate the condition represented and must include the first qualifier from the element to which the condition name element belongs and the word *IS*. For example, the group element CREDIT-CODE contains condition name elements of CREDIT-IS-POOR, CREDIT-IS-GOOD, and CREDIT-IS-EXCELLENT. When elements are related to records, the element names are prefixed by a record code.

- *Modules.* The use of modules is to store user-defined DDR CULPRIT report source code in the data dictionary. The module name consists of the constant DREPORT followed by a space and a sequentially assigned, 3-digit report number. For example, the user-defined Element by User report module is DREPORT 500. Descriptive names of report modules also are documented in the data dictionary.

- *Programs.* The program name is identical to the name of the program member in the program load library. This name consists of the system code of the system to which the program belongs, followed by the letter P (for Program), followed by a 2-digit, sequentially assigned program number, followed by a stage designation letter (A is used for the production copy of the program; any other letter is used for test copies). Program number is unique within a system. For example, S001P01A is assigned to the first program to be documented within the Order Entry system. If test copies of the same program are to be documented, they are assigned the names S001P01B, S001P01C, and so on. Descriptive names of programs also are documented in the data dictionary.

The establishment of naming conventions requires that additional options be supported for some of the entities. To ensure that each naming convention is accommodated, you must review the selected options. The following are the considerations and changes made to selected options for each supported entity type:

- *Users.* Full names of users will be accommodated by the DDDL FULL NAME option of the ADD USER and MODIFY USER statements.
- *Systems.* System codes will be accommodated by a user-defined comment key, SYSTEM CODE.
- *Files.* File external names will be accommodated by the DDDL EXTERNAL NAME option of the FILE clause of the PROGRAM statement.

Because the use of synonyms is not acceptable in this case, you may choose to use separate element occurrences. A relational key named OLD NAME within the element entity type is used to support the element-to-element relationships during the interim between loading the data dictionary and converting the existing programs to use standard names.

Before the existing programs can be converted, a new schema that uses the new names must be created. After the new schema is created, the old schema can be deleted.

Deletion of the old schema causes the old elements to be deleted, and the relationships between the old and new elements no longer exist.

You could have forgone establishment of relationships between old and new element names without causing detriment to either old or new entities. The purpose for the interim relationship is to ensure that the old and new elements can be reported together and to reduce the probablity of losing track of the correspondence between the two.

Had you not planned to change existing programs, the Order Entry database schema would continue to carry the nonstandard element names. However, the nonstandard names must be carried in the data dictionary for as long as the existing programs remain in use. In this case, synonyms would have been chosen. Each existing element would be modified to include the new name as a synonym and to include further information about the element, (e.g., element description, related users).

chapter 7

Data Dictionary Implementation Plan

PREPLANNING ANALYSIS

Requirements for Dictionary Implementation

The successful implementation of a data dictionary requires:

- Management commitment
- Service to the business end user as well as the MIS user
- Planning, coordination, and control
- Effort

Basic Guidelines

The starting point of this whole process is the development of an implementation plan. The implementation plan must be detailed enough to gain management commitment, provide a useful service to end users and MIS personnel, have the controls built in to measure the level of its usefulness, and have the required amount of resources, both human and technology, to make the project a success. In fact, implementation of the dictionary should be handled the same as any major project within the organization.

Since there is no single solution that will tell the DD project manager what categories and services to provide for all cases, the basic recommendations fall into three approaches:

1. Treat the implementation as a project with definite priorities, resources, and objectives.
2. Treat the implementation on a phased basis rather than to try to attempt to do everything for everyone.

3. Define the needs and priorities of the organization as perceived by management, by the users, and by the DD project manager, and focus the implementation toward those needs and priorities.

Questions to Ask

There are critical questions that must be answered by the organization:

- How should the dictionary be used? What should be the evolution of its usage; that is, should it be applied to large projects or should it be applied across the board?
- Based on the answer to the above, what categories of information must be supported by the dictionary? This leads directly to the analysis that results in the establishment of the entity model under which the dictionary operates. As you will realize, this is the key to the practical implementation (i.e., tailoring of the dictionary to suit the needs of the organization).
- What are the benefits of the different types of usage? For example, the application development process support level is quantitatively and qualitatively different from that for operations or security administration.
- What standards should be used? This includes such methods as naming conventions, documentation standards, update procedures, and usage techniques.
- What features of the dictionary can be used to benefit the organization? Such features as extensibility, automatic program access, and copybook generation have to be integrated into the organizational processes and syntax must be transmitted to the users to minimize the reluctance and potential resistance to new ways of doing things.

What the Plan Should Include

Implementation of a dictionary is not unlike implementation of any other major data-based system. A comprehensive implementation plan is necessary in order to communicate the goals of the DD project manager, as well as to obtain support from senior management for the project. A comprehensive implementation plan document should include the following:

- Policy for the use of the dictionary system
- Standards that will be followed in populating the dictionary as well as any naming conventions for dictionary entities
- Decisions that will govern the control functions that exist in the dictionary, such as security, extensions, etc.
- Definition of authority and responsibility for the use of various dictionary system facilities
- Definition of the procedures for storage and retrieval of information in the dictionary system data base
- Specification of the customized applications as well as the extensions that would be needed to support the needs of users of the dictionary system

The Big Picture

In the pages that follow we will review specific steps in implementation planning. Before discussing these steps, let's pull back for a moment and look at the big picture—the overall goals and benefits of dictionary implementation.

The data dictionary can be viewed as an ordered set of entities and the relationships between these entities. The basic concern of the DD project manager is to ensure that the information pertaining to the entities is maintained properly and that the interrelationships portrayed in the dictionary are accurate. The information pertaining to an entity can be broken down into the generic categories shown in Figure 7–1.

For each entity that is in the dictionary, the properties of the entity must be fully defined and updated. Those properties that will be used by programs to perform further processing must be updated using the same format whether the update takes place manually or through an automated mechanism. For example, the attribute of size of data item has to be entered in the format that will be used by a language processor. If the language processor is COBOL, a 7-byte alphanumeric item is defined with a size attribute of PIC X(7). Thus it is important to be precise in defining the rules for the various aspects of an entity.

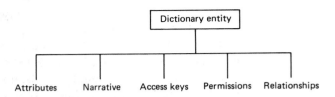

Figure 7–1 Information pertaining to an entity.

The benefit of a data dictionary is that it is a single source of data definitions for system analysts and end users which will result in faster development of systems that can communicate with files in a standardized manner. It is a storage facility for documenting system, subsystem, job, program, inputs, and outputs, and will improve the accuracy and communication of information about the various components of the system to persons in operations, maintenance, and data base administration.

STEPS IN IMPLEMENTATION PLANNING

1. Analyze Functions and User Requirements.

A detailed analysis of selected data dictionary functions and user information requirements has to be performed to arrive at a feasible implementation plan. For each data dictionary function, the corresponding procedures and information flows have to be mapped out in easily understandable terms. This technique can be used for scoping the project at the beginning, and as a tool for planning, controlling, and validating data dictionary activities. This information will also be useful in determining the phases of data dictionary implementation.

2. Interview Users, Prepare Functional Specifications and Flowcharts.

The potential users of the dictionary should be interviewed, as in any system design project. A functional specification should be prepared, combining user informational requirements with the procedures associated with obtaining that service from the data dictionary. Procedure flow charts should be developed which show the manner in which the dictionary functions will be performed under proposed data base or non-data base systems. This will also be useful in user acceptance testing.

3. Develop Entity Categories.

Next, the entity categories that are necessary to service the informational needs of the users must be developed. The more numerous the range of users for a particular entity category, the more critical it becomes to define the category to mean the same thing to multiple users. For example, if the entity category called "program" were used to include manual as well as automated procedures, this should be made clear at the outset. The basis on which entity occurrences are named and the types of secondary names that are required should be fully specified. In all the above, it must be emphasized that for the implementation to be successful, the entity categories should reflect the needs of the users, and be willingly supported by the user. This support extends to the tasks involved in maintaining the entity occurrences for which a user may be responsible.

4. Identify Responsible Individuals.

Construct a chart that identifies the classes of persons responsible for gathering the information pertaining to different entity categories. An example of such a chart is shown in Figure 7–2.

DDS Documentation Responsibility Chart

ENTITY	SA	P	DBA	OP	E–U	DDA	PM	SP
System	*						*	
Job/CLI	*	*	*	*				
Program	*	*						
Item (std)	*				*	*		
Item			*					
Record			*					
File			*					
Subschema			*					
Machine				*				
Function								*
Process								*
Logic. gr.			*			*		*

where

SA = systems analyst
P = programmer
DBA = data base administrator
OP = operations
E–U = end user
DDA = data dictionary administrator
PM = project manager
SP = systems planning

Figure 7–2 Dictionary documentation responsibility chart.

5. Establish Attributes and Relationships.

The definition of which attributes and relationships should be established in the dictionary should be determined very carefully. The users have a definite need for certain where-used information: whether this can be provided via indirect links such as attributes or directly via relationships. Trade-offs must be made as to the effort involved in maintaining attributes versus relationships versus access keys, and the benefits to be derived from each. For example, it may be decided to house both standard data items and file specific data items under the same entity category. The differentiating factor might be the use of "DS" in a qualifier field of the entity containing the standard data item. To relate the specific occurrences of items to the standard, a procedure might be adopted as follows:

- For every standard data item, the qualifier field must be the value "DS."
- For every standard data item, one of the aliases that must be entered into the dictionary must be the entity name of the standard data item.
- For every file-specific occurrence of a data item, one of the aliases must be the standard data item entity name.

When the procedures above are carried out systematically, a question such as "Give me a listing of all the file-specific data items with the standard name of CUST-NO" can be answered easily by using the alias of CUST-NO and obtaining all the entities that have that alias.

In the situation above, an alternative strategy may be to define the standard data item as a separate entity. In such a case, the entity model could be defined to permit the storage of a relationship between the file-specific data item and the standard data item, as shown in Figure 7–3. In the strategy, the procedure would call for the storage of a relationship to the standard data item entity every time a file-specific entity were to be stored. Then to answer the question posed above, one would have to run an entity relationship report that pulled out the entities belonging to a standard item.

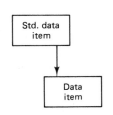

Figure 7–3 Standard data item entity model.

Another strategy to address the situation would be to have the standard data item name as an attribute of the specific item. To answer the question, all data items that had the attribute of CUST-NO could be reported.

From the discussion above, it is apparent that there are several ways to identify entities, attributes, and relationships in order to fulfill a user need. Once a particular method is adopted, the procedures and responsibilities for the loading and maintenance of that information must be specified and the commitment of users to maintain that information must be obtained. This final step is absolutely critical to the success of the dictionary implementation.

6. Develop Procedures for Populating the Dictionary.

Procedures for the initial population of the dictionary must be developed and prioritized. This includes the procedures for loading standards, current data file information, current system information, and current machine loading information. While developing these procedures the administrator will be confronted with the option of letting the users load the data, or having one group have responsibility, or a combination of both. It is important that the expectation of the administrator as to the quality of data expected be made clear beforehand, regardless of who ultimately does the loading. The actual persons who are assigned the responsibility would be a management decision that would depend on the availability of personnel in the various departments affected.

7. Develop Procedures for the Update and Maintenance of the Data in the Dictionary.

These procedures follow on the heels of the population procedures and deal with the ongoing maintenance of the data in the dictionary. A principle that should be followed in this area is that the maintenance should be carried out as close as possible to the occurrence of the event that causes the change to the data in the dictionary. Another principle is that the maintenance should be carried out by the person who is causing the change. Specific procedures with examples are discussed in Chapters 8 and 9.

8. Develop Naming Conventions.

Naming conventions merit a separate activity status because they are so crucial to the overall effort to maintain order in the dictionary. Naming conventions were dealt with in detail in Chapter 6. For each entity that will be supported in the dictionary, a naming convention should be developed. Four other topics should be covered:

- How to handle past inconsistencies
- How to handle conflicts
- When to apply the naming convention
- How to handle exceptions

9. Develop Evaluation Criteria; Select a Data Dictionary System.

This topic is covered in detail in the last part of this chapter.

10. Develop Training Package.

Based on the procedures used to populate and maintain the data in the dictionary, and the specific features of the dictionary, develop general training program to acquaint users with the dictionary. Another purpose served by the training package is that it serves to publicize the availability of the dictionary to the staff.

11. Identify Security Procedures.

Finally, security procedures for using the dictionary must be identified and disseminated to the users. The security procedures must work under several different scenarios, that is, under conditions where the data entry and access are well defined and controlled, to the situation where data entry and access have to be flexible to accommodate various schedules and operating conditions in the departments that are going to be using the dictionary. In short, the security procedures should not hinder the ability to tailor the usage to suit the operating conditions in the organization.

12. Outline Activities for Each Application That Will Be Implemented.

An outline of the activities involved in each of the applications must be prepared. An example that is treated below is the application of the dictionary to the system development life cycle (SDLC):

- **a.** Develop entities required to support the system development life cycle (SDLC).
  - **(1)** Identify type codes and relationships.
  - **(2)** Identify attributes and access keys by entity.
  - **(3)** Assign responsibilities by individual or group.
  - **(4)** Develop samples of entity documentation standard expected in the dictionary.
- **b.** Develop outputs expected from dictionary during SDLC.
  - **(1)** System to data item standard report.
  - **(2)** Copybooks generated from the dictionary of file layouts, screen layouts, report layouts, and working storage.
  - **(3)** System subsystem report containing the narratives for the components within a system, such as programs, reports, screens, files, etc.
- **c.** Provide for training and communication of expectations and roles.
  - **(1)** Train systems development staff in use of the dictionary.

  (2) Develop sample reports to demonstrate workability.
  (3) Update the system development standard to include data dictionary procedures.

d. Select a pilot project for dictionary implementation.

e. Implement and disseminate the results.

f. Obtain management commitment to apply to other system development projects.

13. Create Dependency Graph and Installation Guidelines.

When implementing the pilot project, there will be several other areas that need to be addressed concurrently. This is where a dependency graph can be drawn between the projects that are interrelated. For example, in order to come up with copybooks that conform to data item conventions and standards, the data base administration function has to document and gain commitment to the standards from the system development staff. In many cases, the data base administration function would have to resolve conflicts between different groups of users on the exact definition and attributes of a data item.

 To accommodate concurrent activities that have to go on to make the application of the data dictionary a success, it is important to communicate these dependencies to senior management to gain their commitment. Thus, in the case above, installation of the dictionary system, and the development and documentation of standards, are prerequisites to incorporating the dictionary in the system development life cycle (SDLC). Installation of the dictionary system would require that installation guidelines be developed and implemented. This would include:

a. Determination of the dictionary run-time requirement

b. Determination of the mass storage requirement

c. Assignment of dictionary system defaults

d. Selection of backup and recovery techniques

e. Definition of access control procedure

 The development and documentation of standards would include:

a. Procuring standards from existing sources and documents

b. Developing lists of key data items from systems personnel

c. Developing conventions based on consensus

d. Publishing the standards and ensuring their consistent application.

 When the three different sets of activities are combined in a dependence chart, it would be as shown in Figure 7–4.

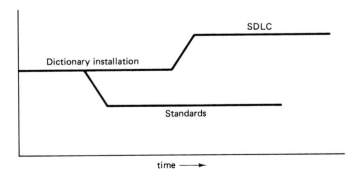

Figure 7–4 Dependence chart.

14. Identify Deliverables for Each Activity.

In addition to outlining the tasks and activities in each area, it is important to identify the deliverables from the end of each major task or activity. Achievement of these deliverables then becomes the measurement of progress on the tasks and activities within the overall project. Examples of deliverables would be:

Activity	Deliverables
Standards	Standard naming convention, primary data item definitions, standards update procedure.
Installation	Hardware requirements, software requirements, system default settings list.
SDLC	Dictionary procedures during various phases of SDLC, sample documentation expected to be part of dictionary processing for SDLC.

15. Estimate Resources and Target Dates for Each Deliverable.

The resources required to achieve each deliverable and the target date for attaining the deliverable must then be presented as part of the project implementation plan. The resources should be broken down into person-hours of effort, hardware costs, development costs, and so on. All of these can be specified in terms of dollar amounts.

16. Quantify Benefits.

To complete the plan, the benefits that were defined previously for implementation of the SDLC application involving the dictionary must be quantified. The quantification can be in terms of person-hours of effort saved during the SDLC utilizing the dictionary, minus maintenance expense, better communication, and so on.
    For example:

Cost to develop standard naming convention:

$$100 \text{ person-hours at } \$30 \text{ per hour} = \$3000$$

Benefits:

$$\text{Reduced maintenance of 60 hours} = \$1800$$
$$\text{Speedier development 60 hours} = \$1800$$

Thus, in the example above, the benefits outweigh the costs by $600. Although there are no easy means of quantifying seemingly difficult-to-measure benefits, any attempt at quantification (with qualifications, of course) is preferable to none. This kind of project implementation planning will ensure that the costs and benefits are understood by management and that there is a measureable set of objectives against which progress on the project can be evaluated.

MANAGING THE IMPLEMENTATION

Project Management

The DD project manager must have an implementation plan that covers all facets of the project and contains the resources needed to complete the project. There are many project management aids in the marketplace that could help the project manager maintain control over the project. An example of a project management and control procedure is shown utilizing the MS Project Manager software from MicroSoft Corporation.

The first task is to identify the activities that are part of the project. These should be at a level of aggregation that makes sense and can be checked and controlled. What this means is that too detailed a level of activity is not necessary here; conversely, too broad or general a level of activity would not provide sufficient benefits in using the Project Manager software tool. Additional pieces of information about each activity need to be entered into the screens—the critical ones are the duration of each activity, the prerequisite activities that have to be completed before that activity can be started (also called predecessors), and who would be able to do it (resources).

ACTIVITIES

1. *Perform DD requirements analysis.* This is an important activity in the project, because this is where the potential users of the dictionary are queried to determine their needs for dictionary information. A result of this activity would be the information flow diagrams that depict the information requirements for each functional set of users (i.e., systems development, operations, end-user computing, etc.).

2. *Define data dictionary requirements.* This is a document that translates information requirements determined in the preceding activity into dictionary entities, access keys, and attributes. The entity relationship diagram is also defined in this activity.

3. *Establish a standard update procedure.* This is the standard update procedure, including forms or screens and the organizational approval steps needed before the data are put into the dictionary.

4. *Determine standard naming conventions.* This includes the development of a naming convention for the various entities that will be supported by the dictionary. There has to be commitment to use the naming convention from MIS and user management. There also must be a migration path for existing naming conventions to change over to the new one.

5. *Evaluate and select a data dictionary system.* This activity results in a detailed list of requirements from a data dictionary software package. The list should be prioritized with weights assigned to the various criteria based on organizational need and implementation objectives. As part of this activity, software vendors are invited to demonstrate their products for evaluation. The evaluation results in a procurement decision. After the package is acquired, it has to be installed.

6. *Develop training package.* The training package should contain organization specific information drawn from the procedures that were defined earlier, tailored to suit the functions in the dictionary software package.

7. *Develop security guidelines and access control lists.* Define authority limits for privileged individuals and for other categories of users of the system.

8. *State primary data definitions.* Using the forms or screens and the procedure specified, the data item definitions are provided by the authoritative sources (i.e. those users who either originate the data or are closest to the data from a use point of view).

9. *Train end users.* This activity teaches the end users how to view the data in the dictionary and how to navigate through the dictionary to get the information they want.

10. *Load data standards.* This activity has to do with loading the data item standard information developed by the authoritative users in a prior step into the dictionary. It makes use of the standard loading features of the dictionary software.

11. *Document reports.* This activity consists of identifying and documenting the reports that are produced by the MIS systems, as well as key reports generated in the user areas that would be of general interest. The documentation should include the report distribution list and a sample page from the report. The data would be entered into the generic data entry screen.

12. *Load report information.* This activity has to do with loading the reports information developed earlier into the dictionary, utilizing standard loading features of the dictionary.

13. *State SDLC integration policy.* This activity is responsible for defining the requirements from the dictionary during the system development life cycle, and defines the interfaces that have to be created to obtain the data.

14. *Implement SDLC Policy.* This activity consists of defining the procedures that have to be specified for the dictionary to be a part of the SDLC, and the controls that need to be placed during the SDLC to ensure that the procedures are being followed. The controls could be either manual or automated, a priori or post facto.

15. *Evaluate SDLC integration.* The integration of any new system into an existing set of procedures, especially where control issues are involved is fraught with problems. Hence this activity is intended to monitor the situation closely to resolve minor problems as they arise, to escalate larger problems, and to report on progress to senior management.

16. *Develop operations user procedures.* This activity consists of identifying current operational procedures that could be affected positively by using the information in the dictionary in an on-line manner, and then defining the procedures and dictionary interfaces required to make this happen.

17. *Document operations procedures.* This activity consists of preparing the information that operations currently has in a manual or automated format into a format that is suitable for loading into the dictionary.

18. *Load operations information.* This activity consists of loading the dictionary with information about the jobs and macros that are run in the computer center, the backup and recovery steps, and the processing interrelationships.

19. *Train operators.* Train operators in dictionary operation and use.

20. *Update operations information.* Set in motion the procedures to maintain the accuracy and integrity of information in the dictionary. Monitor the usage and integrity of the information.

Project Schedule

The activities, their duration, and start and stop times are drawn on a chart by the MS Project Manager system. The chart is shown as a project schedule in Figure 7–5.

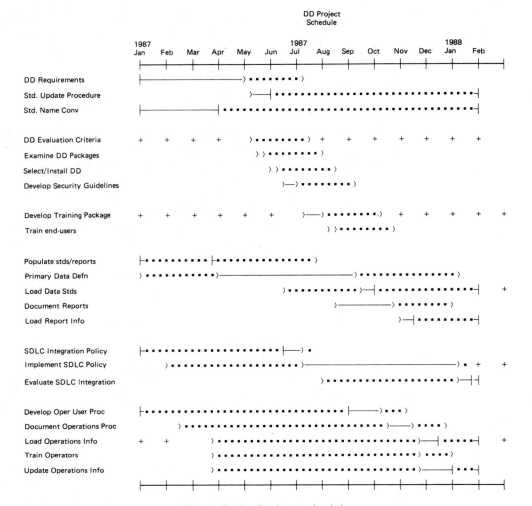

Figure 7-5 Project schedule.

Project Network

The network diagram is a chart that shows the activities and milestones arranged on a precedence basis. It helps visualize the project interdependencies and the critical activities that have to be performed in the project. The network diagram is shown in Figure 7-6.

Project

For a sample set of activities, the details are shown in Figures 7-7 through 7-11. These include the duration, slack time, start and finish times, resources allocated and costs, and predecessors and successors, if any. Also, a short description of the activity is displayed.

Resources

In this example, the following resources are assumed to be available.

Jessup	Project manager
Martin	DD administrator
Davidson	DBA
Larkin	User coordinator
Bianchi	Project leader
Faber	Project leader
Grant	System analyst
Urbano	System programmer

The resources and the amount of time that each is assigned to the activities is shown in Figure 7-12. Based on a cost per person-unit of time, the cost of the project can be calculated. Note that the dictionary system that is procured is a resource that is identified. In addition, where it is not possible to identify individuals, the department is used as a generic identifier.

Resource Histogram

The resource histogram is a plot of the individual's allocation of time over the duration of the project. This allows the project manager quickly to get an idea of where the person is working over capacity and where there is slack time that can be scheduled. Figures 7-13 through 7-18 illustrate the resource histograms for individuals as well as departments. For example, in the histogram for Larkin (Figure 7-16), note that Larkin is overscheduled during April–May and August–September. One possibility is to schedule the activities over a longer period. A second option is to hire another person to assist Larkin during these months.

Changes to Project

Changes in the various parameters affecting the project can be entered into the Project Manager system and the impact quickly determined. The following changes were input into the system:

1. Start date of the project was changed from January 5, 1987 to January 26, 1987.
2. Activity 1 DD requirements' duration was increased from 18 weeks to 22 weeks.
3. Activity 2 standard update procedure duration was expanded from 18 days to 36 days.
4. The cost of the data dictionary was changed from $15,000 to $20,000.

The impact of these changes as of May 22, 1987 was determined by setting the current date to May 22 and running the "analyze" function against the data. The comparison was made between what was forecasted and the actual. The following pages contain several reports that resulted from the "analyzer" function.

Project Variance

The project variance report is a one-page summary showing the status of the project to date and is shown in Figure 7-19.

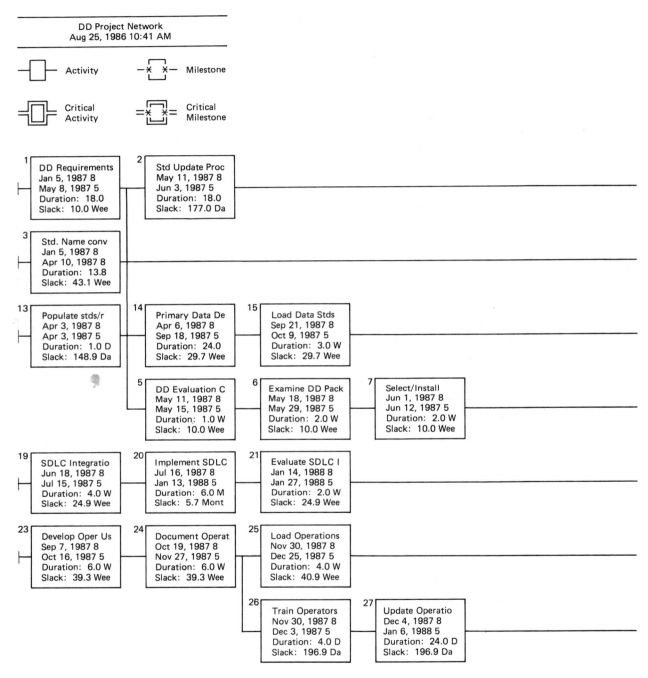

Figure 7-6 Network diagram.

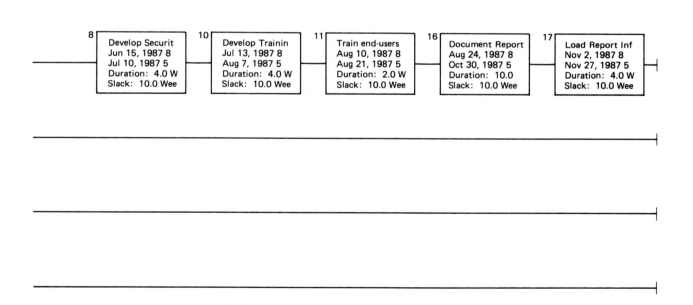

| 8 | Develop Securit
Jun 15, 1987 8
Jul 10, 1987 5
Duration: 4.0 W
Slack: 10.0 Wee | 10 | Develop Trainin
Jul 13, 1987 8
Aug 7, 1987 5
Duration: 4.0 W
Slack: 10.0 Wee | 11 | Train end-users
Aug 10, 1987 8
Aug 21, 1987 5
Duration: 2.0 W
Slack: 10.0 Wee | 16 | Document Report
Aug 24, 1987 8
Oct 30, 1987 5
Duration: 10.0
Slack: 10.0 Wee | 17 | Load Report Inf
Nov 2, 1987 8
Nov 27, 1987 5
Duration: 4.0 W
Slack: 10.0 Wee |

DD Project Detail
Initial Estimate

Project: DDFILE   Date: Aug 25, 1986 10:41 AM

1 DD Requirements   Early Start: Jan 5, 1987 8:00 AM
                                                           Early Finish: May 8, 1987 5:00 PM

  Duration: 18.0 Weeks
  Slack: 10.0 Weeks   Late Start: Mar 16, 1987 8:00 AM
                                                           Late Finish: Jul 17, 1987 5:00 PM

                                                           Sched Start: Jan 5, 1987 8:00 AM
                                                           Sched Finish: May 8, 1987 5:00 PM

Notes:
Develop entity model to support dictionary requirements from the previous step; define facilities that would
be required.

Resources Allocated:

Name	Duration (days)	Amount used	Cost	Cost Basis	Cost to Complete
Jessup	90.0	0.8	$4500.00	Month	$14953.84
Larkin	90.0	0.6	$9.00	Hour	$3888.00
Total:					$18841.84

Predecessors:
None

Successors:

2 Std Update Procedure   Early Start: May 11, 1987 8:00 AM
  Slack avail: 177.0 Days   Late Start: Jan 13, 1988 8:00 AM

5 DD Evaluation Criteria   Early Start: May 11, 1987 8:00 AM
  Slack avail: 50.0 Days   Late Start: Jul 20, 1987 8:00 AM

Figure 7–7   DD requirements activity.

DD Project Detail
Initial Estimate

Project: DDFILE   Date: Aug 25, 1986 10:41 AM

2 Std Update Procedure   Early Start: May 11, 1987 8:00 AM
                                                           Early Finish: Jun 3, 1987 5:00 PM

  Duration: 18.0 Days
  Slack: 177.0 Days   Late Start: Jan 13, 1988 8:00 AM
                                                           Late Finish: Feb 5, 1988 5:00 PM

                                                           Sched Start: May 11, 1987 8:00 AM
                                                           Sched Finish: Jun 3, 1987 5:00 PM

Notes:
Define format for documenting entities; organizational flow of information for update of DD; publish and
disseminate; assign responsibility for sourcing information.

Resources Allocated:

Name	Duration (days)	Amount used	Cost	Cost Basis	Cost to Complete
Martin	18.0	0.6	$8.00	Hour	$691.20
Jessup	18.0	0.5	$4500.00	Month	$1869.23
Total:					$2560.43

Predecessors:
1 DD Requirements   Early Finish: May 8, 1987 5:00 PM
  Slack avail: 50.0 Days   Late Finish: Jul 17, 1987 5:00 PM

Successors:
None

Figure 7–8   Standard update procedure activity.

DD Project Detail
Initial Estimate

Project: DDFILE   Date: Aug 25, 1986 10:41 AM
_____

3 Std. Name conv   Early Start: Jan 5, 1987 8:12 AM
                                                                Early Finish: Apr 10, 1987 8:12 AM
  Duration: 13.8 Weeks
  Slack: 43.1 Weeks   Late Start: Nov 3, 1987 8:00 AM
                                                                Late Finish: Feb 5, 1988 5:00 PM

                                                                Sched Start: Jan 5, 1987 8:12 AM
                                                                Sched Finish: Apr 10, 1987 8:12 AM
_____

Notes:
Establish standard naming conventions for the different types of entities that would be put into the DD; get agreement and sign-up from MIS and users. Write migration from existing conventions.
_____

Resources Allocated:

Name	Duration (days)	Amount used	Cost	Cost Basis	Cost to Complete
Martin	69.0	0.8	$8.00	Hour	$3532.80
Davidson	69.0	1.0	$640.00	Week	$8832.00
Total:					$12364.80

Predecessors:
None
_____

Successors:
None

Figure 7–9   Standard naming convention activity.

DD Project Detail
Initial Estimate

Project: DDFILE   Date: Aug 25, 1986 10:41 AM
_____

5 DD Evaluation Criteria   Early Start: May 11, 1987 8:00 AM
                                                                Early Finish: May 15, 1987 5:00 PM
  Duration: 1.0 Week
  Slack: 10.0 Weeks   Late Start: Jul 20, 1987 8:00 AM
                                                                Late Finish: Jul 24, 1987 5:00 PM

                                                                Sched Start: May 11, 1987 8:00 AM
                                                                Sched Finish: May 15, 1987 5:00 PM
_____

Notes:
Develop evaluation criteria for acquiring/developing dictionary software; prioritize key requirements.
_____

Resources Allocated:

Name	Duration (days)	Amount used	Cost	Cost Basis	Cost to Complete
Jessup	5.0	0.8	$4500.00	Month	$830.76
Total:					$830.76

Predecessors:
1 DD Requirements   Early Finish: May 8, 1987 5:00 PM
  Slack avail: 50.0 Days   Late Finish: Jul 17, 1987 5:00 PM
_____

Successors:
6 Examine DD Packages   Early Start: May 18, 1987 8:00 AM
  Slack avail: 50.0 Days   Late Start: Jul 27, 1987 8:00 AM

Figure 7–10   DD evaluation criteria activity.

DD Project Detail
Initial Estimate

Project: DDFILE   Date: Aug 25, 1986 10:41 AM

6 Examine DD Packages   Early Start: May 18, 1987 8:00 AM
                                                     Early Finish: May 29, 1987 5:00 PM

  Duration: 2.0 Weeks
  Slack: 10.0 Weeks   Late Start: Jul 27, 1987 8:00 AM
                                                     Late Finish: Aug 7, 1987 5:00 PM

                                                     Sched Start: May 18, 1987 8:00 AM
                                                     Sched Finish: May 29, 1987 5:00 PM

Notes:
Get vendors to demonstrate their products; set up benchmarks; test the packages for ease of use and other
functionality.

Resources Allocated:

Name	Duration (days)	Amount used	Cost	Cost Basis	Cost to Complete
Jessup	10.0	0.8	$4500.00	Month	$1661.53
Martin	10.0	0.8	$8.00	Hour	$512.00
Total:					$2173.53

Predecessors:
5 DD Evaluation Criteria   Early Finish: May 15, 1987 5:00 PM
  Slack avail: 50.0 Days   Late Finish: Jul 24, 1987 5:00 PM

Successors:
7 Select/Install DD   Early Start: Jun 1, 1987 8:00 AM
  Slack avail: 50.0 Days   Late Start: Aug 10, 1987 8:00 AM

Figure 7-11 Examine DD packages activity.

DD Resource Cost
Initial Estimate

Project: DDFILE   Date: Aug 25, 1986 10:41 AM

# Resource	Capacity	Unit Cost	Per	Days to Complete	Cost to Complete
1 Martin	No limit	$8.00	Hour	102.0	$6528.00
2 Davidson	No limit	$640.00	Week	146.0	$18688.00
3 Jessup	No limit	$4500.00	Month	117.0	$24299.96
4 Larkin	No limit	$9.00	Hour	214.0	$15408.00
5 Training	No limit	$800.00	Week	30.0	$4800.00
6 Marketing	No limit	$420.00	Week	24.0	$2016.00
7 Field Engg	No limit	$420.00	Week	24.0	$2016.00
8 Personnel	No limit	$420.00	Week	24.0	$2016.00
9 Manufacturing	No limit	$420.00	Week	24.0	$2016.00
10 Finance	No limit	$420.00	Week	24.0	$2016.00
11 Operations	No limit	$340.00	Week	128.8	$8758.40
12 Bianchi	No limit	$600.00	Week	150.0	$18000.00
13 Faber	No limit	$600.00	Week	84.0	$10080.00
14 Grant	No limit	$420.00	Week	130.0	$10920.00
15 Urbano	No limit	$440.00	Week	130.0	$11440.00
16 Data Dictionary	No limit	$15000.00	Fixed	0.0	$0.00
17 Miscellaneous	No limit	$8000.00	Fixed	0.0	$0.00

Cost to Complete: $139002.36   Total Cost of Project: $139002.36

Figure 7-12 Resources.

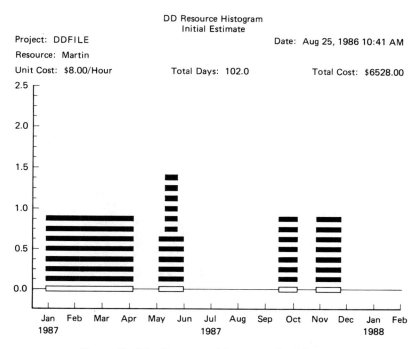

Figure 7–13 Resource histogram for Martin.

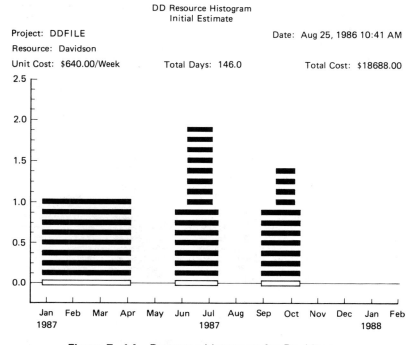

Figure 7–14 Resource histogram for Davidson.

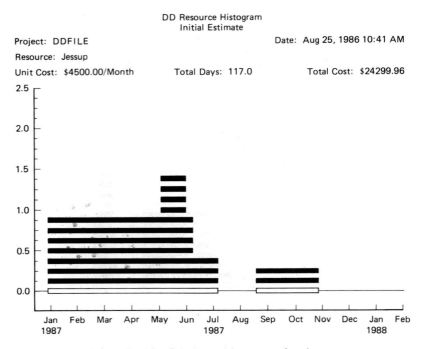

Figure 7–15 Resource histogram for Jessup.

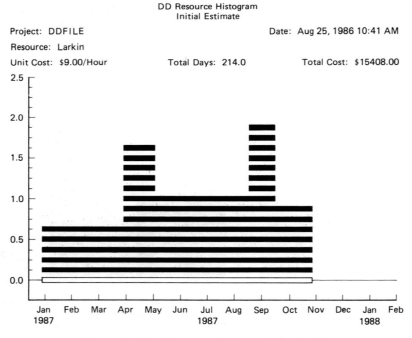

Figure 7–16 Resource histogram for Larkin.

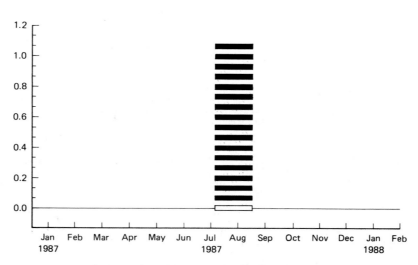

Figure 7–17 Resource histogram for Training.

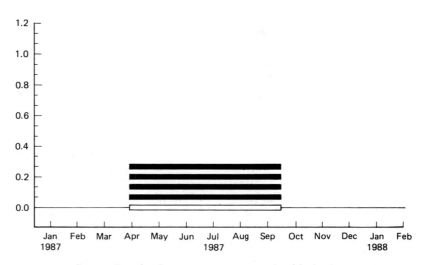

Figure 7–18 Resource histogram for Marketing.

DD Project
as of May 22, 1987

Project: DDFILE   Date: May 22, 1987 12:00 AM

Duration:

	FORECAST	ACTUAL	VARIANCE	
			Difference	Percent
	284.9 Days	283.9 Days	−1.0 Days	−0.3

Cost:

	FORECAST	ACTUAL	VARIANCE	
			Difference	Percent
	$0.00	$145749.87	+$145749.87	+0.0

Event:

	FORECAST	ACTUAL	VARIANCE
Start	Jan 5, 1987 8:12 AM	Jan 5, 1987 8:12 AM	None
Finish	Feb 5, 1988 5:00 PM	Feb 4, 1988 5:00 PM	1 Day Early

Calendar Exceptions:

None

Figure 7-19   Project variance summary.

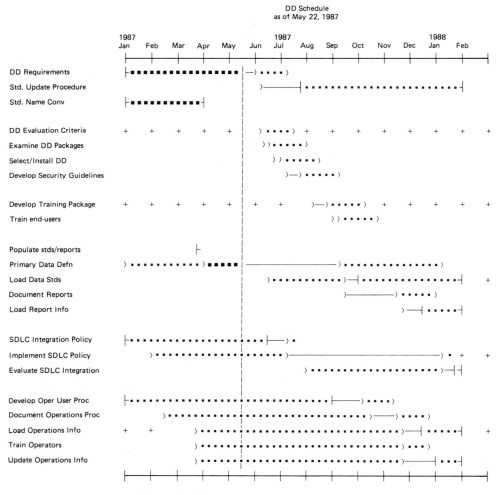

Figure 7-20   Revised project schedule.

DD Project Activity Duration
Forecast vs Actual
as of May 22, 1987

Project: DDFILE

Date: May 22, 1987 12:00 AM
Report Type: DURATION

Activity	FORECAST	ACTUAL	VARIANCE	
			Difference	Percent
1 DD Requirements	89.9 Days	109.9 Days	+20.0 Days	+22.2
2 Std Update Procedure	18.0 Days	36.0 Days	+18.0 Days	+100.0
3 Std. Name Conv	69.0 Days	69.0 Days	0.0 Days	0.0
5 DD Evaluation Criteria	5.0 Days	5.0 Days	0.0 Days	0.0
6 Examine DD Packages	10.0 Days	10.0 Days	0.0 Days	0.0
7 Select/Install DD	10.0 Days	10.0 Days	0.0 Days	0.0
8 Develop Security Guidelines	20.0 Days	20.0 Days	0.0 Days	0.0
10 Develop Training Package	20.0 Days	20.0 Days	0.0 Days	0.0
11 Train end-users	10.0 Days	10.0 Days	0.0 Days	0.0
13 Populate stds/reports	1.0 Day	1.0 Day	0.0 Days	0.0
14 Primary Data Defn	120.0 Days	120.0 Days	0.0 Days	0.0
15 Load Data Stds	15.0 Days	15.0 Days	0.0 Days	0.0
16 Document Reports	50.0 Days	50.0 Days	0.0 Days	0.0
17 Load Report Info	20.0 Days	20.0 Days	0.0 Days	0.0
19 SDLC Integration Policy	20.0 Days	20.0 Days	0.0 Days	0.0
20 Implement SDLC Policy	130.0 Days	130.0 Days	0.0 Days	0.0
21 Evaluate SDLC Integration	10.0 Days	10.0 Days	0.0 Days	0.0
23 Develop Oper User Proc	30.0 Days	30.0 Days	0.0 Days	0.0
24 Document Operations Proc	30.0 Days	30.0 Days	0.0 Days	0.0
25 Load Operations Info	20.0 Days	20.0 Days	0.0 Days	0.0
26 Train Operators	4.0 Days	4.0 Days	0.0 Days	0.0
27 Update Operations Info	24.0 Days	24.0 Days	0.0 Days	0.0
Total Project Duration:	284.9 Days	283.9 Days	−1.0 Days	−0.3

Figure 7-21   Activity variance summary.

Project Schedule

The project schedule that is obtained after the changes have been incorporated by the system is in the same format as the original project schedule, except that the time line has been set to May 22, 1987, and activity durations and start and stop times have been adjusted to reflect the changes that have occurred. This is shown in Figure 7-20.

Activity Variance Summary

The activity variance summary for the project shows actual versus forecast for each activity within the project. An example is shown in Figure 7-21.

Activity Summary Reports

These reports are detailed for each activity, and shown in Figures 7-22 through 7-24. The reports include the duration of each activity, schedule, and resources used to date. With the aid of these reports, the project manager will be able to monitor the progress of the project, and detect and correct any problem before it is too late.

DD Project Activity Summary
Forecast vs Actual
as of May 22, 1987

Project: DDFILE   Date: May 22, 1987 12:00 AM

Activity:

1 DD Requirements

	Planned duration: 90 Days	Duration to date: 99 Days
	Slack avail: 29.0 Days	% Complete: 90

	Start	Finish
Sched:	Jan 5, 1987 8:00 AM	May 8, 1987 5:00 PM
Actual:	Jan 5, 1987 8:00 AM	Jun 5, 1987 5:00 PM
Early:	Jan 5, 1987 8:00 AM	Jun 5, 1987 5:00 PM
Late:	Feb 13, 1987 8:00 AM	Jul 16, 1987 5:00 PM

Notes:

Develop entity model to support dictionary requirements from previous step; define facilities that would be required.

Predecessors:

None

Successors:

Std Update Procedure   Slack avail: 138 Days

Sched Start:	Jun 8, 1987 8:00 AM
Early Start:	Jun 8, 1987 8:00 AM
Late Start:	Dec 17, 1987 8:00 AM

DD Evaluation Criteria   Slack avail: 29 Days

Sched Start:	Jun 8, 1987 8:00 AM
Early Start:	Jun 8, 1987 8:00 AM
Late Start:	Jul 17, 1987 8:00 AM

Resources used to date:

	Forecast	Actual	Variance
Jessup			
Amount	0.8	0.8	0.0
Duration	71.9 Days	79.1 Days	+10.0
Cost	$14933.07	$16428.46	+10.0
Larkin			
Amount	0.6	0.6	0.0
Duration	53.9 Days	59.3 Days	+10.0
Cost	$3880.80	$4269.60	+10.0
Activity total:			
Duration	89.9 Days	98.9 Days	+10.0
Cost	$18813.87	$20698.06	+10.0

Figure 7–22 Activity summary: forecast versus actual for DD requirements activity.

DD Project Activity Summary
Forecast vs Actual
as of May 22, 1987

Project: DDFILE   Date: May 22, 1987 12:00 AM

Activity:

2 Std Update Procedure

	Planned duration: 18 Days	Duration to date: 0 Days
	Slack avail: 138.0 Days	% Complete: 0
	Start	Finish
Sched:	May 11, 1987 8:00 AM	Jun 3, 1987 5:00 PM
Actual:	Jun 8, 1987 8:00 AM	Jul 27, 1987 5:00 PM
Early:	Jun 8, 1987 8:00 AM	Jul 27, 1987 5:00 PM
Late:	Dec 17, 1987 8:00 AM	Feb 4, 1988 5:00 PM

Notes:

Define format for documenting entities; organizational flow of information for update of DD; publish and disseminate; assign responsibility for sourcing information.

Predecessors:

DD Requirements   20 Days Late

  Sched Finish: May 8, 1987 5:00 PM
  Actual Finish: Jun 5, 1987 5:00 PM

Successors:

None

Resources used to date:

	Forecast	Actual	Variance
Martin			
Amount	0.6	0.6	0.0
Duration	5.4 Days	0 Days	−100.0
Cost	$345.60	$0.00	−100.0
Jessup			
Amount	0.5	0.5	0.0
Duration	4.5 Days	0 Days	−100.0
Cost	$934.61	$0.00	−100.0
Activity total:			
Duration	9 Days	0 Days	−100.0
Cost	$1280.21	$0.00	−100.0

Figure 7–23 Activity summary: forecast versus actual for standard update procedure activity.

DD Project Activity Summary
Forecast vs Actual
as of May 22, 1987

Project: DDFILE   Date: May 22, 1987 12:00 AM

Activity:

3 Std. Name Conv

	Planned duration: 69 Days	Duration to date: 69 Days
	Slack avail: 214.9 Days	% Complete: 100

	Start	Finish
Sched:	Jan 5, 1987 8:12 AM	Apr 10, 1987 8:12 AM
Actual:	Jan 5, 1987 8:12 AM	Apr 10, 1987 8:12 AM
Early:	Jan 5, 1987 8:12 AM	Apr 10, 1987 8:12 AM
Late:	Nov 2, 1987 8:00 AM	Feb 4, 1988 5:00 PM

Notes:

Establish standard naming conventions for the different types of entities that would be put into the DD; get agreement and sign-up from MIS and users. Write migration from existing conventions.

Predecessors:

None

Successors:

None

Resources used to date:

	Forecast	Actual	Variance
Martin			
Amount	0.8	0.8	0.0
Duration	55.2 Days	55.2 Days	0.0
Cost	$3532.80	$3532.80	0.0
Davidson			
Amount	1.0	1.0	0.0
Duration	69 Days	69 Days	0.0
Cost	$8832.00	$8832.00	0.0
Activity total:			
Duration	69 Days	69 Days	0.0
Cost	$12364.80	$12364.80	0.0

Figure 7–24 Activity summary: forecast versus actual for standard naming convention activity.

chapter 8

Data Dictionary Selection

DICTIONARY SELECTION CRITERIA

One of the most important decisions facing a data dictionary implementer is the selection of a data dictionary system. This task is greatly facilitated if the steps outlined in the preceding section have been done. The analysis that has been performed in identifying the needs of the organization that the dictionary has to support will form the basis upon which a dictionary can be selected. Since there are several commercial packages available that can perform many of the functions to support information management, it is quite likely that the decision will be made to buy a commercially available package. However, if the requirements of the organization are such that they cannot be met by a single software package, consideration must be given to developing a dictionary system in-house, if that is feasible.

The formation of a selection team is appropriate, to gain the perspectives and support of the different categories of users. If the mix of applications that the dictionary is going to support has been determined, it is wise to involve personnel from those functional areas to be part of the selection team. For example, if the applications to be supported include data administration and end-user computing, a person from each of these groups should be on the team. The objective of the team is to review the analysis that has been done and to enumerate the criteria for selection, assign weights to the selection criteria, and evaluate packages for each selection criterion. The package that has the highest score can then be proposed for acquisition. Let's review some selection criteria that might result from a review of the analysis.

Hardware/Software Compatibility

- Hardware on which the system will work
- Operating system requirement
- Transaction processor requirement
- Network requirement
- Data base management system requirement

Ease of Use

- Ease of learning
- Level of expertise required
- Compatibility with existing procedures
- Operational impact

Entity Support

- Ability to store information about entities of interest to the organization
- Ability to store narratives, and associated keys to access the definition, such as keyword in context (KWIC), aliases, synonyms, homonyms, etc.
- Ability to store and retrieve attributes that include size, type (i.e., numeric, alphanumeric), characteristics, range of values, etc.
- Ability to store assigned responsibility, authoritative source, pointers to physical occurrences in the data base
- Ability to store versions of the definition for cases where there are differences of opinion

Report Capability

- Ability to produce reports of the data definitions upon request, and by subsets that can be defined by the end users
- Ability to obtain where-used reports as well as explosions of components

Data Description Generation

- Ability to generate query record layouts in the host query language
- Ability to interface to primary data management and file management software on the host
- Ability to interface to query processors on the host

Load Facility

- Ability to import descriptions from existing dictionaries, and populate the dictionary
- Ability to import documentation from existing edit mechanisms
- Ability to scan text files with keyword search capability

Vendor Support

- Vendor stability
- Commitment to package
- Reliability and quality of support
- Active user's group
- Documentation

Security Support

- Facilities to protect the data in the data dictionary data base
- Facility to control update access to specific entity categories in the data dictionary data base
- Facility for the creator of an entity to provide access privileges to other authorized users of the system

Special Features

- Extensibility
- Support of system development life cycle
- Support of distributed data base processing

SELECTION PROCESS

Assignment of Weights

Having arrived at a set of criteria, the next step is to assign weights to each criterion. This process represents the "tailoring" of the criteria to the particular needs of the data base environment in question.

The task of deciding on the weights is difficult and critical; it is the one most important activity of the selection team because experience has shown that the process of applying weights will reflect the need for particular features of the data dictionary system. For instance, an installation may already have a DBMS and a source control software package, and special interfaces to these packages would be desirable in the dictionary system. Another installation may wish to incorporate the access to the data dictionary with the office automation software that exists.

The next stage in the selection process is to score the various packages in an objective fashion. This requires that individuals in the selection team review the features advertised by the vendors of data dictionary packages, and then get demonstrations of these features. A still better approach would be to list the benchmark criteria and let the vendors demonstrate that they meet the criteria specified.

An example of a matrix that has weights and some sample scores is given in Figure 8-1. Note that the scores are given for the lowest level at which the criterion exists.

Criteria		Weight-Level				Score		
		1	2	3	4	1	2	3
4.	Security support	10						
4.1	Security attributes		32					
4.1.1	Included in DBMS interface			42		0	0	10
4.1.2	Independent security			58		3	7	0
4.2	Security support-DD		68					
4.2.1	Password control			62				
4.2.1.1	Global				58	5	2	10
4.2.1.2	Local				42	5	0	10

Figure 8-1 Matrix showing weights and sample scores.

Evaluation

The final task is to calculate the results and arrive at a conclusion. In this phase it will become obvious why one data dictionary scored higher or lower than others. One of the advantages of using the weighted evaluation technique is that specific strengths and weaknesses can be isolated and analyzed for their effect on the total selection process. Thus, if a package lacks on-line update capabilities, its final score would clearly reflect the penalty incurred for the absence of this feature. Similarly, scores in particular categories can be compared, to highlight further the relative strengths and weaknesses of the packages under consideration.

In the final stages of evaluation it is important to recognize that the attempt to minimize subjectivity does not completely eliminate individual bias. All the scores were assigned, not measured—these numbers are therefore qualitative, not quantitative, measurements. Thus if two packages are within 5 percentage points of each other, the more subjective criteria, such as ease of use, vendor support, and resource utilization, should be carefully scrutinized.

There may be cases where the consensus might be to develop a package instead of purchasing a commercially available package. In such a case the time to develop a data dictionary system must be taken into account. A simple system may take as long as 9 to 12 months to complete, but the user has the flexibility of tailoring it to the organization's needs.

FEATURES OF COMMERCIALLY AVAILABLE DICTIONARIES

The following pages provide the reader with an overview of several dictionaries that are available in the marketplace.

DATAMANAGER

See Figures 8–2 and 8–3.

Vendor: Manager Software Products Inc.
131 Hartwell Avenue
Lexington, MA 02173

Phone: (617) 863-5800

Hardware/Software Compatibility

- IBM with MVS/XA, VS1, VM/CMS, DOS/VSE operating systems;

Ease of Use

- On-line and batch free-form keyword-based command language
- Set default value feature

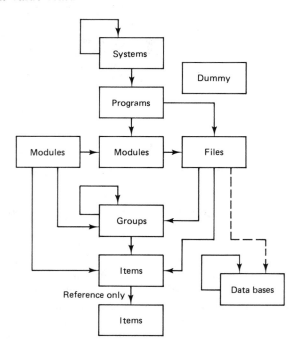

Figure 8–2   DATAMANAGER dictionary entity model.

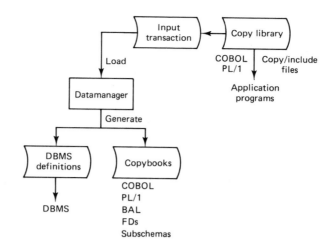

Figure 8-3 DATAMANAGER dictionary interfaces.

- Dummy members for as-yet-unentered lower-level entities automatically produced
- User interface is English-like
- Shorthand abbreviation is optional

Entity Support

- Support for entities such as systems, programs, modules, files, groups, data items, DBMS definition entities, user-defined entities
- Names are 32-character unique identifiers together with status (up to 255 statuses)
- Descriptions up to 65,000 lines
- 16 aliases for all entities
- 15 versions for items
- Unlimited keyword descriptors
- User/owner responsible for
- User-defined characteristics
- User-defined syntax allows choice of unlimited additional dictionary structures

Report Capability

- Glossary, catalog, explosions, selection via entity name, entity type, keyword

Data Description Generation

- ADABAS, TOTAL, IMS/DL1, IDMS, System 2000, COBOL, PL/1, Assembly, MARK IV

Load Facility

- Data definition extracts from COBOL, PL/1
- Utilities copy data between physically separate dictionaries
- User exit facility

Vendor Support

- Product started in Great Britain; established in United States since 1976
- Product is supported in 14 countries

- Active users' group with annual meetings, resulting in a product with few bugs
- Documentation quality is very good

  Security Support

- Has functional access control, user/password scheme with occurrence-level protection

  Special Features

- Very good edit/validation documentation capability
- Capable of supporting distributed data base environment
- Independent dictionary supports several DBMSs

ADABAS™

See Figures 8-4 and 8-5.

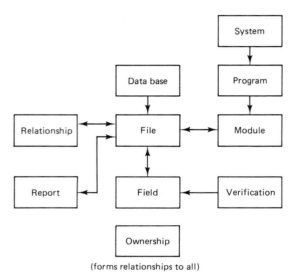

Figure 8-4 ADABAS dictionary entity model. Courtesy Cullinet Software Inc.

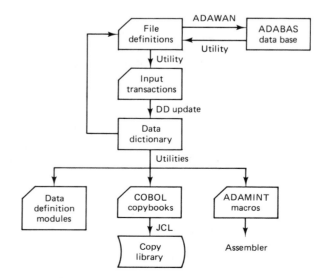

Figure 8-5 ADABAS dictionary interfaces. Courtesy Cullinet Software Inc.

Vendor: Software A.G. of North America Inc.
11800 Sunrise Valley Drive
Reston, VA 22091

(703) 860-5050

Hardware/Software Compatibility

- IBM with DOS, OS/VS, MVS; Univac Series 90 with DOS
- Transaction processors include CICS, TSO, TASKMASTER, CMS, SHADOW II, INTERCOM
- Requires ADABAS Data Base Management System

Ease of Use

- Fixed-format card input transactions
- Pull-forward facility from standard file element definitions
- Intended for the DP-oriented user

Entity Support

- Entity types supported include fields, relationships, files, data bases, field verification procedures, owners/users, programs, modules, systems, reports, response codes, user views
- Names can be up to 32 characters long
- Comments are 30 characters per line, arbitrary number of lines
- Picture, 99 synonyms, range, edit mask, redefines capability, multiple output pictures for fields
- 200 descriptors per ADABAS file

Report Capability

- Via data base query facilities

Data Description Generation

- ADABAS file definitions generated
- COBOL data division statements generated with optional prefixes
- Data definition modules for ADASCRIPT +, ADACOM, and NATURAL generated
- Supplies data for ADAMINT preprocessor

Load Facility

- Existing ADABAS database description input capability
- Descriptors created automatically at file load time
- Initial load utility available

Vendor Support

- Major DBMS vendor
- Commitment to package is at level of commitment to ADABAS data base management system
- Documentation quality is clear and well presented

Security Support

- Functional access control is provided
- Occurrence-level protection is not provided
- Encryption is provided

Special Features

- Good directory model support
- Capable of supporting a distributed data base environment
- Good edit and validation support capability

ADR™/Datadictionary®

See Figures 8–6 and 8–7.

Vendor: Applied Data Research, Inc.
Rt 206 and Orchard Rd. CN-8
Princeton, NJ 08540

(201) 874-9000

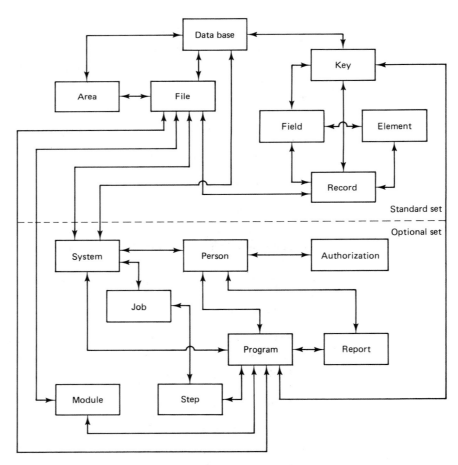

Figure 8–6   DATACOM-DD entity model. Courtesy Manager Software Product Inc.

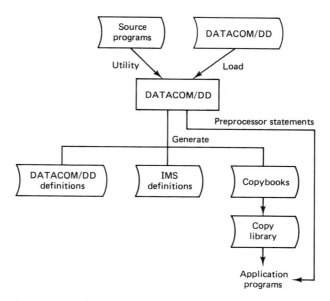

Figure 8-7 DATACOM-DD interfaces. Courtesy Manager Software Product Inc.

Hardware/Software Compatibility

- IBM DOS/VS/VSE/SP, MVS, MVS/XA, VM/CMS systems
- Using CICS, ROSCOE, VOLLIE, and CMS TP monitors
- Using DATACOM/DB Relational Data Base Management System

Ease of Use

- Forms driven input with intelligent defaults, express commands, PF keys, interactive Help, split screens
- Data base prototyping facilities
- Batch transactions for volume updates
- Transport facility for porting definitions
- Automatic, active interfaces to The LIBRARIAN, ADR/IDEAL, and other DATACOM products, including DATAQUERY, PC DATACOM, ADR/DL, D-NET, VSAM TRANSPARENCY, DL/1 TRANSPARENCY, TOTAL TRANSPARENCY, DATACOM/DB, and DATAREPORTER

Entity Support

- Standard entities include data bases, areas, tables, keys, fields, elements, dataviews, systems, programs, modules, reports, panels, persons, authorizations, jobs, steps, nodes, and IMS, TOTAL, and conventional file structure entities
- Unlimited user-defined entities and relationships are supported
- In addition to the dictionary name, assembler, COBOL, PL/1, or FORTRAN names and other aliases are supported
- Names may be up to 32 characters long, with exits for controlling naming standards
- Unlimited text description; author and controller names
- Passwords and three lock levels for read/update security
- Up to eight keyword descriptors may be associated with an entity occurrence

- Multiple versions—999 versions in Test and History status plus one version in Production status

Report Capabilities

- Detailed, summary, and explosion-of-components report types
- Users may specify the desired pathing of entity types and the mixing and nesting of different report types to customize a report, especially for impact analysis
- Data selection may be by entity name/alias/keywords (partial or full), entity type, version, and status
- Ad hoc queries and special reports may be generated by DATAQUERY, IDEAL, and DATAREPORTER

Data Description Generation

- DATACOM/DB data base definitions and dataviews are used directly by ADR's RDBMS and 4GL products
- IMS and TOTAL data base definitions and conventional file record definitions may be generated
- COBOL, PL/1, BAL, and DATAREPORTER copybooks can be generated
- Source programs in The LIBRARIAN can obtain record definitions directly from DATADICTIONARY, without the need for copybook maintenance

Load Facility

- Utility to import and export definitions
- Utility to load DATADICTIONARY from COBOL copybooks
- Utility to regenerate data base definitions from the DATACOM/DB Directory

Vendor Support

- *Vendor stability.* ADR is a major DBMS software vendor.
- *Commitment to package.* DATADICTIONARY is the heart of ADR's RDBMS/4GL product family and is the focal point of its software integration.
- *Active user group.* The independent user group, CADRE (Combined ADR Environment), operates an extensive regional and international organization.
- *Documentation quality.* Excellent.

Security Support

- Multiple levels of user authorizations are available to address the needs of data administration, data base administration, application development, and users.
- Password and three levels of locking are provided to control the displaying reporting and updating of entity occurrences.
- Data encryption is available to provide physical security.
- To ensure auditing integrity, definitions in Production status cannot be changed. When a Test version is promoted to Production, the old Production version is automatically bumped into History status.

Special Features

- *Extensibility.* Unlimited user-defined entity types and relationships may be created, to support any metadata in an enterprise. Once defined, DATA-DICTIONARY automatically generates all the standard supporting facilities for the maintenance and reporting of these user entity types.

- *Dictionary interface.* The DATADICTIONARY Service Facility (DSF) is a high-level command syntax for the accessing and updating of dictionary content. DSF allows other packages and systems to integrate with DATADICTIONARY, toward fostering a single repository of corporate data definitions. An on-line debugging facility is provided for DSF.

- *Distribution support.* DATADICTIONARY acts as a distributed systems directory in support of distributed data base processing using ADR/D-NET. DATADICTIONARY itself may be centralized or distributed.

- *Version management.* In support of the multiple versions of definitions in Test, Production, and History statuses, DATADICTIONARY ensures that all the pieces of a data base definition (tables, fields, etc.) are synchronized to the same version. Commands are available to create new versions or new data base definitions from existing definitions. The COPY command may duplicate entire definition structures or selected substructures, in one step.

- *Life-cycle support.* DATADICTIONARY is updated as a natural by-product of application prototyping, development, execution, and maintenance using IDEAL. In this way DATADICTIONARY serves as an automatic application systems directory and documentation facility.

- *Full-function stand-alone dictionary.* While the majority of DATADICTIONARY users use it in conjunction with ADR's integrated RDBMS/4GL products, DATADICTIONARY possesses the full functionality to be used as a stand-alone dictionary, due to its many interfaces and facilities.

Additional Special Features

- User has the ability to create unlimited entity relationships.
- User-defined exits are available.
- Dictionary automatically records new entity-type information in itself.
- Capability exists for global status change.
- Edit/validation support is via comment statements only.

chapter 9

Populating the Dictionary

OBJECTIVE OF POPULATING THE DICTIONARY

The objective of populating the dictionary is to load the dictionary with the initial data in the shortest possible time in order for the use of the dictionary to be self-sustaining. The term "populate" is commonly used by data dictionary administrators and users to denote the storing into the data dictionary data base of information about different entity categories. The term "populate" implies that there is information about entities in the organization that is available and can be stored in the dictionary. Population also implies a continuing process of update of the initial information that is stored in the dictionary. One other objective of the population strategy is to set in motion processes that support the data in the dictionary as well as provide support for the processes to be effective.

In this book, the initial storage of information is referred to as the "population" process. Chapter 10 is dedicated to the update and maintenance process. This division has been made because the population strategies that are developed and implemented in most installations require perspectives other than ongoing update and maintenance. The administrator has to assess the MIS environment and the maturity of the user community to gain an understanding of the results from the dictionary that would produce a positive impact on the operation and simultaneously produce goodwill and support for the dictionary. The data dictionary administrator has to develop strategies that ensure that the population process is understood and supported at various levels within the organization. Defining the objective of the population process and understanding the organization are key elements in getting the process started.

The objectives of populating the dictionary have to be tied into the implementation strategy that is developed (discussed in Chapter 7). However, it is important to recognize that while the implementation strategy focuses on identifying the deliverables to the users of the dictionary, the population strategy facilitates and supports the implementation strategy. In some cases there may be easier ways to populate certain parts of the dictionary than others which could affect the implementation strategy. For example, if existing copybooks had to be loaded manually, and the time it would take to get them loaded was inordinately long, this step could be a lower-priority item than other steps that would have faster payback, such as loading only new copybooks.

DEALING WITH CHANGES

A complex situation is created because one may be dealing with three sets of changes. One change is the introduction of the dictionary concept itself; the other is the change to existing methods of doing things; the third is the fact that information that as to organization and content with which users are familiar will be transformed to a different style.

It is strongly recommended that the introduction of changes be phased into the organization in stages. A new system requires that users have an orientation and perspective on what the system is going to do for the users much before the actual system is installed or implemented. This is an essential part of selling the new information system and process to the users. The proper use of loading techniques would give the implementer the flexibility to introduce the use of the system utilizing existing information that users are familiar with.

For example, it is well recognized that the information in the dictionary can be used to support the generation of schedules for the computers in the data center. Before this can be implemented, the operations staff must be convinced that the basic data that they require can be stored in the dictionary, and that they can access the data in the dictionary in a reliable manner.

Once support is garnered and a prototype developed, procedures can be put in place to ensure that the data are entered by the authoritative source (in this case, the systems development staff) into the dictionary in the proper sequence and time frames. Note that it would be most convenient to present the same format for the reports that is currently used in the operations department, so that the only change for the operations staff is to use the dictionary to get that information. Most of the data that are used in the production of a schedule come from the systems development staff. In order for the systems development staff to start using the new screens to input information, the process must be introduced gradually. Additional data items to satisfy the needs of the schedule generation mechanism will have to be entered by the development group. It will be much easier to gain their support if they are already used to the dictionary system and its procedures.

GAINING ORGANIZATIONAL SUPPORT

Gaining organizational support and commitment is extremely important. The existence of the right kinds of standards and procedures within the MIS department would make implementation of the dictionary easier. For example, if data item naming conventions are in place and being followed, transition to the dictionary does not have to include procedures for establishing a standard naming convention. Where multiple conventions are being followed by different project teams, the mere fact of having to bring agreement among several groups of people on a standard could result in the dictionary being viewed in a negative light as the conflict resolution process instead of being viewed as the tool that will ease the transition to a standardized and stable environment.

It would be wise to encourage the view of the dictionary as a place to document the agreement of several groups, and to further propagate its usefulness as a communications vehicle among many systems development groups. If an information center is about to be established, or end-user computing procedures are to be put in place, that would be a good time to introduce the dictionary as a place where standard data item conventions are located. An extremely positive reaction would be obtained from end users because they would have a vested interest in ensuring that the definitions are accurate.

Manager's Participation

Standard items are input into the dictionary based on several strategies. A lot depends on the reading of the situation by the DD project manager. Where existing systems are in place and have known data item inconsistencies, a good strategy is to make this fact visible to the managers responsible for the systems. A procedure that involves the participation of the application systems managers is recommended. Depending on the number of managers available, have each manager provide a list of 20 to 30 key data items that they have to deal with. Also ask them to specify the category of data to which the item belongs, its size, and the source file in which it exists. Then input these data into a file that can easily be printed out. Use a sort program to sort this file by data item name. As usually happens, the same item might be called by different names by different groups. The raw data file and the sorted file may appear as shown in Figure 9–1.

1	2	3	4	5	6
C	ORG	ACCT-NO	X(004)	CDSDB	BR. MGR.
C	ORG	ACCT-NO	X(004)	CDSDB	AREA MGR
C	EMPL	ACCT-NO	X(004)	CDSDB	SOC
D	ORG	ACCT-NO	X(008)	CONTR	DATA ENT
D	FAC	ACCT-NO	9(013)	GEN LED	MANUAL
W	ORG	ACCT-NO	X(008)	WDR	DISPATCH

In the file above, the fields have the following meaning:
Field 1 = initial of manager providing the information
Field 2 = data class of data element
Field 3 = data item name
Field 4 = size
Field 5 = data file name
Field 6 = source of update

Figure 9–1 Key data element list.

After the file is sorted by field 3, the printed file will appear as shown in Figure 9–2. One glance at the file reveals certain inconsistencies. The name ACCT-NO has different sizes in different system files. There may be many reasons for this:

- The data item does not mean the same thing to different persons.
- The data item called ACCT-NO is modified in its definition as it goes through various systems but its name is not changed consistent with the new definition.

1	2	3	4	5	6
C	ORG	ACCT-NO	X(004)	CDSDB	BR. MGR.
C	ORG	ACCT-NO	X(004)	CDSDB	AREA MGR
D	ORG	ACCT-NO	X(008)	CONTR	DATA ENT
C	EMPL	ACCT-NO	X(004)	CDSDB	SOC
D	FAC	ACCT-NO	9(013)	GEN LED	MANUAL
W	ORG	ACCT-NO	X(008)	WDR	DISPATCH

Figure 9–2 Sorted key data element list.

Based on the list above, it should be easier to get the cooperation of the managers to address this issue. First, it is now necessary to get the definition of what each manager meant by the data item called ACCT-NO. If the definitions do not match, it is necessary to identify different names for the truly different definitions. If the definitions match, but there are differences in the size, it is necessary to resolve the conflict by identifying the standard name to be associated with the standard definition and size. The process should involve the managers as much as possible.

In the case of some data items, more information may have to be gathered from other parts of the organization to validate and confirm the reasons for coming up with a standard. For example, the data item called part number might be created in the engineering department of the organization but used in the field service systems. In some cases, the field service department may be creating part numbers in response to local needs. Sometimes, these needs may be legitimate, but they work against the interest of overall data integrity.

To resolve these issues, users might have to be brought in from different organizations to help resolve the problem. For example, if part number is created as a 9-byte numeric field, suspicions may be raised if the field is defined as a 10-byte alphanumeric field. This can happen if there is some intelligence embedded in the number, such as: Part number is composed of a three-digit prefix and a six-digit suffix, comprising nine digits in all. Moreover if part numbers were 005000013, 002000123, 017000425, and so on, from a data entry point of view, it might be desirable to break the number into two pieces. Thus, to enter the part 005000013, the operator could enter 5 for the prefix and 13 for the suffix and the system could put the two pieces together after inserting the zeros. If the report formats were made more readable by inserting a period or hyphen between the prefix and the suffix, this would seem a reasonable output function. However, if the data base contained the period, that would be a contravention of data integrity because the format of the data item has been changed. This situation calls for corrective action to be taken.

Staff Participation

Getting different persons to load existing data and system information is another strategy to gain organizational support. The reconciliation of different standards and conventions that have been used in the past is a fairly difficult one. That is because of the erratic quality of the documentation available for analysis. In some cases, there may be little or no documentation available on which to base one's decisions. In other cases, the person with the most knowledge about a system or data base may be working on some other project and thus may not be able to spend the time to figure out the inconsistent definitions of the past. In order to get as much input into the documentation process from all persons with the knowledge, it is important to identify the persons with the expertise and then to develop procedures that make it easy for those persons to interface with the dictionary administrator.

Under no circumstances should the primary authority of the dictionary administrator to set the standards be compromised. When documenting older data structures which may or may not be changed to reflect the standard data item conventions, the primary objective should be to identify as accurately as possible the closest linkage to a standard data definition, if one has already been identified. If a standard definition does not exist, a standard for that data item must be established by the administrator before a linkage or cross-reference is made to the standard name and description from the specific data item. The process involves continuing interaction between the dictionary administrator and the programmer/analyst and end users. As the dictionary gets increasingly populated with the standards, the time it takes to resolve the cross-references should decrease.

System Implication

What does it mean to the DD project manager, who has to decide the features of the dictionary to use, to load the dictionary in the shortest possible time span? First, it means that the features that one would look for in a dictionary should support the loading strategies mentioned above. If the dictionary did not have the capability to support these strategies, and these strategies are deemed to be critical to the successful implementation of the dictionary, it is important that the DD project manager ask if these features could be added to the dictionary.

Second, the project manager has to understand and come to grips with the ways in which the various groups of people within the organization store the information and come up with creative solutions to get these people to use a common format to input this information into the system. With the advent of programs that generate flexible screen formats, it is worth asking whether the dictionary can adjust to differing input screen formats based on users' needs.

Third, the project manager must prepare to load information into the dictionary some time prior to the installation of the dictionary system. This would prepare the users for the different formats that they would face with the introduction of the dictionary system.

Automated Load Mechanisms

One of the major ways to speed up the loading process is to use automated techniques. If the systems are documented in a formal directory structure, this makes the job easier. For instance, if the programs are within the subsystem directory, the subsystem-to-program linkage could be created in the dictionary by scanning the programs within the subsystem directory. If all the copybooks were in a common directory, a scan of that directory could be used to populate the dictionary initially with the entries to identify the copybook. Another useful mechanism is to have a program scanner that can inspect a program and populate the dictionary with the information about the files, records, data items, and copybooks used by that program.

In installations where systems development has not followed well-defined library procedures, the locations of the various entities do not give a clue as to how the entities are related. This means that an initial manual effort must be made to reorganize the subsystems, programs, and file copybooks into a directory structure which can then be scanned by a dictionary program for automated loading.

Automated loading techniques should be incorporated into the dictionary implementation planning process wherever possible. This requires an understanding of the current environment and the ease with which the current environment can be reconfigured to facilitate the use of automated loading mechanisms.

STRATEGIES AND PROCEDURES

For each entity there are two aspects to the loading, as can be observed from the preceding discussion. The portion of the information that exists in non-computer-readable form is immense; it is estimated that only between 15 and 20 percent of the information about data is in a form that can be loaded directly into the dictionary. The rest of the data must somehow be transcribed into a format suitable for loading into the dictionary. This transcription in most instances will have to be done manually. Procedures must be developed for the identification and transcription of information, so that the rules are applied consistently by different persons in the organization. In the discussion that follows, it is evident that the procedures can easily be developed once the strategies have been defined.

Selection of Entities to Load

We have noted that certain entity categories are easier to populate than others. The selection of which entities to load intitially should be based on the following considerations:

- Those entities that have a large payback as far as the implementation strategy is concerned should be implemented first. This is the "biggest bang for the buck" philosophy.
- Those entities that are stand-alone entities should be given preference over the situation where several entities and their interrelationships need to be loaded.
- Those entities that have clearly defined sources and persons that are responsible should be given preference over those entities that would require the administrator to resolve authority or responsibility issues.
- Those entities that have information that can easily be located should be given preference over those that would require the administrator to go to several sources in order to assemble the information.
- Those entities that are in a form that can easily be loaded via automated mechanisms should be given preference over those that have to be entered manually. For example, if the information for a particular entity were in forms that could be scanned via an optical scanner, this would be preferable to another entity's information that is not so organized.

Standard Entity

Standard data items constitute an entity category that must be dealt with in a special way. This is an instance of a single entity, and it would appear that this would be fairly easy to populate. Hence it would be a good tactic to load the standard information ahead of other types of entity occurrences, since there are no dependencies that have to be taken into account. The tasks here would consist of identifying the different attributes that need to be specified for a standard data item, and identifying and tasking the appropriate persons with the knowledge to complete the job.

Figure 9–3 shows the various keys that would be needed by the user to access the standard data. Provision of access keys into the data initially gives the dictionary a user-friendly image which is important to cultivate for its continued and ongoing use.

In some cases it is desirable to provide successive levels of inquiry capability; for example, an end user may want to browse through the dictionary, but may not know the name of the data item that he or she is looking for. In such a case, the user would go through successive searches. The question should be phrased in a way that the dictionary comes up with potential entity names that meet the criteria specified. Let's say the question is: "Give me the data item that tells me the time it takes for the service technician to arrive at the customer's site." A good data dictionary should be able to walk the end user through the data base either by asking further questions or by presenting options and alternatives to the user.

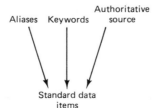

Figure 9–3 Keys to access standard data item.

```
                              Data Dictionary                    Date:  8/25/88

                           Data Standard Proposal

Element Name: _____ Title:_____

Description: _____

         _____

         _____

         _____

         _____

Alias:_____   _____   _____

Keywords: _____   _____   _____

Attributes:  Size:_____ Places after Decimal: ____

        Range:  From: _____ To: _____

        Edits: _____

               _____

        Codes: _____   _____   _____

               _____   _____   _____

Authoritative Source:_____

Data Management Function:_____
```

Figure 9-4   Blank data standard proposal screen.

```
                              Data Dictionary                    Date:  8/25/88

                           Data Standard Proposal

Name:  Symptom Fix Code              Title:  Symptom fault corrective fix code

Description:  The code that is reported to the service technician repairing customer
equipment; there is one symptom fix code reported for each major unit repaired. The
first two digits describe the device-specific symptom, and the last two describe the
corrective action.

Alias:  SYMPTOM FIX          SYMPTOM FAULT FIX          SYMPTOM-FIX-CD

Keyword:  SYMPTOM            FIX                        CODE

Attributes:  Size:  4 bytes numeric

        Range:  From: _____ To: _____

        Edits:  Edit against valid list of symptom fix codes

        Codes:_____   _____   _____

               _____   _____   _____

Authoritative Source:  Service technician
Data Management Function:  HQ administration
```

Figure 9-5   Filled out data standard proposal screen.

Request Procedure

The user should be given convenient procedures to follow in order to request or propose new data standards. It would be preferable to have an on-line data entry screen that the user could fill out whenever the user wishes to propose a new data item. Another feature that should not be overlooked is to give the user the ability to voice disagreement with a standard that is already in the dictionary. A simple data-entry screen can address this purpose. The objective is to give the user the ability to enter the objection when it occurs; the data dictionary administrator will be notified of the objection when he or she logs-on and can respond to the end user right away.

Sample Screens. Figures 9–4 and 9–5 illustrate a blank data standard proposal screen and one that is filled out. If forms are used, they must be multipart forms in order to let the requestor of the standard know of the disposition of the request. In all cases the DDA must have final authority for resolving the standard, and his or her decision must be binding on all parties. Figures 9–6 and 9–7 show a blank data standard form and one that has been filled out.

```
                            Data Dictionary

                     Request for Data Standard Item

   1. Data Name: _____

   2. Recommended Title: _____

   3. Item Narrative (descriptive account, summary, particulars):
      _____
      _____
      _____
      _____
      _____
      _____
      _____
      _____
      _____
      _____

   4. Access Keys: Alias: _____    _____
                   Keywords: _____    _____

   5. Attributes: Recommended size in characters or digits: _____
                  Recommended places after decimal if numeric: _____
                  Range of values: From _____ to _____
                  Edits: _____
                         _____
                         _____
                  Missing value codes (if any): _____
   Authoritative Source: _____
   Data Management Function: _____

                                   Prepared by: _____

  ┌──────────────────────────────────────────────────────────────────┐
  │ To be filled by DDA:                                               │
  │                                                                    │
  │ Standard Name Assigned: _____               │
  │ Status:  ;   Version:01 ;                          Date:_____      │
  │ Narrative: Same as above: __ ;        Different from above:         │
  │ Enterprise name: _____                      │
  │ Alias: _____    _____    _____    │
  │ Keywords: _____    _____    _____   │
  │ Additional attributes:    _____ ;  _____     │
  │                           _____ ;  _____     │
  └──────────────────────────────────────────────────────────────────┘
```

Figure 9–6 Blank data standard request form.

```
                    Data Dictionary

                Request for Data Standard Item

  1. Data Name:  INV-NUMBER

  2. Recommended Title:  Ticket number for inventorying warehouse

  3. Item Narrative (descriptive account, summary, particulars):  INV-NUMBER has a picture clause of
     PIC 9(6) and refers to the Inventory Tag/Ticket Number. It is the preprinted number on the Field
     Engineering Inventory Ticket. It is used in keeping track of the tickets that have been filled out
     (used) or have not been filled out (unused), in doing the inventory of the warehouse. It is also the
     key in the Physical Inventory Data Base "PHYINV."
     _____
     _____

  4. Access Keys:  Alias:              TICKET NUMBER              PHY-INV-NO
                   Keywords:           TAG NUMBER                 PHY-TKT-NUMBER

  6. Attributes:  Recommended size in characters or digits:  9(6)
                  Recommended places after decimal if numeric: __
                  Range of values:  From _____ to _____
                  Edits: _____
                         _____
                         _____

                  Missing value codes (if any): _____

  Authoritative source:  Preprinted numbers resp. RC analyst
  Data Management Function:  Receiving center analyst

                                     Prepared by: _____ Tina F. _____

  ┌──────────────────────────────────────────────────────────────────────────────┐
  │  To be filled by DDA:                                                          │
  │  Standard Name Assigned:  TICKET-NO                                            │
  │  Status:     ;     Version:01;                              Date: 02/01/84     │
  │  Narrative: Same as above: ___ ;  Different from above:  see attached          │
  │  Enterprise name:  INVENTORY TICKET NUMBER                                     │
  │  Alias:  INVENTORY TICKET NUMBER;  TICKET-NO                                   │
  │  Keyword:  INVENTORY;       NUMBER     ;       TICKET                          │
  │  Additional attributes: _____ ; _____ │
  │                                             ; _____  │
  └──────────────────────────────────────────────────────────────────────────────┘
```

Figure 9-7   Filled out data standard request form.

Conflict Resolution

Within every company there are different groups and departments that use some of the same data. Over the course of time, the user originally responsible for the data may be difficult to identify. Moving to a data base environment where data have to be shared may cause disagreements, which must be resolved by the DDA. Figures 9-8 through 9-10 show data definition conflict screens. Once the conflict form or screen reaches the DDA, the DDA must follow a consistent procedure to resolve the conflict. Not every conflict can be resolved to satisfy every party; however, if it can be shown that certain procedures were applied consistently by the DDA, users will generally support the actions taken. See Figure 9-11 for a response to a conflict.

Initially, it is appropriate to involve the systems analyst responsible for an area to get his or her input. If the systems analyst's version and the user still have a disagreement, or if the situation involves several users, it is appropriate to call a meeting of the affected users and get their inputs. The DDA should come up with a definition that he or she believes is appropriate. If there is still disagreement, this should be escalated to the upper management of the users affected. In no case should the DDA delegate or hand over the data definition responsibility to the users.

```
                              Data Dictionary                   Date:  8/25/88

                            Data Definition Conflict


Data name: _____        Status: _____       Version: _____

State as briefly as possible your disagreement, and the changes that you would like
to see made. State reasons, where applicable.

    _____
    _____
    _____
    _____
    _____
    _____
    _____
    _____
    _____
    _____
    _____
    _____
    _____
    _____

If you wish to request a new standard, enter Y: ____
```

Figure 9-8 Data definition conflict screen: I.


```
                              Data Dictionary                   Date:  8/25/88

                            Data Definition Conflict


Name:  CUSTOMER NUMBER                     Status:              Version:01

   Your telephone:  231-4532               Electronic Address:  Nesbit+:kite

   Areas of conflict:    1. Name
                         2. Description
                         3. Aliases
                         4. Attributes
                         5. Cross-references

      Select:  4
      For each, describe your disagreement, and potential resolution.
      The DD Administrator will review your comments and get back to you.
```

Figure 9-9 Data definition conflict screen: II.

Keeping the users, systems analysts, and management informed of the process is extremely important. It is also important to maintain high visibility of this activity by mentioning it in monthly reports and newsletters. Accomplishments in this area should be recognized within the organization and given due publicity because data standards are analogous to any other operating procedures by which the organization operates.

```
                              Data Dictionary                  Date:  8/25/88

                         Data Definition Conflict


Data name:  CUSTOMER NUMBER                Status:              Version:01

State as briefly as possible your disagreement, and the changes that you would like
to see made. State reasons, where applicable.

I would like to propose that the size of the CUSTOMER NUMBER field be a numeric
field rather than an alphanumeric field. This is so that numeric validation by the
system can take place. Also, it is easier for a data-entry operator to key in the
significant digits, than to key in alpha, space, and numeric characters.
_____
_____
_____
_____
_____
_____
_____
_____
_____

If you wish to request a new standard, enter Y:
```

Figure 9–10   Data definition conflict screen: IV.

```
                              Data Dictionary                  Date:  8/25/88

                        Response to Data Conflict
                            CUSTOMER NUMBER


The customer number standard was changed from a numeric format to an alphanumeric
format to take into account subsidiaries of the company that use different customer
numbering conventions. Thus the requirement is that the field in the data base be
defined as a 7-character alpha-numeric field. In your screen, it is possible to
redefine the customer number field to a numeric field if you anticipate only numeric
numbers. You can also apply additional edits to suit the needs of the data-entry
operators at your location.
_____
_____
_____
_____
_____
_____
_____
_____
```

Figure 9–11   Data conflict resolution screen.

Data Load

In case the dictionary system is not in place, forms can be used to collect the data,
and the data can be entered into a temporary holding file as shown in Figure 9–12.
When the dictionary system is installed, a one-shot program can be written to load
the data from the temporary file into the data dictionary data base.

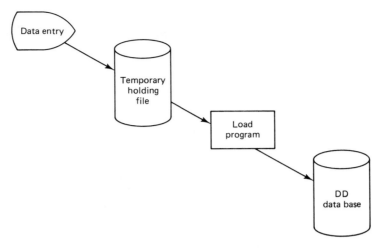

Figure 9–12   Data load via temporary holding file.

File Structures

The files and all the descriptions associated with them must be identified. Some of these components may be embedded in a program source; if that is the case, they must be extracted from the program and stored in a library structure, often referred

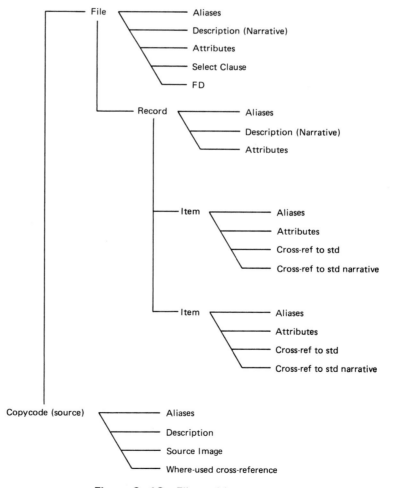

Figure 9–13   File and its components.

to as a source library. Associated with the file would be entries in the dictionary related to record, FD, attributes, cross-references, and so on. All of these entries have to be identified by unique names, so that the first step is to assign unique names to these in the dictionary, and relate the file entry to the other entries. An automatic loader will normally break up the record layout into the individual data items and load each of the data items as independent entries, related to the record entry and to each other. In other words, the file and its components will be as shown in Figure 9–13. The information that is boldfaced in Figure 9–13 will not be loaded into the dictionary automatically, for each of these specific procedures must be developed to assist the person with the knowledge to identify and enter the information. Appropriate naming conventions must be used to identify the different parts of the copybook if they are to be loaded independently of each other. An example of such a situation is that of the COBOL file copybooks, which are broken into FD, Record, Select clause, and so on.

Depending on the type of loader that is used, the information in copybooks will be loaded into the various entities and attributes that comprise the contents of the copybook. Generally, loaders are designed to process different kinds of source descriptions. For example, a loader may be able to process IDMS structures as well as IMS structures. The loader breaks up the structure into generic components which can be combined to produce sources that can work in a different vendor's equipment. For example, the data from an IDMS structure could be used to construct an SQL (structured query language) table definition. Figure 9–14 illustrates how the loader

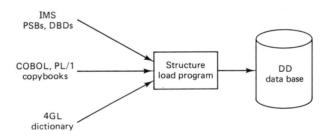

Figure 9–14 Structure load program.

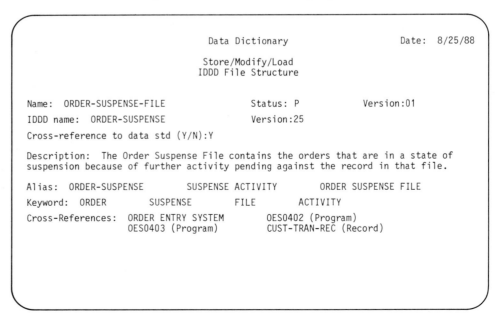

Figure 9–15 Initiate loader screen: I.

```
                           Data Dictionary                      Date:  8/25/88

                         Store/Modify/Load
                         IDDD File Structure

   Name:  ORDER-SUSPENSE-FILE          Status: P          Version:01
   IDDD name:  ORDER-SUSPENSE          Version:25
   Identify data standard corresponding to:

   CUST-NBR                            CUST-NO_____
   ORDER-NBR                           SALES-ORDER-NO____
   SALES-COUNT                         SALES-CNT_____
```

Figure 9–16 Initiate loader screen: II.

can process different structures and store their components in the dictionary. Figures 9–15 and 9–16 are screens that have to be filled out in order to initiate the loader.

Other things the loader will do besides breaking up the source into components include maintaining the integrity of data in the dictionary, including cross-references to standards. The loader will also maintain the integrity of the relationships between the various entities that have been loaded. The loader will also cross-reference the entries to the standard names, provided that you have used standard naming convention in effect at this site. A report will be produced that will tell you the entries that could not be cross-referenced automatically. Figure 9–17 illustrates such a report.

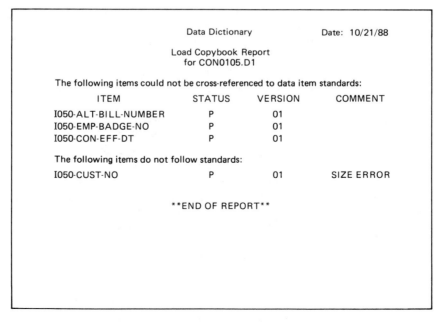

Figure 9–17 Load copybook report.

When the existing record layout follows naming conventions that do not conform to standards as shown in Figure 9–17, there are two options:

1. Change the name in the record layout to match the standard; this would entail changes to the programs that used this record layout and could be time consuming.

2. Leave the name in the record layout the same, but cross-reference it to the data standard manually, especially since the data meanings are the same.

Which approach is taken depends on the resources available to the DD project manager to do the task. The first approach cleans up the existing names and makes them consistent; the second approach may be more practical.

Missing Information

There is, however, additional information that is required of the person who is knowledgeable about the copybook. This information pertains to the definitions of the data items within the copybook, the aliases by which the entity is known, the persons responsible for updating the data item in the data base (the authoritative source), and so on. Depending on the implementation strategy, the updates to complete the information within the dictionary could be entered directly either by the end user or programmer or DBA, or by filling out forms and then submitting them to the dictionary administrator. These include the database, the Select clause, the File Description, the Record description (01), and all the data items within the record(s). The necessary header information for this can be obtained from the previous step.

All data items other than "FILLER(s)" will require a narrative. In entering the narratives include the full English name associated to the data items, the picture clause (PIC XX), a descriptive account, the source (where it comes from), and any validation checks. Once the narrative has been written up, continue on the form where it asks to enter access/alternate keys.

Every specific occurrence of a data item that exists in a copybook must be related to a data standard item. The loader will automatically link the entry to a data standard if one exists. In this manner, as the dictionary gets fully populated, it will be able to answer such questions as: "What are the specific occurrences of the data item in all the copybooks (files)?" In case the data standard item cannot be located automatically, the data standard item can be located either by perusing the dictionary on-line or by looking at cross-reference listings that the DDA will be able to provide. If a data standard item cannot be found in the dictionary, a request for the establishment of a data standard item must be made.

If a data item in your record layout does not have a corresponding data standard item, it is likely that the data standard item is missing in the dictionary. It is your responsibility to request a data standard item from the data dictionary administrator. Use either the on-line screen shown previously or the form to request the data standard item. The data dictionary administrator will return information regarding the data standard item that was finally entered into the system. Then you can go back to the data item that was missing the standard and cross-reference it to the data standard item that was entered by the DDA.

Other Components

Other components of a file definition, such as Select statements, and other vendor-specific or required statements, are stored in the dictionary as is; that is, they are not broken down any further. This facilitates the sourcing of all information from the dictionary. The DDA must have a complete list of all the pieces necessary to complete a file description, and how the dictionary will process them, to ensure that all relevant information is stored in the dictionary. Figure 9–18 illustrates a form that requests the user to provide information about all the components of a file that is used by a COBOL program. Figure 9–19 shows one that is filled out.

Reconciliation

The reader should not be left with the impression that the loading of copybooks is simply a matter of using the structure loader. Before a copybook is loaded into the dictionary, name conflicts should be resolved. Verify that various data items described

Data Dictionary

Missing information request form

Database/File: PHYINV

Select Statement: ______________________________

File Description (FD) ______________________________

Record(s) (01): ____________________;

____________________;

____________________;

To be filled by DBA

Name: ____________

Status: ___ Version: ___ Date: __/__/__

Figure 9–18 Blank missing information request form.

Data Dictionary

Missing information request form

Database/File: PHYINV

Select Statement: PHYINV.SL

File Description (FD) PHYINV.FD

Record(s) (01): PHYINVR.01 ;

____________________;

____________________;

To be filled by DDA

Name: PHYINV.CC

Status: P Version: 01 Date: 01/10/87

Figure 9–19 Filled-out missing information request form.

in the copybooks are described in the dictionary and enter the data standard item if they are not. The people responsible for the system will have to cooperate and provide the narratives for the undefined data items. As more and more information about copybooks, programs, and systems get loaded into the dictionary, the dictionary can be used to determine what copybooks are used by what systems and programs. This brings the benefit of the dictionary to the analysts and programmers who have to deal with large numbers of programs that use several files in a shared environment.

System Entities

If system entities are to be loaded, the DD project manager should look into the entities that the dictionary supports and identify those that are most relevant to system development needs. For instance, it is apparent that information related to the system, subsystems, programs and procedures, and files used by those, as well as reports coming out of the system would be useful. Additionally, information pertaining to the relationships between a system and its subsystems, subsystems to programs and procedures, and programs to files and reports should be stored in the dictionary. Figure 9–20 illustrates the entities and the relationships that need to be maintained in the dictionary.

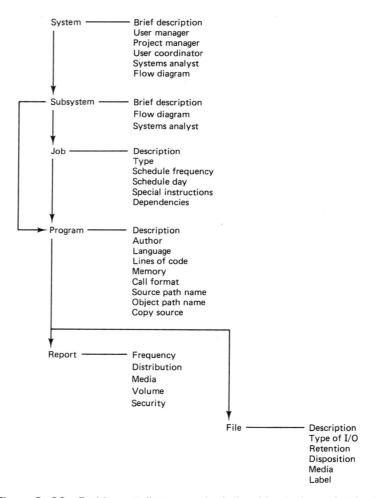

Figure 9–20 Entities, attributes, and relationships to be maintained in the dictionary.

Loading System Information

The loading of information about systems, programs, reports, and job streams and macros is a more difficult proposition. Automated loading techniques are more difficult to apply because the data may not be in a format that is structured and easy to locate. Also, the information is normally located in diverse places and in different formats. Figure 9–21 shows the automated technique that can be used to gather system-related information in one holding file so that the transition to the dictionary is made easier.

Notwithstanding these difficulties, procedures to load these can be put in place, and in conjunction with the loading process, procedures must exist for the continuing update to these entities as they change due to changing business needs. The selection of the first system to load is critical to gaining the support of the application development staff. There are two scenarios that can be discussed here. One of them is to load the dictionary with a visible system, that is, one that is poorly documented and has a number of problems associated with it. In getting it loaded into the dictionary, the systems support staff will be able to realize the utility of the dictionary as a documenting tool. It will demonstrate that documentation helps the support team get up to speed and in training new support staff. A psychological advantage of this is that a person carrying the knowledge in his or her head now has a way to document this information in a logical way and can effectively train other personnel to take over that support role, so that that individual can go onto something new. This will help to improve the morale in the support team.

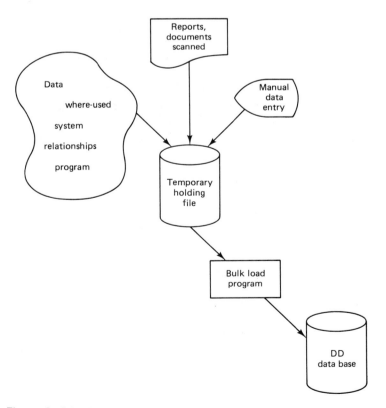

Figure 9–21 Loading system-related information via holding file.

Another scenario occurs when a new system is being developed and the dictionary is used as a tool to document the technical specifications of the system or data base in question. The documentation in the dictionary is easily accessible to all parties on-line and the visibility ensures that the project team can be aware of the levels of activity of members of the team. This serves not only as a measure of the work that is being done, but also as a communications vehicle that people can use to alert others to potential problems in the system.

Another way to look at this is to focus on the system-to-data relationships. In a system where the number of programs have grown to a large number over time, and the data structures have expanded in an unplanned sort of way, there are usually concerns when changes have to be made to the data structure because the full impact of the change on all the programs may not be immediately ascertained. In such a case, loading the program-to-data relationships could prove to be of invaluable help to the system development manager. In one case where there were 300 programs going against 700 data items in a major data base, this sort of where-used analysis proved useful to the manager in ascertaining if certain fields could be eliminated from the data base to conserve space and better utilize the file structure.

Where possible, the loading of system information should be coordinated with the updates to the dictionary of standard data items and the copybooks. This poses the question: Which comes first: the system or the data side? In developing the strategy for loading a system that uses common data files, all the information related to the data files needs to be stored in the dictionary so that when the system information is loaded, it can readily be cross-referenced to the file-related information. This means that shared-file copybooks should be loaded first. Then all the copybooks related to the system should be loaded, and only then should the system-related information be loaded. The above indicates that the sequence in which these activities are carried out is important and should be recognized in the scheduling of time for the loading process.

This brings up another point: Who does the work when the responsibility for the relationships between the system entities and the data entities are shared? It is easy to define the responsibilities where there is a clear line of demarcation between systems and data. The storage of relationships between the system and the data needs to be coordinated with the final control in the hands of the one group that is most affected by the accuracy of the relationship. In this case the data base administrator is the one most affected, because the where-used information is most useful to the DBA in developing new file structures or adding to existing file structures.

System Loading

Loading system information should be done on a system-by-system basis because the responsibility for the entire system can be delegated to the systems analyst or the systems manager. Therefore, all components of a system become the responsibility of the system manager. There are ways in which the loading of system information can be hastened. One is to load the skeleton of the system components and their interrelationships. Once the skeleton is in place, the report generator can be used to produce the system subsystem report, and a scan of this will reveal the missing information, which can then be assigned to individuals to document in the dictionary. System and subsystem names can be loaded manually; job names can be scanned from the directories in which they are stored. If appropriate naming conventions are followed, the acronym for the job will contain the system acronym. The same is true for programs, reports, screens, and input and output files. By scanning the names of these entities, it is possible to relate the jobs to the subsystems, the programs to the jobs, the reports to the programs, and so on. How fast this proceeds ultimately depends on whether certain naming conventions were followed in the environment, and the consistency with which the conventions were followed.

Example. Figures 9–22 through 9–28 are a set of screens that illustrate the discussion above. The screens show the reader the data that have to be entered in order to load system-related information.

```
                              Data Dictionary              Date:  8/25/88

                            Store/Modify/Load
                            System/Subsystem

Name:_____        Status:____        Version:____

Project Manager: _____  User Manager: _____

Systems Analyst: _____  User Coordinator:_____

Description:_____

_____

_____



Cross-References: _____      _____

                  _____      _____
```

Figure 9–22 Load system information screen: I.

```
                              Data Dictionary              Date:  8/25/88

                            Store/Modify/Load
                            System/Subsystem

Name:  FACTS Data Base              Status:  P          Version:01

Project Manager:  Nelson            User Manager:  Risek

Systems Analyst: Bryant             User Coordinator: Cortesa

Description:  The FACTS data base project includes the implementation of a
centralized data base to hold the data that are collected by the area locations by
the central dispatching process. The FACTS data base will be the source of data for
many of the reporting systems that are being developed.

Alias:  FACTS       FIELD ACTIVITY      DATA BASE       CLOSED CALLS
Keyword:  FACTS      FIELD ACTIVITY        CLOSED CALLS
Cross-References: _____      _____

                  _____      _____
```

Figure 9–23 Load system information screen: II.

```
                          Data Dictionary              Date:  8/25/88

                          Store/Modify/Load
                               Job/CLI

Name: _____        Status: ___        Version: ___

Description: _____


    Type: _____        Programmer: _____

    Schedule: _____

    Dependencies: _____

    Special Instructions: _____
```

Figure 9-24 Load job/CLI information screen: I.

```
                          Data Dictionary              Date:  8/25/88

                          Store/Modify/Load
                               Job/CLI

Name:  FACT.0101                 Status:  P          Version:01
Within system/subsystem:  FACT01   Status:  P        Version:01
Description:  The FACT.0101 job takes the tapes from the dispatch centers and loads
them for further processing.

Type:  Batch                     Programmer:  Nelson
Schedule:  Weekly                Estimated Run Time:  30 min
Switches:  None
Dependencies: _____

Special Instructions:  This job can be run for as many tapes as there are from the
dispatch centers.
```

Figure 9-25 Load job/CLI information screen: II.

Programs

Information about programs can be found in many places. Perhaps the primary source is the original documentation, part of the system documentation that was produced during system design and development. This may have been stored in a word processor format. Dictionaries generally have text file import capability that can be used to pull this into the narrative for the program.

```
                              Data Dictionary              Date:   8/25/88

                            Store/Modify/Load
                          Job/CLI Run Instructions

Name:  FACT.0101                        Status:  P          Version:01
Within system/subsystem:  FACT01        Status:  P          Version:01

Run Instructions

QBJ FACT.0101
```

Figure 9-26 Load job/CLI run instructions information screen.

```
                              Data Dictionary              Date:   8/25/88

                            Store/Modify/Load
                         Job/CLI Re-run Instructions

Name:  FACT.0101                        Status:  P          Version:01
Within system/subsystem:  FACT01        Status:  P          Version:01

Rerun Instructions

Restart the job from the beginning.
```

Figure 9-27 Load job/CLI rerun instructions information screen.

The programmer also puts some narrative in the source program itself. This consists of a small number of comment lines at the beginning of the program, indicating the purpose of the program, any special features, and any revisions made to the program. Additional comment lines are scattered throughout the body of the program to help understand the program logic and help debug the program.

Certain attributes, such as author, language, and code set, are required features

```
                         Data Dictionary                 Date:  8/26/88

                          Store/Modify/Load
                       Job/CLI Program File Info

Name:  FACT.0101                    Status:  P           Version:01

Within subsystem:  FACT01          Status:  P           Version:01

   01) Program FACT0101
       Converts RDOS tape format (dispatch system closed calls) to AOS disk format for
       further processing.

       I/O   Filename/File Description    Device    Retention    Format    Copies
       I     FACEXT01S:0                  TAPE      1 YR
             Dispatch system tape (RDOS)
       O     FACTAPEA01                   DISK      EOJ
             FACTS data (AOS format)

   02) Program FACT0102
       Verification against control file

       I/O   Filename/File Description    Device    Retention    Format    Copies
       I     FACTAPEA01                   DISK      EOJ
       O     FACT0101S.W1                 DISK      1 day
       I/O   FACTCTRL                     DISK      PERM
       O     FACT0102.R1                  PRINT                  LONG 6     3
```

Figure 9-28 Load job/CLI program file information screen.

```
                         Data Dictionary                 Date:  8/25/88

                       Load Program Information

                   1. Scan library/directory
                   2. Scan program source
                   3. Import program description
                   4. Load program structure
                   5. Load missing information


                       Select: ____
```

Figure 9-29 Load program information screen: I.

in many programming languages. These can be scanned and the information can be
loaded in the dictionary.

   The programs are generally housed in libraries or directories that are fairly well
structured. An initial pass through the library or directory structure by a scanner
could load the program names into the dictionary.

   Another set of information can be obtained from analyzing the program for

```
                              Data Dictionary                Date:  8/25/86

                             Store/Modify/Load
                                  Program

   Name: _____    Status: _____   Version: _____

   Within Job/CLI: _____    Status: _____   Version: _____

   Within subsystem: _____    Status: _____   Version: _____

   Author: _____    Maintenance Resp: _____

   Language: _____    Code-set: _____

   Description: _____

               _____

               _____

               _____

   Cross-References: _____   _____
```

Figure 9–30 Load program information screen: II.

```
                              Data Dictionary                Date:  8/25/88

                           Load Program Information

                       1. Store/modify
                       2. Scan Library/Directory
                       3. Scan program source
                       4. Import program description
                       5. Load program structure
                       6. Load missing information

                              Select: 1
```

Figure 9–31 Load program information screen: III.

its structure. A scan program can scan the source to pick up the flow of control by keying in on the "PERFORM" or "GO TO" in a COBOL program. A program structure report is obtained which can be loaded into the dictionary. The structure report is an aid during troubleshooting.

Figures 9–29 through 9–33 illustrate the screens involved in loading program-related information.

```
                              Data Dictionary              Date:  8/25/88

                              Store/Modify/Load
                                  Program

   Name:  FACT0101                      Status:  P        Version:01

   Within Job/CLI:  FACT.0101           Status:  P        Version:01

   Within subsystem:  FACT01            Status:  P        Version:01

   Author:  J. Nelson          Maintenance Resp:  J. Nelson

   Language:  COBOL-74              Code set:  ASCII

   Description:  At the end of each week, each dispatch system site will prepare an
   RDOS tape file of all closed calls during the previous week. This tape will be sent
   to the HQ data center. FACT0101 will perform an RDOS-to-AOS format conversion and
   load the file into FACTAPEA01 and record the completion of this process in the
   control file.

   I/O    Filename/File Description      Device    Retention    Format    Copies
   I      FACEXT01S:0                     TAPE      1 YR
          Dispatch system tape (RDOS)

   0      FACTAPEA01                      DISK      EOJ
          FACTS data (AOS format)
```

Figure 9–32 Load program information screen: IV.

```
                              Data Dictionary              Date:  8/25/88

                              Store/Modify/Load
                                  Program

   Name:  FACT0102                      Status:  P        Version:01

   Within Job/CLI:  FACT.0101           Status:  P        Version:01

   Within subsystem:  FACT01            Status:  P        Version:01

   Author:  J. Nelson          Maintenance Resp:  J. Nelson

   Language:  COBOL-74              Code set:  ACSII

   Description:  The AOS file FACTAPEA01 produced from FACT0101 will be verified against
   control information to ensure that the sequence of tapes from the dispatch centers is
   maintained. It will also perform security checks to ensure that tape is from correct
   source.

   I/O    Filename/File Description      Device    Retention    Format    Copies
   I      FACTAPEA01                      DISK      EOJ
   0      FACT0101S.W1                    DISK      1 day
   I/O    FACTCTRL                        DISK      PERM
   0      FACT0102.R1                     PRINT                 LONG 6     3
```

Figure 9–33 Load program information screen: V.

Reports

This is another entity where the documentation would give a fast payback. In addition to entering a narrative about the report, it would be a good idea to include a sample page from the report. The problem with just providing skeletal information

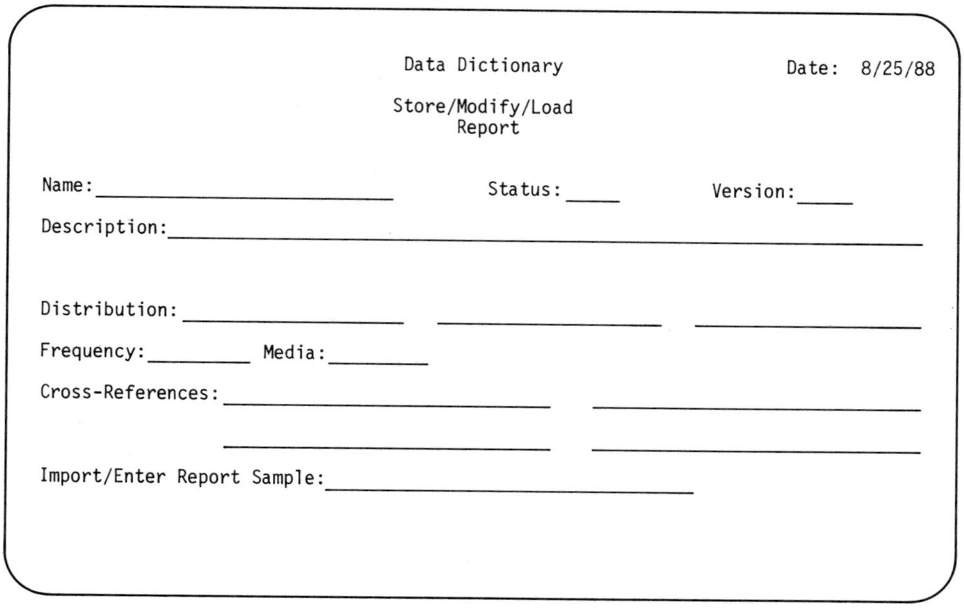

```
                        Data Dictionary          Date:  8/25/88
                        Store/Modify/Load
                              Report

Name:_____      Status:_____    Version:_____
Description:_____


Distribution:_____  _____  _____
Frequency:_____ Media:_____
Cross-References:_____  _____

                 _____  _____

Import/Enter Report Sample:_____
```

Figure 9-34 Load report information screen: I.

```
                        Data Dictionary          Date:  8/25/88
                        Store/Modify/Load
                           Report Sample

Name:_____      Status:_____    Version:_____
Description of data items, files used, etc.



                         sample here
```

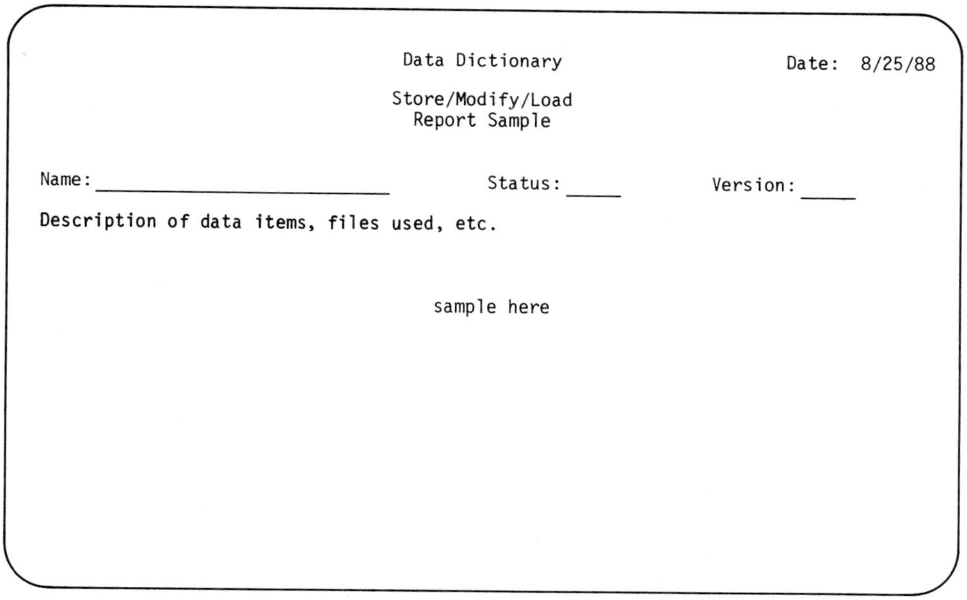

Figure 9-35 Load report information screen: II.

is that someone is going to ask for more information about the data items in the report, the systems and/or programs that produced them, and so on. There would be a temptation to expand the narrative to include these pieces of information as opposed to storing them as separate entity occurrences with the appropriate cross-references. The trade-offs between loading all the information and loading only those that are critically needed must be made by the DD project manager. Figures 9-34 through 9-37 illustrate the screens that are involved in loading into the dictionary information pertaining to a report.

```
                              Data Dictionary              Date:  8/25/88

                             Store/Modify/Load
                                   Report


   Name:  FACT0102.R1                    Status:  P          Version:01

   Produced by:  FACT0102                Status:  P          Version:01

   Description:  FACT0101.R1 is a FACTS load exception report which will be produced
   if there is a discrepancy found in the sequence of tapes sent from the dispatch
   system centers.

   Distribution:  Operations Control; Dispatch Center Supvr; DBA

   Frequency:  When error                    Media:  8 1/2 by 11

   Alias:  FACT0102.R1        LOAD ERROR REPORT        FACTS REPORT

   Keyword:  FACTS        ERROR        LOAD        FACT0102.R1

   Import/Enter Rpt Sample (I/E):  E        File name:_____ Type:_____
```

Figure 9-36 Load report information screen: III.

```
                              Data Dictionary              Date:  8/25/88

                             Store/Modify/Load
                                Report Sample

   Name:  FACT0102.R1                      Status:  P        Version:01

   FACT0102.R1                      FACTS System Report                  2/8/87
                                    LOAD ERROR RPT.

   Error detected on tape for week ending 2/7/87 from Dispatch Center C

   Tape out of sequence; tape for week ending 1/31/87 from Dispatch Center C was not
   processed.


                              ** END OF REPORT **
```

Figure 9-37 Load report information screen: IV.

chapter 10

Data Dictionary Maintenance

NEED FOR MAINTENANCE

The data in the dictionary data base will grow over time to include a variety of information on all facets of information processing within the organization. While some parts of the dictionary data base may remain static, other parts of the data base will be updated quite often and can be classified as dynamic.

A major responsibility of the dictionary project manager is to ensure that update procedures are in place that keep the information in the dictionary as current as possible. Additionally, he or she will have to devise programs and techniques to check the contents of the data base frequently to ensure internal consistency between the various entity occurrences. This is referred to as "change control." An example of the former would be the MIS situation where the enhancements that are made to the operational systems must be reflected in the narratives of the various system components within the dictionary. An example of the latter would be to run procedures and programs against the dictionary data base to check for deviations from standards that may be occurring, and to identify those to the managers concerned.

USER-DEFINED APPLICATIONS

There are certain situations that call for using the "extensibility" feature of the data dictionary. These are:

• Extensions to the data dictionary to include additional entity categories, relationships, and attributes and the reporting thereof. The extensibility of the data dictionary provides the capability to add entity categories and relate these to existing entity categories that come with the dictionary system. The standard report generator can be used to generate reports against the new entities, and user-defined reports can also be created.

- Reports, forms, and input data screens can be defined against the dictionary data base data structure to support site-specific activities. For example, if the functional requirements for a particular process cannot be satisfied with the existing forms, screens, or reports, the site can develop applications against the dictionary data base directly.

- Interfaces to other system components, such as compilers, application generators, and fourth-generation language interfaces, can be made against the dictionary data base, thus providing a link between the data already stored in the data dictionary and other automated components in the MIS installation. These interfaces can be made against data extracts, or directly against the core data structure.

- Distribution of data dictionaries to remote locations and their subsequent control can be handled procedurally as well as via user-defined processing that keeps multiple copies of the dictionary consistently populated. A detailed understanding of the security features of the dictionary is important to have in assigning the responsibilities to the central location as well as the remote location.

PRELIMINARY STEPS

The procedures to address the ongoing maintenance of the dictionary must be the primary concern of the data dictionary project manager.

For maintenance procedures to work smoothly, the DD project manager must perform three preliminary steps:

1. *Define user expectations.*   As in any data base system, the accuracy and integrity of the data in the data base must be maintained to a high degree of user satisfaction. The level of expectation of the users must be determined beforehand, and checks built in to ensure that the required level of data quality is met. This is no mean undertaking since the dictionary will be populated by diverse groups of people with differing perceptions of how to use the dictionary, and more important, their individual commitment to the quality will vary based on individual differences.

2. *Define critical and noncritical data.* The project manager must have a knowledge of the uses and dependencies of the different types of data and the ramifications of incorrect data on downstream applications. For example, the data that are used by compilers must not only be technically consistent but must not be allowed to change without careful scrutiny and control. Narrative data are not so critical; changes can be made to narratives without affecting data-based applications. However, narrative that is related to the recovery steps for a job should be treated with care, because these are the instructions that would be followed by the operator in case of system failure. The critical data must be subject to more controls and audit trails than data that are not so critical. This also determines the extent to which different users will be allowed to update the data without any overseeing authority.

3. *Assign responsibility.*   The ultimate responsibility of the data must be the end user. That is, the quality of the data should be made the responsibility of the persons who are the originators of the data. If the quality of the data deteriorates, the people who are using the data must have the communication channel to the originators of the data to voice their concern and improve the quality level. For example, in most systems organizations, the operations staff are the users

of information that is originated and entered into the dictionary by the development staff. Information about programs, job steps, and recovery procedures are used in the operations environment. If the quality of the documentation is not satisfactory or is not up to date, the DD project manager must make clear to the operations staff that their concern should be directed at the development staff member who entered the information in the first place. Also, wherever possible, it is desirable to build the dictionary update into the procedure as close to the generation or update of the data in the business transaction.

A Few Words of Caution. The data dictionary data base itself is a repository of shared data, and like any other shared data base, there are ramifications in having different groups of people update different parts of the data base concurrently. The integrity of the data in the data base must be protected by the site administrator through procedural as well as systemic means. One of the more important decisions that must be made up front is whether the dictionary will be updated via a single data-entry function through the use of forms, or whether on-line updating will be permitted for each of the entity categories. Also note that some of the automated interfaces update information in the dictionary data base in fairly complicated fashion. An example of this is the copybook loader, which updates copybook, record, group, item, and file entities, and relationships between them. The advantages of single data entry are well known—the ability to control what goes into the system. However, this also introduces a bureaucratic element into the process, which inevitably will tend to slow things down.

A way to combine the best aspects of controlled input and yet have a speedy resolution to bottlenecks is to use the electronic mail functions that are available in today's organizations. Assuming that some data have to be strictly controlled, the discrepancies, if any, should be brought to the attention of the appropriate persons via electronic mail, and reminders should be sent out automatically if the corrections have not been made. This requires that the procedures that are developed be integrated with the office automation system that is in place.

CONFLICTS

One of the more perplexing situations that is often faced by the DD project manager is a result of the inconsistencies and complex interrelationships that exist and need to be mapped and maintained in the dictionary. There is always tremendous pressure to compromise the standards to get the job done. In some instances it may seem a blessing for the dictionary system to have the controls built in so that the DD project manager can just ''blame'' it all on the system!

Most dictionaries are flexible in their design, and they will allow you to store inconsistent information. The problem with storing inconsistent information is that once it is in the data base, there is very little incentive to fix it later. On the other hand, if the quality of the data has to be enhanced or conflicts and inconsistencies have to be resolved prior to entering the data in the dictionary, the dictionary's value is reduced in the eyes of those who expect the dictionary to answer all their questions.

Another conflict-laden situation arises when the users of the dictionary are asked to share in the update and maintenance of the dictionary with a view to popularizing the use of the dictionary. The flip side of the coin is that some users will invariably enter incomplete information or be sloppy in the use of words. Besides the exhortation and constant reminders, feedback of information from the dictionary to concerned persons is suggested as a control measure.

Shared Responsibility Data

For common entities that have to be verified and approved by different groups, a form is preferable since this would leave a paper trail of the approval process. An example of such entities is the standard data item. The definition of a standard data item originates with an end user or systems analyst, and the standard name, aliases, and other attributes are assigned by the data base administrator. In the event of conflicts with an existing definition in the enterprise, the definitions have to be subject to the conflict resolution process. The whole process should be documented with the appropriate signatures at the key points in the process so that the standardization effort is done in a fair and visible manner.

Unshared Responsibility Data

For those entities that are the update responsibility of a certain individual or group, on-line update would be preferable, since these individuals will be the primary users of the data that are input. An example of such an entity is the program entity. To assure the quality of the input, a procedure should be in place that allows changes in a program's narrative to be made on-line by the programmer responsible for the program, as well as a report of the changes to be generated and forwarded to the programmer and to the programmer's supervisor. This will ensure that the organization/persons primarily associated with the entity are also responsible for its documentation and maintenance in the dictionary.

Cross-References

The storage of cross-references between different entity groups that cross organizational boundaries is quite complex. When two entities are the responsibility of the same individual or group, the relationship between the two entities can also be the responsibility of the same person or group. This can be achieved in a practical sense by vesting the authority to store the relationship within that group. However, when a cross-reference is between entities that belong to two or more different groups or functions, the update should be handled by one of the groups or through the data dictionary administration function, and the status of the update should be communicated to both parties affected.

Operations Data

Where forms or reports need to be generated from the dictionary for operational purposes, this should be controlled through a combination of procedures and security privileges that can be assigned by the DDA.

Automated Interfaces

Where automated interfaces to the dictionary exist, the operator of the automated interface must have overall access and update capability against entity occurrences that cross organizational responsibility. Such a user is normally the data dictionary administrator. Therefore, access to automated utilities should be strictly controlled via the security features that are in place. For example, when a utility is used to load entities in the dictionary, it may be appropriate to set the "update" privilege for one person and the "read" privilege to all users. In cases where any one of several individuals within a work group would need access, a group-level access privilege should be granted.

DEVELOPING MAINTENANCE PROCEDURES

The forms, screens, and reports that are necessary to support the update process have to be developed and communicated to the user. In effect, each user of the dictionary will have a subschema view of the data base with which he or she will work. This includes the aspects of the data as well as the procedures that are necessary to keep their data up to date. For example, a ''job'' entity may initially be created by a programmer/analyst but will get updated by the operations department as and when the job is run. Thus it is important that both parties have the ability to view the complete data about the ''job'' entity, but each party should have the ability to only update its own part of the data.

DOCUMENTING

In the coming years, more and more packaged software offerings will be available in the marketplace. This would result in many companies having a hybrid of internally developed as well as externally procured systems. Since the externally procured systems may not necessarily follow the standards prevalent in the company, it is important that policies and procedures be set up to accommodate the documentation of the externally procured system components in the dictionary. Special rules and exemptions may have to be granted these systems, but it is important for the DD project manager to remember that all major systems should be documented in the dictionary; otherwise, the dictionary will cease to be viewed as valuable.

Since most dictionaries are extensible, this can be used to great advantage in documenting systems that do not necessarily utilize standard types of entities. An example of this would be programs written in the APL syntax which treat the grouping of data items in a different way.

Another area that could prove troublesome is the growing popularity of fourth-generation language (4GL) software packages. Most 4GL packages have data dictionaries embedded in them. This is analogous to having to deal with multiple dictionaries. Procedures for the intitial creation and maintenance of the definitions have to be in place before the 4GL packages are encouraged; otherwise, you will be back to an out-of-control situation before long. Remember that the objective is to ensure that there is a single source for data definitions in the organization, not one physical data dictionary. Therefore, the procedures must address the issue of how to tie the different dictionaries together so that the overall objective is achieved.

SAMPLE PROCEDURES: USING THE DICTIONARY DURING THE SYSTEM DEVELOPMENT LIFE CYCLE

Procedures for maintaining and updating the DD are most extensively used during the development phase of a system. For this reason, the following section will walk you through each step of the systems development life cycle (SDLC). It will describe procedures for using and updating the dictionary at each step. The data dictionary can be used effectively to facilitate the definition, design, and implementation phases of system development. This section explains the procedures for using the data dictionary as a resource to aid in system development, and describes the steps the programmer/analyst must take while developing the system.

System Study and Evaluation

The data dictionary serves as a reference to existing systems, programs, files, records, items, and so on. By using the query function within the dictionary, you can reference definitions of standard data items, find out where the item(s) lives on existing file structures, and use descriptions of existing subsystems and programs that are already stored in the data dictionary in preparing your system study and evaluation report.

The data dictionary will indicate whether the data items you need have been entered in the data dictionary, and where they can be found. You must then go to the authoritative source of that data for further information. Figures 10–1 through 10–4 show screens through which information on data items and systems can be obtained.

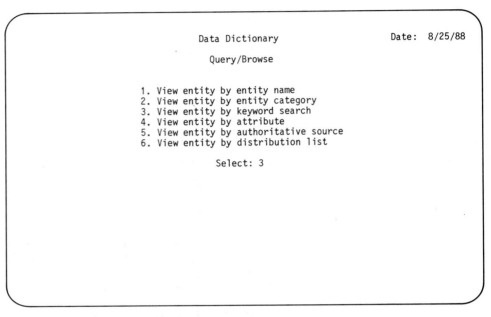

Figure 10–1   Query screen: I.

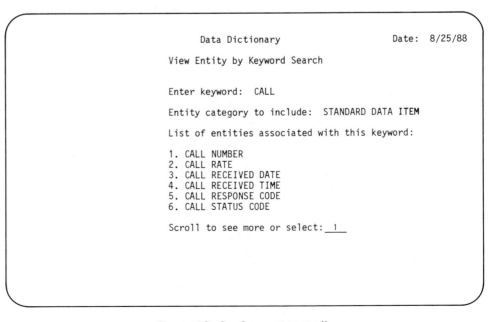

Figure 10–2   Query screen: II.

```
                              Data Dictionary                    Date:  8/25/88
                           Data Item Definition
  Name:  CALL NUMBER                      Title:  Number ID assigned to customer call

  Description:  The CALL NUMBER is the number assigned when a service call is received
  from the customer to the dispatch center. The number is assigned automatically by the
  dispatch system. It consists of two parts: a 1-character identifier for the dispatch
  center, and a 6-digit number assigned in ascending sequence by the system. If the
  system is down, temporary numbers can be assigned by the dispatcher, and when the call
  details are entered into the system, the system will assign the proper number.

  Alias:  CUSTOMER CALL       SERVICE CALL          CALL ID        CALL-NO

  Keyword:  CALL        CUSTOMER      SERVICE       NUMBER      DISPATCH

  Attributes:  Size:  7 bytes:  1 alphabetic and 6 numeric

               Range:

               Edits:  Edit for first character to equal dispatch center ID.
                       Rest of bytes should be numeric.

  Authoritative Source:  Dispatch system

  Data Management Function:
```

Figure 10-3 Query screen: III.

```
                              Data Dictionary                    Date:  8/25/88

                           System Data Definition


  Enter system name:  FACTS Data Base

               1. View information about this entity
               2. Update information about this entity
               3. View list of data items linked to this system
               4. Update list of data items linked to this system
               5. Add new data item to this system

                              Select: 1
```

Figure 10-4 Query screen: IV.

System Development: Identifying Data Items

One of the first steps in the development of a new system is to determine the data items that the system will require. The data dictionary system is the source of what data items exist and where they are used. Assembling a list of required data items for your system can be accomplished by using the query screens of the dictionary system. By using any of the four access methods (entity name, alias, keyword, enterprise name) you can identify standard data name, definition, and attributes for each data item in your systems. Figure 10-5 is a screen by which a data standard proposal is made.

An alternative way to compile your list of data standard items is to refer to the hard-copy data item lists that can be generated from the DD report generator.

```
                         Data Dictionary              Date:  8/25/88
                       Data Standard Proposal


Name:  Symptom Fix Code                Title:  Symptom fault corrective fix code

Description:  The code that is reported to the service technician repairing customer
equipment; there is one symptom fix code reported for each major unit repaired. The
first two digits describe the device-specific symptom, and the last two describe the
corrective action.

Alias:  SYMPTOM FIX          SYMPTOM FAULT FIX            SYMPTOM-FIX-CD

Keyword:  SYMPTOM            FIX                          CODE

Attributes:  Size:  4 bytes numeric

    Range:  From:_____  To:_____

    Edits:  Edit against valid list of symptom fix codes

    Codes: _____   _____   _____

           _____   _____   _____

Authoritative Source:  Service technician

Data Management Function:  HQ administration
```

Figure 10-5 Data standard proposal screen.

```
                         Data Dictionary              Date:  8/25/88

                        Report Generator


              1. Standard data item list
              2. Keyword list
              3. Alias list
              4. System data definition report
              5. System subsystem report
              6. Operations report
              7. Where-used reports

                    Select: 1
```

Figure 10-6 Report generator screen.

Figure 10–6 and 10–7 show the screens that must be filled out to obtain the hard-copy listing of standard data items. The screen provides for a selection of the information pertaining to each entity that can be obtained, such as attributes or descriptions. Figure 10–8 is a sample of a standard item listing.

Occasionally, a conflict arises between a data item that you require and the data standard in the dictionary. For example, an attribute such as the size of a data standard in the dictionary does not satisfy your needs; perhaps the size is too small. This could mean two things; (1) the data standard you have identified in the dictionary is not the same as the one you want, or (2) the standard is incorrect. To resolve case 1, you must query the dictionary further to find the correct data standard. To resolve case 2 you must contact the DDA and work together to find a solution. This may require involving the authoritative source of the data standard and/or others in the organization to resolve.

```
                        Data Dictionary              Date:  8/25/88
                      Standard Data Item List

  Banner:  NARAYAN                    Bin Number:  A110

  Report Heading:  STD ITEM LIST

  Selection Criteria:  Select All or Subset:

  Subset by:  Date created:  From ___/___/___ to ___/___/___
              Date last updated:  From ___/___/___ to ___/___/___

              Category:  ITEM

              Status:_____

              Version:_____

  Report Should Include:  All or Subset (A/S):  S

  Subset:  Attributes:  Y    Aliases:___    Description:___    Cross-references:___
```

Figure 10–7 Standard data item report generation specification screen.

If you cannot locate a data standard in the dictionary for a data item that your system requires, complete the standard data item request form or fill the on-line screen to request a data standard with the information that is required, and submit it to the DDA. If a conflict arises about the data standard itself, or any of the information on the completed form, the DDA will contact you for resolution. This may also require that other persons in the organization become involved. Examples of screens to resolve a data standard conflict are shown in Figures 10–9 through 10–11.

If forms are used, they must be multipart forms in order to let the requester of the standard know of the disposition of the request. In all cases the DDA must have final authority for resolving the standard, and his or her decision must be binding on all parties. Examples of a blank form and one that has been filled out are shown in Figures 10–12 and 10–13.

DDS0705.R1   Data Dictionary   9/05/88

Data Item Standards Report

ARRIVAL DATE (Data item)

The arrival date is the date in YYMMDD format when the technician arrived at the customer's site. Size is 6 bytes numeric.

Authoritative source is field service technician.
Edits: Should be greater than CALL RECEIVED DATE.

ARRIVAL TIME (Data item)

The arrival time is the time in HHMMSS format when the technician arrived at the customer's site. This time is reported on a 24-hour clock. The time is stored relative to GMT in the dispatch system data base. Size is 6 bytes numeric.

Authoritative source is field service technician.
Edits: Edit for limits on hours, minutes, seconds.

BRANCH OFFICE NUMBER (Data item)

The branch office number is the location code assigned to that branch by corporate field administration. It is a unique 8-digit number.

Authoritative source is corporate field administration.
Alias: Location code   Account Number

CALL RECEIVED DATE

The call received date is the date in YYMMDD format when the customer's request for service was received at the central dispatch site. Size is 6 bytes numeric.

Figure 10–8 Data item standards report.

```
                                 Data Dictionary              Date:  8/25/88

                               Data Definition Conflict

Name:   CUSTOMER NUMBER                    Status:            Version:01
    Your telephone:  231-4532             Electronic Address:  Nesbit+:kite
    Areas of conflict:    1. Name
                          2. Description
                          3. Aliases
                          4. Attributes
                          5. Cross-references

        Select:  4
        For each, describe your disagreement, and potential resolution.
        The DD Administrator will review your comments and get back to you.
```

Figure 10–9 Data conflict resolution screen.

```
                        Data Dictionary              Date:  8/25/88
                   Data Definition Conflict

Data name:  CUSTOMER NUMBER            Status:          Version:01

State as briefly as possible your disagreement, and the changes that you would like
to see made. State reasons, where applicable.

I would like to propose that the size of the CUSTOMER NUMBER field be a numeric
field rather than an alphanumeric field. This is so that numeric validation by the
system can take place. Also, it is easier for a data-entry operator to key in the
significant digits, than to key in alpha, space, and numeric characters.
_____
_____
_____
_____
_____
_____
_____
_____

If you wish to request a new standard, enter Y:
```

Figure 10-10 Data definition conflict screen.

```
                        Data Dictionary              Date:  8/25/88

                   Response to Data Conflict
                        CUSTOMER NUMBER

The customer number standard was changed from a numeric format to an alphanumeric
format to take into account subsidiaries of the company that use different customer
numbering conventions. Thus the requirement is that the field in the data base be
defined as a 7-character alpha-numeric field. In your screen, it is possible to
redefine the customer number field to a numeric field if you anticipate only numeric
numbers. You can also apply additional edits to suit the needs of the data-entry
operators at your location.
_____
_____
_____
_____
_____
_____
_____
```

Figure 10-11 Response to data conflict screen.

Defining the system. When you have completed the process of identifying the data standards for the data items in your system, you can define the system itself in the DDS using the store/modify function. You will add the system name (follow

Figure 10-12 Blank request for data standard item form.

naming conventions), alternate access keys, and input a narrative for the system as shown in Figure 10–14.

Relating Standard Data Items to the System Entity. Once the system is defined, you can relate the standard data items, which you defined as part of your system in the previous step, to the system name in the DDS. You can use the on-line store/modify function to accomplish this, as shown in Figure 10–15.

When these relationships have been defined, a system data requirements report can be run from the report generator using the screen shown in Figure 10–16. This report, which consists of an index section and a detailed section (Figures 10–17 and 10–18), lists the system, its description, and all of the standard data items associated with it to provide you with documentation of the data items used by your system.

As the system development life cycle progresses, additional data items which are necessary may be identified. You need to identify the data standards for these items as they surface, and relate them to the system in the data dictionary. This will ensure that that DD is kept current and that the system data requirements report provides accurate information. Conversely, if a relationship between a system and a data standard exists and is no longer needed, use the store/modify function to delete that relationship.

```
┌─────────────────────────────────────────────────────────────────────────┐
│                          Data Dictionary                                  │
│                                                                           │
│                    Request for Data Standard Item                         │
│                                                                           │
│  1. Data Name:  INV-NUMBER                                                │
│                                                                           │
│  2. Recommended Title:  Ticket number for inventorying warehouse          │
│                                                                           │
│  3. Item Narrative (descriptive account, summary, particulars): INV-NUMBER│
│     has a picture clause of PIC 9(6) and refers to the Inventory          │
│     Tag/Ticket Number. It is the preprinted number on the Field           │
│     Engineering Inventory Ticket. It is used in keeping track of the      │
│     tickets that have been filled out (used) or have not been filled out  │
│     (unused), in doing the inventory of the warehouse. It is also the     │
│     key in the Physical Inventory Data Base "PHYINV."                     │
│     ───────────────────────────────────────────────────────────────      │
│     ───────────────────────────────────────────────────────────────      │
│                                                                           │
│  4. Access Keys: Alias:          TICKET NUMBER          PHY-INV-NO        │
│                  Keywords:       TAG NUMBER             PHY-TKT-NUMBER     │
│                                                                           │
│  6. Attributes: Recommended size in characters or digits: 9(6)            │
│                 Recommended places after decimal if numeric: __           │
│                 Range of values: From _____ to _____              │
│                 Edits: _____    │
│                 _____   │
│                 _____   │
│                 Missing value codes (if any): _____   │
│                                                                           │
│  Authoritative source: Preprinted numbers resp. RC analyst                │
│  Data Management Function: Receiving center analyst                       │
│                                                                           │
│                          Prepared by: _____ Tina F. _____      │
│                                                                           │
│     ┌───────────────────────────────────────────────────────────────┐    │
│     │ To be filled by DDA:                                           │    │
│     │                                                                │    │
│     │ Standard Name Assigned: TICKET-NO                              │    │
│     │ Status:    ;    Version:01;                    Date: 02/01/84  │    │
│     │ Narrative: Same as above: __ ; Different from above: see       │    │
│     │            attached                                            │    │
│     │ Enterprise name: INVENTORY TICKET NUMBER                       │    │
│     │ Alias: INVENTORY TICKET NUMBER;  TICKET-NO                     │    │
│     │ Keyword: INVENTORY;      NUMBER    ;      TICKET               │    │
│     │ Additional attributes: _____ ; _____  │    │
│     │                        _____ ; _____  │    │
│     └───────────────────────────────────────────────────────────────┘    │
└─────────────────────────────────────────────────────────────────────────┘
```

Figure 10–13 Filled-out request for data standard item form.

```
╭───────────────────────────────────────────────────────────────────────╮
│                                                                         │
│              Data Dictionary                  Date:   8/25/88           │
│                                                                         │
│                Store/Modify/Load                                        │
│                System/Subsystem                                         │
│                                                                         │
│  Name:  FACTS Data Base              Status: P        Version:01        │
│                                                                         │
│  Project Manager:  Nelson            User Manager:  Risek               │
│                                                                         │
│  Systems Analyst: Bryant             User Coordinator: Cortesa          │
│                                                                         │
│  Description:  The FACTS data base project includes the implementation  │
│  of a centralized data base to hold the data that are collected by the  │
│  area locations by the central dispatching process. The FACTS data base │
│  will be the source of data for many of the reporting systems that are  │
│  being developed.                                                       │
│                                                                         │
│  Alias:  FACTS       FIELD ACTIVITY      DATA BASE      CLOSED CALLS     │
│  Keyword: FACTS      FIELD ACTIVITY      CLOSED CALLS                    │
│  Cross-References: _____  _____   │
│                                                                         │
│                   _____  _____   │
│                                                                         │
╰───────────────────────────────────────────────────────────────────────╯
```

Figure 10–14 Store system/subsystem screen.

189

```
                         Data Dictionary                    Date:  8/25/88

                         Store/Modify/Load
                      System Data Cross-References


System Name:  FACTS Data Base          Status:  P          Version:01

Cross-referenced to:
ALTERNATE BILL TO NUMBER
ARRIVAL DATE
ARRIVAL TIME
CALL RECEIVED DATE
CALL RECEIVED TIME
CUSTOMER NUMBER
CIA CODE
CONTRACT NUMBER
CONTRACT TERRITORY
COST CENTER ACCOUNT NUMBER
COST CENTER OF TECHNICIAN
CUSTOMER ADDRESS
```

Figure 10-15 Store system data cross-references screen.

```
                         Data Dictionary                    Date:  8/25/88

                    System Data Requirements Report

Banner:  NARAYAN                       Bin Number:  A120

Report Heading:  FACTS DB System Data Requirements

System Name:  FACTS Data Base
```

Figure 10-16 System data requirements report generation specification screen.

System Development: Programs, Procedures, Reports, etc.

As you continue with the system development task, the programs, procedures, reports, and so on, that are involved in the system will be identified and must be documented in the dictionary. Figure 10-19 represents a sample structure of relationships that must be preserved. Each of these entities can be input into the dictionary using the set of screens shown in Figure 10-20 through 10-30. Naming conventions must be

```
DDS0715.R1                    Data Dictionary System                  8/26/88

                         FACTS Data Base Data Requirements
                                      INDEX

FACTS DATA BASE
    ALTERNATE BILL TO NUMBER
    ARRIVAL DATE
    ARRIVAL TIME
    BRANCH OFFICE ADDRESS
    CALL RECEIVED DATE
    CALL RECEIVED TIME
    CUSTOMER NUMBER
    CIA CODE
    CONTRACT NUMBER
    CONTRACT TERRITORY
    COST CENTER ACCOUNT NUMBER
    COST CENTER OF TECHNICIAN
    CUSTOMER ADDRESS
    CUSTOMER BILL TO NUMBER
    CUSTOMER CITY
    CUSTOMER EQUIPMENT RECEIVED DATE
    CUSTOMER NAME
    CUSTOMER PURCHASE ORDER NUMBER
    CUSTOMER SHIP TO NUMBER
    CUSTOMER STATE
    CUSTOMER STATUS
    CUSTOMER ZIP CODE
    DIAGNOSTIC REVISION USED
    ECO NUMBER
    EMPLOYEE BADGE NUMBER
    EQUIPMENT INSTALL COMPLETION DATE
    EQUIPMENT WARRANTY PERIOD
    ESP PARTS CODE
    FACTS INCIDENT NUMBER
```

Figure 10–17 FACTS data base requirements report (index).

followed for these entities. Relationships between these entities must be entered along with the descriptions. For example, the jobs and programs must be related to the correct subsystems, the reports must be connected to the program that produced the report, and so on.

It is the responsibility of those working on the systems to ensure that all components of the system (data items, programs, procedures, etc.) and the relationships between them (system to job, job to program, etc.) are properly documented in the data dictionary system. This is a requirement for project manager approval at the time of production turnover.

While the entities are in different phases of being worked upon, the system subsystem report can be run to get an idea of how the entities are related, and to develop a skeleton, which is then filled up with detailed information. An example of the index portion from the system subsystem report is shown in Figure 10–31.

System Development: Files and Record Descriptions

At some point in the system development process, you will begin to visualize the data file interactions and flows that are required to make the system work. The DBA is responsible for defining the file definitions and record descriptions and will actively

DDS0715.R1   Data Dictionary   8/26/88

FACTS Data Base Data Requirements

FACTS DATA BASE (System)

The FACTS DATA BASE project includes the implementation of a centralized data base to hold the data that are collected by the area locations by the central dispatching process. The FACTS data base will be the source of data for many of the reporting systems that are being developed.

ALTERNATE BILL TO NUMBER (Data item)

The alternate bill to number is an identifier of the customer's name and address that should be billed. Size is 7 alphanumeric characters.
Authoritative source is sales administration.

ARRIVAL DATE (Data item)

The arrival date is the date in YYMMDD format when the technician arrived at the customer's site. Size is 6 bytes numeric.
Authoritative source is field service technician.
Edits: Should be greater than CALL RECEIVED DATE.

ARRIVAL TIME (Data item)

The arrival time is the time in HHMMSS format when the technician arrived at the customer's site. This time is reported on a 24-hour clock. The time is stored relative to GMT in the dispatch system data base.
Authoritative source is field service technician.
Edits: Edit for limits on hours, minutes, seconds.

BRANCH OFFICE NUMBER (Data item)

The branch office number is the location code assigned to that branch by corporate field administration. It is a unique 8-digit number.
Authoritative source is corporate field administration.
Alias: Location code   Account Number

CALL RECEIVED DATE (Data item)

The call received date is the date in YYMMDD format when the customer's request for service was received at the central dispatch site. Size is 6 bytes numeric.
Authoritative source is customer.
Edit: Edit for limits on year, month, day.

CALL RECEIVED TIME (Data item)

The call received time is the time in HHMMSS format when the customer's request for service was received at the dispatch center. The time is reported on a 24-hour clock. The time is stored in the central dispatch data base relative to GMT. Size is 6 bytes numeric.
Authoritative source is customer.
Edits: Limits on hours, minutes, seconds.

CUSTOMER NUMBER (Data item)

The customer number is the unique identification given to a customer on customer reference file. It is a 7-character alphanumeric field.
Authoritative source is sales administration.

CIA CODE (Data item)

The CIA code is a code that identifies whether the service technician completed the call or not. The code is 1 byte long and can have the following values: C = Complete; I = Incomplete; A = Assisting.
Authoritative source is field service technician.
Edit: Edit for C, I, or A.

CONTRACT NUMBER (Data item)

The contract number uniquely identifies the service contract. It is an 8 character alphanumeric field.
Authoritative source is field administration.

Figure 10–18 FACTS data base requirements report (data).

```
System
   Subsystem.1
      Job/CLI.11
         Program.111
            Report.1111
            Report.1112
         Program.112
            File.xxx
            Report.1121
      Job/CLI.12
         Program.121
            File.xxx
            File.xxy
            Report.1211
   Subsystem.2
      etc.
```

Figure 10-19 Sample structure relationships.

```
              Data Dictionary                    Date:  8/25/88

        System Subsystem Documentation


           1. Subsystem
           2. Job/CLI
           3. Program/procedure/module
           4. Reports
           5. Files
           6. Copybooks (include files)

               Select:____
```

Figure 10-20 System subsystem documentation menu screen.

```
                      Data Dictionary                  Date:  8/25/88

                      Store/Modify/Load
                      System/Subsystem

Name:  FACT01                    Status:  P          Version:01

Within System:  FACTS Data Base  Status:  P          Version:01

Project Manager:  Nelson      User Manager:  Risek

Systems Analyst:  Bryant      User Coordinator:  Cortesa

Description:  This subsystem within the FACTS data base system covers the loading of
closed call data from the dispatch system to the FACTS data base.

Alias:  FACT01

Keyword:

Cross-References: _____    _____


                  _____    _____
```

Figure 10-21 Store system/subsystem information screen.

```
┌─────────────────────────────────────────────────────────────────────────────┐
│                                                                               │
│                            Data Dictionary                    Date:  8/25/88  │
│                                                                               │
│                            Store/Modify/Load                                  │
│                                Job/CLI                                        │
│                                                                               │
│  Name:  FACT.0101                        Status:  P          Version:01       │
│  Within system/subsystem:  FACT01        Status:  P          Version:01       │
│  Description:  The FACT.0101 job takes the tapes from the dispatch centers and loads │
│  them for further processing.                                                 │
│                                                                               │
│  Type:  Batch                            Programmer:  Nelson                  │
│  Schedule:  Weekly                       Estimated Run Time:  30 min          │
│  Switches:  None                                                              │
│  Dependencies:_____│
│                                                                               │
│  Special Instructions:  This job can be run for as many tapes as there are from the │
│  dispatch centers.                                                            │
│                                                                               │
│                                                                               │
│                                                                               │
└─────────────────────────────────────────────────────────────────────────────┘
```

Figure 10–22 Store job/CLI information screen.

```
┌─────────────────────────────────────────────────────────────────────────────┐
│                                                                               │
│                            Data Dictionary                    Date:  8/25/88  │
│                                                                               │
│                            Store/Modify/Load                                  │
│                          Job/CLI Run Instructions                             │
│                                                                               │
│  Name:  FACT.0101                        Status:  P          Version:01       │
│  Within system/subsystem:  FACT01        Status:  P          Version:01       │
│                                                                               │
│  Run Instructions                                                             │
│                                                                               │
│  QBJ FACT.0101                                                                │
│                                                                               │
│                                                                               │
│                                                                               │
│                                                                               │
│                                                                               │
│                                                                               │
│                                                                               │
└─────────────────────────────────────────────────────────────────────────────┘
```

Figure 10–23 Store job/CLI run instructions screen.

seek your input. During this process the DBA will use the data dictionary and apply the appropriate naming conventions to provide you with file and record descriptions that can be used for preliminary documentation and program development.

Note that the dictionary is the source of all data definitions. This means that any file definitions and record layouts that are required for your system must follow the standard conventions that are part of the dictionary. Although it is mandatory that the file definitions be generated from the dictionary for your program to be

```
                          Data Dictionary                 Date:  8/25/88

                           Store/Modify/Load
                        Job/CLI Re-run Instructions


Name:  FACT.0101                    Status:  P        Version:01

Within system/subsystem:  FACT01    Status:  P        Version:01

Rerun Instructions

Restart the job from the beginning.
```

Figure 10-24 Store job/CLI rerun instructions screen.

```
                          Data Dictionary                 Date:  8/26/88

                           Store/Modify/Load
                        Job/CLI Program File Info


Name:  FACT.0101                    Status:  P        Version:01

Within subsystem:  FACT01           Status:  P        Version:01

  01) Program FACT0101
      Converts RDOS tape format (dispatch system closed calls) to AOS disk format for
      further processing.

      I/O   Filename/File Description    Device    Retention    Format    Copies
      I     FACEXT01S:0                  TAPE      1 YR
            Dispatch system tape (RDOS)
      O     FACTAPEA01                   DISK      EOJ
            FACTS data (AOS format)

  02) Program FACT0102
      Verification against control file

      I/O   Filename/File Description    Device    Retention    Format    Copies
      I     FACTAPEA01                   DISK      EOJ
      O     FACT0101S.W1                 DISK      1 day
      I/O   FACTCTRL                     DISK      PERM
      O     FACT0102.R1                  PRINT                  LONG 6    3
```

Figure 10-25 Store job/CLI program file information screen.

operable in the production environment, there may be cases where because of resource constraints, you could develop the copybooks on your own by following the standards and then use a load function to put it into the dictionary. In any event, you should involve the DBA as early a possible during the system development process so that problems are avoided during the final acceptance procedures prior to production turnover. Once the file and record layouts are finalized they will be enabled for use by your program.

```
                              Data Dictionary              Date:  8/25/88

                         Load Program Information


                            1. Store/modify
                            2. Scan Library/Directory
                            3. Scan program source
                            4. Import program description
                            5. Load program structure
                            6. Load missing information

                                Select: 1
```

Figure 10-26 Load program information screen.

```
                              Data Dictionary              Date:  8/25/88

                            Store/Modify/Load
                                 Program


   Name:  FACT0101              Status:  P           Version:01

   Within Job/CLI:  FACT.0101   Status:  P           Version:01

   Within subsystem:  FACT01    Status:  P           Version:01

   Author:  J. Nelson        Maintenance Resp:  J. Nelson

   Language:  COBOL-74          Code set:  ASCII

   Description:  At the end of each week, each dispatch system site will prepare an
   RDOS tape file of all closed calls during the previous week. This tape will be sent
   to the HQ data center. FACT0101 will perform an RDOS-to-AOS format conversion and
   load the file into FACTAPEA01 and record the completion of this process in the
   control file.

   I/O    Filename/File Description    Device   Retention   Format   Copies
   I      FACEXT01S:0                  TAPE     1 YR
          Dispatch system tape (RDOS)
   O      FACTAPEA01                   DISK     EOJ
          FACTS data (AOS format)
```

Figure 10-27 Store program information screen: I.

  If you are developing a copybook on your own, recognize that you are responsible for ensuring that the complete documentation for every item is entered into the dictionary, including the definition of the data standard and the cross-reference to it in your copybook. You can use the screens shown in Figure 10-32 and 10-33 for that purpose.

  If you already have a copybook that has not been generated from the dictionary,

```
                        Data Dictionary                Date:  8/25/88

                        Store/Modify/Load
                             Program

Name:  FACT0102                    Status:  P          Version:01

Within Job/CLI:  FACT.0101         Status:  P          Version:01

Within subsystem:  FACT01          Status:  P          Version:01

Author:  J. Nelson          Maintenance Resp:  J. Nelson

Language:  COBOL-74               Code set:  ACSII

Description:  The AOS file FACTAPEA01 produced from FACT0101 will be verified against
control information to ensure that the sequence of tapes from the dispatch centers is
maintained. It will also perform security checks to ensure that tape is from correct
source.
```

I/O	Filename/File Description	Device	Retention	Format	Copies
I	FACTAPEA01	DISK	EOJ		
O	FACT0101S.W1	DISK	1 day		
I/O	FACTCTRL	DISK	PERM		
O	FACT0102.R1	PRINT		LONG 6	3

Figure 10-28 Store program information screen: II.

```
                        Data Dictionary                Date:  8/25/88

                        Store/Modify/Load
                             Report

Name:  FACT0102.R1                 Status:  P          Version:01

Produced by:  FACT0102             Status:  P          Version:01

Description:  FACT0101.R1 is a FACTS load exception report which will be produced
if there is a discrepancy found in the sequence of tapes sent from the dispatch
system centers.

Distribution:  Operations Control; Dispatch Center Supvr; DBA

Frequency:  When error              Media:  8 1/2 by 11

Alias:  FACT0102.R1        LOAD ERROR REPORT        FACTS REPORT

Keyword:  FACTS        ERROR        LOAD        FACT0102.R1

Import/Enter Rpt Sample (I/E):  E        File name:_____  Type:_____
```

Figure 10-29 Store report information screen: I.

you will have to load it into the dictionary. Specify the filename (pathname) where the copybook exists and other details that are requested. The automated load facility will break down the copybook into its components and then populate the dictionary with the appropriate entities and relationships. A screen to do this is shown in Figure 10-34. The report from the load process is shown in Figure 10-35.

If your system requires the use of an existing file that has to be modified, this

```
                            Data Dictionary                    Date:  8/25/88

                            Store/Modify/Load
                             Report Sample

   Name:  FACT0102.R1                    Status:  P          Version:01

   FACT0102.R1                    FACTS System Report                  2/8/87
                                  LOAD ERROR RPT.

   Error detected on tape for week ending 2/7/87 from Dispatch Center C

   Tape out of sequence; tape for week ending 1/31/87 from Dispatch Center C was not
   processed.


                            ** END OF REPORT **
```

Figure 10–30 Store report information screen: II.

```
   DDS0713.R1                    Data Dictionary System                9/05/88

                              System Subsystem Report
                                 FACTS Data Base


   FACTS DATA BASE                                                         1
     FACT01                                                                2
       FACT.0101                                                           3
         FACT0101                                                          4
           FACEXT01S:0                                                     5
           FACTAPEA01                                                      6
         FACT0102                                                          7
           FACTAPEA01                                                      8
           FACTCTRL                                                        9
           FACT0102.R1                                                    10
     FACTDB.LOAD                                                          11
       FACT0103                                                           12
         FACT0101S.W1                                                     13
         FACT0102S.W1                                                     14
         FACT0102S.W2                                                     15
         FACT0103S.W3                                                     16
```

Figure 10–31 FACTS data base system/subsystem report (index).

has to be handled by the DBA. You should request the changes that you wish to
make to the file definition, and the DBA will let you know when all modifications
have been made and you can reference that copybook in your program. Note that
in the case of a shared file, there may be several parties involved, and the DBA may
have to coordinate the activities of several individuals in order to make the change
happen.

```
                           Data Dictionary                Date:  8/25/88
                            Define Copybook

   Name:  FACT0105S.W2.CC              Status:  P          Version:01

   Type of Copybook:  File             Language:  COBOL

   Prefix:  S041           Suffix:_____   Indentation:_____

   For Record:  R041-CALL-REC          For File:  FACT0105S.W2

   Organization:  Sequential

      Select data items              Query:
   ___CALL-NO_____
   ___CALL-RECD-DT_____
   ___CALL-RECD-TIME_____
   ___UPDT-DT_____
   ___LCTN-DT_____
   ___ARRIVAL-DT_____
```

Figure 10-32 Define copybook screen.

```
                           Data Dictionary                Date:  8/25/88
                             View Copybook

   Name:  FACT0105S.W2.CC              Status:  P          Version:01

   Type of Copybook:                   Language:  COBOL

   Prefix:  S041           Suffix:_____   Indentation:_____

   For Record:  R041-CALL-REC          For File:  FACT0105S.W2

   Organization:  Sequential

   FD FACT0105S.W2
          RECORD CONTAINS 104 CHARACTERS
          DATA RECORD IS R041-CALL-REC.

   01  R041-CALL-REC.
       05  S041-CALL-NO                          PIC X(7).
       05  S041-CALL-RECD-DT                     PIC 9(6).
       05  S041-CALL-RECD-TIME                   PIC 9(6).
       05  S041-UPDT-DT                          PIC 9(6).
       05  S041-LCTN-CD                          PIC X(8).

       Scroll to see more:___
```

Figure 10-33 View copybook screen.

Figure 10-36 shows the screen that is used to generate the copybook from the dictionary; this function combines the format of the components of the copybook into a source image that the compiler can then process. Figure 10-37 shows the resulting image produced by the generator.

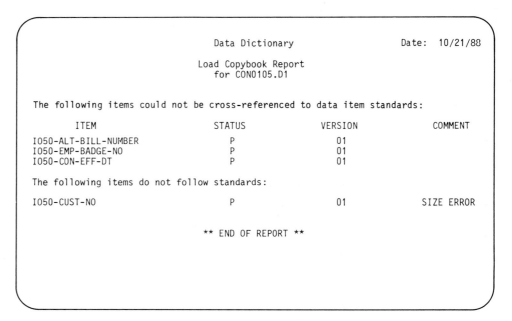

```
                              Data Dictionary                    Date:  8/25/88

                              Store/Modify/Load
                                  Copybook


Name:  CONO105.D1.CC                        Status:  P           Version:01

Directory Path to Copy Source:  :UDD:CONTRACT:CONO105.D1.CC

Cross-Reference to Standard (Y/N):  Y

Type of Copybook:_____     Language:  COBOL

Prefix:_____          Suffix:_____          Indentation:_____

Record:  S012-CONTRACT-REC                  File:  CONO105.D1

Organization:  Sequential
```

Figure 10-34 Load copybook instructions screen.

```
                              Data Dictionary                    Date:  10/21/88

                              Load Copybook Report
                                for CONO105.D1


The following items could not be cross-referenced to data item standards:

        ITEM                    STATUS          VERSION              COMMENT
IO50-ALT-BILL-NUMBER              P               01
IO50-EMP-BADGE-NO                 P               01
IO50-CON-EFF-DT                   P               01

The following items do not follow standards:

IO50-CUST-NO                      P               01              SIZE ERROR


                        ** END OF REPORT **
```

Figure 10-35 Load copybook report screen.

Libraries: Compile for Test and Production

The data base administrator is responsible for setting up the procedures whereby the application programs can access the correct version of the copy source. This not only includes file definitions and record layouts, but could also include source code that

```
                              Data Dictionary              Date:  8/25/88
                            Copy Source Generator

   Name of Copybook:  CON0105.D1.CC        Status:  P        Version:01

   Pathname to File for Storage:  :UDD:COPY:CON0105.D1.CC

   Prefix:  S504              Suffix:_____    Indentation: _____

   Record:  R504-CON-REC                File:  CON0105.D1

   Data Item List File: _____

   Existing Copybook in DD:  Name:  CON0105.D1.CC        Status:  P        Version:01

   Print Output to:  Printer:_____      File:_____
```

Figure 10-36 Copy source generator instruction screen.

is used for I/O drivers attached to a data base. An I/O driver is a part of the program that does the actual access to the data base and includes the data base specific code. Depending on the responsibility of the DBA at a particular site, the dictionary could help control the version of copy source that is available for application programs to use.

The benefits of setting up the procedures to update and maintain central libraries for copy source are:

- Copybooks can be standardized so that they will be easier to use.
- Changes made to copybooks can be controlled, eliminating multiple versions of one copybook.
- There will be one location for all copybooks, making it easier to find a copybook and eliminating unwieldy searchlists required to access copybooks being used in different systems.
- The data dictionary can be used to supply information about copybooks: for example, what copybooks are used in a program or system, or what programs use a particular copybook.
- Narratives for the data items, record, and files which are represented by the copybook will be available from the dictionary.

Procedures for compiling your programs for development, test, and production are based on the premise that the right versions of the copybooks for your program are needed. The compiler will automatically use the copybook with status = P for production and version = 01. If you are compiling your program using a development or test version of the copybook (your DBA will be able to tell you this information), you should add the phrase Status = D; Version = 01 to your copy statement in your program. When your program is turned to production, the DBA will make sure that the right version of the copybooks are available in Production status and also that all other programs using that copybook have been identified and are recompiled so that there are no inconsistencies.

Data Dictionary

Copy Source Generator
COBOL copy source for file CON0105.D1, record R504-CON-REC generated for copybook
CON01015.D1.CC on 9-14-88

R504-CON-REC:
This is a grouping of data items about terms and conditions on the contract header record in the
contracts data base.

S504-CONTRACT-NO:
The contract number uniquely identifies the service contract. It is an 8-character alphanumeric field.

S504-CUST-NO:
The customer number is the unique identification given to a customer on the customer reference file.
It is a 7-character alphanumeric field.

S504-SHIP-TO-SUFFIX:
The ship-to-address suffix is a 3-digit suffix added to the customer number, which indicates the
identifier of the customer's address to which equipment was shipped.

S504-CONTRACT-TYPE:
The contract-type item refers to the type of service contract. This is a 3-character field. The set of
codes includes:

>   DOM = domestic
>   INT = international
>   GSA = government
>   MIL = military
>   OTH = other

S504-ALT-BILL-TO-NO:
The alternate bill to number is an identifier of the customer's name and address that should be billed.
Size is 7-alphanumeric characters.

S504-INSTALL-ADDR:
The installation address is the actual address of the customer at whose location the equipment is
installed. Overall size is 100 bytes, divided into 4 lines of 25 characters each.

S504-INSTALL-CITY:
The installation city is the name of the city of the customer's site at which the equipment is installed.
22 characters long.

S504-INSTALL-STATE:
The installation state is the 3-character state (U.S.) or province (Canada) identifier.

S504-INSTALL-ZIP-CD:
The installation zip code is the postal code and is 9 bytes long.

S504-WKDAY-COVER-BGN:
The weekday coverage-begins item is the start time of service contract during weekdays, in hours
and minutes. 4 bytes long.

S504-WKDAY-COVER-END:
The weekday coverage-ends item is the ending time of service contract during weekdays, in hours
and minutes, military time. 4 bytes long.

S504-SAT-COVER-BGN:
The Saturday coverage-begins item is the start time of service contract during Saturdays, in hours
and minutes. 4 bytes long.

S504-SAT-COVER-END:
The Saturday coverage-ends item is the ending time of service contract during Saturdays, in hours
and minutes, military time. 4 bytes long.

S504-SUN-COVER-BGN:
The Sunday coverage-begins item is the start time of service contract during Sunday, in hours and
minutes. 4 bytes long.

S504-SUN-COVER-END:
The Sunday coverage-ends item is the ending time of service contract during Sundays, in hours
and minutes, military time. 4 bytes long.

S504-LCTN-CD:
The location code is the 8-digit identifier that uniquely identifies the branch office within the region
within the area.

Figure 10-37 Copy source report.

```
FD  CON0105.D1
    RECORD CONTAINS 210 CHARACTERS
    DATA RECORD IS S504-CON-REC.

01  S504-CON-REC.

    05    S504-CONTRACT-NO            PIC X(8).
    05    S504-CUST-NO                PIC X(7).
    05    S504-CUST-SHIP-TO-SUFFIX    PIC 9(3).
    05    S504-CONTRACT-TYPE          PIC X(3).
    05    S504-ALT-BILL-TO-NO         PIC X(7).
    05    S504-INSTALL-ADDR           PIC X(100).
    05    S504-INSTALL-CITY           PIC X(22).
    05    S504-INSTALL-STATE          PIC X(3).
    05    S504-INSTALL-ZIP-CD         PIC X(9).
    05    S504-WKDAY-COVER-BGN        PIC 9(4).
    05    S504-WKDAY-COVER-END        PIC 9(4).
    05    S504-SAT-COVER-BGN          PIC 9(4).
    05    S504-SAT-COVER-END          PIC 9(4).
    05    S504-SUN-COVER-BGN          PIC 9(4).
    05    S504-SUN-COVER-END          PIC 9(4).
    05    S504-LCTN-CD                PIC 9(8).
```

Figure 10–37 Continued

System Subsystem Report

When the system development process is completed, the system and all its components have been entered into the data dictionary system and the relationships have been established, a system subsystem report can be run from the report generator. This report lists all of the components of a system in a hierarchical fashion beginning at the system level. The report contains the subsystems, procedures, programs, reports, files, and so on, that are part of the system. A sample of this report follows.

DDS0713.R1

Data Dictionary System
System Subsystem Report
FACTS DATA BASE

9/05/88
Pg   ii

DDS0713.R1   Data Dictionary System   9/05/88
                          System Subsystem Report   Pg   1
                                 FACTS DATA BASE

FACTS DATA BASE   (System)   Status: P   Version:01

The FACTS data base project includes the implementation of a centralized data base to hold the data that are collected by the area locations by the central dispatching process. The FACTS data base will be the source of data for many of the reporting systems that are being developed. The FACTS (Field Activity Collection and Tracking) system is designed to organize data from the field into a data base to satisfy the information needs of the field and headquarters. The FACTS data base will contain the previous week's closed calls as reported by each central dispatch center. In addition, the data base will contain the contract and configuration changes that are reported by the customer, service technician, and branch manager.

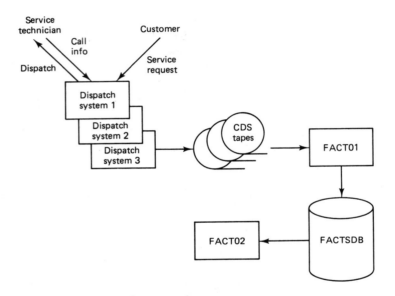

FACTS data flow diagram.

DDS0713.R1   Data Dictionary System   9/05/88
        System Subsystem Report   Pg   2
        FACTS DATA BASE

FACT01   (Subsystem)   Status: P   Version:01

The FACT01 subsystem within the FACTS system includes the steps needed to process the closed call data from the dispatch centers into the FACTS data base

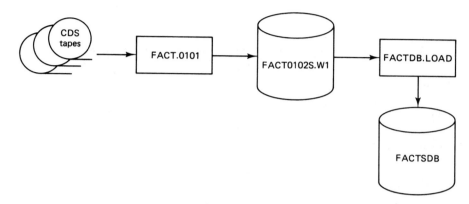

FACT01 subsystem diagram.

DDS0713.R1	Data Dictionary System	9/05/88
	System Subsystem Report	Pg 3
	FACTS DATA BASE	

FACT.0101   (Job/CLI)   Status: P   Version:01

The FACT.0101 job takes the tapes from the dispatch centers and loads them for further processing.

Type: Batch   Programmer: Nelson
Schedule: Weekly   Estimated Run Time: 30 min
Switches: None
Dependencies:
Special Instructions: This job can be run for as many tapes there are from the dispatch centers.

Run Instructions:

   QBJ FACT.0101

Rerun Instructions:

   Restart the job from the beginning.

Program/File Information

   01) Program FACT0101
      Converts RDOS tape format (dispatch system closed calls) to AOS disk format for further processing.

I/O	Filename/File Description	Device	Retention	Format	Copies
I	FACEXT01S:0	TAPE	1 YR		
	Dispatch system tape (RDOS)				
O	FACTAPEA01	DISK	EOJ		
	FACTS data (AOS format)				
I/O	FACTCTRL	DISK	PERM		

   02) Program FACT0102
      Verification against control file

I/O	Filename/File Description	Device	Retention	Format	Copies
I	FACTAPEA01	DISK	EOJ		
O	FACT0101S.W1	DISK	1 day		
I/O	FACTCTRL	DISK	PERM		
O	FACT0102.R1	PRINT		LONG 6	3

FACT.0101   (Job/CLI)   Status: P   Version:01

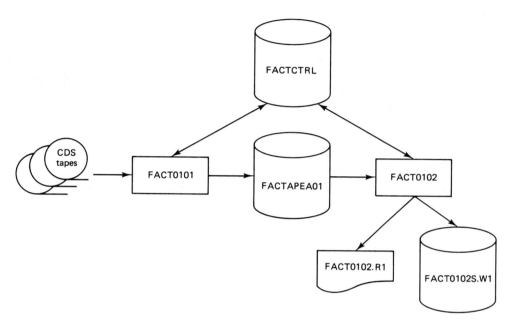

FACT.0101 job flow diagram.

DDS0713.R1	Data Dictionary System	9/05/88
	System Subsystem Report	Pg 5
	FACTS DATA BASE	

FACT.0101   (Program)   Status: P   Version:01

Author: J. Nelson   Maintenance Resp: J. Nelson
Language: COBOL-74   Code set: ASCII

Description: At the end of each week, each dispatch system site will prepare an RDOS tape file of all closed calls during the previous week. This tape will be sent to the HQ data center. FACT0101 will perform an RDOS-to-AOS format conversion, load the file into FACTAPEA01, and record the completion of this process in the control file.

Operations Doc:

Program FACT0101
Converts RDOS tape format (dispatch system closed calls) to AOS disk format for further processing.

I/O	Filename/File Description	Device	Retention	Format	Copies
I	FACEXT01S:0	TAPE	1 YR		
	Dispatch system tape (RDOS)				
O	FACTAPEA01	DISK	EOJ		
	FACTS data (AOS format)				
I/O	FACTCTRL	DISK	PERM		

DDS0713.R1   Data Dictionary System   9/05/88
System Subsystem Report   Pg   6
FACTS DATA BASE

FACEXT01S: (File)   Status: P   Version:01

FACEXT01S:0 is the filename under which the tape of closed calls from the dispatch center is loaded at the HQ data center.

Short Desc: Dispatch system tape (RDOS)
Retention: 1 year
Organization: Sequential
Record Size: 309 bytes max.

DDS0713.R1	Data Dictionary System	9/05/88
	System Subsystem Report	Pg 7
	FACTS DATA BASE	

FACTAPEA01   (File)   Status: P   Version:01

FACTAPEA01 is the disk filename of the AOS file that will hold the data from the dispatch center after they have been converted from RDOS format to AOS format. It consists of variable-length records, representing the different types of transaction records generated by the dispatch system. The first 28 characters of the transaction records have a common format:

Bytes		
	1–3	Record ID
	4–10	Call number
	11–16	Date of service
	17–22	Time of service
	23–28	Employee badge number

Short Desc: FACTS data (AOS format)
Retention: EOJ
Organization: Sequential
Record Size: 309 bytes max.

FACTCTRL   (File)   Status: P   Version:01

FACTCTRL is an ISAM file that contains the control information required to ensure that the proper
sequence of tapes are processed from each dispatch center. The tape from the dispatch center contains
a header record and a trailer record that has information which can be used for verification. In addition
to control totals, the header and trailer records contain extract sequence indicators (ESI), which are
compared with the ESIs in the FACTCTRL file to ensure that tapes are processed in the correct
sequence.

Short Desc: Control file for tape sequencing
Retention: PERM
Organization: ISAM
Record Size: 180 bytes
Copybook:

```
          SELECT FACTCTRL ASSIGN INDEX TO WS-FACTCTRL-INDX
          ASSIGN DATA TO WS-FACTCTRL-DATA
          KEY IS WS-CTRL-KEY KEY LENGTH IS WS-KEY-LENGTH
          FILE STATUS IS WS-FILE-STAT.

          FD FACTCTRL
          RECORD CONTAINS 180 CHARACTERS
          DATA RECORD IS 1276-CTRL-REC.

       01 1276-CTRL-REC.
              05      1276-CTRL-KEY.
                  10      1276-CREATE-DATE            PIC 9(6).
                  10      1276-CREATE-TIME            PIC 9(6).
                  10      1276-DISPATCH-AREA          PIC X(1).
                  10      1276-DISPATCH-CENTER-ID     PIC X(1).
                  10      1276-DISPATCH-CENTER-LOC    PIC X(8).
                  10      1276-LOW-ESI                PIC 9(8).
                  10      1276-HIGH-ESI               PIC 9(8).
                  10      1276-SEQ-NO                 PIC 9(4).
                  10      1276-CTRL-DATA              PIC X(138).
```

Name: FACT0102   (Program)   Status: P   Version:01

Author: J. Nelson   Maintenance Resp: J. Nelson
Language: COBOL-74   Code set: ASCII

Description: The AOS file FACTAPEA01 produced from FACT0101 will be verified against control information to ensure that the sequence of tapes from the dispatch centers is maintained. It will also perform security checks to ensure that the tape is from the correct source. It appends to FACT0101S.W1.

Operations Doc:

> Program FACT0102
> Verification against control file.

I/O	Filename/File Description	Device	Retention	Format	Copies
I	FACTAPEA01	DISK	EOJ		
O	FACT0101S.W1	DISK	1 day		
	Holding file				
I/O	FACTCTRL	DISK	PERM		
O	FACT0102.R1	PRINT		LONG 6	3

FACTAPEA01   (File)   Status: P   Version:01

FACTAPEA01 is the disk filename of the AOS file that will hold the data from the dispatch center
after they have been converted from RDOS format to AOS format. It consists of variable-length
records, representing the different types of transaction records generated by the dispatch system. The
first 28 characters of the transaction records have a common format:

Bytes		
	1–3	Record ID
	4–10	Call number
	11–16	Date of service
	17–22	Time of service
	23–28	Employee badge number

Short Desc: FACTS data (AOS format)
Retention: EOJ
Organization: Sequential
Record Size: 309 bytes max.

DDS0713.R1	Data Dictionary System	9/05/88
	System Subsystem Report	Pg 11
	FACTS DATA BASE	

Name: FACT0101S.W1   (File)   Status: P   Version:01

File FACT0101S.W1 is the file that holds the data from FACTAPEA01. The data from FACTAPEA01 are appended to any other data that may already be in FACT0101S.W1 from another dispatch center.

Short Desc: Holding file
Retention: 1 day
Organization: Sequential
Record Size: 309 bytes max.

DDS0713.R1   Data Dictionary System   9/05/88
                          System Subsystem Report   Pg   12
                              FACTS DATA BASE

FACTCTRL   (File)   Status: P   Version:01

FACTCTRL is an ISAM file that contains the control information required to ensure that the proper sequence of tapes are processed from each dispatch center. The tape from the dispatch center contains a header record and a trailer record that has information which can be used for verification. In addition to control totals, the header and trailer records contain extract sequence indicators (ESI) which are compared with the ESIs in the FACTCTRL file to ensure that tapes are processed in the correct sequence.

Short Desc:
Retention: PERM
Organization: ISAM
Record Size: 180 bytes
Copybook:

```
SELECT FACTCTRL ASSIGN INDEX TO WS-FACTCTRL-INDX
ASSIGN DATA TO WS-FACTCTRL-DATA
KEY IS WS-CTRL-KEY KEY LENGTH IS WS-KEY-LENGTH
FILE STATUS IS WS-FILE-STAT.


FD FACTCTRL
RECORD CONTAINS 180 CHARACTERS
DATA RECORD IS I276-CTRL-REC.

01-I276-CTRL-REC.
    05    I276-CTRL-KEY
          10    I276-CREATE-DATE            PIC 9(6).
          10    I276-CREATE-TIME            PIC 9(6).
          10    I276-DISPATCH-AREA          PIC X(1).
          10    I276-DISPATCH-CENTER-ID     PIC X(1).
          10    I276-DISPATCH-CENTER-LOC    PIC X(8).
          10    I276-LOW-ESI                PIC 9(8).
          10    I276-HIGH-ESI               PIC 9(8).
          10    I276-SEQ-NO                 PIC 9(4).
          10    I276-CTRL-DATA              PIC X(138).
```

DDS0713.R1   Data Dictionary System   9/05/88
                                  System Subsystem Report   Pg   13
                                  FACTS DATA BASE

Name: FACT0102.R1   (Report)   Status: P   Version:01
Produced by: FACT0102   Status: P   Version:01

Description: FACT0101.R1 is a FACTS load exception report which will be produced if there is a
discrepancy found in the sequence of tapes sent from the dispatch centers.

Distribution: Operations control; dispatch center supvr; DBA

Frequency: When error   Media:8 1/2 by 11

Alias: FACT0102.R1   LOAD ERROR REPORT   FACTS REPORT
Keyword: FACTS   ERROR   LOAD   FACT0102.R1

****

Report Sample

FACT0102.R1   FACTS System Report   2/8/89
                                  LOAD ERROR RPT.

Error detected on tape for week ending 2/7/89 from Dispatch Center C

Tape out of sequence; tape for week ending 1/31/89 from Dispatch Center C was not processed.

** END OF REPORT **

****

FACTSDB.LOAD   (Job/CLI)   Status: P   Version:01

The FACTSDB.LOAD is a job stream that takes the data from job FACT.0101 as input, breaks them down into smaller files by record category, sorts these files, and then loads the FACTS data base with these files. It consists of the execution of four programs: FACT0103 (sort input data), FACT0105 (format data into FACTS format), FACT0106 (sort FACTS records), and FACT0107 (load records to FACTS data base).

Type: Batch   Programmer: Nelson
Schedule: Weekly   Estimated Run Time: 1 hr
Switches: None
Dependencies:
Special Instructions

Run Instructions:

```
)SEA FACTSDB [!SEA]        set searchlist to FACTSDB
)QBJ FACTSDB.LOAD
```

Rerun Instructions:

If program modules FACT0103, FACT0105, or FACT0106 abort, the entire job can be restarted from the beginning. To do this, just make sure that the searchlist is set to find FACTSDB; then

```
)QBJ FACTSDB.LOAD
```

If program module FACT0107 is to be restarted, the operator types out the file FACT0107S.A2:

```
)TY FACT0107S.A2
```

This file will tell the operator which switch to use when restarting the job. Then the operator will make sure that the searchlist is set to find FACTSDB; then

```
)QBJ FACT0107/s  where s = the restart switch
```

Program/File Information

| DDS0713.R1 | Data Dictionary System
System Subsystem Report
FACTS DATA BASE | | 9/05/88
Pg　15 |

FACTSDB.LOAD　(Job/CLI)　　　　　　　　　　　　　Status: P　Version:01
Operations Doc:

ST	MODULE	I/O	FILE NAME	FILE DESCRIPTION	DEV	RET	PRINTER
1	FACT0103	I	FACT0101S.W1	ADS/FACTS file	D	Eoj	
	Sort	O	FACT0102S.W1	FACTS file w/o F53 records	D	1 day	
		O	FACT0102S.W2	F53 activity records	D	1 day	
	Sort	I	FACT0102S.W2	F53 activity records	D		
		O	FACT0102S.W3	Sorted activity records	D	1 day	
	Merge	I	FACT0102S.W1	Sorted CDS/FACTS records	D	1 day	
		I	FACT0102S.W3	Sorted activity records	D		
		O	FACT0103S.W1	Merged FACTS records	D		
2	FACT0105	I	FACT0103S.W1	Merged FACTS records	D	1 day	
		O	FACT0105S.W1	Location code file	D	1 day	
		O	FACT0105S.W2	Call record file	D	1 day	
		O	FACT0105S.W3	Part used file	D	1 day	
		O	FACT0105S.W4	Model number file	D	1 day	
		O	FACT0105S.W5	Contract number file	D	1 day	
		O	FACT0105S.W6	Activity record	D	1 day	
		O	FACT0105S.W8	Employee record	D	1 day	
		O	FACT0105S.W9	Employee time record	D	1 day	
		O	FACT0105S.W10	Equipment record	D	1 day	
		O	FACT0105S.W12	Expense record	D	1 day	
		O	FACT0105S.A1	Status report	D	1 day	short 6
3	FACT0106	I	FACT0105S.W1	Location code file	D	1 day	
		O	FACT0106S.W1	Location code file	D	1 day	
	Sort	I	FACT0105S.W2	Call record file	D	1 day	
		O	FACT0106S.W2	Call record file	D	1 day	
	Sort	I	FACT0105S.W3	Part used file	D	1 day	
		O	FACT0106S.W3	Part used file	D	1 day	
	Sort	I	FACT0105S.W4	Model number file	D	1 day	
		O	FACT0106S.W4	Model number file	D	1 day	
	Sort	I	FACT0105S.W5	Contract number file	D	1 day	
		O	FACT0106S.W5	Contract number file	D	1 day	
	Sort	I	FACT0105S.W6	Activity record	D	1 day	
		O	FACT0106S.W6	Activity record	D	1 day	
	Sort	I	FACT0105S.W8	Employee record	D	1 day	
		O	FACT0106S.W8	Employee record	D	1 day	
	Sort	I	FACT0105S.W9	Employee time record	D	1 day	
		O	FACT0106S.W9	Employee time record	D	1 day	
	Sort	I	FACT0105S.W10	Equipment record	D	1 day	
		O	FACT0106S.W10	Equipment record	D	1 day	
	Sort	I	FACT0105S.W12	Expense record	D	1 day	
		O	FACT0106S.W12	Expense record	D	1 day	
4	FACT0107	I	FACT0106S.W1	Location code file	D	1 day	
		I	FACT0106S.W2	Call record file	D	1 day	
		I	FACT0106S.W3	Part used file	D	1 day	
		I	FACT0106S.W4	Model number file	D	1 day	
		I	FACT0106S.W5	Contract number file	D	1 day	
		I	FACT0106S.W6	Activity record	D	1 day	
		I	FACT0106S.W8	Employee record	D	1 day	
		I	FACT0106S.W9	Employee time record	D	1 day	
		I	FACT0106S.W10	Equipment record	D	1 day	
		I	FACT0106S.W12	Expense record	D	1 day	
		I-O	FACTSDB　　FACTS data base		D	perm	
		O	FACT0107S.A1	Stat report	D		short 6

DDS0713.R1   Data Dictionary System   9/05/88
                   System Subsystem Report   Pg   16
                       FACTS DATA BASE

FACTSDB.LOAD   (Job/CLI)   Status: P   Version:01

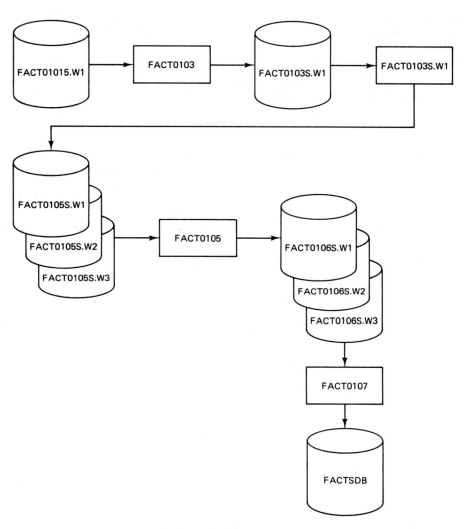

FACTSDB.LOAD job flow diagram.

FACT0103   (Program)   Status: P   Version:01

Author: J. Nelson   Maintenance Resp: J. Nelson
Language: SORT   Code-set:

Description: This is a sort procedure that consists of four steps: (1) replace the nulls in the
FACT0101S.W1 file with spaces; (2) separate the F53 activity records into a separate file called
FACT0102S.W2; (3) sort the outputs; and (4) merge the sorted records into file FACT0103S.W1.

Operations Doc:

ST	MODULE	I/O	FILE NAME	FILE DESCRIPTION	DEV	RET	FORMAT
1	FACT0103	I	FACT0101S.W1	CDS/FACTS file	D	Eoj	
	Sort	O	FACT0102S.W1	FACTS file w/o F53 records	D	1 d	
		O	FACT0102S.W2	F53 activity records	D	1 d	
	Sort	I	FACT0102S.W2	F53 activity records	D		
		O	FACT0102S.W3	Sorted activity records	D	1 d	
	Merge	I	FACT0102S.W1	Sorted CDS/FACTS records	D	1 d	
		I	FACT0102S.W3	Sorted activity records	D		
		O	FACT0103S.W1	Merged FACTS records	D		

DDS0713.R1

Data Dictionary System
System Subsystem Report
FACTS DATA BASE

9/05/88
Pg   18

FACT0101S.W1   (File)   Status: P   Version:01

FACT0101S.W1 is the file in which dispatch system records have been stored from the FACT0102 program.

Short Desc: AOS FACTS file
Retention: EOJ
Organization: Sequential
Record Size: 309 bytes max.

DDS0713.R1   Data Dictionary System   9/05/88
                               System Subsystem Report   Pg   19
                                   FACTS DATA BASE

FACT0102S.W2   (File)   Status: P   Version:01

FACT0102S.W2 is a sorted file from FACT0101S.W1, but without the F53 activity records.

Short Desc: FACTS file w/o F53 records
Retention: EOJ
Organization: Sequential
Record Size: 309 bytes max.

FACT0102S.W3   (File)   Status: P   Version:01

FACT0102S.W3 is the file that contains the sorted activity records.

Short Desc: Sorted activity records
Retention: 1 day
Organization: Sequential
Record Size: 309 bytes max.

FACT0103S.W1   (File)   Status: P   Version:01

FACT0103S.W1 is the result of merging the FACT0102S.W2 and FACT0102S.W3 files.

Short Desc: Merged FACTS records
Retention: 1 day
Organization: Sequential
Record Size: 309 bytes max.

DDS0713.R1

Data Dictionary System
System Subsystem Report
FACTS DATA BASE

9/05/88

Pg   22

FACT0105   (Program)   Status: P   Version:01

Author: J. Nelson   Maintenance Resp: J. Nelson
Language: COBOL   Code set: ASCII

Description: This is a program that will use the file FACT0103S.W1 as input and create files with record formats similar to the records in the FACTS data base. There will be separate files for location codes, calls, parts used, model number, contract number, activity, employee, employee time, equipment, expense, and status.

Operations Doc:

ST	MODULE	I/O	FILE NAME	FILE DESCRIPTION	DEV	RET	FORMAT
2	FACT0105	I	FACT0103S.W1	Sorted CDS/FACTS tape	D	1 day	
		O	FACT0105S.W1	Location code file	D	1 day	
		O	FACT0105S.W2	Call record file	D	1 day	
		O	FACT0105S.W3	Part used file	D	1 day	
		O	FACT0105S.W4	Model number file	D	1 day	
		O	FACT0105S.W5	Contract number file	D	1 day	
		O	FACT0105S.W6	Activity record	D	1 day	
		O	FACT0105S.W8	Employee record	D	1 day	
		O	FACT0105S.W9	Eployee time record	D	1 day	
		O	FACT0105S.W10	Equipment record	D	1 day	
		O	FACT0105S.W12	Expense record	D	1 day	
		O	FACT0105S.A1	Status report	D		short6

FACT0103S.W1   (File)   Status: P   Version:01

FACT0103S.W1 is the result of merging the FACT0102S.W2 and FACT0102S.W3 files.

Short Desc: Merged FACTS records
Retention: 1 day
Organization: Sequential
Record Size: 309 bytes max.

DDS0713.R1
Data Dictionary System
System Subsystem Report
FACTS DATA BASE
9/05/88
Pg   24

FACT0105S.W1   (File)   Status: P   Version:01

FACT0105S.W1 is the file that contains location-code-related information.

Short Desc: Location code file
Retention: 1 day
Organization: Sequential
Record Size: 8 bytes
Copybook:

```
            SELECT FACT0105S-W1
                    ASSIGN TO FACT0105S-W1-FILE-NAME
                    ORGANIZATION IS SEQUENTIAL
                    ACCESS IS SEQUENTIAL
                    FILE STATUS IS WS-FACT0105S-W1-COB-STAT.

            FD FACT0105S-W1
                    RECORD CONTAINS 8 CHARACTERS
                    DATA RECORD IS R040-ARBO-REC.

            01   R040-ARBO-REC.
                 05 S040-LCTN-CD                          PIC X(8).
```

FACT0105S.W2   (File)   Status: P   Version:01

FACT0105S.W2 is the file that contains call-related information.

Short Desc: Call record file
Retention: 1 day
Organization: Sequential
Record Size: 104 bytes
Copybook:

```
            SELECT FACT0105S-W2
                    ASSIGN TO FACT0105S-W2-FILE-NAME
                    ORGANIZATION IS SEQUENTIAL
                    ACCESS IS SEQUENTIAL
                    FILE STATUS IS WS-FACT0105S-W2-COB-STAT.


            FD FACT0105S-W2
                    RECORD CONTAINS 104 CHARACTERS
                    DATA RECORD IS R041-CALL-REC.

      01    R041-CALL-REC.
            05 S041-CALL-NO                        PIC X(7).
            05 S041-CALL-RECD-DT                   PIC 9(6).
            05 S041-CALL-RECD-TIME                 PIC 9(6).
            05 S041-UPDT-DT                        PIC 9(6).
            05 S041-LCTN-CD                        PIC X(8).
            05 S041-ARRIVAL-DT                     PIC 9(6).
            05 S041-ARRIVAL-TIME                   PIC 9(6).
            05 S041-CALL-CLOSE-DT                  PIC 9(6).
            05 S041-CALL-CLOSE-TIME                PIC 9(6).
            05 S041-CIA-CD                         PIC X(1).
            05 S041-STOP-TIME                      PIC 9(6).
            05 S041-TOT-SVC-HRS                    PIC 9(3)V9.
            05 S041-CNTRCT-FLAG                    PIC X.
            05 S041-ERROR-FLAG                     PIC X(1).
            05 S041-ERROR-FLAG-DT                  PIC 9(6).
            05 S041-REVIEW-FLAG                    PIC X(1).
            05 S041-REVIEW-FLAG-DT                 PIC 9(6).
            05 S041-EDIT-FLAG                      PIC X.
            05 S041-EDIT-FLAG-DT                   PIC 9(6).
            05 S041-BILL-FLAG                      PIC X(1).
            05 S041-BILL-FLAG-DT                   PIC 9(6).
            05 S041-CUST-NO                        PIC X(7).
```

DDS0713.R1

Data Dictionary System
System Subsystem Report
FACTS DATA BASE

9/05/88
Pg   26

FACT0105S.W3   (File)   Status: P   Version:01

FACT0105S.W3 is the file that contains the parts used information.

Short Desc: Part used file
Retention: 1 day
Organization: Sequential
Record Size: 116 bytes
Copybook:

```
              SELECT FACT0105S-W3
                      ASSIGN TO FACT0105S-W3-FILE-NAME
                      ORGANIZATION IS SEQUENTIAL
                      ACCESS IS SEQUENTIAL
                      FILE STATUS IS WS-FACT0105S-W3-COB-STAT.


              FD FACT0105S-W3
                      RECORD CONTAINS 116 CHARACTERS
                      DATA RECORD IS R042-PART-USED.

        01    R042-PART-USED.
              05 S042-LCTN-CD                      PIC X(8).
              05 S042-CALL-NO                      PIC X(7).
              05 S042-ACT-REC-NO                   PIC 9(3).
              05 S042-FRU-NO                       PIC X(10).
              05 S042-FRU-REV-NO                   PIC 9(2).
              05 S042-FRU-SERIAL-NO                PIC X(10).
              05 S042-SYMPTOM-FIX                  PIC X(4).
              05 S042-HRS-WRKD-FRU                 PIC 9(2)V9(1).
              05 S042-HRS-FRU-BILLED               PIC 9(2)V9(1).
              05 S042-PART-NO                      PIC X(10).
              05 S042-PART-REV-NO                  PIC 9(2).
              05 S042-PART-SERIAL-NO               PIC X(15).
              05 S042-ESP-PARTS-CD                 PIC 9(1).
              05 S042-ESP-PARTS-BILLED             PIC 9(1).
              05 S042-QTY-PART-USED                PIC 9(3).
              05 S042-QTY-PART-BILLED              PIC 9(3).
              05 S042-PART-SHIP-DT                 PIC 9(6).
              05 S042-HRS-WRKD-PART                PIC 9(2)V9.
              05 S042-SELL-PRICE                   PIC 9(11).
              05 S042-COST-PRICE                   PIC 9(11).
```

FACT0105S.W4   (File)   Status: P   Version:01

FACT0105S.W4 is the file that contains the model-number-related information.

Short Desc: Model number file
Retention: 1 day
Organization: Sequential
Record Size: 10 bytes
Copybook:

```
            SELECT FACT0105S-W4
                    ASSIGN TO FACT0105S-W4-FILE-NAME
                    ORGANIZATION IS SEQUENTIAL
                    ACCESS IS SEQUENTIAL
                    FILE STATUS IS WS-FACT0105S-W4-COB-STAT.


            FD FACT0105S-W4
                    RECORD CONTAINS 10 CHARACTERS
                    DATA RECORD IS R043-MODEL-REC.

            01    R043-MODEL-REC.
                  05 S043-MODEL-NO                              PIC X(10).
```

DDS0713.R1

Data Dictionary System
System Subsystem Report
FACTS DATA BASE

9/05/88
Pg   28

FACT0105S.W5   (File)   Status: P   Version:01

FACT0105S.W5 is the file that contains contract-number-related information.

Short Desc: Contract number file
Retention: 1 day
Organization: Sequential
Record Size: 16 bytes
Copybook:

```
SELECT FACT0105S-W5
        ASSIGN TO FACT0105S-W5-FILE-NAME
        ORGANIZATION IS SEQUENTIAL
        ACCESS IS SEQUENTIAL
        FILE STATUS IS WS-FACT0105S-W5-COB-STAT.


FD FACT0105S-W5
        RECORD CONTAINS 16 CHARACTERS
        DATA RECORD IS R044-CONTRACT-REC.

01   R044-CONTRACT-REC.
     05 S044-CONTRACT-NO                       PIC X(8).
     05 S044-LCTN-CD                           PIC X(8).
```

FACT0105S.W6   (File)   Status: P   Version:01

FACT0105S.W6 is the file that contains the activity records.

Short Desc: Activity record
Retention: 1 day
Organization: Sequential
Record Size: 198 bytes
Copybook:

```
            SELECT FACT0105S-W6
                    ASSIGN TO FACT0105S-W6-FILE-NAME
                    ORGANIZATION IS SEQUENTIAL
                    ACCESS IS SEQUENTIAL
                    FILE STATUS IS WS-FACT0105S-W6-COB-STAT.


            FD FACT0105S-W6
                    RECORD CONTAINS 198 CHARACTERS
                    DATA RECORD IS R045-ACTIVITY-REC.


        01    R045-ACTIVITY-REC.
                05 S045-FACT-SVC-CD                          PIC X(3).
                05 S045-SVC-DT                               PIC 9(6).
                05 S045-SVC-TIME                             PIC 9(6).
                05 S045-ACT-REC-NO                           PIC 9(3).
                05 S045-STOP-TIME                            PIC 9(6).
                05 S045-CALL-NO                              PIC X(7).
                05 S045-CONTRACT-NO                          PIC X(8).
                05 S045-EMP-BADGE-NO                         PIC 9(6).
                05 S045-EMP-OFFICE-NO                        PIC X(8).
                05 S045-EMP-TERR-NO                          PIC 9(3).
                05 S045-LCTN-CD                              PIC X(8).
                05 S045-ACCT-TERR-NO                         PIC 9(3).
                05 S045-MODEL-NO                             PIC X(10).
                05 S045-MODEL-SERIAL-NO                      PIC X(15).
                05 S045-UPGRADE-MODEL-NO                     PIC X(6).
                05 S045-SYMPTOM-FIX-CD                       PIC X(4).
                05 S045-SALES-ORDER-NO                       PIC X(20).
                05 S045-CUST-PO-NO                           PIC X(20).
                05 S045-ISC-NO                               PIC X(20).
                05 S045-CUST-STATUS                          PIC X(1).
                05 S045-SCHDL-ID                             PIC X(1).
                05 S045-REG-HRS                              PIC 9(3)V9(1).
                05 S045-REG-HRS-BILLED                       PIC 9(3)V9(1).
                05 S045-PRM-HRS                              PIC 9(3)V9(1).
                05 S045-PRM-HRS-BILLED                       PIC 9(3)V9(1).
                05 S045-PARTS-RUN                            PIC 9(3)V9(1).
                05 S045-PARTS-RUN-BILLED                     PIC 9(3)V9(1).
                05 S045-FCO-NO                               PIC X(10).
```

DDS0713.R1

Data Dictionary System
System Subsystem Report
FACTS DATA BASE

9/05/88
Pg   30

FACT0105S.W8   (File)   Status: P   Version:01

FACT0105S.W8 is the file that contains the employee information.

Short Desc: Employee record
Retention: 1 day
Organization: Sequential
Record Size: 6 bytes
Copybook:

```
        SELECT FACT0105S-W8
                ASSIGN TO FACT0105S-W8-FILE-NAME
                ORGANIZATION IS SEQUENTIAL
                ACCESS IS SEQUENTIAL
                FILE STATUS IS WS-FACT0105S-W8-COB-STAT.


        FD FACT0105S-W8
                RECORD CONTAINS 6 CHARACTERS
                DATA RECORD IS R047-EMP-REC.

    01   R047-EMP-REC.
         05 S047-EMP-BADGE-NO                      PIC 9(6).
```

FACT0105S.W9   (File)   Status: P   Version:01

FACT0105S.W9 is the file that contains the employee-time-spent information.

Short Desc: Employee time record
Retention: 1 day
Organization: Sequential
Record Size: 81 bytes
Copybook:

```
                SELECT FACT0105S-W9
                        ASSIGN TO FACT0105S-W9-FILE-NAME
                        ORGANIZATION IS SEQUENTIAL
                        ACCESS IS SEQUENTIAL
                        FILE STATUS IS WS-FACT0105S-W9-COB-STAT.


                FD FACT0105S-W9
                        RECORD CONTAINS 81 CHARACTERS
                        DATA RECORD IS R048-TIME-REC.

        01   R048-TIME-REC.
                05 S048-EMP-BADGE-NO                        PIC 9(6).
                05 S048-FISCAL-DATE.
                        10 S048-FISCAL-YEAR                 PIC X(2).
                        10 S048-FISCAL-PERIOD-OF-YEAR       PIC X(2).
                        10 S048-FISCAL-WEEK-OF-PERIOD       PIC 9.
                05 S048-UNAVAILABLE-DT       OCCURS 7 TIMES PIC 9(6).
                05 S048-UNAVAILABLE-CD       OCCURS 7 TIMES PIC X(1).
                05 S048-UNAVAILABLE-HRS      OCCURS 7 TIMES PIC 99V9.
```

DDS0713.R1

Data Dictionary System
System Subsystem Report
FACTS DATA BASE

9/05/88
Pg   32

FACT0105S.W10   (File)   Status: P   Version:01

FACT0105S.W10 is the file that contains customer-site-equipment information.

Short Desc: Equipment record
Retention: 1 day
Organization: Sequential
Record Size: 102 bytes
Copybook:

```
        SELECT FACT0105S-W10
                ASSIGN TO FACT0105S-W10-FILE-NAME
                ORGANIZATION IS SEQUENTIAL
                ACCESS IS SEQUENTIAL
                FILE STATUS IS WS-FACT0105S-W10-COB-STAT.

        FD FACT0105S-W10
                RECORD CONTAINS 102 CHARACTERS
                DATA RECORD IS R198-EQPMT-REC.

01      R198-EQPMT-REC.
        05 S198-LCTN-CD                         PIC X(8).
        05 S198-CALL-NO                         PIC X(7).
        05 S198-ACT-REC-NO                      PIC 9(3).
        05 S198-TYPE                            PIC X(2).
        05 S198-LINE-NO                         PIC X(2).
        05 S198-DATA                            PIC X(80).
```

FACT0105S.W12   (File)   Status: P   Version:01

FACT0105S.W12 is the file that contains the employee-expenses information.

Short Desc: Expense record
Retention: 1 day
Organization: Sequential
Record Size: 693 bytes
Copybook:

```
SELECT FACT0105S-W12
        ASSIGN TO FACT0105S-W12-FILE-NAME
        ORGANIZATION IS SEQUENTIAL
        ACCESS IS SEQUENTIAL
        FILE STATUS IS WS-FACT0105S-W12-COB-STAT.


FD FACT0105S-W12
        RECORD CONTAINS 693 CHARACTERS
        DATA RECORD IS R199-EXPENSE-REC.


01   R199-EXPENSE-REC.
     05 S199-CALL-NO                            PIC X(7).
     05 S199-EMP-BADGE-NO                       PIC 9(6).
     05 S199-EXPENSE-GRP OCCURS 20 TIMES.
        10 S199-BILL-CD                          PIC X(1).
        10 S199-SVC-DT                           PIC 9(6).
        10 S199-SVC-TIME.
           15 S199-SVC-HHMM                      PIC 9(4).
           15 S199-SVC-SS                        PIC 9(2).
        10 S199-TRVL-TO-HRS                      PIC 99V9.
        10 S199-TRVL-FROM-HRS                    PIC 99V9.
        10 S199-DISTANCE                         PIC 9(3)V9.
        10 S199-EXPENSES                         PIC 9(11).
```

FACT0105S.A1   (File)   Status: P   Version:01

FACT0105S.A1 is the audit trail report file from program FACT0105.

Short Desc: Audit trail report
Retention: 1 day
Organization: Sequential
Record Size: 325 bytes
Copybook:

```
            SELECT FACT0105S-A1
                      ASSIGN TO FACT0105S-A1-FILE-NAME
                      ORGANIZATION IS SEQUENTIAL
                      ACCESS IS SEQUENTIAL
                      FILE STATUS IS WS-FACT0105S-A1-COB-STAT.


            FD FACT0105S-A1
                      RECORD CONTAINS 325 CHARACTERS
                      DATA RECORD IS R200-AUDIT-REC.

      01    R200-AUDIT-REC.
            05 S200-PROGRAM                          PIC X(30).
            05 S200-FUNCTION                          PIC X(30).
            05 S200-DATE                              PIC 9(6).
            05 S200-TIME                              PIC 9(6).
            05 S200-CALL-NO                           PIC X(7).
            05 S200-EMP-BADGE-NO                      PIC 9(6).
            05 S200-AUDIT-INFO                        OCCURS 3 TIMES.
            10 S200-AUDIT-CD                          PIC 9(2).
            10 S200-AUDIT-DATA                        PIC X(78).
```

FACT0106   (Program)   Status: P   Version:01

Author: J. Nelson   Maintenance Resp: J. Nelson
Language: Sort   Code set:

Description: This is a series of sorts of the files created in program FACT0105 so that the records in these files will be in the correct order for loading into the FACTS data base.

Operations Doc:

ST	MODULE	I/O	FILE NAME	FILE DESCRIPTION	DEV	RET	FORMAT
3	FACT0106	I	FACT0105S.W1	Location code file	D	1 day	
		O	FACT0106S.W1	Location code file	D	1 day	
	sort	I	FACT0105S.W2	Call record file	D	1 day	
		O	FACT0106S.W2	Call record file	D	1 day	
	sort	I	FACT0105S.W3	Part used file	D	1 day	
		O	FACT0106S.W3	Part used file	D	1 day	
	sort	I	FACT0105S.W4	Model number file	D	1 day	
		O	FACT0106S.W4	Model number file	D	1 day	
	sort	I	FACT0105S.W5	Contract number file	D	1 day	
		O	FACT0106S.W5	Contract number file	D	1 day	
	sort	I	FACT0105S.W6	Activity record	D	1 day	
		O	FACT0106S.W6	Activity record	D	1 day	
		I	FACT0105S.W8	Employee record	D	1 day	
		O	FACT0106S.W8	Employee record	D	1 day	
	sort	I	FACT0105S.W9	Employee time record	D	1 day	
		O	FACT0106S.W9	Employee time record	D	1 day	
	sort	I	FACT0105S.W10	Equipment record	D	1 day	
		O	FACT0106S.W10	Equipment record	D	1 day	
	sort	I	FACT0105S.W12	Expense record	D	1 day	
		O	FACT0106S.W12	Expense record	D	1 day	

DDS0713.R1

Data Dictionary System
System Subsystem Report
FACTS DATA BASE

9/05/88

Pg   56

FACT0107   (Program)   Status: P   Version:01

Author: J. Nelson   Maintenance Resp: J. Nelson
Language: COBOL   Code set: ASCII

Description: This is a program that will read in the sorted files from FACT0106 and update the FACTS
data base. It will be loading location, models, and contract numbers that are missing on the data base.
The employee, employee time, and call files are loaded in that sequence next. The expenses and activity
files are loaded last. Each file is treated as a DBMS transaction; if there is program abort, the program
can be restarted at the beginning of whichever input file was being processed.

Switches: In case of program abort, the program can be restarted by using one of the following switches:

A:	Restart with models file	(FACT0106S.W4)
B:	Restart with contract numbers file	(FACT0106S.W5)
C:	Restart with employee numbers file	(FACT0106S.W8)
D:	Restart with employee time file	(FACT0106S.W9)
E:	Restart with call file	(FACT0106S.W2)
F:	Restart with employee expense file	(FACT0106S.W12)
H:	Restart with activity file	(FACT0106S.W10)

Operations Doc:

ST	MODULE	I/O	FILE NAME	FILE DESCRIPTION	DEV	RET	FORMAT
4	FACT0107	I	FACT0106S.W1	Location code file	D	1 day	
		I	FACT0106S.W2	Call record file	D	1 day	
		I	FACT0106S.W3	Part used file	D	1 day	
		I	FACT0106S.W4	Model number file	D	1 day	
		I	FACT0106S.W5	Contract number file	D	1 day	
		I	FACT0106S.W6	Activity record	D	1 day	
		I	FACT0106S.W8	Employee record	D	1 day	
		I	FACT0106S.W9	Employee time record	D	1 day	
		I	FACT0106S.W10	Equipment record	D	1 day	
		I	FACT0106S.W12	Expense record	D	1 day	
		I-O	FACTSDB FACTS database		D	perm	
		O	FACT0107S.A1	Stat report	D		short 6

DDS0713.R1   Data Dictionary System   9/05/88
                                   System Subsystem Report   Pg   69
                                      FACTS DATA BASE

FACT02   (Subsystem)   Status: P   Version:01

The FACT02 subsystem within the FACTS system is the on-line query (based on call number) and print function. It consists of a query program FACT0201 and a print program FACT0202.

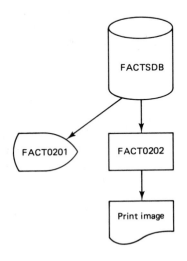

FACT02 subsystem diagram.

DDS0713.R1   Data Dictionary System   9/05/88
System Subsystem Report   Pg   70
FACTS DATA BASE

FACT0201   (Program)   Status: P   Version:01

Author: J. Nelson   Maintenance Resp: J. Nelson
Language: COBOL   Code set: ASCII

Description: This is the FACTS data base query program. It is an interactive program.

A screen with header information is displayed initially, and the user enters the call number that is to be queried. All information pertaining to this call will be displayed. The user has the option to view more data about this call, start over with the current call, print the current call, or look at another call. If the user wished to print the call, header information that will appear on the report header will have to be entered. This program will batch program FACT0109, which will actually print the call.

Files used: FACTSDB
             FACTSxxyyyyyy.W1 - print call job file
             FACTSxxyyyyyy.A1 - audit file
                where xx = terminal number
                   yyyyyy = time of job

```
FACT0201                    FACTS Data Base System            Date:  8/25/87
                                Call View Screen

Call No.:  M012548     Arrival Date:  08/08/87      Call Close Date:  08/08/87

Customer No.:  001245     Total Service Hours:  001.3

ST No.:  018943   Travel to:  00.5   From:  00.5   Mileage:  020   Expenses:  000.00

              Service Date:  08/08/87        Stop Time:  00:00

Contract No.:  A026780         Account No.:  46781244           ISC No.:

   PO No.:                       SO No.:                   Cust. Status:  1

M/S:  8053  0045732       SVC:  CO       Part Run:  000.0      Stop:  10:30
```

FACTS call view screen.

DDS0713.R1	Data Dictionary System	9/05/88
	System Subsystem Report	Pg 71
	FACTS DATA BASE	

FACT0202   (Program)   Status: P   Version:01

Author: J. Nelson   Maintenance Resp: J. Nelson
Language: COBOL   Code set: ASCII

Description: This is program that prints all the details pertaining to the call number that has been requested by the user from the interactive screen program FACT0108. If the call can be found, the expense information is totaled, and for each activity the parts-used information is obtained and formatted
for the printer. If the call does not exist on the data base, the program aborts and an abort message is
logged on FACTSDBLOGS.

Switches: CALL—the number of the call that is requested
                    QUEUE—output file name FACTSxxyyyyyy.R1

Outputs: FACTSxxyyyyyy.R1—image of the call requested
                    where xx = terminal number
                       yyyyyy = time of job
                    FACTSDBLOGS—error log report for FACTS data base

chapter 11

Data Dictionary Training

NEED FOR TRAINING

The variety of users of the data dictionary make training a challenge; the training program must be able to adapt to differing technical and business orientations of the users and also meet the individual user's needs. The training goal is for the end user to understand and accept new technology.

Over time the scope of the dictionary will continue to expand. As new uses of the dictionary are developed, a training program would be necessary to bring the existing users up to an acceptable level of proficiency. In some cases the vendor of the dictionary system would have made functional improvements to the product which have to be brought to the attention of the users. In most MIS installations, there is a steady turnover of staff for various reasons, and it is imperative that new hires be given training in dictionary concepts and procedures, since they will interact with the dictionary significantly over the course of their day-to-day activities.

DICTIONARY USERS

It is necessary to provide training for a wide variety of users in the workings of the data dictionary and the procedures surrounding its use. This training should be directed to the potential user and the ways in which that user would view, use, and update information in the Dictionary. Care must be taken to ensure that people understand that the dictionary is a multiple-user system, and the impact of using the system for various purposes, such as report generation during prime time, will have an impact on other users. There are three general groups of dictionary users. Because each group uses the dictionary in a different way, training for each group must be customized to meet its needs.

1. *Dictionary administrators:* personnel who are responsible for designing, maintaining, and customizing the content of dictionary data bases. The dictionary

administrator normally supports the data administration and the data base administration activities in an installation. In many cases, the data administration and data base administration staff have complementary roles with respect to the dictionary and may have an equal role and responsibility in updating the dictionary with the most accurate information.

2. *Active users:* the staff who use the dictionary as a tool while maintaining and developing application programs and their related data bases. These users enter data into the dictionary relating to systems, subsystems, jobs, programs, and so on, use the language structures generated out of the dictionary, and extract other data in the form of reports. In cases where the operations department uses the dictionary, it may be necessary to provide them with specific screens to use to view their data, or use a facility to feed operational data into the dictionary.

3. *General users:* personnel who refer to reports prepared by the data processing installation, who may be occasional data dictionary users. These users could be end users as well as managers and others who are trying to resolve the meaning of a certain term. Often these users only care to know what they need to know to get their job done and are less willing to invest long study hours. They want training that relates to their experience. Therefore, the training should grab their attention quickly and keep it.

PROJECT-ORIENTED TRAINING

Special consideration should be given to the training of individuals or groups that form a critical part of the implementation process. This is especially important for those user departments that are tasked with definitions of data items and reports. To start with, a handout covering the objectives of the project and the role of the group of persons being trained should be developed with a clear explanation of what is expected, and the assignments.

If the dictionary training is too general and nondirectional, it may lose its impact over time. Therefore, it is preferable to have specific objectives for each group being trained, so that results can be measured. Training end users who have an interest in accessing and manipulating data is far easier if an example of how they would use the dictionary in achieving their objectives and what they would be expected to do are clearly identified. In the case of the dictionary administrator, it may be preferable to send the person to any one of a number of generic courses on data dictionary that are offered by vendors.

One efficient way to begin end-user training is to categorize the end users by organizational or skill level. For purposes of this training program, let's say that it is directed toward three classes: managers, analysts, and administrative personnel. Managerial end users do not want to appear computer illiterate, and therefore a personalized training approach is recommended. In addition, more time will be required because they may be unfamiliar with keyboards. Analysts, on the other hand, are used to the computer and would easily adapt to the new technology, and look forward to the use of new tools and techniques. Administrative personnel are primarily interested in developing skills for a specific application of the dictionary. During the training session, the dictionary administrator should be identified as a resource person to users if they have any questions or problems while using the system.

DOCUMENTATION

Effective documentation pays off with multiple benefits for the project manager. It enables the average employee to perform complex computer tasks by breaking them down into simple step-by-step procedures. Documentation also makes the training process go easier and at a faster pace because the documentation aids the training process by setting down the task expectations. By codifying the procedures, documentation makes the DD project manager's job easier, thus saving time and raising employee satisfaction. The training program must be in synchronization with the procedural documentation on the dictionary and its usage within the organization. The documentation can be broken up into several manuals:

- *Implementation plan.* This document provides the description of the objectives of the dictionary as visualized by the DD project manager, and also contains the current and planned DD applications. This document should be updated on a periodic basis to reflect changing priorities as well as status reports. This document can be used as an informational tool for the senior managers of the organization, to keep them appraised of the progress on implementing the dictionary.
- *Dictionary concepts overview.* This is a brief document that gives an executive-level summary of what a dictionary is, and how it is proposed to be used in the organization, and its current and planned usage.
- *Dictionary user's manual.* This is the most important document because it will govern the day-to-day working relationships between the user and the dictionary staff and/or dictionary. It will document the procedures that have to be followed and the rules for proper update and maintenance of the data in the dictionary.

Note that the DD administrator should keep track of who has copies of the manuals so that users will receive updated versions. An additional aspect that should be examined is the use of the computer not only for the storage of the manuals (via a word processor) but also for distributing this information on the computer system.

ORGANIZATION OF DICTIONARY MANUAL

The dictionary user's manual should have a table of contents that reflects the operating philosophy of the data dictionary administrator. The following list of topics is suggested as a guideline for a typical user's manual.

- *Introduction:* what the dictionary can do for the user; basic concepts
- *Entity terminology:* entity types that are in the dictionary and their relationships; how data are stored in the dictionary; role of data standards; importance of concise nonambiguous textual descriptions and how to develop these; how attribute classes are developed and their specification in the dictionary
- *Query function:* the query command and how to use it to browse through the dictionary; different ways to access data with examples of different access techniques and the use of cross-references to traverse the superior and subordinate entities
- *Naming conventions:* explanation of the reason for having naming conventions; naming conventions that are in use in the installation with examples; application development and maintenance standards
- *Access controls:* explanation of the security features in the dictionary as well as the different types of access granted to users
- *Store, modify, and delete:* procedures for storing, modifying, and deleting the data in the dictionary; includes cross-references, attributes, and access keys
- *Report generator:* description of the features of the report generator and procedures for its use
- *Data dictionary administrator:* outline of the role and functions of the data dictionary administrator; procedures that need to be enforced by the DDA for

gathering and inputting data; brief description of the specific services provided by the DDA

- *End-user computing usage of the dictionary:* capabilities of the end users to use hardware and software in conjunction with the dictionary to access and manipulate data; how to use the dictionary to obtain information about data availability and access requirements
- *Systems development:* definition, design, and implementation phases of developing new systems and the relationship to the dictionary; the use of the dictionary as a reference for systems maintenance; roles and responsibilities; the ability to produce source code for the program development phase; documentation capability of the dictionary
- *Operations:* use of the dictionary as a reference for restart and recovery steps in case of production failure
- *Appendix:* forms to be used for the storage, modification, and deletion of data in the dictionary
- *Glossary:* terms relevant to the dictionary

COMPUTER ASSISTED INSTRUCTION (CAI)

The use of computer assisted instruction (CAI) techniques as a method of delivering training has spread rapidly in recent years. The dictionary concepts and training program described earlier can be delivered via CAI. A brief discussion of the advantages of CAI over conventional training methods is presented below.

CAI is a technique whereby the student interacts with a lesson that is stored in the computer. The basic system consists of a display of information that may consist of sentences, line drawings, graphs, or animations. The display is generally followed by a response from the student. The response could consist of a single keystroke (–HELP– or –CR– keys), or by typing a word, sentence, or mathematical expression, or even by making a geometrical construction. Lesson authors provide enough details about the possible student responses so that the computer system can maintain a dialogue with the student.

Advantages of CAI

The advantages of CAI stem from the fact that the lesson is available as long as the student has access to the computer, and the system can keep track of the student's interaction with the lesson and tailor the sequence of the lessons to the ability and needs of the student.

The CAI technique is especially suited to dissemination of consistent information about concepts and procedures to large groups of people with varying requirements. Because of the ability to tailor the course to different audiences, the students can quickly gain the knowledge they need for their specific job. The ability of the system to keep track of the student's progress gives the administrator the assurance that the course was completed. Tests and review sessions can be built into the course to ensure that certain minimal levels of understanding and competency are demonstrated.

Since the CAI system is computer-based, it follows that any application system can be simulated by CAI. Thus, a practical training program for learning an installed dictionary system can be based on CAI. As the system evolves, the CAI lesson can evolve simultaneously, thus giving the users of the system an easy way to upgrade their skill level.

In assisting with dictionary implementation, CAI can play a useful role in attaining the following objectives:

1. To convey the basic concepts and functions of the dictionary.
2. To communicate a uniform system development life cycle methodology (SDLC) and how the dictionary supports the different phases of the SDLC.
3. To provide different users of the dictionary, such as analysts, data base administrators, programmers and operators, the specific ways in which they would interact with the dictionary during the SDLC.
4. To provide a clear understanding of the entity model as the basis on which most dictionaries function.
5. To provide the capability to navigate through the entity structure utilizing store, modify, query, and report commands.
6. To disseminate the site-specific standards and procedures, such as naming conventions, security controls, and update procedures, that will be followed to ensure program and data control.
7. To explain and simulate the actual workings of the installed dictionary system.

TRAINING SESSION EXAMPLE

The following pages are illustrative of the topics covered in a training session. The session is oriented toward end users and is composed of two parts. The first part goes over the generic functions of the dictionary with specific reference to the functions of interest to the end user. The second half covers the way an end user would use the dictionary, with an example.

Introduction to the Data Dictionary

What Is It?

- A tool to document, organize, and control information about data items, files, systems, programs, and reports
- A resource, that is, an organized repository of information describing the source, use, and responsibility of information in the business.

The data dictionary resource is created as it is used as a tool.

Benefits

- Answers questions about what data are where and enables you to access the data from production files.
- Enhances communication through the use of standard conventions in MIS systems as well as end-user-developed applications.
- Identifies and enforces accountability for data integrity, leading to better data quality, orderly data sourcing, and flow.
- Provides documentation about systems, programs, files, and reports that can be accessed easily and quickly.

Generic Functions

- Querying based on different access keys, aliases.
- Load/store/modify entity occurrences (i.e., data items, files, reports, system).
- Report generation, providing tailored and ad hoc reports.
- COPY (INCLUDE) code generation.
- Run-time interface to compilers, operating systems, and other DBMS.

How Information Is Organized within DD. An entity is an object in the data processing environment that is described in the dictionary. Examples are

- Data item
- File/data base
- Report
- System, etc.

For each entity occurrence in DD, other descriptive data are also stored, such as

- Attributes
- Text
- Graphics
- Cross-references
- Keywords, aliases

Figures 11–1 through 11–14 illustrate the different kinds of information available in the dictionary.

Conventions

- There can only be one name for a ''thing'' that is described in the dictionary.
- This name is called the ''enterprise'' name; other names, such as aliases and keywords, can be used to access this ''thing.''
- MIS- or machine-recognizable names, such as COBOL names, and the rules in force for these must be used so that systems developed by different persons can talk to each other.

```
                          Data Dictionary                Date:  1/5/88


Information in this dictionary is stored under these categories:

                          1. Applications
                          2. Reports
                          3. Data items
                          4. Programs
                          5. Files/data bases


Enter a number, or Q to quit:  3
```

Figure 11–1 DD information menu screen.

```
                              Data Dictionary              Date:  1/5/88


Data item information can be obtained via different methods:

                              1. Name of the data item
                              2. Alias or alternative name
                              3. Keyword
                              4. Logical data category


Enter a number, or Q to quit:_4__

Enter name:_PART_____
```

Figure 11-2   Data item menu screen.

```
                              Data Dictionary              Date:  1/5/88

Entries that are available in the dictionary:

   1. ____PART NUMBER_____    12. ____PART REPAIR FLAG_____

   2. ____PART DESCRIPTION_____    13. ____PART REPAIR LOCATION_____

   3. ____PART REVISION NUMBER_____    14. ____PART REPLACED NUMBER_____

   4. ____PART SERIAL NUMBER_____    15. _____

   5. ____PART TYPE_____    16. _____

   6. ____PART TYPE FAMILY_____    17. _____

   7. ____PART SELL PRICE_____    18. _____

   8. ____PART SWAP PRICE_____    19. _____

   9. ____PART TOOL FLAG_____    20. _____

  10. ____PART SHIP DATE_____    21. _____

  11. ____PART PRODUCT CLASS_____    22. _____


There are more. Scroll to see more, or make your choice:

Press a number, or Q to quit:_1__

Enter name:_____
```

Figure 11-3   Data entries screen for PART.

```
                              Data Dictionary                    Date:  1/5/88


  Versions of the data item you chose are:

                    Data item                    Version        Status          Comment

  1.  BASE PART NUMBER
  2.  PART NUMBER
  3.  VENDOR PART NUMBER
  4.  PRIME PART NUMBER
  5.  FIELD REPLACEMENT UNIT NUMBER


  There are more. Scroll to see more, or make your choice:  2
```

Figure 11-4 Data element versions screen for PART NUMBER.

```
                              Data Dictionary                    Date:  1/5/88


  Data Item:      Part number

  Description:    The part number is a unique number assigned to a part by Engineering.
                  The first 3 digits represent the class of the part, and the last 6
                  digits represent the sequential number of that part within the class.
                  Vendor-produced parts are assigned a part number by Engineering. Each
                  part can have many revision numbers, which are carried in a separate
                  field called PART REVISION NUMBER.

  Other names for this data item:  PART-NO (COBOL); PART_NO (PL1); PART; NUMBER;
                                   VENDOR PART;


  Scroll to see more, Q to quit:_____
```

Figure 11-5 Data element description screen for PART NUMBER.

How to Get Access

- Identify the functions that you need to perform in order to do your job. Refer to Figures 11-15 through 11-24.
- Determine the entities to which you need access. Refer to entity model diagram on Figure 11-25.
- Determine if the access is going to be for query only or also for update.
- Request access profile from data dictionary administrator using the user permission request form shown in Figure 11-26.

```
                              Data Dictionary                    Date:   1/5/88


 Information about applications can be obtained via one of these methods:

                    1. Specify the name (if you happen to know it)
                    2. Ask for a list of names stored in the directory
                    3. Ask for a list of applications by type (i.e., service)


 Enter a number, or Q to quit:   2
```

Figure 11-10 DD applications information menu screen.

```
                              Data Dictionary                    Date:   1/5/88


 Select the type of applications that you want more information on:

                              1. Contract administration
                              2. Service call handling
                              3. Parts distribution
                              4. Spreadsheet
                              5. Data base
                              6. Account management

 There are more. Scroll to see more or make your choice.


 Enter a number, or Q to quit:    5
```

Figure 11-11 Application selection menu screen.

Procedure

1. Look up data items in the dictionary to ensure that they are available:
   a. Data may be available as an extract.
   b. Data may have to be specified item by item.
2. Create a grouping of the data items.
3. Specify selection criteria.

```
                                    Data Dictionary                    Date:  1/5/88


  Type of Application:  Data base

                                   1. PFS/file
                                   2. Condor III
                                   3. DBASE III


  Enter a number, or Q to quit: __3__
```

Figure 11-12   Application selection screen.

```
                                    Data Dictionary                    Date:  1/5/88


  Enter application name:_____

    Application              Revision           Status              Comment
    1. DBASE III               1.1                                  Supported
    2. DBASE II                4.5                                  Not supported
    3. DBASE PLUS              1.0                                  Future release


  Choose one: __1__
```

Figure 11-13   DBASE III version selection screen.

4. Get appropriate approvals, submit end-user computing request forms shown in Figure 11-27.
5. Get the data extract from the production data base; format of extract shown in Figure 11-28.
6. Use a report writer to process the data to get the desired report.

```
                            Data Dictionary              Date:  1/5/88


Application:  DBASE III

Description:  DBASE III is a data base management software package that consists of
              a relational data base management system and enables you to manipulate
              information in that data base. It has programming features for inter-
              active use and programmed applications development.

Vendor:       Ashton-Tate
              10150 West Jefferson Blvd.
              Culver City, CA 90230

              Phone:  (213) 204-5570


Scroll to see more, or Q to quit:  Q
```

Figure 11-14 DBASE III information screen.

```
                            Data Dictionary              Date:  8/25/88

                     Enter Username:

                     Enter Password:
```

Figure 11-15 Log-on screen.

Identify Extended Hour Coverage Contracts

This extract has all the header information from a contract image, format of sequential file shown in Figure 11-29.
Used sort/merge to pull out Canadian and internal contracts from the strip.
Used PRESENT to select contracts with coverage hours outside normal working hours.

```
                        Data Dictionary              Date:  8/25/88

                           Job Functions


                      1. Data planning
                      2. DBA
                      3. System development
                      4. Operations
                      5. Security administration
                      6. End-user computing
                      7. DD project implementation
                      8. DD administration


                      Select Job Function:_____
```

Figure 11-16 Job functions menu screen.

```
                        Data Dictionary              Date:  8/25/88

                           Job Function


                         Data Planning Menu
                      1. Query/browse
                      2. Report generator
                      3. Data convention standards
                      4. Logical data groups
                      5. Data model
                      6. System data matrix


                         Select: _____
```

Figure 11-17 Data planning menu screen.

Program listings shown in Figure 11-30.
The macro sorted the information by Area Region Branch Office (ARBO) and made page breaks after each area. Each area's section was mailed to the area controller. The report is used to allocate work load.

Output Report

A page from the report that was produced is shown in Figure 11-31. The abbreviations of the column headings are as follows:

```
                            Data Dictionary                Date:  8/25/88

                            Job Function


                   Data Base Administration Menu

                       1. Query/browse
                       2. Report generator
                       3. Logical DB design
                       4. Physical DB design
                       5. Load copy source
                       6. Edit copy source
                       7. Generate copy source
                       8. Data base documentation


                            Select:_____
```

Figure 11-18 Data base administration menu screen.

```
                            Data Dictionary                Date:  8/25/88

                            Job Function


                        System Development Menu

                       1. Query/browse
                       2. Report generator
                       3. System data requirements
                       4. System subsystem documentation
                       5. Operations documentation
                       6. Program analyzer
                       7. Operations turnover


                            Select:_____
```

Figure 11-19 System development menu screen.

- WKBG is the hour and minute during the weekday when service coverage begins;
- WKEN is the hour and minute during the weekday when service coverage ends;
- SABG is the hour and minute during Saturdays when service coverage begins;
- SAEN is the hour and minute during Saturdays when service coverage ends;
- SUBG is the hour and minute during Sundays when service coverage begins;
- SUEN is the hour and minute during Sundays when service coverage ends.

The report subtotals at the branch, region, and area levels.

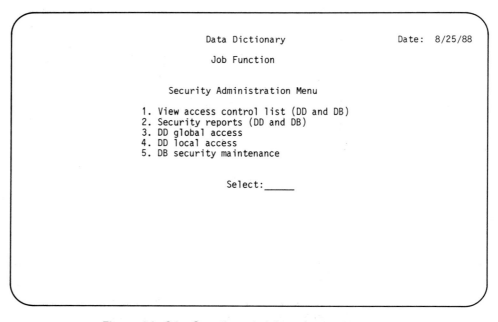

```
                         Data Dictionary              Date:  8/25/88

                         Job Function


                         Operations Menu

                         1. Query/browse
                         2. Report generator
                         3. Run instructions
                         4. Restart instructions
                         5. Schedule information
                         6. Resources


                              Select:_____
```

Figure 11-20   Operations menu screen.

```
                         Data Dictionary              Date:  8/25/88

                         Job Function


                         Security Administration Menu

                         1. View access control list (DD and DB)
                         2. Security reports (DD and DB)
                         3. DD global access
                         4. DD local access
                         5. DB security maintenance


                              Select:_____
```

Figure 11-21   Security administration menu screen.

```
Data Dictionary                    Date:  8/25/88

Job Function


End-User Computing Menu

1. Query/browse
2. Report generator
3. Data extract request
4. Data definition request


         Select:_____
```

Figure 11–22   End-user computing menu screen.

```
Data Dictionary                    Date:  8/25/88

Job Function


DD Project Management Menu

1. Query/browse
2. Report generator
3. Standards exception reports
4. Population statistics
5. Percent documentation complete


         Select:____
```

Figure 11–23   DD project management menu screen.

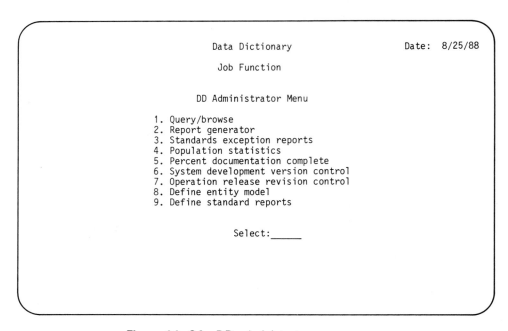

```
                    Data Dictionary              Date:  8/25/88

                    Job Function


                    DD Administrator Menu
                 1. Query/browse
                 2. Report generator
                 3. Standards exception reports
                 4. Population statistics
                 5. Percent documentation complete
                 6. System development version control
                 7. Operation release revision control
                 8. Define entity model
                 9. Define standard reports


                      Select:_____
```

Figure 11-24 DD administrator menu screen.

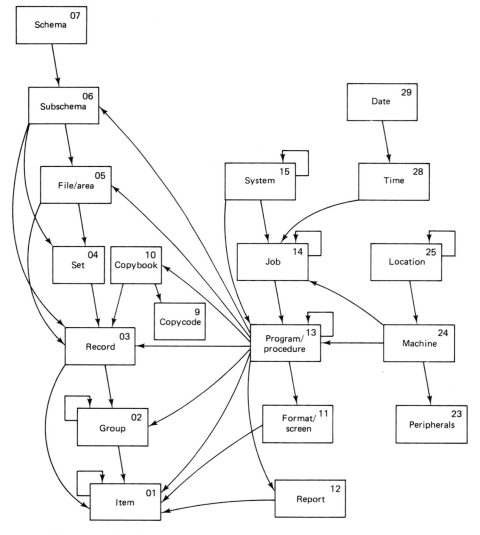

Figure 11-25 Entity model diagram representing logical relationships between data, process, machine, and time variables.

```
┌──────────────────────────────────────────────────────────────────────────┐
│                               Data Dictionary                              │
│                            User Permission Request                         │
│                                                                            │
│  1. Name of Requester: ___Lisa Jones___    Date of Request: __1/13/88__    │
│                                                                            │
│  2. Position ___Contract Analyst___    Manager/Approval: __J. Davidson__   │
│                                                                            │
│  3. Department ___Contracts Administration___    Phone: __478-4000 X2238__ │
│                                                                            │
│  4. Badge No. ___37522___                                                  │
│                                                                            │
│  5. Entities Requested/Permission (Read (R), Modify (M), Create (C))       │
│                                                                            │
│        System          __R__                                               │
│        Job/CLI         __R__                                               │
│        Program         __R__                                               │
│        File/Data Base  __R__                                               │
│        Record          __R__                                               │
│        Data Item       __R__                                               │
│        Report          __R__                                               │
│        Schedule Date   _____                                               │
│        Schedule Time   _____                                               │
│        Machine         _____                                               │
│        Peripheral      _____                                               │
│        Copybook        __R__                                               │
│                                                                            │
│  6. Manual Issued/Date _____    Manual No. _____     │
│                                                                            │
│  7. DDS to be used for:                                                    │
│                                     Job Functions                          │
│                          1. Data planning                                  │
│                          2. DBA                                            │
│                          3. System development (SDLC)                      │
│                          4. Operations                                     │
│                          5. Security administration                        │
│                         (6.) End-user computing                            │
│                          7. DD project implementation                      │
│                          8. DD administration                              │
│                                                                            │
│  8. User Name Requested     ___L. Jones_____                           │
│                                                                            │
│  9. Password Requested      ___ENLTP___                                    │
│                                                                            │
│                          DBA/DDA Approved __(signature)__                  │
│                                                                            │
│                          Date: _____                           │
└──────────────────────────────────────────────────────────────────────────┘
```

Figure 11-26 Data dictionary User permission request form.

END-USER COMPUTING REQUEST

NOTE: YOU MUST ATTACH A LIST OF DATA ELEMENTS REQUIRED.
       (Attach selection criteria as applicable.)

Request # _E U C ϕ1ϕ5_   Date _7/24/88_

Requested by __LARRY LOPEZ__   Tel. Ext. _____   M.S. _____

Department Name ____MARKET_____   Account # _____

Username _____

Describe Request: __SEE ATTACHED SPECIFICATION SHEET — 2 DATA__
__STRIPS FROM CONTRACTS DB_____

Handware Requirements: CPU: _____

Memory: _____

Disk Storage: _____

Software Requirements: Operating System: _____

Application System: _____   Frequency of Run _QUARTERLY_

Retention Days (default is 30) __3 PERIODS__

Requesting Department Approval _____Larry Lopez_____

Data Security Approval _____   Date _8/8/88_

Security Level: _____

MIS USE ONLY

Date Recd. _8/12/88_   Target Date __/__/__   DBA Mgr._Ron Warera_

Date Assigned __/__/__   Date Completed __/__/__

File Name _____

Retention Period (in terms of days) _____

Comments _____
_____
_____

Figure 11–27 End-user computing request form.

— Data Items:
- Contract Number
- Customer Number
- Installed-ARBO
- Contract Effective Date
- Contract Cancel Date
- Model Number
- Serial Number
- Model Add-Date
- Model Remove-Date
- Price
- Type Code

— Required Frequency
- Quarterly

— Selection Criteria
- Skip the record if the model remove date is before 13 months back from the date the data strip is generated.
- Skip the record if the contract cancel date is before 13 months back from the date the data strip is generated.

Load both data strips onto FS1Z29 in directory: EUCFILES.

Assign read access to following usernames:

Contracts, Jones L

Figure 11–27 Continued

Data Standard Name	Picture Clause	Start/End	Total Bytes
CONTRACT-NO	PIC X(8)	1/8	8
CUST-NO	PIC X(7)	9/15	7
CUST-SHIP-TO-SUFFIX	PIC 9(3)	16/18	3
CONTRACT-TYPE	PIC X(3)	27/29	3
ALT-BILL-TO-NO	PIC X(10)	30/39	10
INSTALL-ADDR	PIC X(100)	40/139	100
INSTALL-CITY	PIC X(22)	140/161	22
INSTALL-STATE	PIC X(3)	162/164	3
INSTALL-ZIP-CD	PIC X(9)	165/173	9
WKDAY-COVER-BGN	PIC X(4)	174/177	4
WKDAY-COVER-END	PIC X(4)	178/181	4
SAT-COVER-BGN	PIC X(4)	182/185	4
SAT-COVER-END	PIC X(4)	186/189	4
SUN-COVER-BGN	PIC X(4)	190/193	4
SUN-COVER-END	PIC X(4)	194/197	4
DOLLAR-BASE	PIC S9(6)V99	199/205	8
CON-LAST-CHANGE-DT	PIC 9(6)	206/211	6
CONTRACT-EFT-DT	PIC 9(6)	212/217	6
CONTRACT-CANCEL-DT	PIC 9(6)	218/223	6
CON-INIT-TERM-DT	PIC 9(6)	224/229	6
ORG-PRFX	PIC X(4)	230/233	4
ORG-ARBO	PIC X(4)	234/237	4
CUST-TEAM-ID	PIC 9(3)	238/240	3
EMP-BADGE-NO	PIC 9(5)	241/245	5
SALES-ORDER-NO	PIC 9(10)	246/255	10

Figure 11–28 Extract file record layout (COBOL).

```
SEQUENTIAL FILE

        CONEUC0105_REC FIXED LENGTH 437,
        05 CONTRACT_NO                  CHARACTER (8),
        05 CUST_NO                      CHARACTER (7),
        05 CUST_SHIP_TO_SUFFIX          UNPACKED DECIMAL UNSIGNED (3),
        05 CPU_TYPE                     UNPACKED DECIMAL UNSIGNED (8),
        05 CONTRACT_TYPE                CHARACTER (3),
        05 ALT_BILL_TO_NO               CHARACTER (10),
        05 INSTALL_ADDR                 CHARACTER (100),
        05 WKDAY_COVER_BGN              UNPACKED DECIMAL UNSIGNED (4),
        05 WKDAY_COVER_END              UNPACKED DECIMAL UNSIGNED (4),
        05 SAT_COVER_BGN                CHARACTER (4),
        05 SAT_COVER_END                CHARACTER (4),
        05 SUN_COVER_BGN                CHARACTER (4),
        05 SUN_COVER_END                CHARACTER (4),
        05 DOLLAR_BASE                  UNPACKED DECIMAL (6,2),
        05 CON_LAST_CHANGE_DT           UNPACKED DECIMAL UNSIGNED (6),
        05 CONTRACT_EFT_DT              UNPACKED DECIMAL UNSIGNED (6),
        05 CONTRACT_CANCEL_DT           UNPACKED DECIMAL UNSIGNED (6),
        05 CON_INIT_TERM_DT             UNPACKED DECIMAL UNSIGNED (6),
```

Figure 11-29 Data extract record layout for "PRESENT" report generator.

```
AUTHOR  "L JONES"

MHELP   "THIS REPORT LISTS EXTENDED HOUR CONTRACTS"
        "THE SOURCE FILE IS     EUC0105.D1          "

NOTES   "EXTENDED.PR.MAC"
NOTES   "RAN SORT TO ELIMINATE CONTRACTS WHICH     "
        "CANCELLED BEFORE 06/01/86                  "

REPORT  1 BAS_AREA          COL  3
          BAS_REGION        COL  4
          BAS_BRANCH        COL  5
          BAS_OFFICE        COL  6
          BAS_HDR_CONT_FNT  COL  9
          BAS_HDR_CONT_BCK  COL 10
          BAS_WKDY_BEG_HRS  COL 18
          BAS_WKDY_BEG_MIN  COL 20
                     "-"    COL 22
          BAS_WKDY_END_HRS  COL 23
          BAS_WKDY_END_MIN  COL 25
          BAS_SAT_BEG_HRS   COL 30
          BAS_SAT_BEG_MIN   COL 32
                     "-"    COL 34
          BAS_SAT_END_HRS   COL 35
          BAS_SAT_END_MIN   COL 37
          BAS_SUN_BEG_HRS   COL 41
          BAS_SUN_BEG_MIN   COL 43
                     "-"    COL 45
          BAS_SUN_END_HRS   COL 46
          BAS_SUN_END_MIN   COL 48
          BAS_INSTALL_ADDR1     COL 53
```

Figure 11-30 "PRESENT" program listing.

```
HEADER     BAS_AREA          "A"
HEADER     BAS_REGION        "R"
HEADER     BAS_BRANCH        "E"
HEADER     BAS_OFFICE        "A"
HEADER     BAS_HDR_CONT_FNT "C"
HEADER     BAS_HDR_CONT_BCK "ONTRACT"
HEADER     BAS_WKDY_BEG_HRS "WK"
HEADER     BAS_WKDY_BEG_MIN "BG"
HEADER     BAS_WKDY_END_HRS "WK"
HEADER     BAS_WKDY_END_MIN "EN"
HEADER     BAS_SAT_BEG_HRS  "SA"
HEADER     BAS_SAT_BEG_MIN  "BG"
HEADER     BAS_SAT_END_HRS  "SA"
HEADER     BAS_SAT_END_MIN  "EN"
HEADER     BAS_SUN_BEG_HRS  "SU"
HEADER     BAS_SUN_BEG_MIN  "BG"
HEADER     BAS_SUN_END_HRS  "SU"
HEADER     BAS_SUN_END_MIN  "EN"
HEADER     BAS_INSTALL_ADDR1  "INSTALL CUSTOMER"

SELECT     BAS_SAT_BEG_HRS   > 0
OR         BAS_SAT_BEG_MIN   > 0
OR         BAS_SAT_END_HRS   > 0
OR         BAS_SAT_END_MIN   > 0
OR         BAS_SUN_BEG_HRS   > 0
OR         BAS_SUN_BEG_MIN   > 0
OR         BAS_SUN_END_HRS   > 0

OR         BAS_SUN_END_MIN   > 0
OR         BAS_WKDY_BEG_HRS  < 07
OR         BAS_WKDY_END_HRS  > 18

BREAK BEFORE BAS_BRANCH
1
2
BREAK AFTER BAS_BRANCH
                     "BRANCH TOTAL =" COL+2 COUNT REPEAT
BREAK BEFORE BAS_REGION
1
2
BREAK AFTER BAS_REGION
                     "REGION TOTAL =" COL+2 COUNT REPEAT

BREAK BEFORE BAS_AREA "EXTENDED HOUR CONTRACTS IN AREA: " CENTER
BAS_AREA
BREAK AFTER BAS_AREA
                     "AREA TOTAL =  " COL+2 COUNT EJECT REPEAT

SORT BAS_AREA BAS_REGION BAS_BRANCH BAS_OFFICE

TITLE 1 DATE LEFT TIME CENTER PAGE RIGHT
TITLE 2
TITLE 3 "FIELD SERVICE" CENTER
TITLE 4
TITLE 5 "EXTERNAL EXTENDED COVERAGE CONTRACTS" CENTER
TITLE 6
TITLE 7
```

Figure 11–30 Continued

```
8/19/88                          FIELD SERVICE

                        EXTERNAL EXTENDED COVERAGE CONTRACTS


   AREA      CONTRACT     WKBG WKEN     SABG SAEN     SUBG SUEN     INSTALL CUSTOMER

                    EXTENDED HOUR CONTRACTS IN AREA: 1

   1111       37065      8 0-2359      0 0- 0 0      0 0- 0 0      WEST IND
   1111       35310      8 0-2359      8 0-2359      0 0- 0 0      SOMERSET TRAVEL
   1111       24322      7 0-23 0      7 0-23 0      7 0-23 0      BEDFORD PRESS
   1111       33819      8 0-2359      0 0- 0 0      0 0- 0 0      BEDFORD PRESS

   BRANCH TOTAL =                 4
   1121       03500      9 0-21 0      0 0- 0 0      0 0- 0 0      BRANDEIS UNIV
   1121       05402      830-2030      0 0- 0 0      0 0- 0 0      FIRST TRUST
   1121       14428      830-2030      0 0- 0 0      0 0- 0 0      HONEYWELL INSTR
   1121       24241      8 0-20 0      0 0- 0 0      0 0- 0 0      ANACOMP
   1121       44261      8 0-17 0      8 0-17 0      8 0-17 0      ANACOMP
   1121       44222      0 1-2359      0 1-2359      0 1-2359      ANACOMP

   BRANCH TOTAL =                 6
   1141       24426      0 1-2359      0 1-2359      0 1-2359      CRESSEY
   1141       33790      0 1-2359      0 1-2359      0 0- 0 0      NYNEX
   1141       33428      830-2030      0 0- 0 0      0 0- 0 0      NYNEX

   BRANCH TOTAL =                 3
   REGION TOTAL =                13

   1211       36652      0 1-2359      0 1-2359      0 1-2359      ATLANTIS SHOP
   1213       05681      8 0-20 0      0 0- 0 0      0 0- 0 0      CHARMING SHOPPES

   BRANCH TOTAL =                 2
   1221       08249      8 0-2359      0 0- 0 0      0 0- 0 0      FIRST TRUST
   1221       28244      8 0-2359      8 0-2359      0 0- 0 0      FIRST TRUST
   1221       32336      8 0-20 0      0 0- 0 0      0 0- 0 0      VANDERBILT
   1221       38421      0 1-2359      0 1-2359      0 1-2359      CBT COMPUTER
   1221       43249      830-2030      0 0- 0 0      0 0- 0 0      APOLLO STRUCTURES
   1223       19119      8 0-2359      0 0- 0 0      0 0- 0 0      CHEMICAL BANK

   BRANCH TOTAL =                 6
   1231       06052      6 0-22 0      0 0- 0 0      0 0- 0 0      SIEBERT
   1231       26671      830-2030      0 0- 0 0      0 0- 0 0      MIDLANTIC STATES
   1231       28952      6 0-22 0      6 0-22 0      0 0- 0 0      GE
   1231       38533      9 0-18 0      9 0-18 0      0 0- 0 0      GE
   1231       44752      6 0-22 0      0 0- 0 0      0 0- 0 0      GE
   1231       45324      830-2030      0 0- 0 0      0 0- 0 0      GE
   1231       46652      0 1-2359      0 1-2359      0 1-2359      RCA RECORDS
   1231       46653      0 1-2359      0 1-2359      0 1-2359      RCA RECORDS

   BRANCH TOTAL =                 8
   1241       53267      830-1730      830-1730      0 0- 0 0      COMM MASS

   BRANCH TOTAL =                 1
   REGION TOTAL =                17
   AREA   TOTAL =                30
```

Figure 11–31 Final report on extended coverage contracts.

chapter 12

Monitoring DDS Usage and Performance

INTRODUCTION

Performance does not become an issue until a problem situation arises. Performance issues can arise from many different sources; performance issues also tend to become apparent over a period of time. For example, the amount of data in the data dictionary would govern the amount of time spent by the query program to search for and locate a particular piece of information that the user is looking for. As the amount of data in the data dictionary grows, the access paths to the data become large and unwieldy. This results in the response time to a simple query getting longer and longer.

This chapter is organized into three parts. The first part discusses the typical manifestations of performance problems. The second part deals with the reasons and etiology of these problems. The third part discusses the steps that should be taken to monitor the system and diagnose the nature of these problems and how to deal with each.

TYPICAL PERFORMANCE PROBLEMS

Performance problems are generally manifested to the end user by unusually long response times. Examples of some typical performance problems follow:

Poor Response Time When Using Function Keys

The response time between function keys is not acceptable. Traditionally, a 3- to 8-second response time has been considered acceptable. The response time is generally a function of the load on the system, that is, the number of other users who are performing tasks on the system. Since the computer can handle only a certain number of users adequately, the response time will vary over the day.

Poor Response Time When Generating Reports

Another area where there may be problems would be in user-specified report generation. In a typical dictionary system, there will exist a facility to specify the selection criteria for a report, and then the dictionary system would produce the report based on the criteria specified. An example of such a request would be when the user requests a report that provides all the components within a system, or when the user wants to get a list of all the standard data items. To produce these reports, the system would have to traverse the data base to pull out the information that the user is looking for. This is expensive in terms of computer resources and takes a considerable length of time to complete. If several of these requests came in at about the same time, the overall response time would suffer as well as the fact that the jobs would take longer to complete, since there will be contention among the jobs.

Poor Response Time during Data Entry

Another area where there may be problems would be in handling updates to the Dictionary data base. If forms are used as the primary source of input into the Dictionary, and the forms are entered by a data-entry person, the system may not be able to keep up with the speed of the data-entry person. There may be two reasons for this: The system may not have been designed with heavy-duty data entry in mind and as a result may not be able to handle the throughput required; also, the system itself may not have the horsepower to respond to the speed of the data-entry person in keying in the data.

Poor Response Time When Networking

In situations where the user has to be connected to the system via a network connection from a remote location, the response time is affected by factors such as line transmission speed and network software access time.

REASONS FOR PERFORMANCE PROBLEMS

There are several factors that affect response time. In general, a single factor or a combination of factors can cause deterioration in system performance. In this discussion we focus on the data structure, the effect of design factors, and the network.

Data Structure

Most dictionaries work on the basis of an indexing scheme, that is, the data content can be retrieved through a keyed access technique. Some technical terms that are used to describe these techniques are ISAM (indexed sequential access method) and DBAM (data base access method). The common property of these techniques is that in addition to the data content, a key (or pointer) to the data content is stored as a separate piece of information in the dictionary data base. Therefore, when the user requests data from the dictionary based on an entity name or an alias, the dictionary system will look for the key, and then use the information in the key to retrieve the data content in the dictionary data base. Therefore, a request for data from the dictionary requires at least two accesses to the data base, one for the key and another one for the data.

As the amount of data grows and the number of keys expands, the situation becomes more complicated—to get a key may take more than one access, because an index to the index of keys would have to be set up automatically by the system to handle the larger number of keys. Also, once the key is obtained, several accesses may be required to pull all the data together because different pieces may have been stored at different times and hence may not be physically co-located.

The last point leads to another interesting phenomenon called "fragmentation." Since the physical disk is shared by many users, the disk space is allocated based on the space needed at any moment in time. Thus if the data were entered at different times, it is quite likely that the data are scattered across many disk areas (or sectors), making the access that much more time consuming.

Another thing to remember about file systems is that when data are deleted from the data base, "holes" are left in the data base that lead to inefficiencies in trying to obtain the appropriate data later because the file system has to jump over the holes, and this takes additional effort and time.

Effect of Design Factors

The way the dictionary system is designed and implemented can cause performance issues to come up. Some dictionaries are active in the sense that they are referenced during the compile and run-time phases. Examples of such dictionaries are Cullinet's IDD, 4GLs such as EXSYS, and Data General's DG/SQL product among others. The major problem that could develop is that the dictionary is being accessed so frequently that contention takes place and the dictionary performance suffers.

Another design feature that affects performance is the fact that the dictionary maintains the data in their raw form rather than in semifinished form. For example, where a dictionary is used for program compilations, the dictionary can contain the data in their raw form, in which case another step in the process has to be added to recombine the raw data into the file definition source code, which can then be compiled. This additional step takes time and resources. In some dictionaries, a source code image can be generated and stored within the dictionary itself, so that when the compiler asks the dictionary for the source code it is available immediately.

A design feature that improves performance in a dictionary is the availability of several access paths. These access paths ensure that the information can be obtained quickly for the end user. Yet the existence of these access paths means that every time a new entity is added or an existing one is modified, these access paths have to be updated, and that is expensive in terms of machine resources.

Another design feature that affects performance is whether the dictionary uses the features of the hardware and operating system on which it is based. In many cases dictionaries are designed to be portable, so they use standard features. Some dictionaries that work only in certain hardware and software configurations can be fine-tuned to be more efficient precisely because they have been designed to take advantage of the strengths of the operating system and file handler.

Dictionaries possess a feature called "extensibility." This feature allows the user of the dictionary to extend the dictionary to define entities over and above the standard set that comes with the dictionary. One consequence of this is that the design and operation of the dictionary to accommodate extensibility will compromise the performance of the system, since the dictionary will have to be made for general-purpose usage. It is important to find out from the vendor of the software the performance impact of utilizing the extensibility features and the trade-offs.

Dictionaries that are designed to work with a fixed set of entities and relationships will be more efficient than those designed to be extensible. Depending on whether the installation wants to go beyond the subset of applications that come with the dictionary will govern the need for extensibility. The trade-off between performance and flexibility must be kept in mind, though.

Network Considerations

Dictionaries that are designed with network access in mind will be more efficient than those that are designed to work on a single machine. Generally, as the network gets more complex, the software layers that need to be navigated increase and consequently the response time deteriorates. For example, in a distributed situation, a dictionary can exist on the mainframe but have an interface to a personal computer so that users who are logged onto the personal computer can use the dictionary without even knowing where the dictionary is located. For the user, this means that he or she must have the functional capabilities and power available on the mainframe at his or her desk via the personal computer. If the dictionary is not designed with this in mind, it will not be able to meet the needs of the remote user. In a situation where there are different machines and there must be some form of communication between them, the performance implications could become important.

PERFORMANCE MONITORING

Performance monitoring procedures should be set up as an ongoing set of procedures that are executed on a regular schedule by the operations department. These monitoring procedures produce statistics on file growth and record placement within the data dictionary data base. They should be analyzed to examine points of potential contention by the sudden growth in certain types of records. These could be the cause of delays in response time. When response-time degradation can be traced to file growth and fragmentation problems, the data base should be reorganized. Reorganization procedures and programs are generally provided by the vendors of the data dictionary software.

Users who report response-time problems should be tracked carefully to see what they were doing that caused the system problems. In some cases the execution of a large query could cause the other users to suffer response-time delays. In such cases it would be wise to have a deferred query execution process such that the query is automatically put into execution by the system during off-peak hours. If deferred execution is not possible, the users should be taught to use the system resource judiciously.

Run-time dictionaries have other aspects that should be monitored, since the run-time dictionary could be a bottleneck that contributes to delay. Some active dictionaries pull all the data that are needed into memory in order to reduce the input/output (I-O) to the disk file that is required for the dictionary itself to operate. In other cases, the data to run the dictionary itself have to be obtained from disk storage every time and could add to the time lag. One important indicator that should be available is the ratio of I-O for the dictionary versus the I-O for the data base. The smaller this ratio, the better. When the run-time performance deteriorates, steps should be taken to increase the amount of operating system resource allocated to the dictionary process by increasing the priority of that process. Another tack is to remove from the system altogether other jobs that may be consuming resources. The preceding steps, together with fine-tuning the system, will make the system more responsive.

chapter 13

Data Dictionary Role in Data Planning

INTRODUCTION

This and the following five chapters comprise a set of topics called DD applications. Each chapter treats an important subject within the information management area, with specific reference to the role the data dictionary can play. The topics are: data planning, data base administration, the systems development life cycle, computer operations, data security, and end-user computing.

While reading these chapters the reader will note that the following themes that have been interwoven throughout the chapters:

- The results of the business planning, systems planning, and data planning exercises are reflected in each individual application system project through the data models, logical data base design, and physical data base design.
- All functional or organizational groups working on the application system development project follow the same system development life cycle.
- The dictionary plays a role for each group involved in a system development project, but its key role is to propagate the data conventions by being a single point of reference for all the groups involved.
- Systems that are built on a data foundation that reflect aggregate business plans and direction will require less reorganization, maintenance, and administration than will those that are developed in an ad hoc manner. Also, the data foundation can be shared by many systems, thus contributing to the productivity of the business.

In this chapter we explain the relationships among business planning, systems planning, and data planning at the aggregate level. Examples of outputs of these planning exercises are shown, with further breakdowns into individual systems and data base projects on a time schedule. The relationship between the output from the data planning exercise (i.e., the data models) and the systems projects that are carried out in support of the business is examined. The systems projects follow a life cycle approach called the systems development life cycle (SDLC). The life cycle requires logical data base design and physical data base design for the system project. The logical data base design for each individual application system has to be consistent with the data model derived from the data planning exercise. This not only ensures that the planned data base direction is incorporated into the system projects, but also assures that the different systems developed in different points in time can share the data base owing to the fact that the underlying data model is consistent. Finally, the role of the dictionary in supporting and documenting the results of the planning process is explained, with a list of entity categories that are necessary in the dictionary itself.

WHAT IS DATA PLANNING?

Data planning is the process of deriving data models and data base models that can be used as a basis for individual application system or data base development projects within a business. Data models and data base models embody the rules about data that a company wishes to propagate throughout the organization.

Reasons for Data Planning

There are several important reasons for data planning. Such planning:

- Results in clearly defined systems projects
- Encourages clarity of thinking about data base planning
- Reduces the number of data bases resulting in greater integration
- Prevents continuous restructuring of data bases and application programs (called "maintenance" in most companies, this activity often comprises 80 percent of the data processing dollar)
- Reduces the number of isolated applications which cannot be easily combined with others within a reasonable development horizon

Links

This chapter starts out by providing the reader with an overview of the links among business planning, systems planning, and data planning. A business plan is a statement of direction about the business; based on this, systems plans can be formulated. Although systems are implemented on the needs of the business, they all draw on a common set of data. In order that systems that are developed build on one another and the data, it is important to have a good foundation of data. The data foundation is constructed from views of the data called data models. In this chapter the focus is not so much on the methods of systems planning or data planning as much as on defining the outputs from each of these processes and how these outputs can be portrayed in a dictionary for use by persons in the organization doing system development.

Figure 13-1 shows the links among business planning, systems planning, and data base planning. Note that there are definite outputs expected from each of the above. These outputs will be in the form of diagrams that represent the end point toward which the business should be striving.

The actual projects and programs that lead to the implementation will be handled

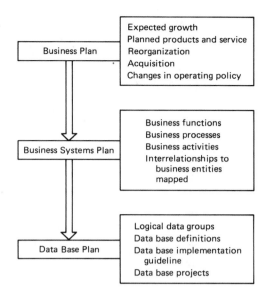

Figure 13-1 Links among business plan, business systems plan, and data base plan.

through project prioritization committees, also called steering committees. These committees look at the current needs of the business for systems and data base projects, balance these needs with future requirements, and come up with a set of projects that need to be implemented at various points in time to meet the needs of the business.

Terminology

- *Function:* highest-level summary of action that must take place to perpetuate the business
- *Process:* ongoing set of related activities that support one of an organization's functions
- *Activity:* repetitive well-defined set of tasks or transactions usually completed according to a given schedule
- *Logical grouping:* ties together the data elements that correspond to something that has separate and distinct existence; also referred to as "entity"

For each function (e.g., production, marketing, etc.) a set of business processes may be defined. Additionally, each business process has a set of specific business actions, referred to as business activities, which must be completed on a continuous basis in order to achieve the objectives of a process. Each of these activities requires data groups in order to achieve the objectives of a process.

Connection between Plans and Systems Development

The connection between the various outputs of the planning process and systems development goes beyond the schedules of implementation. There are interrelations between systems and data bases, data bases and data models, and systems and business processes that enter into the system design and development activity at the lowest level of implementation. These relationships are shown in Figure 13-2.

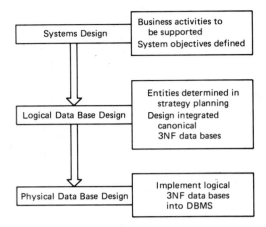

Figure 13-2 Relationships between plan outputs and system development.

BUSINESS PLANNING

The foundation of both systems and data planning is the business plan. Business planning produces information about the following items:

- Business growth expected
- Diversification of products and services
- Reorganization of business functions
- Acquisitions planned
- Changes in operating philosophy

The results of the business planning process are objectives for the business as a whole; these objectives could be in the form of process objectives, such as implementing a different way of conducting the business. An example of an endpoint picture for a service-call-handling process could be stated simply as: "Give the customer a single point of contact within the company for service support and administrative support."

Certain assumptions are generally made that have to be stated explicitly so that persons executing the business strategy can clearly understand them. Assumptions could be as follows:

- Business will be consolidated into fewer support locations.
- There will only be one technical support group; it will be feasible to fly technical support personnel to any customer site rather than maintain technical support personnel close to major customer locations.
- There will be a problem management system for all products which includes the capability of alerting problem status to appropriate persons, meets management information needs, and provides symptom-fix data.

Information Flow Diagrams

Any business organization may be generally viewed as depicted in the information flow diagram shown in Figure 13-3. In this diagram all the business functions are represented in the broadest sense. These are the main functions for which business planning occurs. Arrows between the major business functions indicate information

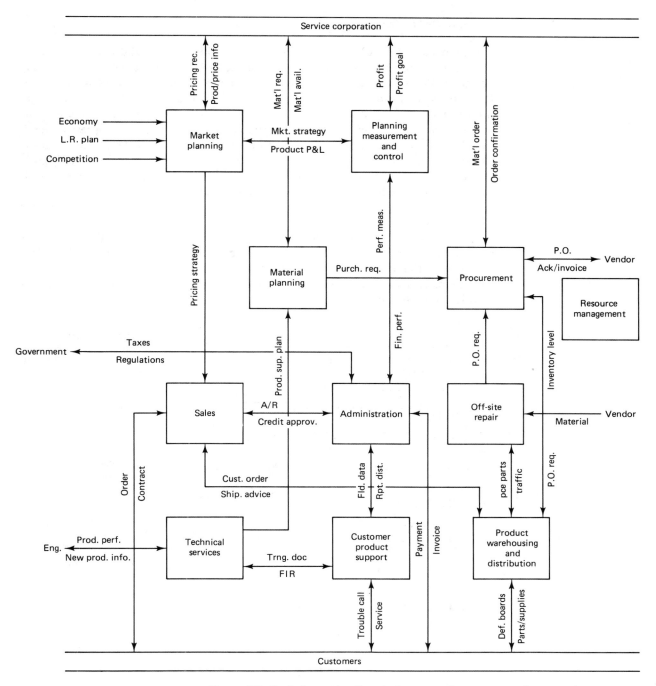

Figure 13-3 Information flow between major processes for a service organization.

flow and dependency between the various functions of business. Collective information regarding business plans flow to the business systems planning process.

To create the information flow diagram, functions in the business and the interactions between them must be defined and portrayed. This diagram can often be shown to a chief executive officer to get his or her concurrence and support. An example of an information flow diagram for a service organization is shown in Figure 13-3.

System Data Map

It is necessary to have a clear understanding of the business and the data that are of critical importance to the functioning of the business. If the term "system" can be used to denote manual systems and automated ones, one can draw a picture where the systems and the data interact to support the functioning of the business. The other missing pieces of this diagram would be the persons or functions that interact with the systems, and the flow of parts that need to be represented. Such a representation is called a "system data map." There can be a system data map of the current situation and one to represent the future. In any event they must represent the relationship between systems and data as viewed by the persons in the organization responsible for conducting the business. The map should be the view that is agreed upon by the user managers as representing the business information flow necessary to conduct the business.

The system data map illustrates the importance of having thought through the information processing that is going on in the organization. It consists of symbols representing the data bases, the processes, and the individuals/customers/parts that have to interact with the processes. An example of a section of a systems data flow map is shown in Figure 13–4.

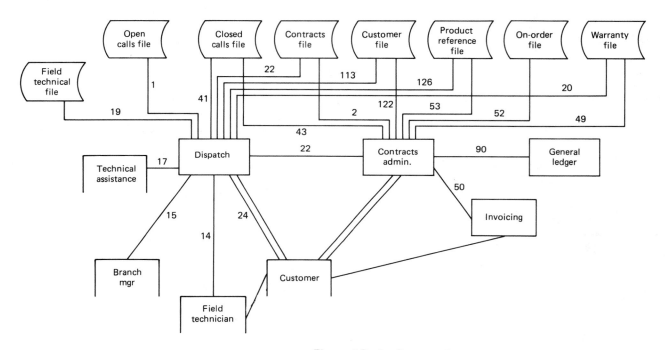

Figure 13–4 System data map.

System Data Map Explanations

1. *Data base interactions.* This is the process by which information systems retrieve and store data from their associated data bases.

24. *CDS/customer interface.* A customer initiates a service call when he or she calls the central dispatch system (CDS) to complain about a computer problem. The customer service representative (CSR) who answers the call asks questions to determine the type of customer, the type of problem, and whether or not the trouble call is to be passed on to others. The same link is used when the customer calls to inquire about the progress of the trouble call.

14. *Service technician/CDS interface.* A dispatcher initiates a page when a service call request appears on his or her CDS screen. The service technician, upon receiving the call, calls CDS. A dispatcher then informs the ST about the location of the customer and the nature of the problem. Any additional information about this problem may be given at this time. The ST may call CDS at any time during a service call to obtain warranty information on parts. When the ST has successfully completed a trouble call, he or she calls CDS to give all the field incident information related to the service call, such as configuration changes, parts exchanges, and billing information. An ST can call CDS to request that diagnostics be run on the customer's machine.

15. *Branch management/CDS interface.* Branch offices have a terminal which can be logged onto CDS to inform the branch management about the status of service calls. If too much time passes during a service call, CDS escalates the call. A dispatcher then calls the branch manager to inform him or her of the action taken. The branch manager gives CDS the exact schedule for visits from the office.

17. *TAC/CDS interface.* The technical assistance center (TAC) is able to access the open calls files to retrieve information relating to service calls that have entered alert status. TAC can access the open calls files to retrieve information to verify that the person calling for technical assistance is the ST assigned to the service call. TAC tells CDS the action plans for the escalated calls that TAC is monitoring.

19. *Employee reference file/CDS interface.* The employee reference file provides CDS with up-to-date information about employees.

20. *CDS/warranty interface.* CDS interacts with the warranty system to indicate which parts have been installed into the customers' machines and therefore are covered under a new warranty. The warranty system indicates if the replaced parts are under warranty.

22. *Contracts/CDS interface.* The contracts system provides information to CDS about service contracts, equipment, hours of coverage, and related areas, on a regular basis.

113. *Customers/CDS interface.* Customers provides CDS with customer information.

126. *Product reference/CDS interface.* Product reference provides CDS with parts information for verification purposes.

90. *Contracts/general ledger interface.* The contracts system provides the general ledger with journal entries.

2. *Data base interactions.* This is the process by which information systems retrieve and store data from their associated data bases.

22. *Contracts/CDS interface.* The contracts system provides information to CDS about service contracts, equipment, hours of coverage, and related areas, on a regular basis.

43. *FACTS/contracts interface.* FACTS provides the contracts system with information from CDS regarding changes in basic contract information (e.g., contact name, configuration, etc.). The contracts system provides FACTS with service contract information for billing purposes.

49. *Shipped equipment file/contracts interface.* The contracts system has access to the shipped equipment file so that a customer's contract can be referenced to the model configuration that was shipped to that customer.

50. *Contracts/invoicing interface.* Invoicing receives billing information on service contracts customer from the contracts system.

52. *Contracts/on order interface.* The contracts system provides on-order information with valid sales order numbers as a validation procedure.

53. *Product reference/contracts interface.* The contracts system receives information on prices, configurations, and so on, from the product reference system.

90. *Contracts/general ledger interface.* The contracts system provides the general ledger with journal entries.

122. *Customer/contracts interface.* The contracts system can access customer information from the customer system.

41. *Open calls files/FACTS interface.* This is the process of transferring and consolidating closed call information from CDS into the FACTS system. Certain open call information may also be transferred for time reporting purposes.

43. *FACTS/contracts interface.* FACTS provides the contracts system with information from CDS regarding changes in basic contract information (e.g., contact name, configuration, etc.). The contracts system provides FACTS with service contract information for billing purposes.

SYSTEMS PLANNING

Many companies have developed their own business systems planning methodology. Even the mainframe computer vendors have developed such methods to support their clients. IBM supports its clients through Business Systems Planning (BSP). The major thrust of such methods is to integrate business plans with systems plans in order to generate project priority, development schedule, and resources required for major systems development efforts. Once the business processes and activities have been defined for current and new business plans, they may be very clearly divided among various systems projects. These projects may, in turn, be prioritized and scheduled according to resources available.

Function Process Activity

Functions, processes, and activities can be portrayed in the form of matrix tables. These tables can be used to cross-reference the impact of an activity on the various processes of which it is a part. It is important to realize that the number of functions that one could end up with would be between 20 and 30 in number. There could be between 150 and 200 business processes, and anywhere from 200 to 800 business activities. This may seem like a large number to deal with initially; it is highly recommended that an initial cut include only those functions and processes that are critical to the business (i.e., the mainstream processes).

An example of function, process, and activities for a service business is shown in Figure 13-5. Only one example of process, activities, and entities is given; however, a company can expect to have many business processes under a function, many activities under a business process, and many entities required to support an activity.

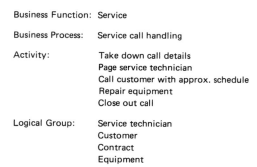

Figure 13-5   Example of function, process, activities.

Precedence Chart

It is not unusual in medium-sized to large corporations to find that several systems projects have been established with the same objectives. This results in wasted resources that could have been directed toward the achievement of other systems objectives. Therefore, one purpose of the strategic planning process is to define the blocks of business activities that need to be addressed by an information system.

Many companies decide on a list of system projects to attend to by means of a steering committee. This committee is composed of senior persons from the business and information sectors of the company. In many cases, the steering committee settles on too many projects to develop concurrently. The majority of companies should have only three or four systems development efforts under way at any time, in order to derive the best benefit from the resources available. This is so that the technical and data base specialists who need to be involved in integrated projects can be utilized effectively over a smaller number of projects rather than having their efforts dissipated over a large number of projects.

The systems design effort is bounded by the set of activities defined in the strategic planning process. Once the system boundaries are set, it is the responsibility of management to develop the schedule of the order of systems development, the interfaces that need to be built, and to schedule the detailed activities accordingly. Figure 13–6 shows the results of laying out the systems development on a time line that covers four years.

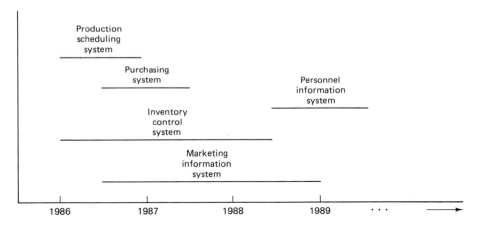

Figure 13–6 Precedence development chart for systems.

DATA BASE PLAN

Traditionally, data base development has occurred in a sporadic manner. This is because most data bases have been developed as adjuncts to the application systems rather than as important projects in their own right. In examining the system data map, it will become obvious that data bases of information are shared by many application systems, and a business case could be made to develop the data base as a separate project. Once the data base is developed, diverse application systems can utilize the data base.

This task is made easier by the development and use of structured programming methodologies. These methodologies emphasize that the data base access routines be segregated into separate modules that can be tested independently of the program. Once these modules are tested, they can be "called" from the application program whenever access to the data base is required for retrieval or update of information. This makes it possible for two things to happen:

1. The access routines can be shared by many application programs.
2. Changes can be made to the structure of the data base, with minimal or no changes to the application program.

Data Base Plan Definition

The data base plan is composed of the following:

1. Overall set of data bases that have to be developed to satisfy the needs of the business; i.e., data base portfolio
2. Logical groupings of data that go into these data bases
3. Implementation interdependencies, if any, and plans to address these
4. Schedule of implementation of the data bases as separate projects, with a time line

Data Base Portfolio

The portfolio of data bases that are needed by the business, as reflected in the system data flow map, is the focal point of this discussion. These are the data bases that are key to the information processing for the business. This is not to suggest that other data bases should be ignored; on the contrary, a second level of inquiry should be directed at these at the appropriate time.

The data bases that have been defined in the system data flow map are the ones that users have identified as meeting the current needs of the business and also have the potential to meet the future needs of the business. Therefore, there is value to the business in implementing these as stand-alone projects, or in conjunction with other system development projects.

Then it is necessary to look at each of these data bases and identify what they should contain. In doing this analysis, it may be necessary to break one data base into two or more data bases. As long as the function of the data base is maintained, this would be a very practical way to proceed. The next section delves into the process of coming up with the logical data groups within each of the data bases identified in the data map.

In developing the list of data bases that need to be worked on, note that it is important to understand that the same data base may be extended by each application systems project that is implemented. This is something that carries a significant design implication. Data base design and development have generally taken place based on the demonstrated need of an application system. What we are saying here is that data base design and development must proceed at least concurrently in order to arrive at a portfolio of data bases that serve several application projects. If this is not done, what happens is that data bases get designed on the requirements of the first application system project that comes along, and the projects that are implemented later require restructuring of the data base, because the needs were not taken into account when initially designing the data base.

Other ways of meeting current needs of application projects, yet providing for the future, is to use the techniques of normalization and canonical analysis to arrive at data models that are generic to the business. It will be apparent that a data base that is based on a data model will have less extensive restructuring done to it than one that has been developed in an ad hoc manner. Normalization and canonical structuring are discussed in more detail at the end of this chapter.

Logical Design

A data base can be viewed in a logical context as well as a physical context. The logical structure of a data base includes the data item groupings, interrelationships between these groupings, access paths, and so on, to meet the needs of the applications surrounding the data base. The physical context is the translation of the logical structure into an implementable structure on any one of a number of data base management systems. The physical design will take into account the strengths and weaknesses of the DBMS and the physical constraints of the operating environment.

Although the data structure is designed with applications in mind, it is independent of any one application and represents inherent properties of the data. The structure that results may be adjusted in anticipation of possible new applications of the data not yet specified. The relational model, by its very nature, does not have to consider the usage paths of the data by the applications. However, to implement the model and to achieve a reasonable performance, knowledge of the paths needed should be incorporated into the derivation of the canonical structure.

The data bases that are to be developed should be identified, and the logical groups of data that each is composed of should be identified. Note that the same logical group in two data bases could contain different subsets of data items. To understand this, let us use the following example. A service call can be in either an active state or a closed state. Many components of the service call are similar in both states. However, there are some differences. To begin with, all the components of the logical group called "CALL" should be identified. The resulting list is shown in Figure 13–7. Subsets 1 and 2 contain data items that are important for the processing while the call is open, whereas the data items in subset 3 are important for further analysis after the call is closed. The logical structure diagrams for the open calls data base and the closed calls data base is described below. Each logical diagram is preceded

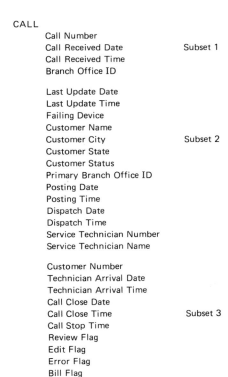

Figure 13–7 Subsets of data within "CALL" logical group entity.

by a short description and a statement of data requirements. Although the CALL record occurs in both data structures, the content of the record would be different. The positioning of data groups in a logical structure diagram based on overall requirements affects the contents of the group.

Open Calls File. The open calls file (or central dispatch system data base; Figure 13-8) is a decentralized data base (one to an area) that contains the data required to support:

- Recording of a customer service call
- Dispatch of a service technician to the customer site
- Escalation of the call to other technical and/or managerial levels based on elapsed time, and the closing of the call

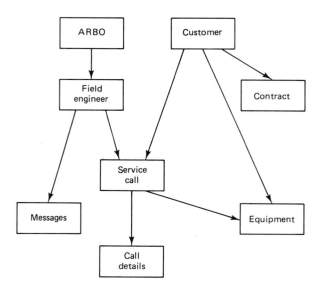

Figure 13-8 Logical data structure of "OPEN CALLS" file.

The open call file is a tactical data base.

Data Requirements

The data carried in the open calls file include but are not restricted to:

- Branch and team organization, service technician assignments to customers, availability, and messages
- Customer service contracts, and equipment identification/configuration data
- Service call dates, times, activities, and status

Closed Calls File. The closed calls file (sometimes referred to as the FACTS data base; Figure 13-9) contains information about service calls that have been processed by the area service operations centers (SOCs) using the central dispatch system. The data from the SOC are transmitted on a regularly scheduled basis to headquarters, where they are loaded into the closed calls file.

The data in the closed calls file are arranged in a format that enables data consolidation and ease of inquiry at a multinational level. All reports for field management and product performance are generated from the closed calls file. In addition, "time and material" (T and M) calls are billed to customers based on the data in this file.

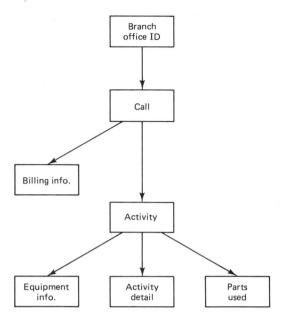

Figure 13-9 Logical data structure of "CLOSED CALLS" file.

All call data pertaining to an office within a branch within a region within an area are grouped together. These data can then be rolled up the area–region–branch-office hierarchy. The call itself is broken up into activity records, one for each type of activity. An activity is any discrete service action step taken against a particular model by a service technician. In a more general sense, actions taken by other functions, such as TAC related to a service call, can also be classified as activities within a particular type code.

Data Requirement

The data items that will be placed in the closed calls file will consist of a subset of the items in the open calls file (CDS). At the close of each call at the SOC, additional data items will be collected from the field engineer for analysis by headquarters technical personnel.

Access Requirement

Access to the call activity data must be available through employee, model, contract, and organization (ARBO) keys.

Data Base Projects

As a result of the steps described above, data base projects will be defined and resources allocated for systems development. Many corporations attempt the development of too many systems projects concurrently. Most companies do not have the resources to attempt such an effort. It is generally recommended that a company attempt no more than three concurrent system developments. In the systems precedence chart (Figure 13–6), note that through 1989, a maximum of three systems are being designed at the same time. Inspection of the data base implementation schedule (Figure 13–10) reveals that more than three data bases are being designed within the same time frame. Many data base projects have to be addressed in order to meet the needs of a few major application systems development projects.

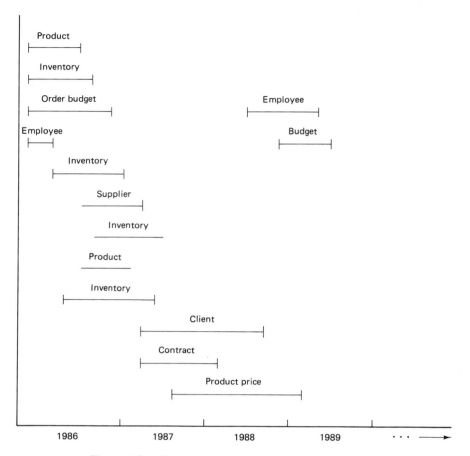

Figure 13-10 Data base implementation schedule.

Data Base Implementation Schedule

The implementation schedule for the data bases must be synchronized with the systems development schedule. In some cases, a data base development can stand on its own merit if it is a reference file that can be used by many application systems. Although data bases have been developed to meet an application need, and expanded, over time to include other application's requirements, pure data base development will take priority as the company understands the role of a stable portfolio of data bases in the information management context. Figure 13-10 is a chart containing the data bases that would be implemented over a period of time. Note that the same data base appears several times, indicating that the different facets of the data base will be implemented at different periods of time.

Dictionary's Role

The role of the data dictionary consists of being a central reference point for identifying the components of the system data map for the mainstream information processing systems and data bases of the business. Information about the system and files utilized is stored in the dictionary so that a common base of information can be used to generate reports and diagrams, as well as matrices, for further analysis. The information about the components of the system data map stored in the dictionary will provide the basis on which the data base plan can be done. In an interactive dictionary, graphics front-end software would be the tool that facilitates the process.

Several tools are available in the marketplace under the general category of computer-aided systems engineering (CASE).

Steps to Develop a Data Base Plan

The summary of steps necessary to complete a data base plan are listed below:

1. Represent the organization as business functions at the highest level possible (i.e., production, marketing, top management, support service).
2. Identify the business processes and activities that occur within the business functions described in step 1 (activities within processes within functions).
3. Establish specific decisions, questions, transactions, and informational transfer required for each of the activities described in step 2.
4. Determine the data groups required to support the business function activities (by decisions, questions, transactions, and informational education) developed in the previous steps.
5. Group and name related activities by business function into systems projects with well-defined objectives (i.e., which activities will be supported by each systems project). List these projects by name.
6. Develop a system data map that displays the information gathered in the previous steps.
7. Determine a priority of development for the systems projects determined in step 5. This would result in a systems priority listing.
8. Group the previously defined logical groups and show interrelationships necessary to provide the data to support the activities that occur in each of the systems projects defined in previous steps.
9. Establish data base boundaries for the logical data groups determined in step 8.
10. Determine the time requirements for developing each system defined in previous steps. Display the result of this step as a systems precedence development chart.
11. Develop an association list between system projects and data bases, and identify any interdependencies between them.
12. Complete the association of data base development to systems projects by drawing a precedence development chart of data base development over the planning horizon of the systems projects. Thus the chart developed in this step must be coordinated with the one developed in step 10. This step displays the time frame for data base development. As a result, the company has a set of interrelated data bases that will evolve to the future support of all systems.

DATA MODEL

Data Orientation

More and more organizations are utilizing a data model over their business systems and data base plans. These are the progressive organizations of the future which will significantly reduce maintenance costs, provide program and data independence, add new applications with ease, and enjoy an effective user environment.

Reasons for Data Model

It is of the utmost importance, both from a design standpoint and a communication standpoint, that the data model of the organization be the basis on which data base designs are created. There are many different techniques that can be used to come up with the data model. The techniques themselves are not that important, only that they help produce models that are clear and can be communicated with precision to the users that need them. Once the users have the models, methods and procedures need to be developed to ensure that these models are incorporated into the designs being developed. Another approach is to use the model as a yardstick against which the designs are evaluated and any deviations are reported and dealt with.

Once the nonredundant data groups have been identified and the interrelationships specified, it is possible to develop a diagrammatic representation of the groups and their relations to individual items. These relationships can be linked to the business model as represented by functions, processes, and activities within processes.

The end result of data modeling is to come up with the set of logical data structures needed to support the business requirements. The structures would be the basis on which the data base administrator will design and develop the physical data bases to meet the development schedule of different application systems. What the data model affords the DBA is an overall perspective and direction that would result in a stable set of data bases no matter which data base or application was implemented first.

Data Model Definition

The data model consists of establishing the entities necessary to support business activities and, in turn, processes. Entities should be thought of as an information group needed for a business activity. In that sense, entities and logical groups are synonymous. Both systems plans and the data model are passed to the actual systems development process once the strategic planning is complete.

There are two aspects to the derivation of the data model:

1. Grouping of data items to form logical records where the data items within the record have been subject to the process of normalization
2. Relationships between these logical data groups based on the ideas of canonical structuring, that is, the derivation of those relationships such that they provide a near-optimal grouping of data which can be used by many applications

There are several design methods that one could use to come up with the data models. Techniques such as normalization and canonical analysis are aids to the intuitive methods of identifying data groups. Theoretically, it should be possible for the data groups to be identified, and then for relationships between these data groups to be derived from the knowledge of the processing rules. In actual fact, most vendors of data modeling techniques combine the analytical approach with experiential and heuristic data from the current and proposed environment to add a touch of reality to the model that is developed.

Data Analysis

Data item analysis has long been the focal point of data base implementation. However, it has become evident that data item analysis alone is insufficient; the delineation of the contexts in which the data items are used is an additional dimension that is required. In short, it is the modeling of what the organization does, with an emphasis on how the information fits in. Data models are basically "created"; given the same set of data items, many data models can be derived. Although each data model lends itself to certain types of meaningful information use, the data model with the highest productive value is the one that best lends itself to the meaning of the context.

The success of a centralized data resource depends on its relevance and usefulness to end users; unless the needs of these users are considered and included in the model, their commitment will decline. User participation is a must for a successful data base project. Finally, data structures must be attuned to the processing requirements; a workable physical data structure is possible only when the data model is well constructed. Organizations may be able to survive with structures that do not conform to any set of data models, but the long-term stability of the systems that are constructed on these premises is doubtful.

Data analysis is the process by which the data items can be grouped together to reflect the association (or strength of relationship) that exists between the items. An assumption that is often made in data analysis is that there is a natural hierarchy of relationships between data items that can be identified. Once these items and groups of data items (entities) are identified, the associations between the items for each of these relationships can be identified. These functional dependencies are analyzed to obtain optimal third-normal-form data structures. Data analysis identifies the corporate groups of data and attempts to avoid redundancies in the groups of data themselves. For example, it would recognize that client and customer and account have the same data definition. There are associations between data items. For example, one branch office has many salespersons; one salesperson has many customers.

Existing tree, plex, and pointer linked structures can be reduced to tabular form with the addition of redundancy. It is possible to use a step-by-step process to reduce tree, plex, and pointer linked structures to two-dimensional table formats. Conversely, tree, plex, and pointer structures can be derived from tabular form; thus tabular form is a good starting point for the physical data base design process. Further details on the normalization process and the derivation of canonical structures are given toward the end of this chapter.

Given that data items could be grouped together at different levels of aggregation, the focus here is on deriving the lowest-level records or user view (also referred to as "tuples" in the relational language terminology).

By means of DBMS software, it is possible to keep the user's view of the data completely separate from the physical representation of data on the data base, and it is possible to change the physical representation and the hardware without changing the user's logical description of the data. One consideration is of overriding importance in the logical data description: the convenience of the majority of application programmers and users. The tabular method of representing the data can easily be understood by users with minimal training in programming. It makes it possible to add new data items, records, and relationships to the data base without changing the existing user views, and permits maximum flexibility in handling ad hoc queries.

The combination of the tabular method of representation and the data management software associated with the data definition and manipulation facilities are called relational data base management systems. The tables that would be derived would have the following properties:

- Each entry in a table represents one data item; there are no repeating groups.
- They are column homogeneous; that is, in any column all items are of the same kind.
- Each column is assigned a distinct name.
- All rows are distinct; duplicate rows are not allowed.
- Both the rows and the columns can be viewed in any sequence at any time without affecting either the information content or the semantics of any function using the table.

Dictionary's Role

Thus far, we have discussed the role of the dictionary in propagating the standard data definitions, which included the usage rules for these items. Another role is associated with the rules concerning the positioning of a data item within a hierarchy of data items. It is important to understand why this is important, so that the reader can keep the rest of the discussion in perspective.

The data model that is obtained through the process of normalization and canonical analysis would be stored in the final form in the dictionary. The interim steps that one would have to go through to derive the model may be stored in the dictionary at the discretion of the user. There are two reasons for this:

1. It may be necessary to redo the process starting at an intermediate point rather than at the beginning. It would be necessary in such cases to track the iteration level in the dictionary.

2. It may be necessary to perform simulations or what-if types of analysis by modifying the parameters manually or in an automated fashion. Under these circumstances, until the appropriate model is selected, the interim data must be available in the dictionary.

Therefore, the dictionary should have the capability to store the following types of data:

- Data about the function, process, activity, and logical group entities
- Data about the attributes of each of the above
- Data about the relationships between the various entities above, and their relationships to the standard data items
- Control data about the various steps in the iterative data modeling process
- Data about the planned data bases and their relationships to standard data items, for potential use in graphic presentation

Typical Dictionary Entities to Support Data Models

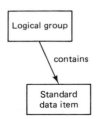

Figure 13-11
Logical group and data element entity model.

The part of the data dictionary that would be most useful for data modeling is the list of standard data item definitions that is maintained by the data base administrator. An entity type to represent a logical group is necessary. The logical group would consist of one or more individual standard data items. This is shown in Figure 13-11.

In addition to storing information about the characteristics of the data items, information about the nature of the relationship between the logical group and the data item will need to be stored. Such factors as how many occurrences of the item could exist per occurrence of the logical group, and whether the item is a key to accessing the logical record, need to be stored along with all other relevant information.

The dictionary can also be used to hold documentation about other information collected during the systems and data planning effort. Figure 13-12 illustrates

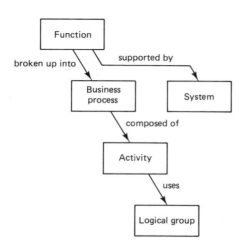

Figure 13-12 Entities that support planning.

an entity model that can store information about several such entities. In the entity model there are linkages to the "system" entity category from the "function" category. The systems that support a particular function can be linked to that function. Note that the "activity" entity is linked to the "logical group" entity. This allows the logical groups of data that support a particular business activity to be portrayed in the dictionary.

Since the dictionary is a central reference point, there is widespread accessibility to the data base, and the dictionary is used for the purpose of documenting systems and data planning information. Most dictionary vendors do not support these entities as part of the standard implementation; however, with the aid of the extensibility feature, entity categories related to systems and data planning can be stored and accessed.

NOTES ON NORMALIZATION

Ideal Structure

The ideal data base structure should include as many as possible of the following:

- Fast access for updating and reading any data in it
- Logical structure that is easy to understand, and thus to maintain and change
- Easy to expand to add in new tables and attributes, anywhere
- Structure independent of the procedures that use the data, so that new procedures may be easily designed
- Minimization of data redundancy (multiple occurrences of the same item) and storage space usage

To a large extent, in real systems the requirement for "fast access" conflicts with the other requirements. To raise the performance level of a system, the data base normally has to be tailored to the particular access paths that will produce the quickest input/output processing. Since program complexity is directly related to data structure complexity, they tend to be both difficult to understand and maintain, and inflexible to other application requirements. Furthermore, systems are usually only "fast" for certain applications (i.e., fast read access), which may make other applications comparatively slower (i.e., data update), due mainly to the fact that special indexes or inversions need to be maintained to get the fast read access.

If an ideal data base structure is to be achieved, it must be measured in terms of the cost to the organization using and maintaining the system over its life cycle; when the costs of software maintenance and ongoing development and enhancements are included, it can be shown that the ideal data base structure is normalized and relational.

Relational Method

Until recently, relational methods were considered too slow for many applications. This is rapidly changing, due mainly to the availability of improved relational data base management systems and the availability of faster machines which perform larger amounts of I/O per unit of time.

In many other respects, a relational structure will have the following advantages:

- Easier to design, since there is a simple, logical, standardized basis
- Easier to document, for the same reasons as above, and there tend to be fewer specially customized features to handle special applications

- Easier to maintain and update, as the structure is relatively independent of the applications that use it
- Able to minimize data redundancy and space usage without having to resort to special design methods

Normalized data groups are better able to accommodate future organizational and business change, and to minimize the impact of that change on computer systems. There are many ways of grouping large numbers of data items; experience has shown that when data items are organized in normalized form, the resulting data structures are more stable and better able to accommodate changing business requirements without having to go through the costly restructuring process associated with conventional file structures.

First Normal Form

A file that is "flat" except for a repeating group can be normalized by removing the repeating group into a separate table or flat file. This is often referred to as first normal form. For example, let us consider the case of a purchase order. The file layout is shown in Figure 13–13.

```
ORDER-NO
SUPPLIER-NO
ORDER-DT
DELIVERY-DT
LINE-ITEM-1
    PART-NO
    PART-PRICE
    PART-QTY
LINE-ITEM-2
    PART-NO
    PART-PRICE
    PART-QTY
repeat occurrences of LINE-ITEM-n
TOTAL-AMT
```

Figure 13–13 File layout of "PURCHASE ORDER" file.

```
ORDER-NO
SUPPLIER-NO
ORDER-DT
DELIVERY-DT
TOTAL-AMT

ORDER-NO
PART-NO
PART-PRICE
PART-QTY
```

Figure 13–14 File layout after repeating groups are removed.

If the repeating group LINE-ITEM is removed to form another table, the layouts would be as shown in Figure 13–14. Note that the second flat file layout has the ORDER-NO as part of the key; this increases the amount of redundancy, although it does not necessarily imply an increase in storage requirements, because normalization is concerned with logical structures—the user's view of data—and not with the way they are physically represented in storage. If repeating groups are not separated through normalization, further evolution of the data base may necessitate their separation at a much higher maintenance cost. Note also that each normalized record has a key associated with it (shown underlined). The key must have two properties:

1. The value of the key must uniquely identify that record (or tuple).
2. No attribute in the key can be discarded without destroying the property of unique identification.

```
PURCHASE-ORDER (ORDER-NO, SUPPLIER-NO,
            ORDER-DT, DELIVERY-DT, TOTAL-AMT)

PURCHASE-ITEM (ORDER-NO, PART-NO,
            PART-PRICE, PART-QTY)
```

Figure 13–15 "PURCHASE_ORDER" and "PURCHASE_ITEM" relations. PURCHASE-ORDER and PURCHASE-ITEM are names of the relation, the items within the parentheses are the names of the domains, and the underlined items are the primary keys needed to identify the tuple.

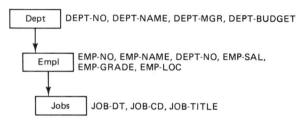

Figure 13–16 Tree structure.

A shorthand notation to represent the flat file layouts (also called relations) has been developed, as shown in Figure 13–15. Similar types of logic can be applied to tree and plex structures to reduce them to normalized relations. In the case of tree structures, the child segment or member record would have a key that included the owner identification key. Consider the structure shown in Figure 13–16. The normalized form of this tree structure would be represented as shown in Figure 13–17.

DEPT (DEPT-NO, DEPT-NAME, DEPT-MGR,
      DEPT-BUDGET)

EMPL (EMP-NO, EMP-NAME, DEPT-NO, EMP-SAL,
      EMP-GRADE, EMP-LOC)

JOBS (EMP-NO, JOB-DT, JOB-CD, JOB-TITLE)

Figure 13–17 Normalized form of tree structure.

In normalizing a structure, extra data items may be added, for two reasons. First, primary-key data items may be added to make the resulting concatenated key identify the tuple uniquely. Second attribute data items may be added to represent the paths that are shown on conventional schemas by lines and arrows. The normalized form of the traditional bill of materials structure (a plex structure) is shown in Figure 13–18. Note that in the situation above, the answer to the where-used question would require manipulation of the BREAKDOWN relation.

ITEM (ITEM-NO, CATEGORY, ITEM-DESC)

BREAKDOWN (ITEM-NO, COMPONENT-ITEM-NO,
           USAGE-QTY)

Figure 13–18 Normalized form of traditional bill of materials structure.

In attempting to lay out the relationships between data items, designers must concern themselves with which attributes are dependent on which others. Saying that item B is functionally dependent on item A is equivalent to saying that A identifies B. In other words, if the value of A is known at a point in time, the value of B is determined. In the relation shown in Figure 13–19, EMP-NO is not functionally dependent on EMP-SALARY, because more than one employee could have the same salary. Similarly, EMP-NO is not functionally dependent on PRJCT-NO, but PRJCT-COMP-DT is. No other attribute in the relation is fully dependent on PRJCT-NO.

EMPLOYEE (EMP-NO, EMP-NAME, EMP-SALARY,
          PRJCT-NO, PRJCT-COMP-DT)

EMP-NO is dependent on EMP-NAME;
EMP-NAME is dependent on EMP-NO;
EMP-SALARY is dependent on either EMP-NO or
EMP-NAME;
PRJCT-NO is dependent on either EMP-NAME or
EMP-NO;
PRJCT-COMP-DT is dependent on EMP-NAME,
EMP-NO, or PRJCT-NO.

Figure 13–19 Dependency of attributes.

Second Normal Form

Note that a data item can be functionally dependent on a combination of data items or on a concatenated key. Thus we can define second normal form of a relation if it is already in first normal form and a functional dependency can be shown for each of the nonkeyed data items. For example, the relation shown in Figure 13–20 is not in second normal form. This relation has only one candidate key. SUPPLIER-NAME

SUPPLY SOURCE (<u>SUPPLIER-NO, PART-NO,</u>
SUPPLIER-NAME, SUPPLIER-DTL, PART-PRICE)

Figure 13–20   Relation not in second normal form.

does not participate in a candidate key because the same supplying firm at different locations has different supplier numbers. Supplier name does not identify supplier number. The nonprime data items SUPPLIER-NAME and SUPPLIER-DTL are functionally dependent on SUPPLIER-NO, not on the whole concatenated key. Some of the problems in not being in second normal form are:

- We cannot enter details about a supplier until that supplier supplies a part. If the supplier does not supply a part, there is no key.
- If a supplier should temporarily cease to supply a part, the deletion of the last segment or record or tuple containing that SUPPLIER-NO will also delete the data item SUPPLIER-DTL. It would normally be desirable that SUPPLIER-DTL be preserved.
- Problems will arise when the details for a particular supplier need to be updated. Every record would have to be searched that contains the supplier as part of the key, thus increasing the amount of processing.

These types of irregularities can be removed by splitting the relation into two relations in second normal form, as shown in Figure 13–21.

SUPPLIER-INFO (<u>SUPPLIER-NO,</u> SUPPLIER-NAME,
SUPPLIER-DTL)

SUPPLIER PARTS (<u>PART-NO, SUPPLIER-NO,</u>
PART-PRICE)

Figure 13–21   Relation in second normal form.

Third Normal Form

Anomalies similar to the above can occasionally occur in a relation that is in second normal form. To remove them, the last normalization step is used, which converts second normal form to third normal form. This step removes what is referred to as "transitive dependence." Suppose that A, B, C are three data items within a relation. Assume also that C is functionally dependent on B, and B is functionally dependent on A. This implies that C is functionally dependent on A. Now, if the inverse mapping is nonsimple (i.e., if A is not functionally dependent on B, or B is not functionally dependent on C), C is said to be transitively dependent on A. In the employee relation example, PRJCT-COMP-DT is functionally dependent on PRJCT-NO, and PRJCT-NO is functionally dependent on EMP-NO. PRJCT-COMP-DT is therefore transitively dependent on EMP-NO. This relation can be converted to third normal form by splitting it as shown in Figure 13–22. The pair of relations above is preferable because information about projects will be needed independently of the employee information, and the completion date is primarily a fact about a project rather than about the employee. If the relation were not in third normal form:

EMPL (<u>EMP-NO</u>, EMP-NAME, EMP-SALARY, PRJCT-NO)

PROJECT (<u>PRJCT-NO</u>, PRJCT-COMP-DT)

Figure 13-22   Relation in third normal form.

- Before any employees are recruited for a project, the completion date of the project cannot be recorded.
- If all the employees should leave the project so that the project has no employees until others are recruited, all records containing the completion date would be deleted.
- If the completion date is changed, it will be necessary to search for all records containing that completion date, and update them all.

The concept of third normal form applies not only to relational data bases, but to all data bases. Experience has shown that the records of a CODASYL system and of other file-based systems can benefit from being in third normal form. An analyst may sometimes choose to allow a record not to be stored in third normal form, but when this is so, the analyst should at least know what he or she is doing, understand the reasons, and understand the possible consequences when new data items and relationships are added. A record not in third normal form may occasionally be used for performance reasons.

NOTES ON CANONICAL STRUCTURES

Structure Rules

It is necessary not only to identify the third-normal-form records of the relational model, but also to identify the uses for the records in the model and come up with structuring rules for the interrecord relationships. In many cases this would result in the integration of the new record into the developing canonical model. The derivation of optimal relationships between groups of data is called canonical analysis.

Canonical analysis begins with the logical views of data, which may be current user views, records, documents, or displays used in current applications, or views of how the data may be used in the future. The procedure of combining the views into a schema—a minimal set of canonical records with the requisite links between records—is tedious to do by hand but easy by computer.

The process of canonical analysis is an iterative one. The base data for canonical analysis are the user views. In addition, data about the access paths, the frequency of access, and the response-time requirements should also be stated. As has been stated before, there are many ways to organize the data into a canonical schema. The best way to come up with the model would include the maximum number of parameters about the context, to make it as realistic as possible. One parameter that should not be included in the initial iterations is that covering the various physical characteristics of the machines. The reason for this is that the performance characteristics of computer hardware and software tend to improve over time; to be limited by current processing limitations would tend to cloud the issues and lead to a less-than-optimal data model.

Dictionary's Role

The data dictionary provides storage for the various normalized views of the schema. Once the logical groups have been stored in the dictionary, a report can be generated that will display in matrix form the data items that are part of each logical group and the common data items between logical groups. A measure of the association between logical groups is the number of data items in common between them. Other measures, such as common access frequency and response time for related retrievals, should be input and considered. When the matrix is built and displayed in graphic form, a team composed of representatives from the planning, data base, and systems development functions should review the data on the associations and make the decisions as to which entities should be associated in the entity model diagram. These decisions have to be made; otherwise, all possible relationships would have to be specified. For a 10 × 10 logical groups matrix, this amount to 45 pairwise associations. For a 20 × 20 logical groups matrix, this would amount to 190 possible associations. Fortunately, not all of the possible associations occur in the business world. Thus the major role of the advisory team would be to weed out the weak associations and identify the strong ones.

The collection of data definitions and data item groupings in the data dictionary, the logical groups matrix (LGM), and the final diagrams taken together constitute the final data model. Since the model does change as a business changes, it must be validated at least once a year.

Physical Implementation

The final step is the physical implementation of the data model. If truly relational data base systems were available, the physical implementation would be identical to the logical model just completed, and the association between the logical groups would be performed dynamically. But the capacities of the commercially available data base management systems (DBMS), and the capacities of the machines to run relational structures for production applications, prove to be obstacles to direct implementation of the model. Until the capacities of relational file handlers and the underlying machines improve, the model would have to be implemented using a combination of the file structures and machine combinations available today. Thus the DBA has to keep in mind the data model that one is striving toward, but gear the compromises that have to be made during physical data base design so that attainment of the data model is possible in the long run.

chapter 14

Data Dictionary Role in Data Base Administration

INTRODUCTION

We begin this chapter by discussing the evolution of MIS organizations to the data base approach. The role of data base administration (DBA), and the functions that are part of a typical DBA organization are listed. Then the DBA role in the systems development life cycle (SDLC) is outlined in terms of the data base documentation that is needed from the DBA at each stage. Particular emphasis is placed on the logical data base design, the physical data base design, and the operational data base recovery procedures for which the DBA is solely responsible. The DBA plays the key role in ensuring that the data models and data conventions that have been developed as part of the data planning exercise are incorporated into the logical and physical data base designs for that system project. The role of the dictionary in documenting the data conventions, and then generating source code reflecting these conventions directly from the data dictionary, are illustrated via an example of a field activity data base development project.

DATA BASE APPROACH

Application systems are typically designed to satisfy specific, usually carefully defined output requirements (such as payroll, accounts payable, order entry, bill of materials, etc.). Each application is set up with its own input files (with specific processing rules) and generates its own set of data files. Hence the same data items reside in several files subject to different processing rules. With the advent of end-user computing, the ability to create data files increases geometrically. This could result in several versions of the same data, some of them inconsistent.

Application systems have been developed for individual managers and departments, reflecting the organization structure and information requirements at a given point in time. They also reflect the individual styles and preferences of the managers and analysts who built them. Changes in organization, management philosophy, or style tended to have a significant impact on application systems because they redefine information needs. Since the data files, and their underlying structures, were developed with an application in mind, these changes have resulted in data structure changes which have been expensive and time-consuming to make.

The data processing environment created by using the "applications" approach to developing computer systems results in data processing input, storage, and processing techniques geared to specific output needs. The "applications" approach implies that:

- Systems are built for individual managers, not for the company as a whole.
- Justifications for data processing services are based on cost trade-offs on an application-by-application basis rather than on company plans to improve overall efficiency or productivity.
- The data processing environment services managers who want computerization; that is, it evolves along the path of least resistance subject to managers with budget dollars.
- The data processing department is viewed as a program development shop.

The data base approach, however, is characterized by the recognition by top levels of management that data are a corporate resource and must be subject to the same disciplines and controls as assets and labor. A data base is a repository of data, not information. Information can be generated from the stored data. A data base is the starting point from which information processes are constructed. The data base must provide sufficient breadth to permit an information system to "weather the storms of change."

The raw data that describe a company and its relationship to its environment would be independent of the organization of the company. The operational functions and the data necessary to support the operational functions do not change once the functions are well defined and incorporated into the data model. Only the information produced from the data base reflects the personality of management.

The data base approach requires corporate data planning so the data bases will be able to serve a variety of applications through the use of common shared data. Using common data implies that trade-offs must be made. The data base environment that results from the adoption of the data base approach consists of the following three structures.

1. The data base input control systems collect and manage input to data bases and ensure data quality and integrity. Input data validation against control or reference data files is an essential part of this function. The data base input control systems, once established, should not undergo many changes because they deal with relatively stable business functions.

2. The data base output control systems operate completely differently from the input control systems because they are subordinate to both organizational structure and management information requirements. In a properly developed data base, changes in output requirements should rarely cause changes in the data base input control system, because the information required to satisfy 80 to 90 percent of management's decision-making needs is, in most companies, developed from combining, arranging, analyzing, sorting, and reporting a subset of between 400 and 800 basic items of data.

3. The data base storage and processing control systems manage the operations (storage retrieval) within the data base and include capabilities for backup, recovery, data availability, security, and so on.

The descriptions above do not imply three sets of data bases; they represent three ways of structuring data bases. They may be optimized separately or together; the data base approach implies that these structures should be optimized together. This is where the trade-offs occur. The data base and system designers must be aware of the variations in requirements as data are entered, processed, and output as information. The data base environment is the result of implementation of a data base plan that is in synchronization with the corporate plan.

Data Base Utility

The end result of the data base approach is the creation of a set of data bases that reflect business strategy and meet the information processing needs of the business. In the literature, these have been referred to as "subject" data bases, "reference" files, data base "portfolio," or data base "utility"—in the sense that these data bases are available for everybody to utilize. Once these data bases have been built, minor fine tuning would be required in order to meet the expansion of the business. Major restructuring should be avoided by skillfully designing the data base to accommodate nominal swings in business direction.

To achieve this data base utility is not a trivial task. It requires the definition of the data structures that need to be developed, a migration plan for moving from the existing file structures and processes to the new one, implementation of a set of data bases and maintenance procedures, while not disturbing the processing that is carried out on a day-to-day basis. In most cases the construction of a data base utility will be perceived by users as overhead activity that takes resources away from the applications backlog that exists. Then there is the inertia that exists in any organization that works against this activity. The reasoning would be: "Why do something differently when the existing files and data bases manage to do the job!"

DATA BASE ADMINISTRATION

Data base administration (DBA) encompasses all the technical and management activities required for organizing, maintaining, and directing the data base environment. The DBA optimizes usage of data in a shared data base environment, implements a systematic methodology for the centralized management and control of data resources, and balances conflicting objectives with respect to the organization's mission and the overall economy of data handling.

Objectives of DBA

The achievement of the data base utility is without question the primary purpose of data base administration. To guide the current and future systems development projects so that they assist in achieving the data base utility, the DBA has to gain control over the current environment. The DBA concurrently develops and implements the data conventions consistently throughout the organization. The DBA has a dual role: to nudge the current system development efforts along a set of data plans, while at the same time implementing data bases that meet long-term needs.

The effectiveness of DBA has to be tied into how closely the application systems and data bases mirror the data plans. The data dictionary is the repository of these data plans. Other objectives, such as integrity of data and nonredundancy, are tied into the data plans. For example, if the data plan states that the engineering department is the originator of part numbers within the organization, it is the duty of the DBA to ensure that nobody else is creating part numbers in any other system without a reference to the authoritative source. Whether data are duplicated in different files or not, the DBA is responsible for ensuring that the values of similar data items stay consistent with each other if they are duplicated.

The DBA must have complete authority over the decisions related to the design, development, and maintenance of the data base in order to fulfill the foregoing objectives. Together with the authority goes the responsibility for the performance of the data base to meet application system and user needs.

Traditionally, the data base administration function has had the most use for a data dictionary. This is because the data base administrator has to sort out the complexity of the data interactions with the programs and systems, and thus simplify the task of managing and controlling the data base environment. To do this without an automated tool would be a herculean effort requiring a lot of manual labor. The data dictionary fulfills the requirement for a tool for the DBA and is often the justification for purchasing a data dictionary.

Functions of DBA

A sample charter for a data base administration function follows:

1. Data base definition. The DBA is responsible for cataloging the data resources of the organization and maintaining an accurate representation of the relationships between data items and their usage in business processes, application systems, programs, and files. The above includes:

- Definition of common (or reference) data items
- Identification of appropriate organization(s) and person(s) within those organizations who have responsibility for sourcing and maintaining data items
- Assignment of standard definitions of data items and ensuring that the standard definitions are used in application systems and files
- Maintenance of where-used information for data items, records, and so on.

2. Data base design. The major design activity is the design and structuring of the data bases to meet application system needs for on-line and batch processing and user needs for query/ad hoc processing, taking into consideration the overall business needs as identified in the business system plan. The above includes:

- Initial definition of the data base portion of the business system plan and making revisions to the plan based on changing business needs and technology availability
- Derivation of the normalized data structures from the planning process to be used as guidelines in application data structure design; identification of data flows from authoritative source persons, documents, and files to the systems utilizing the data; design and development of reference files
- Involvement in application systems planning and design, to provide input on the impact of new application systems on existing data base processing, transaction processing, and query processing loads
- Design of the data structure (schema, subschema), storage structure, mapping, and search strategies
- Review of data base design in light of user experience and redesign involving restructure and reorganization of data, based on input from application systems personnel and end users
- Establishment of short- and long-term strategies for data integration; anticipation of the need to distribute the data base and plan accordingly.

3. Data base administration. The DBA is responsible for the creation of the data base files, specifying the subschema to application systems personnel and for providing support and technical assistance related to the data base management system (DBMS). The above includes:

- Specification of subschemas and recommended access paths to application systems personnel and provision of necessary training
- Provision of sufficient data base capacity to facilitate concurrent development of applications using shared files, including the allocation, control, and monitoring of file space for the test and production environments
- Definition of application programming procedures to follow to enable recovery from "soft" and "hard" types of failures; definition of responsibilities and action cycle in case of program abort in production mode, including the responsibility to resolve data base problems
- Provision of guidelines to process the data base efficiently, including the establishment and enforcement of data base access logic and procedures; monitoring the efficiency and responsiveness of the data base; reorganization of data bases to improve processing speeds.

4. Query processing administration. The DBA is responsible for providing appropriate views (subschemas) of the data base to the end user for query purposes. The above includes:

- Ascertaining, through discussions with application systems personnel and user management, the query processing requirements and incorporating them in the data base design
- Monitoring the query processing load on the system and data bases and giving feedback to the end users regarding the efficiency of their query programs
- Educating end users in proper use of the query system
- Providing data extracts of the production data base to satisfy the needs of end-user computing.

5. Transaction processing system administration. Since the transaction processing (TP) system could affect overall system performance, the TP administration functions will be carried out in close consultation with the technical staff in operations. The DBA is responsible for specifying the TP system generation parameters to operators for starting the TP system and also the procedures for restart of the TP system in case of failure. The above includes:

- Monitoring TP system performance and fine tuning to obtain the desired response time
- Provision of test TP system to application systems personnel for development and testing
- Definition and implementation of backup procedures for files accessed via TP
- Definition of parameters to be used in transaction programs (e.g., I/Os per transaction, screen mode, conversational mode, etc.)
- Assessing the need for distributing the transaction processing load via different mechanisms (e.g., distributed data entry, remote concentration facility, cooperating transactions, etc.) across a network and plan accordingly.

6. Data security. The DBA is responsible for providing mechanisms that enable authorized individuals to control access to the appropriate parts of the computerized data base to those persons with a designated need to know. The DBA is ultimately responsible and accountable to monitor and control access to the data base. The above includes:

- Usage of security locks and keys and other implementer-defined security features that already exist; development of security monitors and procedures, if none are available
- Definition (and implementation) of security validation procedures to be followed by users of the TP and query processors; ensuring that these procedures are incorporated into the application programs; ensuring the segregation of program testing from production data base systems.

7. Data integrity. Data integrity is related to the accuracy and correctness of the data from the stage where the user has performed the data-entry function to the stage where the data are manipulated by application system programs and ultimately stored in the data base by system software programs such as DBMS. The DBA is responsible for ensuring that the TPMS and DBMS software perform their functions properly and back out of an incorrect update situation. It is the responsibility of the application system personnel, in conjunction with the end user, to build in validation checks for editing purposes, consistency checks such as hash totals, and audit trails and reports that will lead to identification of breaches in data integrity. It is the DBA's responsibility to bring to the attention of application systems personnel the need for the data integrity checks. It is also the responsibility of the DBA to monitor the quality of the data, report potential problems to the appropriate persons for resolution, and take appropriate action (where it is warranted) to protect the integrity of the data base.

8. Program change control. All file and data base layouts will be maintained by the DBA in central libraries. Any change in a file layout (copybook) will only be made after its impact on all programs has been identified. Version control of copybooks in the development and production environments will be enforced by the DBA through the use of standardized procedures and policies. All programs (batch and TP) that read from or write to the data base will be reviewed by the DBA to ensure that all data base and TP standards for processing the data base have been followed. This would also enable the DBA to update the where-used information for the data items that are affected by the program. After the review, the programs will be placed on the production library by authorized personnel.

Major Activities of DBA

- Maintains the data dictionary
- Plans the data base
- Designs data base structures (i.e., schema, subschema, FD, sort files, etc.)
- Creates data base procedures, documentation, and standards
- Provides assistance to all users of the data base (i.e., programmers, analysts, end users)
- Maintains data base integrity and availability via implementation of adequate backup and recovery procedures
- Manages the on-line and query processors and provision of concurrent access controls

DBA ROLE IN SDLC

Following is an outline of the system development life cycle (SDLC) process, which highlights and identifies the role of the data base administrator (DBA). As the system development process takes place, the DBA should be aware of the documentation that will play a critical role during and after the process. These are indicated in the appropriate phases after the tag "DB documentation."

System development can be divided into five main phases, with smaller divisions within each phase. On the following pages is a sample system development life cycle. Each phase and/or division contains details about who does the tasks, who participates, what resources are relied on, exactly what the tasks are, what the results will be, and the role of the data dictionary within this life cycle. The five main phases of the SDLC are: (1) system study and evaluation, (2) system design, (3) system development, (4) implementation, and (5) audit.

1. System study and evaluation. The primary purpose of the system study and evaluation phase is to define the system from the business point of view and to have the system design approved by the relevant user organizations. The user of the system must be fully cognizant of the various features of the system and the implications of the system in the areas of user training, conversion to new procedures, and hardware and software requirements. In addition, this is the phase where a preliminary cut is taken at defining all the data items that the system will use, so that the DBA will begin to plan the logical structures and visualize the impact on existing files and data bases.

Scope done by:

Analyst, user

Resource documents:

System documentation
Project request
Existing documentation

Tasks:

Analyze needs and benefits.
Analyze current business practices.
Prepare proposed system overview, narratives, and diagrams.
Prepare cost/benefit analysis and evaluation.
Perform system evaluation.

Comment:

DBA consulted to determine impact of system on existing and proposed data bases. DBA notified of impact on other systems. DBA consulted to investigate similarities in utilization of data resources.

Outputs:

Finalized user-supplied requirements
Finalized project scope
Finalized information required
System performance criteria—ballpark (includes hardware proposal)
System overview—narrative and diagrams (conceptual design)
Sign-offs
System study and evaluation
Analyst has a written document defining the information the system should generate
Analyst creates a description of the proposed system and a schematic of the proposed system

Analyst creates a cost/benefit analysis for the proposed system, if required

User signs off on and understands the system

DB documentation:

Bubble chart of applications interfacing with data base. This is a diagram illustrating the flow of data between the applications and the data base.

2. System design

The system design phase includes two activities: (a) data requirements and design and (b) program design. These two activities should proceed in close synchronization with each other, because changes in one could affect the other. For example, if a response-time requirement was set to close tolerances, an existing file may not be usable to get the response. On the other hand, if the application requires that data be sourced from different parts of the organization, the time it would take to build these interfaces must be factored into the project schedule.

A. DATA REQUIREMENTS AND DESIGN

Done by:

Analyst, DBA

Resource document:

System study, evaluation document

Tasks:

Define data flows.

Prepare data item definitions for data dictionary.

Develop a list of the access paths needed.

Develop a generic diagram of new or revised data structure.

Review a data base design and data items.

Develop a security plan.

Develop a backup and recovery plan.

Comment:

With the assistance of the data dictionary and the DBA, the programmer/analyst will develop a list of the data items. These standard data items and their narratives are added to the dictionary only after appropriate approvals have been obtained.

Outputs:

Preliminary file design

Logical data flow diagram

Standard data items

Understanding of information the system will use and generate

DB documentation:

Data dictionary with all data items, narratives, and attributes that will be required for the system

Sources and users of all data items in the data base; should include the authoritative source for each data item

Logical structure diagrams illustrating data groups and relationships between the groups; should include data base entry points required and the organization of the data within the data base

B. PROGRAM DESIGN

Done by:

Analyst/programmer, user, DBA

Resource documents:

Completed and approved system specifications
Programming standards
Finalized user-supplied requirements

Tasks:

Define input/output (screens, FDs, DB copybooks, files, etc.).
Prepare program narratives, specifications, and detailed test specifications.
Prepare development schedule and estimates.
Define user-prepared system acceptance criteria.

Outputs:

Program specifications: charts, narratives, etc.
Testing specifications
System acceptance criteria

DB documentation:

Physical data base structures with which the programs will work; these include DBMS schemas and subschemas, contents of included files and copybooks, diagrams illustrating the entry points and access paths, record descriptions, file definitions, etc.

3. Development

The purpose of the development phase is to build and test the components of the system as specified in the prior phases. Concurrent with the development should be the process of user training, building conversion interfaces and strategies, ensuring that the operations department is kept up to date about the new system and the additional processing loads being placed on existing files and machines. This will allow the operations department to schedule the impact of the new system and balance the load. The development phase consists of four parts: (a) data base preparation, (b) program preparation, (c) subsystem development, and (d) systems integration testing.

A. DATA BASE PREPARATION

Done by:

DBA, programmer/analyst

Resource documents:

File design
Data base standards

Tasks:

Analyze data items.
Review data base design.
Finalize data base security/recovery.
Load/update data dictionary.
Create data base.

Test data base.
Create/alter copybooks, schema.

Outputs:

Finalized file design
Updated data dictionary
Test data base

Comment:

Any changes at this stage have to be approved by the managers concerned. Any
new data items *must be completely entered* in the data dictionary.

DB documentation:

Backup and recovery procedures, including listing of all applications accessing
the data base, and the kind of backup and recovery procedure needed to maintain data integrity for each of the given applications against the data base
Test data base plan which includes the approach to maintain an abbreviated
but adequate subset of the production data base for testing

B. PROGRAM PREPARATION

Done by:

Programmer/analyst

Resource documents:

Program specifications
Testing specifications
Programming standards
Data base specifications

Tasks:

Prepare flowcharts.
Write code and incorporate data base error handling in *all* programs.
Prepare program test data.
Test program.

Outputs:

Error-free program
Program documentation
Dictionary updated with program narrative

C. SUBSYSTEM DEVELOPMENT

Done by:

Programmer/analyst

Resource documents:

System documentation
User-supplied requirements
Acceptance criteria
Operations standards

Tasks:

Prepare operations procedures.

Prepare subsystem test data.

Test subsystem.

Prepare user procedures.

Familiarize training staff.

Outputs:

Preliminary operations procedures

Preliminary user procedures

Error-free subsystems

Approved test results

D. SYSTEMS INTEGRATION TESTING

Done by:

Programmer/analyst, DBA, operations

Resource documents:

Preliminary operations and user procedures

System documentation

Preliminary implementation plan

Acceptance criteria

Tasks:

Perform system test.

Perform system review and approval (includes standards).

Finalize operations and user procedures.

Start training users.

Finalize implementation plan.

Outputs:

Finalized operations and user procedures

Finalized implementation

Accepted system, including list of outstanding issues

Training material

DB documentation:

Reorganization procedures, including the programs, flowcharts, and operation instructions needed to reorganize the production data base

Operational procedures and considerations, including special instructions to operations for handling the data base

4. Implementation

Implementation phase consists of two steps: (a) data base preparation and, (b) beta or parallel test and implementation.

A. DATA BASE PREPARATION

Done by:

Programmer/analyst, DBA

Resource documents:

Finalized implementation plan
Operations procedures
System specifications

Tasks:

Create data bases.
Expand existing data bases.
Load data bases.
Monitor performance.
Install data bases.
Perform capacity (load) tests.
Check data integrity.
Check security requirements.

Outputs:

Data bases are on appropriate machines.
Communication networks are in working condition.
System subsystem report is issued from data dictionary.

B. BETA OR PARALLEL TEST AND IMPLEMENTATION

Done by:

Analyst, user, operations

Resource documents:

Entire system documentation

Tasks:

Install system.
Train users.
Test system.
Review and approve results.
Implement.

Outputs:

Approval to implement
Completed system
Completed procedures

DB documentation:

Monitor the physical characteristics of the data base, such as use of records
and file growth.

Monitor the users of the data base and the access privileges of each person;
brief explanation of the type of access and the reason.

Document any data base modification requests and the impact caused by making the modifications.

5. Audit

System evaluation done by:

Analyst, user

Resource documents:

Entire system documentation
System processing results

Tasks:

Evaluate user satisfaction.
Evaluate performance.
Evaluate security.
Evaluate control.
Evaluate backup and recovery.

Outputs:

Evaluation report with recommendations

DB documentaion:

A list of data items that have been inserted into the data base to ensure audit-ability, for the purpose of monitoring the accuracy and evaluating the integrity of the data content

Logical Design

The logical design of the data base is an important part of system development, because this is where the DBA injects the data definitions and directions that have been developed as part of the overall data planning process discussed in an earlier chapter. The logical data groups, the relationships between the groups, and the access paths must conform to the plans developed earlier. This will ensure that no matter which system is being developed, the same data definitions and directions are being applied consistently.

The logical design process starts with the user functional specification, and based on the requirements, a logical view of the data requirements can be established. For example, if the processing of service call information requires on-line access by call number, a key of call number would seem appropriate. This is shown in Figure 14–1.

However, if the processing of the service call information requires processing by a branch office in an aggregated fashion, it would only be necessary to have all the information pertaining to the branch office stored together for quick access, as shown in Figure 14–2.

Thus the logical models could vary significantly depending on the application's requirements. However, the rules underlying the model would not be different. In the example above, if the governing data standard was that one branch office could service many calls, and calls would remain the responsibility of one branch office

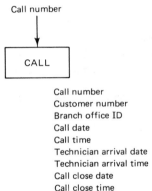

Call number

CALL

Call number
Customer number
Branch office ID
Call date
Call time
Technician arrival date
Technician arrival time
Call close date
Call close time

Figure 14–1 ''Call processing'' logical model: I.

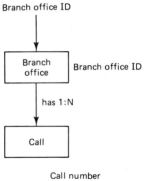

Branch office ID

Branch office ID

has 1:N

Call

Call number
Customer number
Call date
Call time
Technician arrival date
Technician arrival time
Call close date
Call close time

Figure 14-2 "Call processing" logical model: II.

only, even if personnel from another branch responded or assisted in resolving the service call. We see that the data standard clearly defines the underlying relations that can be permitted in the logical data design for a particular application. If the application tried to operate on a different underlying standard, that would be exposed clearly for all to see, and the conflict could be resolved only by the data standard being changed, which would require changes in the data plan.

Physical Design

The physical design process is one where the DBA translates the logical design into implementable physical file and record structures that can meet the performance requirements of the application. Therefore, there can be variability in the physical design, depending on the hardware and software systems that are being used. Again, it should be noted that the data standards are still respected; that is, data standards for data item size, validation criteria, and so on, are followed through faithfully in the physical design process.

A logical model such as described above could be represented by many physical designs. For example, if the implementation data base management system is a CODASYL DBMS, the structure shown in Figure 14-3 may be appropriate. Or if the data management system is an indexed sequential file structure, the physical design could be like the one shown in Figure 14-4.

The branch office record would carry multiple occurrences of call data in the branch office record. Another way to improve the design is to add the call number as the key to the branch office record, so that each record now carries the detail for only one call, but recognize that the relationship between branch office and call that exists in the data standard has been followed through in the logical design and hence in the physical designs that follow.

Branch office ID

SYS-BRANCH-SET

Branch office

BRANCH-CALL-SET

Call

Figure 14-3 "Call processing" physical design in CODASYL format.

Branch office ID

Branch office

Figure 14-4 "Call processing" physical design in sequential file format.

Data Items for Monitoring Data Base

The tools to monitor the data base should be defined as part of the development project, and not after the fact. This is because the addition of additional data items that ensure auditability and control have to be defined as part of the logical and physical design. The procedures should be clear regarding who gets the control reports and the responsibilities should the control reports indicate data integrity problems.

DATA DICTIONARY ROLE IN DATA BASE ADMINISTRATION

The data dictionary catalogs an organization's data resources: what data exist, where they originate, who uses them, their format, and so on. Data dictionaries can produce various reports based on the catalog as well as data description code for inclusion in application programs. There are three parts of the dictionary that will play an important part in data base administration activity:

1. Documentation of the data definitions, including data items, logical groups, and process-to-system interrelationships, used in logical design
2. Documentation of existing program-to-data interrelationships that contain where-used and how-used information, used in physical design; in addition, the capability of the dictionary to hold and generate files and copybooks for inclusion in programs
3. Documentation of operational information relating to recovery procedures, timings of jobs, and file space statistics will enable the DBA to monitor the growth of files and prevent mishaps from occurring by enabling the DBA to take preventive measures

Entity Model

The entities that exist in the dictionary must at a minimum provide support for the above-mentioned areas. Depending on the type of hardware and software that are in use, the dictionary must be capable of supporting the DBMSs that are in use. Active interfaces to compilers, run-time units, and 4GLs make the job of data base administration easier to perform. Where networks are in use, the capability to describe and support data that are located in distributed data bases should be available. See Figure 14–5 for an entity model to support data base administration.

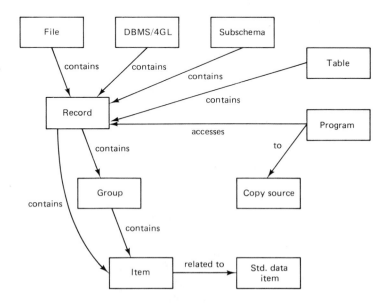

Figure 14–5 Entity model to support data base administration

DB Documentation Requirements

Guidelines. Documentation in the dictionary should assist in the maintenance and recovery process. Normally, recovery is done under extreme time pressure to repair the data base as quickly as possible and to get the application systems on-line again. Therefore, documentation in the dictionary should be geared to the person performing the recovery or maintenance; that is, the information should be presented in a concise manner and in a format that can be easily understood. The use of graphics should be maximized, for as the saying goes, a picture is worth a thousand words.

For example, note the information needed by a person doing maintenance to locate a system problem. At the minimum, in addition to a program source listing, the following are required:

- System specification
- System narrative
- System flowchart
- System data flow
- Program data flow
- Program narrative
- Program specification
- Edit and validation criteria for data items
- Where-used information about data items

The data dictionary can provide much of this information, detailing definitions and relationships as well as general operation data. The following is some of the information that can be obtained from the dictionary and its value to the DBA.

- Summary documentation about systems
  - Quick look-up by maintenance personnel
  - Training new hires
  - Centralized summary documentation
- Relationships between program and data variables
  - Plan the impact of changes in data size, definition, etc.
  - Reduce the amount of redundancy as a result of using existing data items
  - Reduce development expenditures by using existing programs to obtain the data, if possible
- What information is where
  - Reduce time spent in searching for data about different entities
- Sources and users of data
  - Assign responsibility for data, thus enhancing integrity
  - Save time and avoid duplication of effort
- Edit and validation criteria
  - Ensure consistency of values in data items
  - Provide better intersystem communication because standard processing rules have been applied
  - Provide better control of data
- File and subschema definitions
  - Ensure consistency of presentation of file structures
  - Lead to standardization and centralized control of files by data base administration
- Interactive access to data dictionary
  - Leads to resolution of terminology conflicts
  - Identifies redundant items

— Settles issues regarding name, abbreviation, size, etc.

— Results in consistency and control

• Jobs, programs, time schedule, machine

— Is a base that can be used for producing a schedule

— Leads to better machine utilization

Audit Controls. In a transaction-oriented DBMS environment, the auditor faces the unique problem of having to assess the impact of each transaction on the data base itself. Specifically, the DD can provide complete and accurate information relating transaction programs to records and data items. Using the information above, the auditor can understand exactly how each transaction enters the data base and how it traverses from one record type to another. This allows proper evaluation of the degree to which controls are necessary during the transaction processing. An understanding of the requirements of the auditor will enable the DBA to store the proper types of information that will assist the auditor. The DD functions that assist the auditor are:

• Documentation of data and systems

Audit trail from where-used information

Control through generation of file descriptions and the inherent facility for change control procedures

Access control information that can be stored in the DD and used actively at program execution

Example. The documentation that would be produced by the DBA in support of the data base design and development process is outlined below. Every major data base must be identified and documented in full. As the data bases evolve to meet the changing needs of the business, the documentation for the data bases is kept current by updating the relevant portions of the documentation in the data dictionary.

1. Bubble chart of applications interfacing with data base, illustrating all data flow between the applications and the data base.
2. Data definitions for all data items, their narratives and attributes; data dictionary will be the source for the information.
3. List of authoritative sources of all data elements in the data base.
4. Logical structure diagrams:
   a. Data groupings and the relationships between the groupings.
   b. Data base entry points and organization of the data.
5. File structure definition:
   a. If file is DBMS, a schema listing produced from the DBMS schema processor.
   b. Listing of all subschemas and their contents.
   c. Diagram illustrating the logical view of each subschema.
   d. Copybooks, record descriptions, selects, etc.
6. Backup and recovery procedures listing, all applications accessing the data base and the kind of backup and recovery procedure needed to maintain data integrity for each of the given applications against the data base.
7. Test data base plan for maintaining an abbreviated but adequate representation of the production data base for testing.
8. Reorganization procedures, including programs, flowcharts, and operation instructions needed to reorganize the production data base.

9. Special operational procedures and considerations for operations required in order to handle data base.

10. Physical characteristics (monitor and record use and growth of data base): diagram, chart, or the like which records the ongoing use and growth of data base.

11. Current access control list and reason for type of access assigned:
    a. List of users, systems using data base, and the type of access.
    b. Brief explanation, qualifying the type of access assigned.

12. Data base modification request document, containing request for data base modification, requester, and the impact caused by making modifications.

13. Data auditability and control considerations listing the data items that have been inserted into the data base for the purpose of monitoring the accuracy and evaluating the integrity of the data content.

EXAMPLE OF DB DOCUMENTATION

The section that follows contains the system overview, the data flow, and the supporting logical and physical data structures that were derived for the field activity subsystem. The physical structure is much more detailed because of the data items and access paths that are required for processing various applications. The logical model is consistently applied and carried over into the physical side.

Purpose of the System

The FACTS Data Base project is a set of programs and procedures that is executed by MIS Operations and monitored by MIS Data Base Administration. This system will assure users that the data collected at the Service Operations Center (SOC) are transmitted to headquarters on a scheduled basis. These data are updated on the FACTS data base, and are available for further use in a timely manner.

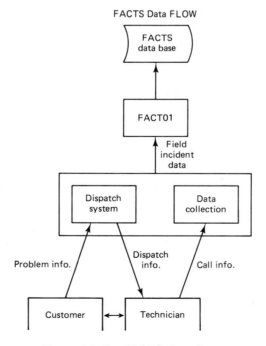

Figure 14-6 FACTS data flow.

System Narrative

FACTS (The Field Activity Collection and Tracking System) is designed to organize data from the field. This program was designed and written specifically to satisfy the data needs of the field and headquarters. All FACTS information reported through the SOC will be sent to headquarters on a weekly basis. The FACTS data base will be made available to Users for individualized processing.

The FACTS Data Base will contain the previous week's closed calls as reported by each SOC. In addition, the data base will contain contract and configuration changes that are reported by the Customer, Service Technician, or the Branch Manager to the Dispatcher.

FACTS Data Flow

The FACTS system data flow is shown in Figure 14–6. Note the data produced by the different kinds of interactions between the customer calling for service, the dispatch system dispatching the technician, and the technician relaying the results of the call to the system. The field incident data are aggregated on a weekly basis, and transmitted to the FACTS data base processing subsystem FACT01, at headquarters. The processing steps under sybsystem FACT01 are shown in Figure 14–7.

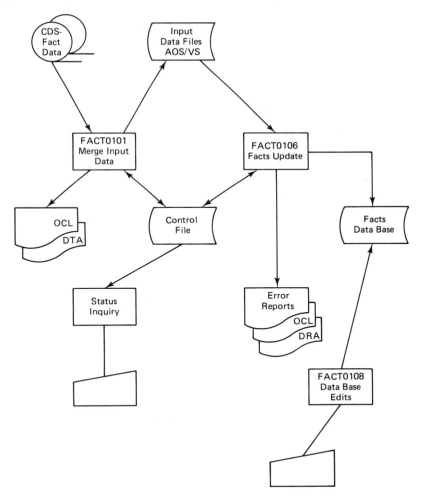

Figure 14–7 FACTS subsystem Ø1 diagram.

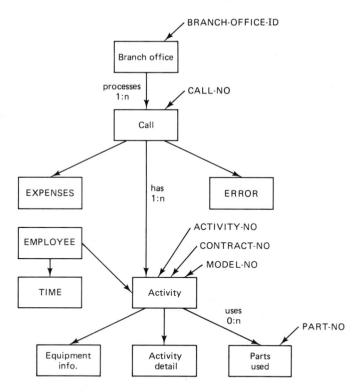

Figure 14-8   FACTS data base logical data structure diagram.

Logical Model

The logical model that is derived for the field activity subsystem is shown in Figure 14-8. The call record has an error record subordinate to it; this is to track errors in processing call-related information and for making corrections to appropriate data files so that future consistency and integrity of data is maintained. The activity record is broken down further at a lower level into an equipment record, an activity detail, and parts used. The following narratives comprise the key data items that are needed to constitute each logical group or record.

BRANCH OFFICE RECORD.   The BRANCH OFFICE RECORD is a record that is keyed on the branch office ID (e.g., 49822121 represents Division 4982, Area 2, Region 1, Branch 2, Office 1). All call records are stored under the corresponding branch office record by call-received date in descending sequence, so that the most recent call will appear first in a query of the data.

BRANCH OFFICE ID.   The BRANCH OFFICE ID is the eight-digit account number that is assigned by corporate administration. These first two digits are the division code, the next two are the cost center code, and the last four are the area region branch office (ARBO) code.

CALL RECORD.   The CALL RECORD is the record that ties together all the information pertaining to the call in terms of individual activities. Each activity within a call is identified uniquely by the combination of service code, service date, and the major unit (type serial or model serial) that was worked on by the service technician. Several activities can be reflected under a call: for example, preventive activity, technical support activity, remote activity, installation, and the regular service repair activity. The CALL RECORD is uniquely identified by the call number that is assigned by the system.

CALL NUMBER.   The CALL NUMBER item is composed of two parts: The first part consists of alphabetic character and represents the dispatch system–assigned call identifier. The second part is six digits long and is the call number that is assigned by the dispatch system. The six-digit field is a unique number that is assigned by each system.

CALL RECEIVED DATE.   The CALL RECEIVED DATE field is a six-digit item that represents the date in YYMMDD format on which the customer's call for service was received at the central dispatch location.

CALL RECEIVED TIME.   The CALL RECEIVED TIME is a six-digit item that represents the time at which the customer's service call was received by the central dispatch location. The time is stored in the central dispatch system relative to Greenwich Mean Time (GMT).

UPDATE DATE.   UPDATE DATE is the date this record was last modified. The first two characters are the year, the second two characters are the month, and the last two characters are the days in the month. It is an audit and control data item.

ARRIVAL DATE.   ARRIVAL DATE is a six-digit item that represents the arrival date of a technician at a customer site. The date is stored in the form YY-MM-DD. The technician is the source of the data.

ARRIVAL TIME.   The ARRIVAL TIME item is a six-digit item that represents the arrival time of a technician at the customer site. The time is stored as hours (two digits), minutes (two digits), and seconds (two digits). As stored in the Dispatch System, it is the time relative to Greenwich Mean Time at the location from which dispatching originates.

CALL CLOSE DATE.   The CALL CLOSE DATE is the date in year, month, day format on which the call was closed either by the technician or branch manager. This is recorded automatically by the Dispatch System.

CALL CLOSE TIME.   The CALL CLOSE TIME is the time in hours, minutes, seconds format at which the call was closed either by the technician or branch manager. This is recorded automatically by the dispatch system.

CIC CODE.   The CIC CODE is a one-character item that indicates complete (C) or incomplete (I) status of a call. It stands for "complete incomplete call." This indicator will be passed back to the dispatch system.

STOP TIME.   The STOP TIME is the time at which the technician stopped working on the call. This is reported to the dispatch system as a separate field and is based on a 24-hour clock. This is required in order to determine billing.

TOTAL SERVICE HOURS.   The TOTAL SERVICE HOURS is the number of hours that the technician reported that he or she spent on the call for chargeback purposes. The technician should report the time in hours and tenths of hours (e.g., 1.6 equals 1 hour and 36 minutes).

ERROR FLAG.   The ERROR FLAG is a flag that is set to the value "E" to indicate that the data in the call record has errors. If there are no errors, the error flag is set to space.

ERROR FLAG DATE.   ERROR FLAG DATE is the date when a call was last edited and an error was detected.

REVIEW FLAG.   The REVIEW FLAG is a one-character item which is set to the value "R" whenever the call is flagged as being under review by the branch manager for billing purposes. If the call is not under review, the flag is set to space.

REVIEW FLAG DATE.   The REVIEW FLAG DATE data item is the date at which the call went under review.

EDIT FLAG.   The EDIT FLAG is a flag that is used by the edit validation procedures within the data base implementation to flag calls that have failed to pass all the edit validation checks.

EDIT FLAG DATE.   The EDIT FLAG DATE item is the date at which the call did not pass validation process.

BILL FLAG.   The BILL FLAG is a one-character item that is set to spaces by default. When the billing extract program has processed a call for billing purposes, that program will set the bill flag to "B."

BILL FLAG DATE.   The BILL FLAG DATE item is the date on which the call was passed on to invoicing for billing.

CUSTOMER NUMBER.   The CUSTOMER NUMBER is a seven-character item as defined in the corporate customer reference file. Normally, the CUST-NO has a three-digit or three-character suffix, depending on the type of address to which it pertains (e.g., a BILL-TO or an ALTERNATE-BILL-TO or a SHIP-TO number). If the suffix is all spaces, the combined field represents a BILL-TO address or an ALTERNATE-BILL-TO address; if the suffix is all zeros, the combined item represents a SHIP-TO address that is the same as the BILL-TO address; if the suffix is a number other than zeros, it will represent other SHIP-TO addresses for the same CUSTOMER.

EXPENSE.   The EXPENSE record contains the expense information pertaining to a call, such as mileage, travel to and from hours, parts run times, out-of-pocket expenditures incurred during a service call, and so on. One of these records will be stored for each time the technician calls in the information.

EMPLOYEE BADGE NUMBER.   The EMPLOYEE BADGE NUMBER is a six-digit item and is the official number that is assigned to the technician employee upon hire or rehire. This data item identifies the technician and the associated expense. If there were more than one technician on a call, there would be an EXPENSE for each additional technician.

BILL CODE.   This BILL CODE data item is used to indicate if the expenses are billable. It is a one-character field. When the expenses are initially loaded to the FACTS data base, the BILL CODE will contain a "B." The "B" indicates that the expenses are to be billed.

SERVICE DATE.   The SERVICE DATE item is the date on which the technician performed the field service and the associated expense.

SERVICE TIME.   The SERVICE TIME item is the time when the technician performed the field service and the associated expense.

TRAVEL TO HOURS.   The TRAVEL TO HOURS item is a 99v9 field that represents the amount of time spent by the technician in traveling to the customer site to perform the service. This is stored in hours and fractions of an hour.

TRAVEL FROM HOURS.   The TRAVEL FROM HOURS item is a 99v9 field that represents the time in hours and fractions of an hour that it took the technician to travel from the customer site back to the office after completion of that day's service activity.

DISTANCE.   The DISTANCE data item contains the actual distance the field engineer traveled to and from the customer site. The data item will contain miles or kilometers, depending on the location of the call. The DISTANCE field is a 9(3)V9.

EXPENSES.   The EXPENSES is the amount spent by the technician in responding to the call. This amount will include taxi, airfare, lodging, meals, or fixed-rate charges. It does not include mileage charges, parts, tolls, and parking. The field is numeric with 11 whole numbers. This is to accommodate all denominations.

ERROR RECORD.   The ERROR RECORD is a record which contains the data that are used to support the edit/validation of the closed call information that is received from the dispatch center.

ERROR TYPE.   The ERROR TYPE represents the type of error that could be found in the data that are passed up to headquarters from the service operations center.

SERVICE DATE.   The SERVICE DATE is the calendar date (MM/DD/YY) that service activity was performed on the product. It is stored as six numeric positions, YY-MM-DD. The source of the data is the technician.

CALL NUMBER.   The CALL NUMBER item is composed of two parts. The first part consists of one alphabetic character and represents the dispatch system–assigned call identifier. The second part is six digits long and is the call number that is assigned by the dispatch center. The six-digit field is a unique number that is assigned by each system.

CONTRACT NUMBER.   The CONTRACT NUMBER item is seven characters long. It will contain the contract number of the call that received an error during edit validation of the load to the FACTS data base.

OTHER CONTRACT NUMBER.   The OTHER CONTRACT NUMBER refers to the contract number under which the equipment is listed in the dispatch center (other than the one under which it should be listed according to the customer). This field is required in order to correct the contract files and put the equipment under the proper contract.

EMPLOYEE BADGE NUMBER.   The EMPLOYEE BADGE NUMBER is a six-digit item that is used to identify the technician who worked on the call.

SERVICE CODE.   The SERVICE CODE indicates the type of service the technician is performing on-site. Each service code is a separate activity. The item is three numeric positions long. The source of the data is the technician. The service code description is in the technician's reporting manual.

MODEL NUMBER.   The MODEL NUMBER is a 10-character item that is the official model number assigned to a product. The source for model information is the product reference data base.

MODEL SERIAL NUMBER.   The MODEL SERIAL NUMBER is a 15-character field that represents the serial number that is stamped on the model by the manufacturing location. In cases where the model serial number is incorrect or missing, the technician may attach a serial-number tag in consultation with administration personnel.

PART NUMBER.   The PART NUMBER is a nine-digit item that is assigned by the engineering staff to identify a part. The first three digits represent the class of the part, and the last six digits represent the sequential number of the part within that class. Each part can have several revision numbers, which are carried in the PART REVISION NUMBER data item (two digits).

SITE NAME.   The SITE NAME item is a 35-character field. The item is used to identify SITE name changes.

SITE ADDRESS.   The SITE ADDRESS is a 137-character item. It is used to contain any SITE address changes.

CUSTOMER BILL TO NAME.   The CUSTOMER BILL TO NAME is a 35-character item. The data item is used to identify customer bill-to-name changes.

CUSTOMER BILL ADDRESS.   The CUSTOMER BILL ADDRESS is a 137-character item. It is used to contain any customer bill-to-address changes.

PART USED RECORD.   The PART USED record contains data about the field-replaceable unit that was serviced by the technician, and the part that was used to fix the service call problem. In most cases, the replacement part used will be the same kind that failed. That is, the part serviced and the part used are the same; only their serial numbers will be different. In the rare instance of several parts being used to repair a failed part, a new PART USED record will be created for each part that is used.

PART NUMBER.   The PART NUMBER is a nine-digit field that is assigned by the engineering staff to identify a part. The first three digits represent the class of the part, and the last six digits represent the sequential number of the part within that class. Each part can have several revision numbers, which are carried in the PART REVISION NUMBER data item (two digits).

PART REVISION NUMBER.   The PART REVISION NUMBER is a two-digit item that represents the revision number of a particular part (see PART NUMBER). Values can range from 0 to 99.

PART SERIAL NUMBER.   The PART SERIAL NUMBER is a 15-character item that will contain the serial number that is stamped on a part or assembly by the manufacturing department. The serial number may contain alphanumeric characters.

SYSTEM FIX CODE.   SYMPTOM FIX CODE is a four-character item that contains further explanation of the service code used to explain a field incident. The first two digits describe the device-specific symptoms and the last two describe the corrective action taken. The source of the data is the technician.

HOURS WORKED.   The HOURS WORKED item represents the number of hours worked (to one decimal place) on a particular part within a model unit.

ESP PARTS CODE.   The ESP PARTS CODE is an item that indicates whether a part that was used for a repair is to be charged to the customer at the exchange sales price.

QTY PART USED. The QTY PART USED is an item that contains the number of parts of the same kind that were used in a particular repair situation.

PART SHIP DATE. The PART SHIP DATE field contains the date in YYMMDD on which a particular part was shipped for a given customer repair situation.

ACTIVITY RECORD. The ACTIVITY RECORD belongs to a particular call record. One of these records is created for a unique occurrence of service code, service date, and optionally, the model serial. In addition, if two or more Technicians worked on the same call, separate activity records would be created even though the service code, service date, and the major unit are the same. The SYMPTOM FIX data in the activity record would be filled with SYMPTOM FIX data by default if no replacement part is associated with the SYMPTOM FIX CODE. This may happen in certain instances. In all other cases, the SYMPTOM FIX is associated with a specific replacement part, and should be updated in the part used record.

SERVICE CODE. The SERVICE CODE indicates the type of service the Technician is performing on-site. Each service code is a separate activity. The item is three numeric positions long. The source of the data is the Technician. The service code description is in the Technician's reporting manual.

ACTIVITY SERVICE DATE. The ACTIVITY SERVICE DATE is a six-digit item that represents the date in YYMMDD format on which a particular activity was performed by a technician at a customer site.

ACTIVITY SERVICE TIME. The ACTIVITY SERVICE TIME is a six-digit item that represents the time in YYMMDD format on which a particular activity was performed by a Technician at a customer site.

ACTIVITY RECORD NUMBER. ACTIVITY RECORD NUMBER is a two-digit item that can be used to keep track of the number of an "activity" within a "call."

ACTIVITY STOP TIME. The ACTIVITY STOP TIME is the time at which the Technician stopped working on a activity. This is reported to the dispatch system as a separate field and is based on a 24-hour clock. This is required in order to determine billing.

UPGRADE MODEL NUMBER. UPGRADE MODEL NUMBER refers to the model number of the upgrade kit to be applied to the product. The item is 10 alphanumeric positions long.

SYMPTOM FIX CODE. SYMPTOM FIX CODE is a four-character item that contains further explanation of the service code used to explain a field incident. The first two digits describe the device-specific symptoms and the last two describe the corrective action taken. The source of the data is the technician.

SALES ORDER NUMBER. The SALES ORDER NUMBER is a 10-digit number assigned by sales administration, the first six digits representing the sales order contact number.

CUSTOMER PO NUMBER. The CUSTOMER PO NUMBER is a 20-character item containing the purchase order number supplied by the outside customer to link the field incident to their purchase order system.

ISC NUMBER. The ISC NUMBER or internal service charge number is the account number to which internal charges can be made. It is defined as a 20-character field.

PARAMETER RECORD. The PARAMETER RECORD is a general-purpose record that is used for storing reporting parameters and other values that are useful for processing the data base. Since much of the processing will be date sensitive, it is important to maintain the last processed dates in parametric format.

TECHNICIAN RECORD. The TECHNICIAN RECORD is a record that contains key employee information, such as badge number, cost center, and employment start and termination dates. This record serves two purposes. It is the header record for query access to all the calls and activities relating to any one employee via the ACTIVITY RECORD and it is the header under which time records will be maintained for each technician, so that 100 percent time reporting can be carried out. The time data will be kept in TIME RECORD.

EMPLOYEE BADGE NUMBER. The EMPLOYEE BADGE NUMBER is a six-digit item and is the official number that is assigned to an employee upon hire or rehire.

TIME RECORD. The TIME RECORD is a record that will store the weekly time data that are sent up from the dispatch system for each Technician. The time data, broken down into various categories (e.g., unavailable, training, unavailable sick, etc.), will be entered into the dispatch system by the branch manager before the end of the week.

YEAR PERIOD WEEK. The YEAR PERIOD WEEK data item is a five-digit field containing the year, period, and week at which the technician accumulated unavailable time. The format is 84124, where 84 = year, 12 = period, 4 = week.

UNAVAILABLE DATE. UNAVAILABLE DATE is the date against which unavailable code and unavailable hours will be recorded by the dispatch system for the technician.

UNAVAILABLE CODES. UNAVAILABLE CODES are the codes that represent the reason for the technician being unavailable for service call activity on any particular date. The codes are: V, vacation; T, training; H, holiday; L, leave of absence; M, meeting; S, sick; O, other.

UNAVAILABLE HOURS. The UNAVAILABLE HOURS is a 9(2)v9(1) item. This data item is used to contain the number of hours a technician was unavailable to perform customer service work for a specific unavailable code for a specific week.

EQUIPMENT RECORD. The EQUIPMENT RECORD is a record that contains the data on equipment that has been installed, changed, or relocated by the technician. This is a holding place for data that will eventually be moved to the contract data file to keep the customer configuration up to date. Another category of data that is related to new products and special data items that have to be obtained from the Technician regarding these.

TYPE OF DATA. TYPE OF DATA is a two-character item indicating the type of data that are stored within the EQUIPMENT RECORD (a general-purpose record containing equipment-related data from the Technician).

LINE NUMBER.   LINE NUMBER is a two-digit signed item that is used to assign sequential identification numbers to the EQUIPMENT records.

ACTIVITY DETAIL RECORD.   The ACTIVITY DETAIL RECORD is a record that contains the action plans and comments pertaining to a service activity by technicians or branch managers.

Physical Structure

The physical representation of the logical model is shown in Figure 14–9. The physical structure is a Codasyl DBMS implementation and contains some extra items in the records for application processing control. The subschema follows the diagram to give the reader a clear picture of the mapping from the logical to the physical side.

Subschema.   The FACTSS subschema contains all the items, records, and sets that correspond to the physical CODASYL structure diagram.

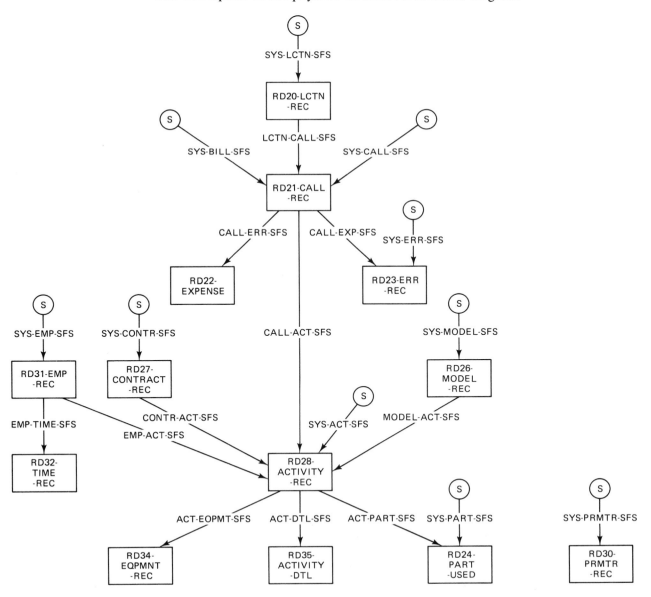

Figure 14–9 FACTS data base schema diagram.

```
          SUBSCHEMA NAME IS ''FACTSS''
                   WITHIN ''FACTDB''
                   ALLOWS ERASE GET MODIFY STORE

          SET NAME IS ACT-DTL-SFS
                   ALLOWS RECONNECT
                   OWNER IS RD28-ACTIVITY-REC
                   MEMBER IS RD35-ACTIVITY-DTL
                   INSERTION AUTOMATIC
                   RETENTION MANDATORY
    *              ORDER IS SORTED BY KEY ASCENDING
    *              DD35-ACT-TYPE
    *              DD35-ACT-LINE-NO
    *              DUPLICATES NOT ALLOWED
    *         MEMBER LIMIT IS NONE

          SET NAME IS ACT-EQPMT-SFS
                   ALLOWS RECONNECT
                   OWNER IS RD28-ACTIVITY-REC
                   MEMBER IS RD34-EQPMNT-REC
                   INSERTION AUTOMATIC
                   RETENTION MANDATORY
    *              ORDER IS SORTED BY KEY ASCENDING
    *              DD34-TYPE
    *              DD34-LINE-NO
    *              DUPLICATES NOT ALLOWED
    *         MEMBER LIMIT IS NONE

          SET NAME IS ACT-PART-SFS
                   ALLOWS RECONNECT
                   OWNER IS RD28-ACTIVITY-REC
                   MEMBER IS RD24-PART-USED
                   INSERTION AUTOMATIC
                   RETENTION MANDATORY
    *              ORDER IS SORTED BY KEY ASCENDING
    *              DD24-FRU-NO
    *              DUPLICATES ALLOWED
    *         MEMBER LIMIT IS NONE

          SET NAME IS ARBO-CALL-SFS
                   ALLOWS RECONNECT
                   OWNER IS RD20-ARBO
                   MEMBER IS RD21-CALL-REC
                   INSERTION MANUAL
                   RETENTION OPTIONAL
    *              ORDER IS SORTED BY KEY ASCENDING
    *              DD21-CALL-RECD-DT
    *              DUPLICATES ALLOWED
    *         MEMBER LIMIT IS NONE

          SET NAME IS CALL-ACT-SFS
                   ALLOWS RECONNECT
                   OWNER IS RD21-CALL-REC
                   MEMBER IS RD28-ACTIVITY-REC
                   INSERTION AUTOMATIC
                   RETENTION MANDATORY
    *              ORDER IS SORTED BY KEY ASCENDING
    *              DD28-FACT-SVC-CD
    *              DD28-SVC-DT
```

```
     *            DD28-SVC-TIME
     *               DUPLICATES ALLOWED
     *            MEMBER LIMIT IS NONE


     SET NAME IS CONTR-ACT-SFS
                ALLOWS RECONNECT
                OWNER IS RD27-CONTRACT-REC
                MEMBER IS RD28-ACTIVITY-REC
                INSERTION MANUAL
                RETENTION OPTIONAL
     *               ORDER IS SORTED BY KEY ASCENDING
     *               DD28-SVC-DT
     *               DUPLICATES ALLOWED
     *            MEMBER LIMIT IS NONE


     SET NAME IS EMP-ACT-SFS
                ALLOWS RECONNECT
                OWNER IS RD31-EMP-REC
                MEMBER IS RD28-ACTIVITY-REC
                INSERTION MANUAL
                RETENTION OPTIONAL
     *               ORDER IS SORTED BY KEY ASCENDING
     *               DD28-SVC-DT
     *               DD28-SVC-TIME
     *               DUPLICATES NOT ALLOWED
     *            MEMBER LIMIT IS NONE


     SET NAME IS EMP-EXP-SFS
                ALLOWS RECONNECT
                OWNER IS RD31-EMP-REC
                MEMBER IS RD22-EXPENSE
                INSERTION AUTOMATIC
                RETENTION MANDATORY
     *               ORDER IS SORTED BY KEY ASCENDING
     *               DD22-CALL-NO
     *               DUPLICATES ALLOWED
     *            MEMBER LIMIT IS NONE


     SET NAME IS EMP-TIME-SFS
                ALLOWS RECONNECT
                OWNER IS RD31-EMP-REC
                MEMBER IS RD32-TIME-REC
                INSERTION AUTOMATIC
                RETENTION MANDATORY
     *               ORDER IS SORTED BY KEY ASCENDING
     *               DD32-YR-PER-WK
     *               DUPLICATES NOT ALLOWED
     *            MEMBER LIMIT IS NONE


     SET NAME IS MODEL-ACT-SFS
                ALLOWS RECONNECT
                OWNER IS RD26-MODEL-REC
                MEMBER IS RD28-ACTIVITY-REC
                INSERTION MANUAL
                RETENTION OPTIONAL
     *               ORDER IS SORTED BY KEY ASCENDING
     *               DD28-SVC-DT
     *               DUPLICATES ALLOWED
     *            MEMBER LIMIT IS NONE
```

```
        SET NAME IS SYS-ACT-SFS
              ALLOWS RECONNECT
              OWNER IS SYSTEM
              MEMBER IS RD28-ACTIVITY-REC
              INSERTION MANUAL
              RETENTION OPTIONAL
  *               ORDER IS SORTED BY KEY ASCENDING
  *               DD28-SVC-DT
  *               DUPLICATES ALLOWED
  *           MEMBER LIMIT IS NONE


        SET NAME IS SYS-ARBO-SFS
              ALLOWS RECONNECT
              OWNER IS SYSTEM
              MEMBER IS RD20-ARBO-REC
              INSERTION AUTOMATIC
              RETENTION MANDATORY
  *               ORDER IS SORTED BY KEY ASCENDING
  *               DD20-ARBO
  *               DUPLICATES NOT ALLOWED
  *           MEMBER LIMIT IS NONE


        SET NAME IS SYS-BILL-SFS
              ALLOWS RECONNECT
              OWNER IS SYSTEM
              MEMBER IS RD21-CALL-REC
              INSERTION MANUAL
              RETENTION OPTIONAL
  *               ORDER IS SORTED BY KEY ASCENDING
  *               DD21-CALL-RECD-DT
  *               DUPLICATES ALLOWED
  *           MEMBER LIMIT IS NONE


        SET NAME IS SYS-CALL-SFS
              ALLOWS RECONNECT
              OWNER IS SYSTEM
              MEMBER IS RD21-CALL-REC
              INSERTION AUTOMATIC
              RETENTION MANDATORY
  *               ORDER IS SORTED BY KEY ASCENDING
  *               DD21-CALL-NO
  *               DUPLICATES NOT ALLOWED
  *           MEMBER LIMIT IS NONE


        SET NAME IS SYS-CONTR-SFS
              ALLOWS RECONNECT
              OWNER IS SYSTEM
              MEMBER IS RD27-CONTRACT-REC
              INSERTION AUTOMATIC
              RETENTION MANDATORY
  *               ORDER IS SORTED BY KEY ASCENDING
  *               DD27-CONTRACT-NO
  *               DUPLICATES NOT ALLOWED
  *           MEMBER LIMIT IS NONE


        SET NAME IS SYS-EMP-SFS
              ALLOWS RECONNECT
              OWNER IS SYSTEM
              MEMBER IS RD31-EMP-REC
```

```
                    INSERTION AUTOMATIC
                    RETENTION MANDATORY
*              ORDER IS SORTED BY KEY ASCENDING
*                  DD31-EMP-BADGE-NO
*                  DUPLICATES NOT ALLOWED
*              MEMBER LIMIT IS NONE

SET NAME IS SYS-MODEL-SFS
                    ALLOWS RECONNECT
                    OWNER IS SYSTEM
                    MEMBER IS RD26-MODEL-REC
                    INSERTION AUTOMATIC
                    RETENTION MANDATORY
*              ORDER IS SORTED BY KEY ASCENDING
*                  DD26-MODEL-NO
*                  DUPLICATES NOT ALLOWED
*              MEMBER LIMIT IS NONE

SET NAME IS SYS-PART-SFS
                    ALLOWS RECONNECT
                    OWNER IS SYSTEM
                    MEMBER IS RD24-PART-USED
                    INSERTION MANUAL
                    RETENTION OPTIONAL
*              ORDER IS SORTED BY KEY ASCENDING
*                  DD24-PART-NO
*                  DUPLICATES ALLOWED
*              MEMBER LIMIT IS NONE

SET NAME IS SYS-PRMTR-SFS
                    ALLOWS RECONNECT
                    OWNER IS SYSTEM
                    MEMBER IS RD30-PRMTR-REC
                    INSERTION AUTOMATIC
                    RETENTION MANDATORY
*              ORDER IS SORTED BY KEY ASCENDING
*                  DD30-PRMTR-CD
*                  DUPLICATES ALLOWED
*              MEMBER LIMIT IS NONE

SET NAME IS CALL-ERR-SFS
                    ALLOWS CONNECT DISCONNECT RECONNECT
                    OWNER IS RD21-CALL-REC
                    MEMBER IS RD23-ERR-REC
                    MANUAL
                    OPTIONAL
*              ORDER IS SORTED BY KEY ASCENDING
*                  DD23-ERR-TYPE
*                  DUPLICATES ALLOWED
*              MEMBER LIMIT IS NONE

SET NAME IS SYS-ERR-SFS
                    ALLOWS RECONNECT
                    OWNER IS SYSTEM
                    MEMBER IS RD23-ERR-REC
                    AUTOMATIC
                    MANDATORY
*              ORDER IS SORTED BY KEY ASCENDING
*                  DD23-ERR-TYPE
```

```
*          DD23-SVC-DT
*             DUPLICATES ALLOWED
*          MEMBER LIMIT IS NONE

   DBMS STATUS IS DBMS-STATUS.

01 RD20-LCTN-REC                        ALLOWS ERASE GET MODIFY STORE
   05 DD20-LCTN-CD                      PIC X(8)
                                        USAGE IS DISPLAY
                                        ALLOWS GET MODIFY.

01 RD21-CALL-REC                        ALLOWS ERASE GET MODIFY STORE
   05 DD21-CALL-NO                      PIC X(7)
                                        USAGE IS DISPLAY
                                        ALLOWS GET MODIFY.

   05 DD21-CALL-RECD-DT                 PIC 9(6)
                                        USAGE IS DISPLAY
                                        ALLOWS GET MODIFY.

   05 DD21-CALL-RECD-TIME               PIC 9(6)
                                        USAGE IS DISPLAY
                                        ALLOWS GET MODIFY.

   05 DD21-UPDT-DT                      PIC 9(6)
                                        USAGE IS DISPLAY
                                        ALLOWS GET MODIFY.

   05 DD21-LCTN-NO                      PIC X(8)
                                        USAGE IS DISPLAY
                                        ALLOWS GET MODIFY.

   05 DD21-ARRIVAL-DT                   PIC 9(6)
                                        USAGE IS DISPLAY
                                        ALLOWS GET MODIFY.

   05 DD21-ARRIVAL-TIME                 PIC S9(6)
                                        USAGE IS DISPLAY
                                        ALLOWS GET MODIFY.

   05 DD21-CALL-CLOSE-DT                PIC 9(6)
                                        USAGE IS DISPLAY
                                        ALLOWS GET MODIFY.

   05 DD21-CALL-CLOSE-TIME              PIC 9(6)
                                        USAGE IS DISPLAY
                                        ALLOWS GET MODIFY.

   05 DD21-CIC-CD                       PIC X(1)
                                        USAGE IS DISPLAY
                                        ALLOWS GET MODIFY.

   05 DD21-STOP-TIME                    PIC 9(6)
                                        USAGE IS DISPLAY
                                        ALLOWS GET MODIFY.

   05 DD21-TOT-SVC-HRS                  PIC 9(3).9(1)
                                        USAGE IS DISPLAY
                                        SIGN IS TRAILING
                                        ALLOWS GET MODIFY.
   05 DD21-ERROR-FLAG                   PIC X(1)
                                        USAGE IS DISPLAY
                                        ALLOWS GET MODIFY.

   05 DD21-ERROR-FLAG-DT                PIC 9(6)
                                        USAGE IS DISPLAY
                                        ALLOWS GET MODIFY.

   05 DD21-REVIEW-FLAG                  PIC X(1)
                                        USAGE IS DISPLAY
                                        ALLOWS GET MODIFY.
```

DD23-SVC-DT

```
        05 DD21-REVIEW-FLAG-DT          PIC 9(6)
                                        USAGE IS DISPLAY
                                        ALLOWS GET MODIFY.
        05 DD21-EDIT-FLAG               PIC X(1)
                                        USAGE IS DISPLAY
                                        ALLOWS GET MODIFY.
        05 DD21-EDIT-FLAG-DT            PIC S9(6)
                                        USAGE IS DISPLAY
                                        ALLOWS GET MODIFY.
        05 DD21-BILL-FLAG               PIC X(1)
                                        USAGE IS DISPLAY
                                        ALLOWS GET MODIFY.
        05 DD21-BILL-FLAG-DT            PIC 9(6)
                                        USAGE IS DISPLAY
                                        ALLOWS GET MODIFY.
        05 DD21-CUST-NO                 PIC X(7)
                                        USAGE IS DISPLAY
                                        ALLOWS GET MODIFY.

01 RD22-EXPENSE                         ALLOWS ERASE GET MODIFY STORE
        05 DD22-EMP-BADGE-NO            PIC 9(6)
                                        USAGE IS DISPLAY
                                        ALLOWS GET MODIFY.
             10 DD22-BILL-CD            PIC X(1)
                                        USAGE IS DISPLAY
                                        ALLOWS GET MODIFY
                                        OCCURS 20 TIMES.
             10 DD22-SVC-DT             PIC 9(6)
                                        USAGE IS DISPLAY
                                        ALLOWS GET MODIFY
                                        OCCURS 20 TIMES.
             10 DD22-SVC-TIME           PIC 9(6)
                                        USAGE IS DISPLAY
                                        ALLOWS GET MODIFY
                                        OCCURS 20 TIMES.
             10 DD22-TRVL-TO-HRS        PIC 9(2).9(1)
                                        USAGE IS DISPLAY
                                        ALLOWS GET MODIFY
                                        OCCURS 20 TIMES.
             10 DD22-TRVL-FROM-HRS      PIC 9(2).9(1)
                                        USAGE IS DISPLAY
                                        ALLOWS GET MODIFY
                                        OCCURS 20 TIMES.
             10 DD22-DISTANCE           PIC 9(3).9(1)
                                        USAGE IS DISPLAY
                                        OCCURS 20 TIMES
                                        ALLOWS GET MODIFY.
             10 DD22-EXPENSES           PIC 9(11)
                                        USAGE IS DISPLAY
                                        ALLOWS GET MODIFY.

01 RD23-ERR-REC                         ALLOWS ERASE GET MODIFY STORE
        05 DD23-ERR-TYPE                PIC X(2)
                                        USAGE IS DISPLAY
                                        ALLOWS GET MODIFY.
        05 DD23-SVC-DT                  PIC X(6)
                                        USAGE IS DISPLAY
                                        ALLOWS GET MODIFY.
```

```
        05 DD23-CALL-NO                    PIC X(7)
                                           USAGE IS DISPLAY
                                           ALLOWS GET MODIFY.
        05 DD23-CONTRACT-NO                PIC X(7)
                                           USAGE IS DISPLAY
                                           ALLOWS GET MODIFY.
        05 DD23-OTHER-CONTRACT-NO          PIC X(8)
                                           USAGE IS DISPLAY
                                           ALLOWS GET MODIFY.
        05 DD23-BADGE-NO                   PIC 9(6)
                                           USAGE IS DISPLAY
                                           ALLOWS GET MODIFY.
        05 DD23-LCTN-CD                    PIC X(8)
                                           USAGE IS DISPLAY
                                           ALLOWS GET MODIFY.
        05 DD23-SVC-CD                     PIC X(3)
                                           USAGE IS DISPLAY
                                           ALLOWS GET MODIFY.
        05 DD23-MODEL-NO                   PIC X(10)
                                           USAGE DISPLAY
                                           ALLOWS GET MODIFY.
        05 DD23-SERIAL-NO                  PIC X(15)
                                           USAGE IS DISPLAY
                                           ALLOWS GET MODIFY.
        05 DD23-FRU-NO                     PIC X(10)
                                           USAGE IS DISPLAY
                                           ALLOWS GET MODIFY.
        05 DD23-PART-NO                    PIC X(10)
                                           USAGE IS DISPLAY
                                           ALLOWS GET MODIFY.
        05 DD23-SITE-NAME                  PIC X(35)
                                           USAGE IS DISPLAY
                                           ALLOWS GET MODIFY.
        05 DD23-SITE-ADDR                  PIC X(137)
                                           USAGE IS DISPLAY
                                           ALLOWS GET MODIFY.
        05 DD23-BILL-NAME                  PIC X(35)
                                           USAGE IS DISPLAY
                                           ALLOWS GET MODIFY.
        05 DD23-BILL-ADDR                  PIC X(137)
                                           USAGE IS DISPLAY
                                           ALLOWS GET MODIFY.
01 RD24-PART-USED                          ALLOWS ERASE GET MODIFY STORE
        05 DD24-FRU-NO                     PIC X(10)
                                           USAGE IS DISPLAY
                                           ALLOWS GET MODIFY.
        05 DD24-FRU-REV-NO                 PIC X(2)
                                           USAGE IS DISPLAY
                                           ALLOWS GET MODIFY.
        05 DD24-FRU-SERIAL-NO              PIC X(15)
                                           USAGE IS DISPLAY
                                           ALLOWS GET MODIFY.
        05 DD24-SYMPTOM-FIX                PIC X(4)
                                           USAGE IS DISPLAY
                                           ALLOWS GET MODIFY.
        05 DD24-HRS-WRKD-FRU               PIC 9(2).9(1)
                                           USAGE IS DISPLAY
                                           ALLOWS GET MODIFY.
```

```
      05 DD24-PART-NO                    PIC X(10)
                                         USAGE IS DISPLAY
                                         ALLOWS GET MODIFY.
      05 DD24-PART-REV-NO                PIC X(2)
                                         USAGE IS DISPLAY
                                         ALLOWS GET MODIFY.
      05 DD24-PART-SERIAL-NO             PIC X(15)
                                         USAGE IS DISPLAY
                                         ALLOWS GET MODIFY.
      05 DD24-ESP-PARTS-CD               PIC 9
                                         USAGE IS DISPLAY
                                         ALLOWS GET MODIFY.
      05 DD24-QTY-PART-USED              PIC 9(3)
                                         USAGE IS DISPLAY
                                         ALLOWS GET MODIFY.
      05 DD24-PART-SHIP-DT               PIC 9(6)
                                         USAGE IS DISPLAY
                                         ALLOWS GET MODIFY.
      05 DD24-HRS-WRKD-PART              PIC 9(2) .9(1)
                                         USAGE IS DISPLAY
                                         ALLOWS GET MODIFY.
 01 RD26-MODEL-REC                       ALLOWS ERASE GET MODIFY STORE
      05 DD26-MODEL-NO                   PIC X(10)
                                         USAGE IS DISPLAY
                                         ALLOWS GET MODIFY.
 01 RD27-CONTRACT-REC                    ALLOWS ERASE GET MODIFY STORE
      05 DD27-CONTRACT-NO                PIC X(8)
                                         USAGE IS DISPLAY
                                         ALLOWS GET MODIFY.
      05 DD27-LCTN-CD                    PIC X(8)
                                         USAGE IS DISPLAY
                                         ALLOWS GET MODIFY.
 01 RD28-ACTIVITY-REC                    ALLOWS ERASE GET MODIFY STORE
      05 DD28-FACTS-SVC-CD               PIC X(3)
                                         USAGE IS DISPLAY
                                         ALLOWS GET MODIFY.
      05 DD28-SVC-DT                     PIC 9(6)
                                         USAGE IS DISPLAY
                                         ALLOWS GET MODIFY.
      05 DD28-SVC-TIME                   PIC 9(6)
                                         USAGE IS DISPLAY
                                         ALLOWS GET MODIFY.
      05 DD28-ACT-REC-NO                 PIC S9(2)
                                         USAGE IS DISPLAY
                                         SIGN IS TRAILING
                                         ALLOWS GET MODIFY.
      05 DD28-STOP-TIME                  PIC 9(6)
                                         USAGE IS DISPLAY
                                         ALLOWS GET MODIFY.
      05 DD28-CALL-NO                    PIC X(7)
                                         USAGE IS DISPLAY
                                         ALLOWS GET MODIFY.
      05 DD28-CONTRACT-NO                PIC X(8)
                                         USAGE IS DISPLAY
                                         ALLOWS GET MODIFY.
      05 DD28-EMP-BADGE-NO               PIC 9(6)
                                         USAGE IS DISPLAY
                                         ALLOWS GET MODIFY.
```

```
        05 DD28-LCTN-CD                    PIC X(8)
                                           USAGE IS DISPLAY
                                           ALLOWS GET MODIFY.
        05 DD28-MODEL-NO                   PIC X(10)
                                           USAGE IS DISPLAY
                                           ALLOWS GET MODIFY.
        05 DD28-MODEL-SERIAL-NO            PIC X(15)
                                           USAGE IS DISPLAY
                                           ALLOWS GET MODIFY.
        05 DD28-UPGRADE-MODEL-NO           PIC X(6)
                                           USAGE IS DISPLAY
                                           ALLOWS GET MODIFY.
        05 DD28-SYMPTOM-FIX-CD             PIC X(4)
                                           USAGE IS DISPLAY
                                           ALLOWS GET MODIFY.
        05 DD28-SALES-ORDER-NO             PIC X(20)
                                           USAGE IS DISPLAY
                                           ALLOWS GET MODIFY.
        05 DD28-CUST-PO-NO                 PIC X(20)
                                           USAGE IS DISPLAY
                                           ALLOWS GET MODIFY.
        05 DD28-ISC-NO                     PIC X(20)
                                           USAGE IS DISPLAY
                                           ALLOWS GET MODIFY.

    01 RD30-PRMTR-REC                      ALLOWS ERASE GET MODIFY STORE
        05 DD30-PRMTR-CD                   PIC X(2)
                                           USAGE IS DISPLAY
                                           ALLOWS GET MODIFY.
        05 DD30-PRMTR-DATA                 PIC X(80)
                                           USAGE IS DISPLAY
                                           ALLOWS GET MODIFY.

    01 RD31-EMP-REC                        ALLOWS ERASE GET MODIFY STORE
        05 DD31-EMP-BADGE-NO               PIC 9(6)
                                           USAGE IS DISPLAY
                                           ALLOWS GET MODIFY.

    01 RD32-TIME-REC                       ALLOWS ERASE GET MODIFY STORE
        05 DD32-YR-PER-WK                  PIC X(5)
                                           USAGE IS DISPLAY
                                           ALLOWS GET MODIFY.
        05 DD32-UNAVAILABLE-DT             PIC 9(6)
                                           USAGE IS DISPLAY
                                           ALLOWS GET MODIFY
                                           OCCURS 20 TIMES.
        05 DD32-UNAVAILABLE-CD             PIC X(1)
                                           USAGE IS DISPLAY
                                           ALLOWS GET MODIFY
                                           OCCURS 7 TIMES.
        05 DD32-UNAVAILABLE-HRS            PIC 9(2) .9(1)
                                           USAGE IS DISPLAY
                                           ALLOWS GET MODIFY.

    01 RD34-EQPMT-REC                      ALLOWS ERASE GET MODIFY STORE
        05 DD34-TYPE                       PIC X(2)
                                           USAGE IS DISPLAY
                                           ALLOWS GET MODIFY.
        05 DD34-LINE-NO                    PIC 9(2)
                                           USAGE IS DISPLAY
                                           ALLOWS GET MODIFY.
```

```
          05 DD34-DATA                    PIC X(80)
                                          USAGE IS DISPLAY
                                          ALLOWS GET MODIFY.
    01 RD35-ACTIVITY-DTL                  ALLOWS ERASE GET MODIFY STORE.
          05 DD35-ACT-TYPE                PIC X(2)
                                          USAGE IS DISPLAY
                                          ALLOWS GET MODIFY.
          05 DD35-ACT-LINE-NO             PIC 9(2)
                                          USAGE IS DISPLAY
                                          ALLOWS GET MODIFY.
          05 DD35-ACT-DTL                 PIC X(80)
                                          USAGE IS DISPLAY
                                          ALLOWS GET MODIFY.
```

chapter 15

Data Dictionary Role in the System Development Life Cycle

INTRODUCTION

In this chapter we examine the role of the dictionary as a documentation tool for some of the outputs from the phases of the SDLC. Throughout the SDLC, the dictionary can be used interactively to look up information as well as to enter information pertaining to the system being developed. Since the dictionary is a common repository of information, the reports that are produced in support of a system contain the same common information that would appear on a report for data base administration and computer operations. Thus the dictionary actively propagates data definitions because it is stored once in the dictionary and then placed in different reports from the same source. The dictionary entities needed to support SDLC are listed. Throughout this chapter, examples of documentation produced from the field activity data base development project are presented.

SYSTEM DEVELOPMENT IN A SHARED DATA BASE ENVIRONMENT

Reasons for Shared Files

The pressure for application systems to share data files and data bases has increased for the following reasons:

- Not sharing files leads to duplication of effort involved in maintenance of data and the programs that store the data.
- Over time, the data integrity becomes questionable if multiple users are creating and maintaining the same data item; reports from different systems concerning the same data item do not match.

- If application systems development is done by different teams following their own data definitions (which is very likely), the different application systems cannot talk to each other.

The result of the above has been a continuing pressure on MIS staff to develop systems that share data files, where the integrity of data is maintained by single source update, and where the same data definitions are followed from one system to the next.

Change Control

As the number of application systems grows within the organization, and the amount of sharing of common resources such as files and program modules increases, any change to one application or data file can have consequences on other applications and files. This is generally true with any complex system. When the system is implemented at first, this may not seem like such a big problem because the analyst and programmers involved with the system know everything about the system. As time passes, and changes are made in the system, often by persons other than those who initially developed the system, it becomes necessary to keep track of the changes and enhancements that are made in a systematic manner, so that an understanding of the changes can be passed on to others. This aspect is called "change control," and the dictionary can play a very important role in maintaining statuses of descriptions and relationships accurately. As changes are made in components of a system, the descriptions of those components in the dictionary should be updated to reflect the latest status. When it is time to release the system to "production," the components in the dictionary should be checked to ensure that all the relevant changes have been made and a release process implemented to certify that all component descriptions reflect the released version. In the rest of this chapter, change control will not be treated as a separate topic; this is because whatever documentation requirements apply to the development of a new application system applies to the enhancements and changes in an existing system.

Basic Information Unit

The basic building blocks of information are data items, which are combined into groups and records, and occurrences of records are stored in files which are used to build information processes. It is clear from Chapter 14 that the focus of the DBA is to ensure that the appropriate file structures are made available to the various systems that are under production or development. In coming up with these file structures, the DBA used the concepts of data planning, data modeling, and normalization. The dictionary is the place where the definitions of these file structures were documented by the DBA. These definitions can be accessed by the systems analyst or programmer via access keys such as aliases, keyword in context, or enterprise name. The systems analyst who is responsible for developing a new system that uses many existing data items can save considerable time and effort, because he or she can use the definitions that are already stored in the dictionary. The systems analyst's time is therefore freed to define the user functional requirements and the procedures that are required to meet user needs.

DDS Role

The role of the dictionary in documenting and propagating the data item definitions and the record and file structures should be clear by now. Its role in the systems development life cycle is really tied to the fact that there is a need to maintain the relationships between the programs/modules and the data bases that they affect, so that the impact of changing a data item's attributes in terms of the number of programs that would have to be changed can be determined. Conversely, if a program is changed, and the changes affect the data items being accessed, the dictionary is also updated with these data.

During the system development process, a lot of documentation corresponding to the several phases is produced by the systems analyst and programmer. Although the documentation may be produced by one of several word processing systems, they are generally stored and distributed in hardcopy format. Although this is changing with the advent of office automation, the capacity of a human being to read through large documents on a screen is limited. Not only is it a strain on the eyes, but the ability to go back and forth to get clarification is more difficult on an electronic document than on a paper document. In many situations, only key aspects of a system are needed by the operator or systems analyst on-line. This is where the capabilities of a dictionary can be usefully employed. The dictionary is used to store key information about systems, subsystems, jobs, programs, reports, screens, and so on. Also, these entities can be related together in the dictionary so that the query capability of the dictionary can be used to obtain quickly the information that is needed. For example, if the analyst wanted a quick summary of the jobs that need to be executed within a subsystem, this information could be obtained quickly via the on-line screens. The dictionary also prompts the analyst to other information that is available, thus enhancing the knowledge of the analyst.

It may be argued that the dictionary is not the right place to store summary information about systems, subsystems, and so on. It is possible to devise another application data base that contains all this information. This author contends that if a dictionary is implemented, it is probably cheaper to utilize the dictionary to include summary documentation than to create another data base and application to store this information. Also, since the dictionary effort is fairly large and comprehensive, the documentation and training are required for the dictionary implementation in any case. Therefore, it is more cost-effective to train users to access different kinds of information through one set of dictionary screens than to have them learn two different kinds of access techniques. The rest of this discussion assumes that the DD project manager has made a decision to utilize the dictionary data base to store information related to the system and its components.

The data dictionary is the key information system that supports systems development, operation, and support activities. What will become clear is that the dictionary is not referenced or updated in a single sequence of activities; on the contrary, a good dictionary will be used iteratively in the system development process. The data dictionary system is used as a checklist or note pad that can be continuously refined and updated with new ideas and data. To do this, the project has to be divided into subsystems, and within each subsystem will be the jobs (a collection of procedures), the programs, the inputs, and the outputs. Once the skeleton has been formed by the designer, it is a matter of continuously updating the information about these entities in the dictionary as they become clearer. The output of this process is depicted in a report called the system subsystem report.

Entities Required to Support SDLC

The entities that are required to support SDLC generally follow the order in which these are created during the system development process. Thus system and subsystem entities are created early during the process, whereas job, program, and other operational data are created later. Figure 15–1 illustrates the entities and the relationships that will support the system development life cycle.

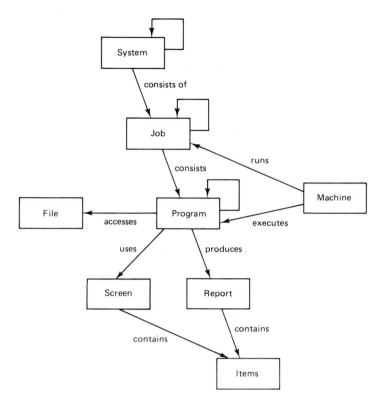

Figure 15-1   Entity model to support SDLC.

DICTIONARY SUPPORT FOR SYSTEMS DEVELOPMENT

Organization

The remaining topics in this chapter are oriented to giving you a description of the phases of an SDLC, and then show the role of the dictionary within each of these phases. Examples are used to highlight the role.

Role in SDLC Phases

System development can be divided into five main phases, with smaller divisions within each phase. On the following pages is a sample system development life cycle. Each phase and/or division contains details about who does the tasks, who participates, what resources are relied on, exactly what the tasks are, what the results will be, and the role of the data dictionary within this life cycle. The five main phases of the SDLC are (1) system study and evaluation, (2) system design, (3) system development, (4) implementation, and (5) audit.

1. System Study and Evaluation.   The primary purpose of the system study and evaluation phase is to define the system from the business point of view and to have the system design approved by the relevant user organizations. This phase is done by the analyst with the full participation and concurrence of the user. The user of the system must be fully cognizant of the various features of the system and the implications of the system in the areas of user training, conversion to new procedures, and hardware and software requirements. In addition, this is the phase where a preliminary cut is taken at defining all the data items that the system will use, so that the DBA will begin to plan the logical structures and visualize the impact on existing files and data bases.

Existing documentation related to manual and automated procedures are analyzed, as well as other systems that do a similar function. The documentation that is produced would give a system overview, cost/benefit analysis, and evaluation so that the user can make a "go/no go" decision at this stage. The data dictionary is consulted to look up summary documentation of existing systems and data bases, so that preliminary estimates can be made. For example, if the data that the user is requesting already exist in automated form, only a conversion utility program needs to be written; if the data exist on paper, an edit screen as well as a load program would have to be provided. The DBA is consulted to determine the impact of adding an application to an existing data base; the operational considerations of performance (response time), transaction processing capacity, disk storage capacity, and the time windows for batch processing are taken into account.

2. System Design

The system design phase includes two activities: (a) data requirements and design and (b) program design. These two activities proceed in close synchronization with each other, because changes in one could affect the other. For example, if a response-time requirement were set to close tolerances, an existing file might not be able to get the response. On the other hand, if the data required by an application are sourced from different parts of the organization, the time it would take to build these interfaces must be factored into the project schedule.

A. DATA REQUIREMENTS AND DESIGN

Data requirements and design include the definition of the data flows, identifying the data items that are required by the system, as well as the key paths by which the data will be accessed by the application. This forms the basis for a logical data structure diagram, with the data items aggregated in the normalized form. With the assistance of the data dictionary and the DBA, the programmer/analyst will develop a list of the data items that are added to the dictionary only after appropriate approvals have been obtained.

This phase results in a more detailed understanding of the information that will be used and generated by the application system. The logical data structures are used by the DBA as a basis for the physical structures that will be defined later in the SDLC.

B. PROGRAM DESIGN

Program design refers to the specifications that are produced by the analyst and programmer that when implemented in a programming language with the appropriate file structures will make the application work. This includes the finalization of screen and report layouts, programming standards, test specifications, program specifications, a development schedule, and estimates.

3. Development

The purpose of the development phase is to build and test the components of the system as specified in the prior phases. Concurrent with the development should be the process of user training, building conversion interfaces, and implementation strategies, ensuring that the operations department is kept up to date about the new system and the additional processing loads being placed on existing files and machines. This will allow the operations department to schedule the impact of the new system and balance the load. The development phase consists of four parts: (a) data base preparation, (b) program preparation, (c) subsystem development, and (d) systems integration testing.

A. Data Base Preparation

Data base preparation is the activity that results in the physical data base structure design and specification. It is in this phase that the DBA has a full set of activities that must be performed, and in which the dictionary is used extensively.

The DBA produces a data design, updates the dictionary in the process, and produces a test data base that can be used by the programmer for program development and testing. The data dictionary is used to generate the file definitions and "include files" so that the standard data definitions are propagated throughout.

B. Program Preparation

Program preparation refers to the process of flowcharting the procedure, writing the code, incorporating all the error-handling procedures that are required, and testing the program to make sure that it works. In some installations where I/O drivers are prevalent, the programmer would issue "call" statements with the appropriate arguments to the I/O drivers, which would get the data back from the data base to the program. The programmer documents the program in the data dictionary and establishes the relationship of the program to the files that are used by the program, the reports produced by the program, and the jobs that execute the program.

C. Subsystem Development

Subsystem development is concurrent with program development and refers to the operational and procedural aspects of the system that have to be developed. These include operations procedures, user procedures, subsystem tests, and getting training programs under way.

D. Systems Integration Testing

Systems integration testing involves testing the automated and manual portions of the system to determine if they mesh together, and if there are any problems, to resolve these as soon as possible. These tests also reveal inadequacies in the documentation. The finalized operations and user procedures are documented in summary form in the dictionary. At this time, the training material can be released for wider dissemination.

4. Implementation

The implementation phase consists of two steps: (a) data base preparation and (b) beta or parallel test and implementation.

A. Data Base Preparation

Data base preparation consists of a series of activities that the DBA performs to ensure that the skeletal data bases are created for new data bases, and that the correct versions of existing data bases are available in the production environment. The DBA also uses load utilities to load the data bases and monitors the performance of the data bases once operational. In addition, any security-related work such as loading user profiles is taken care of at this stage. The system subsystem report from the dictionary is produced to verify that all system components have been adequately documented in the dictionary. The program analyzer is run against all the programs so that the program to file relationships in the dictionary are updated.

B. BETA OR PARALLEL TEST AND IMPLEMENTATION

This is the phase when the system is installed on the appropriate machine, the network links are brought up, users are trained, and the system starts functioning. Users, analysts, programmers, DBA, and operations personnel are all involved in making it happen.

5. Audit

The audit phase is a postimplementation review after the system has been operational for some time. The audit evaluates the user's satisfaction with the system, the performance, and security, control, backup, and recovery procedures. An evaluation report with recommendations is produced which becomes the basis for further work on the system to implement the recommendations.

Dictionary Query Facility

The typical dictionary provides many ways in which to access the data. Mention has already been made of access by keywords, aliases, and other names that are used in the business context. One method of query is to get more information about a particular occurrence of an entity, such as a system, or a program, or a data item. This will generally be the route taken by somebody who wishes quickly to gain knowledge about a particular entity. Another form of query would require information about related entities. An example of this kind of query would occur where the user wants to know what reports are produced from a system, or what data items are in a particular data base. Another form of query is to get a list of entities by some category, such as version, or status, or prefix. A query of this kind occurs when the user wants to get a list of all the data items that are "data standard." Screens that would be used to obtain information from the dictionary are shown in Figures 15-2 through 15-12.

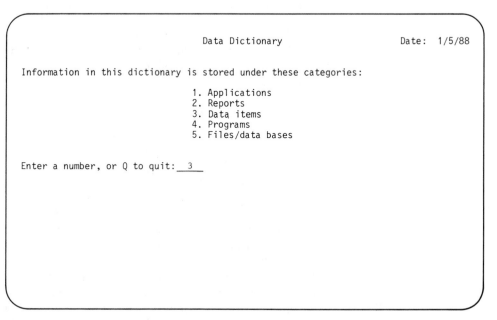

```
                              Data Dictionary                    Date:  1/5/88


   Information in this dictionary is stored under these categories:

                            1. Applications
                            2. Reports
                            3. Data items
                            4. Programs
                            5. Files/data bases


   Enter a number, or Q to quit:  3
```

Figure 15-2 DD information menu screen.

```
                              Data Dictionary                   Date:  1/5/88

  Data item information can be obtained via different methods:

                        1. Name of the data item
                        2. Alias or alternative name
                        3. Keyword
                        4. Logical data category


  Enter a number, or Q to quit:  4

  Enter name:  PART
```

Figure 15-3 Data item information menu screen.

```
                              Data Dictionary                   Date:  1/5/88

  Entries that are available in the dictionary:

   1.    PART NUMBER                     12.    PART REPAIR FLAG

   2.    PART DESCRIPTION                13.    PART REPAIR LOCATION

   3.    PART REVISION NUMBER            14.    PART REPLACED NUMBER

   4.    PART SERIAL NUMBER              15.

   5.    PART TYPE                       16.

   6.    PART TYPE FAMILY                17.

   7.    PART SELL PRICE                 18.

   8.    PART SWAP PRICE                 19.

   9.    PART TOOL FLAG                  20.

  10.    PART SHIP DATE                  21.

  11.    PART PRODUCT CLASS              22.

  There are more. Scroll to see more, or make your choice:

  Press a number, or Q to quit:  1

  Enter name:
```

Figure 15-4 Data item entries screen for PART.

```
                          Data Dictionary                    Date:  1/5/88


Versions of the data item you chose are:

              Data item                   Version      Status        Comment
1.  BASE PART NUMBER
2.  PART NUMBER
3.  VENDOR PART NUMBER
4.  PRIME PART NUMBER
5.  FIELD REPLACEMENT UNIT NUMBER


There are more. Scroll to see more, or make your choice:  2
```

Figure 15-5 Data item versions screen for PART.

```
                          Data Dictionary                    Date:  1/5/88


Data Item:     Part number

Description:   The part number is a unique number assigned to a part by Engineering.
               The first 3 digits represent the class of the part, and the last 6
               digits represent the sequential number of that part within the class.
               Vendor-produced parts are assigned a part number by Engineering. Each
               part can have many revision numbers, which are carried in a separate
               field called PART REVISION NUMBER.

Other names for this data item:   PART-NO (COBOL); PART_NO (PL1); PART; NUMBER;
                                  VENDOR PART;

Scroll to see more, Q to quit:_____
```

Figure 15-6 Data item description screen for PART NUMBER.

Dictionary Reporting Facility

Besides the on-line query facilities that can be used, reports of entities can be produced from the dictionary for reference purposes. These listings make the job of
locating the entities easier for the analyst. The standard items list is one such report
that should be available to the analyst and the user in print form from the dictionary.
If the data item that the user is going to want to use is within this list, the analyst

```
                              Data Dictionary                    Date:  1/5/88


Data Item:      Part number

Attributes:     Size:  (9)
                Range:  1 to 9999999999
                Data Mgmt:  Engineering
                Authoritative Source:  Engineering manager

Cross-References:

                Files:   1. Product reference
                         2. BOM
                         3. OES.D1
         Applications:   4. Order entry
                         5. Manufacturing scheduling
                         6. Distribution
                         7. Bill of materials


Press a number to go to cross-reference; B to go back; Q to quit:_____
```

Figure 15-7 Data element attributes screen for PART NUMBER.

```
                              Data Dictionary                    Date:  1/5/88


Information about applications can be obtained via one of these methods:

           1. Specify the name (if you happen to know it)
           2. Ask for a list of names stored in the directory
           3. Ask for a list of applications by type (i.e., service)


Enter a number, or Q to quit:__2__
```

Figure 15-8 DD applications information menu screen.

would reference that data item in the dictionary on-line to get the latest information about that data item. The screens to specify the report selection criteria are shown in Figure 15-13 and Figure 15-14. The resulting report (sample) is shown in Figure 15-15.

Another report that can be useful in this context is a cross-reference list of aliases to the standard data name. This list enables the analyst to locate the standard name even though it may be called something different by the user. An example of an alias

```
                              Data Dictionary                    Date:  1/5/88


Select the type of applications that you want more information on:

                              1. Contract administration
                              2. Service call handling
                              3. Parts distribution
                              4. Spreadsheet
                              5. Data base
                              6. Account management

There are more. Scroll to see more or make your choice.


Enter a number, or Q to quit:   5
```

Figure 15-9 Application selection menu screen.

```
                              Data Dictionary                    Date:  1/5/88


Type of Application:  Data base

                      1. PFS/File
                      2. Condor III
                      3. DBASE III


Enter a number, or Q to quit:   3
```

Figure 15-10 Application selection screen.

list is given in Figure 15-16. From this alias list, the analyst can access the dictionary to obtain more information about the item.

The keyword in context (KWIC) listing is another cross-reference list that could prove to be valuable in locating the standard data item. A sample listing is provided in Figure 15-17.

```
                          Data Dictionary                    Date:  1/5/88


    Enter application name:_____


       Application           Revision          Status           Comment
       1. DBASE III            1.1                             Supported
       2. DBASE II             4.5                             Not supported
       3. DBASE PLUS           1.0                             Future release


    Choose one:
```

Figure 15–11   DBASE III version selection screen.

```
                          Data Dictionary                    Date:  1/5/88


    Application:  DBASE III

    Description:  DBASE III is a data base management software package that consists of
                  a relational data base management system and enables you to manipulate
                  information in that data base. It has programming features for inter-
                  active use and programmed applications development.

    Vendor:       Ashton-Tate
                  10150 West Jefferson Blvd.
                  Culver City, CA 90230

                  Phone:  (213) 204-5570


    Scroll to see more, or Q to quit:__Q__
```

Figure 15–12   DBASE III information screen.

EXAMPLE OF DICTIONARY USAGE DURING SDLC

System Study and Evaluation Phase

The system scope and requirements analysis phase of the SDLC will include the data items or data classes that would be required by the system. If the data item has already been defined, it would have to be cross-referenced in the dictionary to the system

```
                            Data Dictionary              Date:  8/25/88

                            Report Generator


                        1. Standard data item list
                        2. Keyword list
                        3. Alias list
                        4. System data definition report
                        5. System subsystem report
                        6. Operations report
                        7. Where-used reports

                              Select: 1
```

Figure 15-13 Report generator menu screen.

```
                            Data Dictionary              Date:  8/25/88

                          Standard Data Item List

Banner:  NARAYAN                          Bin Number:  A110

Report Heading:  STD ITEM LIST

Selection Criteria:  Select All or Subset:

Subset by:  Date created:  From ___/___/___ to ___/___/___
            Date last updated:  From ___/___/___ to ___/___/___

            Category:  ITEM

            Status:_____

            Version:_____

Report Should Include:  All or Subset (A/S):  S

Subset: Attributes: Y    Aliases:___   Description:___   Cross-references:___
```

Figure 15-14 Report generator standard data item report
specification screen.

or subsystem entity that would use it. However, if it is a new data item, it must first
be standardized, then added to the standard set of data items. If the data item that
is needed already exists, but the system users have a different meaning for that data
item than the one in the dictionary, it is incumbent on the data dictionary administrator to reconcile the differences between the two definitions. If the data dictionary

Authoritative source is customer.
Edit: Edit for limits on year, month, day.

CALL RECEIVED TIME (Data item)

The call received time is the time in HHMMSS format when the customer's request for service was received at the dispatch center. The time is reported on a 24-hour clock. The time is stored in the central dispatch data base relative to GMT. Size is 6 bytes numeric.

Authoritative source is customer.
Edits: Limits on hours, minutes, seconds.

CUSTOMER NUMBER (Data item)

The customer number is the unique identification given to a customer on customer reference file. It is a 7-character alphanumeric field.

Authoritative source is sales administration.

CIC CODE (Data item)

The CIC code is a code that identifies whether the service technician completed the call or not. The code is 1 byte long and can have the following values: C = Complete; I = Incomplete.

Authoritative source is field service technician.
Edit: Edit for C, I

CONTRACT NUMBER (Data item)

The contract number uniquely identifies the service contract. It is an 8-character alphanumeric field.

Authoritative source is field administration.

Figure 15-15 Standard data element report.

Alias	Standard Data Item
ACTUAL CALL RATE	CALL RATE
CALL DATE	CALL RECEIVED DATE
CALL NUMBER	CALL NUMBER
CALL RATE	CALL RATE
CALL RECEIVED DATE	CALL RECEIVED DATE
CALL RECEIVED TIME	CALL RECEIVED TIME
CALL RATE ACTUAL	CALL RATE
CALL TIME	CALL RECEIVED TIME
CALL-NO	CALL NUMBER
CALL-RATE	CALL RATE
CALL-RECD-DT	CALL RECEIVED DATE
CALL-RECD-TIME	CALL RECEIVED TIME
DATE OF CALL	CALL RECEIVED DATE
NUMBER OF CALL	CALL NUMBER

Figure 15-16 DD alias report.

administrator cannot get agreement on the definition, it must be escalated to the necessary level of management for further review. The reviews are to ensure that each affected user can determine the impact the change would have on his or her operation. If a data item is identified that is not in the dictionary, it is the responsibility of the analyst and the user to bring this to the attention of the data base administrator responsible for the project, who will then make arrangements to standardize the data item; assign a suitable name, size, and so on; and then put it into the dictionary.

Keyword	Standard Data Item
CALL	CALL NUMBER
	CALL RATE
	CALL RECEIVED DATE
	CALL RECEIVED TIME
	CALL RESPONSE CODE
	CALL STATUS CODE
	CALL STATUS TYPE
CODE	ABC CODE
	APPLICATION CODE
	CALL RESPONSE CODE
	CALL STATUS CODE
	CONTRACT ADMINISTRATOR CODE
	CUSTOMER TAX CODE
DATE	AGING DATE
	CALL RECEIVED DATE
	CONTRACT AUTHORIZATION DATE
	CONTRACT CANCEL DATE
	CONTRACT RENEW DATE

Figure 15–17 DD keyword in context report.

As each data item for the system is identified by the analyst and the user, it must be noted on paper and later transferred to the dictionary as a cross-reference from the system entity to the standard data item entity. This presupposes that the analyst has already entered the system entity into the dictionary. The cross-references are noted in the format shown in Figure 15–18. Once the cross-references are stored in the dictionary, a report called the system data requirement report can be generated via the screen shown in Figure 15–19. The report that is produced becomes a part of the system documentation for the users. A few pages from a system data requirement report is shown in Figures 15–20 and 15–21.

The system data requirements report gives the analyst, data base designer, and the users a preview of the data requirements for the project. Why is this important? In many cases, the data item required by one system may already exist in a file. A parallel investigation can now proceed as to the possibilities of sharing that data item. This would involve getting the persons responsible for that data item to get together with the persons asking for the new system, and getting agreements on sharing the data.

So, let's trace the steps as far as interactions with the dictionary are concerned:

1. Analyst enters system narrative into dictionary.
2. Analyst looks up standard items in dictionary or via the cross-reference alias lists.
3. Analyst identifies new data item required for system.
4. DBA standardizes the new items and enters them into dictionary.
5. Analyst maintains a running list of all data items using the standard names.
6. Analyst cross-references system entity to the standard data item entity.
7. Analyst generates system data definition report and incorporates it into the system documentation.

Data Definition Conflicts

If a data item is already being updated by one user group within the company, it should not be necessary for another user group to create the same item. A way should be found by which the second user group can piggyback off the efforts of the first user. Now it may so happen that the sourcing and update procedure for the second user may be different from the first. This can be resolved by one of the following methods:

- Have the second user modify his or her procedures to adapt to the first; this will require a redefinition of the procedures in the system design document.
- Have the two users compromise on the procedure to be followed; this will require that procedures for both the existing system and the new system will be subject to change.
- Maintain the single sourcing, but by duplicating the data item and/or creating appropriate user views, create an environment that suits both parties. From a data base administration viewpoint, this is the least desirable alternative because sooner or later the data item in the two files could become out of synchronization. Also, it adds to the amount of work that the operations center has to perform to keep the two files in synchronization.

Once agreement has been reached among the DBA, analyst, and the concerned users, the results should be documented in the data dictionary. In the event that the data item is replicated in another file, the principle of single sourcing and the vesting of responsibility in one authoritative source should be followed.

```
SYSTEM ENTITY                          STANDARD DATA ITEM

FACTS DATA BASE                        ALTERNATE BILL TO NUMBER
                                       ARRIVAL DATE
                                       ARRIVAL TIME
                                       BRANCH OFFICE ADDRESS
                                       CALL RECEIVED DATE
```

Figure 15-18 Cross-references between system entity and standard data items.

```
                        Data Dictionary              Date:  8/25/88

                   System Data Requirements Report

Banner:  NARAYAN                    Bin Number:  A120

Report Heading:  FACTS DB System Data Requirements

System Name:  FACTS Data Base
```

Figure 15-19 System data requirements report generation screen.

```
DDS0715.R1                        Data Dictionary System                        8/26/88

                              FACTS Data Base Data Requirements

                                          INDEX


FACTS DATA BASE
      ALTERNATE BILL TO NUMBER
      ARRIVAL DATE
      ARRIVAL TIME
      BRANCH OFFICE ADDRESS
      CALL RECEIVED DATE
      CALL RECEIVED TIME
      CUSTOMER NUMBER
      CIA CODE
      CONTRACT NUMBER
      CONTRACT TERRITORY
      COST CENTER ACCOUNT NUMBER
      COST CENTER OF TECHNICIAN
      CUSTOMER ADDRESS
      CUSTOMER BILL TO NUMBER
      CUSTOMER CITY
      CUSTOMER EQUIPMENT RECEIVED DATE
      CUSTOMER NAME
      CUSTOMER PURCHASE ORDER NUMBER
      CUSTOMER SHIP TO NUMBER
      CUSTOMER STATE
      CUSTOMER STATUS
      CUSTOMER ZIP CODE
      DIAGNOSTIC REVISION USED
      ECO NUMBER
      EMPLOYEE BADGE NUMBER
      EQUIPMENT INSTALL COMPLETION DATE
      EQUIPMENT WARRANTY PERIOD
      ESP PARTS CODE
      FACTS INCIDENT NUMBER
```

Figure 15-20   FACTS data base data requirements report (index).

System Design Phase: Documentation

We have already mentioned that the dictionary is used to document summaries of the system, subsystems, programs/procedures, inputs, and outputs. This should be something that the analyst does on a continuing basis. It is important to develop the skeleton of the overall organization of the system design and its components and establish a skeleton in the data dictionary in the beginning. Once this has been done, the report generator can be used to generate the system/subsystem report. This is a report of the components arranged in a hierarchical fashion, one subsystem at a time. The skeleton can be fleshed out as the components become clearer. Additional components can be added and related to the skeleton as the need arises. Since the dictionary is on-line to the analysts and users, the components and their descriptions are visible to the users. Thus the dictionary can be used as a common point of communication and verification during the design process by users and the analyst/designer.

As each entity is identified during the development process, it should be entered into the dictionary and the appropriate relationships stored. Thus the initial reports from the dictionary will be skeletal in nature, but will become filled with details in the course of time. Figure 15-22 illustrates this. An index from a system/subsystem report is shown in Figure 15-23.

DDS0715.R1   Data Dictionary   8/26/88

FACTS Data Base Data Requirements

FACTS DATA BASE (System)

The FACTS DATA BASE project includes implementation of a centralized data base to hold the data that are collected by the area locations by the central dispatching process. The FACTS data base will be the source of data for many of the reporting systems that are being developed.

ALTERNATE BILL TO NUMBER (Data item)

The alternate bill to number is an identifier of the customer's name and address that should be billed. Size is 7 alphanumeric characters.
Authoritative source is sales administration.

ARRIVAL DATE (Data item)

The arrival date is the date in YYMMDD format when the technician arrived at the customer's site. Size is 6 bytes numeric.
Authoritative source is field service technician.
Edits: Should be greater than CALL RECEIVED DATE.

ARRIVAL TIME (Data item)

The arrival time is the time in HHMMSS format when the technician arrived at the customer's site. This time is reported on a 24-hour clock. The time is stored relative to GMT in the dispatch system data base.
Authoritative source is field service technician.
Edits: Edit for limits on hours, minutes, seconds.

BRANCH OFFICE NUMBER (Data item)

The branch office number is the location code assigned to that branch by corporate field administration. It is a unique 8-digit number.
Authoritative source is corporate field administration.
Alias: Location code   Account Number

CALL RECEIVED DATE

The call received date is the date in YYMMDD format when the customer's request for service was received at the central dispatch site. Size is 6 bytes numeric.

Figure 15–21   FACTS data base data requirements report (detail).

Data Base Structure

While the system design specifications are being written, the data base analyst is looking to see how the data requirements for the system can be satisfied. The first task is to look at the current file structures to see if the data items exist and whether they will satisfy the processing needs of the system. New file structures should be proposed only after a thorough examination of the current systems and with con-

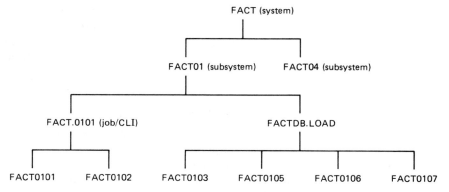

Figure 15–22   FACTS system structure.

```
  DDS0713.R1                        Data Dictionary System                   9/05/88

                                    System Subsystem Report
                                        FACTS Data Base


  FACTS DATA BASE                                                               1
      FACT01                                                                    2
         FACT.0101                                                              3
            FACT0101                                                            4
               FACEXT01S:0                                                      5
               FACTAPEA01                                                       6
            FACT0102                                                            7
               FACTAPEA01                                                       8
               FACTCTRL                                                         9
               FACT0102.R1                                                     10
         FACTDB.LOAD                                                           11
            FACT0103                                                           12
               FACT0101S.W1                                                    13
               FACT0102S.W1                                                    14
               FACT0102S.W2                                                    15
               FACT0103S.W3                                                    16
```

Figure 15–23 FACTS data base system/subsystem report (index).

siderable justification. If data items are going to be duplicated in a new file structure, the appropriate data flows to maintain integrity must be stated.

The file structures that are required for the system to work are determined by the data base administrator in conjunction with the systems analyst. In some cases, this may be an expansion of existing file structures; in other cases, new file structures would have to be defined. During this process, the DBA will actively utilize the data dictionary and apply the appropriate naming conventions to come up with file and record descriptions that can be used for preliminary documentation and program development.

It is important to note that the valid file structures have to be entered into the dictionary (either manually or through the copybook loader) and then generated from the dictionary in order to be operable in the MIS production environment. A sample of the output from the copy generator function in the dictionary is shown in Figure 15–24. The narratives that appear in front of the actual copybook give the application programmer the rules for edit/validation for a data item that has been stored in the dictionary by the data base administrator. This makes it easier for the programmer to put the proper edits into the program.

When the file and record layouts are finalized, they are placed in the copybook library by the data base administrator. Whether the copybooks are loaded automatically or manually, certain other information about the data items within the copybook must be entered into the dictionary. The data items that have been defined for the file layout already follow the standard data item conventions. Therefore, it is necessary to ensure that the data items within the copybook are cross-referenced to the standard narrative in the dictionary. This serves two purposes:

1. When querying the dictionary for the narrative for a particular data item in the file or record, the standard information will be available to the user.

2. The copy generator has an option that produces the narratives of each data item that is included as part of the copy file that is to be used by the programmer; this is useful documentation to the programmer because valuable edit and validation rules will be part of the copy file.

Data Dictionary

Copy Source Generator
COBOL copy source for file CON0105.D1, record R504-CON-REC generated for copybook
CON01015.D1.CC on 9-14-88

R504-CON-REC:
This is a grouping of data items about terms and conditions on the contract header record in the contracts data base.

S504-CONTRACT-NO:
The contract number uniquely identifies the service contract. It is an 8-character alphanumeric field.

S504-CUST-NO:
The customer number is the unique identification given to a customer on the customer reference file. It is a 7-character alphanumeric field.

S504-SHIP-TO-SUFFIX:
The ship-to-address suffix is a 3-digit suffix added to the customer number, which indicates the identifier of the customer's address to which equipment was shipped.

S504-CONTRACT-TYPE:
The contract-type item refers to the type of service contract. This is a 3-character field. The set of codes includes:

        DOM = domestic
        INT = international
        GSA = government
        MIL = military
        OTH = other

S504-ALT-BILL-TO-NO:
The alternate bill to number is an identifier of the customer's name and address that should be billed. Size is 7-alphanumeric characters.

S504-INSTALL-ADDR:
The installation address is the actual address of the customer at whose location the equipment is installed. Overall size is 100 bytes, divided into 4 lines of 25 characters each.

S504-INSTALL-CITY:
The installation city is the name of the city of the customer's site at which the equipment is installed. 22 characters long.

S504-INSTALL-STATE:
The installation state is the 3-character state (U.S.) or province (Canada) identifier.

S504-INSTALL-ZIP-CD:
The installation zip code is the postal code and is 9 bytes long.

S504-WKDAY-COVER-BGN:
The weekday coverage-begins item is the start time of service contract during weekdays, in hours and minutes. 4 bytes long.

S504-WKDAY-COVER-END:
The weekday coverage-ends item is the ending time of service contract during weekdays, in hours and minutes, military time. 4 bytes long.

S504-SAT-COVER-BGN:
The Saturday coverage-begins item is the start time of service contract during Saturdays, in hours and minutes. 4 bytes long.

S504-SAT-COVER-END:
The Saturday coverage-ends item is the ending time of service contract during Saturdays, in hours and minutes, military time. 4 bytes long.

S504-SUN-COVER-BGN:
The Sunday coverage-begins item is the start time of service contract during Sunday, in hours and minutes. 4 bytes long.

S504-SUN-COVER-END:
The Sunday coverage-ends item is the ending time of service contract during Sundays, in hours and minutes, military time. 4 bytes long.

S504-LCTN-CD:
The location code is the 8-digit identifier that uniquely identifies the branch office within the region within the area.

Figure 15-24 FACTS data base system/subsystem report (detail).

```
FD  CON0105.D1
    RECORD CONTAINS 210 CHARACTERS
    DATA RECORD IS S504-CON-REC.

01  S504-CON-REC.
        05    S504-CONTRACT-NO          PIC X(8).
        05    S504-CUST-NO              PIC X(7).
        05    S504-CUST-SHIP-TO-SUFFIX  PIC 9(3).
        05    S504-CONTRACT-TYPE        PIC X(3).
        05    S504-ALT-BILL-TO-NO       PIC X(7).
        05    S504-INSTALL-ADDR         PIC X(100).
        05    S504-INSTALL-CITY         PIC X(22).
        05    S504-INSTALL-STATE        PIC X(3).
        05    S504-INSTALL-ZIP-CD       PIC X(9).
        05    S504-WKDAY-COVER-BGN      PIC 9(4).
        05    S504-WKDAY-COVER-END      PIC 9(4).
        05    S504-SAT-COVER-BGN        PIC 9(4).
        05    S504-SAT-COVER-END        PIC 9(4).
        05    S504-SUN-COVER-BGN        PIC 9(4).
        05    S504-SUN-COVER-END        PIC 9(4).
        05    S504-LCTN-CD              PIC 9(8).
```

Figure 15-24 Continued

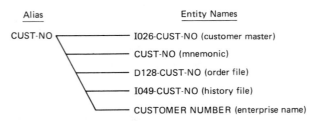

Figure 15-25 Alias to entity cross-references.

Access keys should be entered for each data item; it is recommended that, at the least, the standard data item name be made an alias. For example, the access key to the data item called I026-CUST-NO will be the mnemonic of CUST-NO, which will be stored as an alias. If this procedure is followed consistently for every data item, we are provided with a means of connecting the occurrences of the data items with the same mnemonic. Thus a query of the kind ''give me the occurrences of all data items that refer to CUST-NO'' can be answered because the required connections have been made in the dictionary, as shown by the set of relationships in Figure 15-25.

Permissions must be adjusted so that other persons can access the data item. When the copy loader stores the copybook in the dictionary, it automatically creates an entity occurrence for each data item, record, and file associated with that copybook. The relationships between these entity occurrences and the attributes for them are also loaded automatically. However, only the username of the person loading the copybook has permission to create and modify against the entities. If other users are required to view the entities associated with the copybook, the original user must give specific access rights to the other users or give general access to everybody to view the data item, record, or file descriptions in the data dictionary.

Development Phase: System Subsystem Report

During the development phases, the system and its components are documented by the programmer or analyst. As stated previously, this is an iterative process. The skeleton of the components that were inserted in the dictionary are fleshed out over time. An example of a system subsystem report is shown on the following pages.

DDS0713.R1   Data Dictionary System   9/05/88
                     System Subsystem Report   Pg   1
                       FACTS DATA BASE

FACTS DATA BASE   (System)   Status: P   Version:01

The FACTS data base project includes the implementation of a centralized data base to hold the data that are collected by the area locations by the central dispatching process. The FACTS data base will be the source of data for many of the reporting systems that are being developed. The FACTS (Field Activity Collection and Tracking) system is designed to organize data from the field into a data base to satisfy the information needs of the field and headquarters. The FACTS data base will contain the previous week's closed calls as reported by each central dispatch center. In addition, the data base will contain the contract and configuration changes that are reported by the customer, service technician, and branch manager.

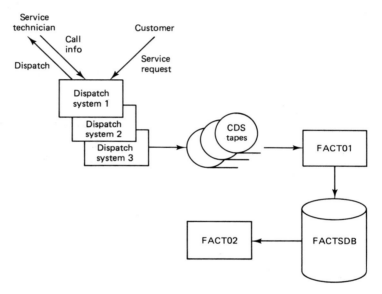

FACTS data flow diagram.

DDS0713.R1	Data Dictionary System	9/05/88
	System Subsystem Report	Pg 2
	FACTS DATA BASE	

FACT01 (Subsystem)   Status: P   Version:01

The FACT01 subsystem within the FACTS system includes the steps needed to process the closed call data from the dispatch centers into the FACTS data base

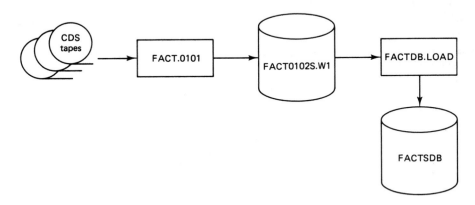

FACT01 subsystem diagram.

DDS0713.R1	Data Dictionary System	9/05/88
	System Subsystem Report	Pg 3
	FACTS DATA BASE	

FACT.0101   (Job/CLI)   Status: P   Version:01

The FACT.0101 job takes the tapes from the dispatch centers and loads them for further processing.

Type: Batch   Programmer: Nelson
Schedule: Weekly   Estimated Run Time: 30 min
Switches: None
Dependencies:
Special Instructions: This job can be run for as many tapes as are there from the dispatch centers.

Run Instructions:

    QBJ FACT.0101

Rerun Instructions:

    Restart the job from the beginning.

Program/File Information

    01) Program FACT0101
         Converts RDOS tape format (dispatch system closed calls) to AOS disk format for further processing.

I/O	Filename/File Description	Device	Retention	Format	Copies
I	FACEXT01S:0	TAPE	1 YR		
	Dispatch system tape (RDOS)				
O	FACTAPEA01	DISK	EOJ		
	FACTS data (AOS format)				
I/O	FACTCTRL	DISK	PERM		

    02) Program FACT0102
         Verification against control file

I/O	Filename/File Description	Device	Retention	Format	Copies
I	FACTAPEA01	DISK	EOJ		
O	FACT0101S.W1	DISK	1 day		
I/O	FACTCTRL	DISK	PERM		
O	FACT0102.R1	PRINT		LONG 6	3

FACT.0101   (Job/CLI)   Status: P Version: 01

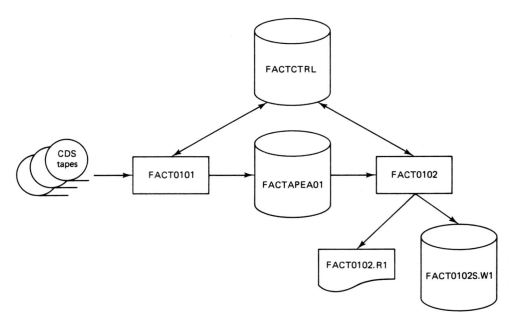

FACT.0101 job flow diagram.

DDS0713.R1

Data Dictionary System
System Subsystem Report
FACTS DATA BASE

9/05/88

Pg   5

FACT0101   (Program)   Status: P   Version:01

Author: J. Nelson   Maintenance Resp: J. Nelson
Language: COBOL-74   Code set: ASCII

Description: At the end of each week, each dispatch system site will prepare an RDOS tape file of all closed calls during the previous week. This tape will be sent to the HQ data center. FACT0101 will perform an RDOS-to-AOS format conversion, load the file into FACTAPEA01, and record the completion of this process in the control file.

Operations Doc:

    Program FACT0101
    Converts RDOS tape format (dispatch system closed calls) to AOS disk format for further processing.

I/O	Filename/File Description	Device	Retention	Format	Copies
I	FACEXT01S:0	TAPE	1 YR		
	Dispatch system tape (RDOS)				
O	FACTAPEA01	DISK	EOJ		
	FACTS data (AOS format)				
I/O	FACTCTRL	DISK	PERM		

DDS0713.R1	Data Dictionary System	9/05/88
	System Subsystem Report	Pg 6
	FACTS DATA BASE	

FACEXT01S:2   (File)   Status: P   Version:01

FACEXT01S:2 is the filename under which the tape of closed calls from the dispatch center is loaded at the HQ data center.

Short Desc: Dispatch system tape (RDOS)
Retention: 1 year
Organization: Sequential
Record Size: 309 bytes max.

DDS0173.R1   Data Dictionary System   9/05/88
                   System Subsystem Report   Pg   7
                       FACTS DATA BASE

FACTAPEA01 (File)   Status: P   Version:01

FACTAPEA01 is the disk filename of the AOS file that will hold the data from the dispatch center after they have been converted from RDOS format to AOS format. It consists of variable-length records, representing the different types of transaction records generated by the dispatch system. The first 28 characters of the transaction records have a common format:

Bytes		
	1–3	Record ID
	4–10	Call number
	11–16	Date of service
	17–22	Time of service
	23–28	Employee badge number

Short Desc: FACTS data (AOS format)
Retention: EOJ
Organization: Sequential
Record Size: 309 bytes max.

FACTCTRL   (File)   Status: P   Version:01

FACTCTRL is an ISAM file that contains the control information required to ensure that the proper sequence of tapes are processed from each dispatch center. The tape from the dispatch center contains a header record and a trailer record that has information which can be used for verification. In addition to control totals, the header and trailer records contain extract sequence indicators (ESI) which are compared with the ESIs in the FACTCTRL file to ensure that tapes are processed in the correct sequence.

Short Desc:

Retention: PERM

Organization: ISAM

Record Size: 180 bytes

Copybook:

```
            SELECT FACTCTRL ASSIGN INDEX TO WS-FACTCTRL-INDX
            ASSIGN DATA TO WS-FACTCTRL-DATA
            KEY IS WS-CTRL-KEY KEY LENGTH IS WS-KEY-LENGTH
            FILE STATUS IS WS-FILE-STAT.

            FD FACTCTRL
            RECORD CONTAINS 180 CHARACTERS
            DATA RECORD IS 1276-CTRL-REC.

        01 1276-CTRL-REC.
            05   1276-CTRL-KEY.
                 10   1276-CREATE-DATE             PIC 9(6).
                 10   1276-CREATE-TIME             PIC 9(6).
                 10   1276-DISPATCH-AREA           PIC X(1).
                 10   1276-DISPATCH-CENTER-ID      PIC X(1).
                 10   1276-DISPATCH-CENTER-LOC     PIC X(8).
                 10   1276-LOW-ESI                 PIC 9(8).
                 10   1276-HIGH-ESI                PIC 9(8).
                 10   1276-SEQ-NO                  PIC 9(4).
                 10   1276-CTRL-DATA               PIC X(138).
```

Name: FACT0102   (Program)   Status: P   Version:01

Author: J. Nelson   Maintenance Resp: J. Nelson

Language: COBOL-74   Code set: ACSII

Description: The AOS file FACTAPEA01 produced from FACT0101 will be verified against control information to ensure that the sequence of tapes from the dispatch centers is maintained. It will also perform security checks to ensure that the tape is from the correct source. It appends to FACT0101S.W1.

Operations Doc:

     Program FACT0102
     Verification against control file.

I/O	Filename/File Description	Device	Retention	Format	Copies
I	FACTAPEA01	DISK	EOJ		
O	FACT0101S.W1	DISK	1 day		
	Holding file				
I/O	FACTCTRL	DISK	PERM		
O	FACT0102.R1	PRINT		LONG 6	3

DDS0713.R1	Data Dictionary System	9/05/88
	System Subsystem Report	Pg 10
	FACTS DATA BASE	

FACTAPEA01 (File)   Status: P   Version:01

FACTAPEA01 is the disk filename of the AOS file that will hold the data from the dispatch center
after they have been converted from RDOS format to AOS format. It consists of variable-length
records, representing the different types of transaction records generated by the dispatch system. The
first 28 characters of the transaction records have a common format:

Bytes		
	1–3	Record ID
	4–10	Call number
	11–16	Date of service
	17–22	Time of service
	23–28	Employee badge number

Short Desc: FACTS data (AOS format)
Retention: EOJ
Organization: Sequential
Record Size: 309 bytes max.

DS0713.R1   Data Dictionary System   9/05/88
System Subsystem Report   Pg   11
FACTS DATA BASE

FACT0101S.W1   (File)   Status: P   Version:01

File FACT0101S.W1 is the file that holds the data from FACTAPEA01. The data from FACTAPEA01 are appended to any other data that may already be in FACT0101S.W1 from another dispatch center.

Short Desc: Holding file
Retention: 1 day
Organization: Sequential
Record Size: 309 bytes max.

DDS0713.R1	Data Dictionary System	9/05/88
	System Subsystem Report	Pg 12
	FACTS DATA BASE	

FACTCTRL   (File)   Status: P   Version:01

FACTCTRL is an ISAM file that contains the control information required to ensure that the proper sequence of tapes are processed from each dispatch center. The tape from the dispatch center contains a header record and a trailer record that has information which can be used for verification. In addition to control totals, the header and trailer records contain extract sequence indicators (ESI) which are compared with the ESIs in the FACTCTRL file to ensure that tapes are processed in the correct sequence.

Short Desc:
Retention: PERM
Organization: ISAM
Record Size: 180 bytes
Copybook:

```
        SELECT FACTCTRL ASSIGN INDEX TO WS-FACTCTRL-INDX
        ASSIGN DATA TO WS-FACTCTRL-DATA
        KEY IS WS-CTRL-KEY KEY LENGTH IS WS-KEY-LENGTH
        FILE STATUS IS WS-FILE-STAT.

        FD FACTCTRL
        RECORD CONTAINS 180 CHARACTERS
        DATA RECORD IS 1276-CTRL-REC.

        01 I276-CTRL-REC.
           05   I276-CTRL-KEY.
                10   I276-CREATE-DATE              PIC 9(6).
                10   I276-CREATE-TIME              PIC 9(6).
                10   I276-DISPATCH-AREA            PIC X(1).
                10   I276-DISPATCH-CENTER-ID       PIC X(1).
                10   I276-DISPATCH-CENTER-LOC      PIC X(8).
                10   I276-LOW-ESI                  PIC 9(8).
                10   I276-HIGH-ESI                 PIC 9(8).
                10   I276-SEQ-NO                   PIC 9(4).
                10   I276-CTRL-DATA                PIC X(138).
```

Name: FACT0102.R1 (Report)   Status: P   Version:01
Produced by: FACT0102   Status: P   Version:01
Description: FACT0101.R1 is a FACTS load exception report which will be produced if there is a discrepancy found in the sequence of tapes sent from the dispatch centers.

Distribution: Operations control; dispatch center supvr; DBA

Frequency: When error   Media:8 1/2 by 11

Alias: FACT0102.R1   LOAD ERROR REPORT   FACTS REPORT
Keyword: FACTS   ERROR   LOAD   FACT0102.R1

Report Sample

FACT0102.R1   FACTS System Report   2/8/89
                               LOAD ERROR RPT.

Error detected on tape for week ending 2/7/89 from Dispatch Center C

Tape out of sequence; tape for week ending 1/31/89 from Dispatch Center C was not processed.

** END OF REPORT **

Implementation Phase: Operations Documentation

Operations documentation includes the procedures necessary to ensure that the operator can look up relevant information in the dictionary. Depending on the usage of the dictionary by the operations department, additional information may be required. Screens that are used to enter the operations documentation are shown in Figures 15–26 through 15–29.

```
                         Data Dictionary              Date:  8/25/88

                         Store/Modify/Load
                              Job/CLI

 Name:  FACT.0101                    Status:  P          Version:01
 Within system/subsystem:  FACT01    Status:  P          Version:01
 Description:  The FACT.0101 job takes the tapes from the dispatch centers and loads
 them for further processing.

 Type:  Batch                        Programmer:  Nelson
 Schedule:  Weekly                   Estimated Run Time:  30 min
 Switches:  None
 Dependencies:_____

 Special Instructions:  This job can be run for as many tapes as there are from the
 dispatch centers.
```

Figure 15–26 Store job/CLI information screen.

```
                         Data Dictionary              Date:  8/25/88

                         Store/Modify/Load
                         Job/CLI Run Instructions

 Name:  FACT.0101                    Status:  P          Version:01
 Within system/subsystem:  FACT01    Status:  P          Version:01

 Run Instructions

 QBJ FACT.0101
```

Figure 15–27 Store job/CLI run instructions screen.

```
                          Data Dictionary              Date: 8/25/88

                            Store/Modify/Load
                          Job/CLI Re-run Instructions


  Name:  FACT.0101                    Status:  P       Version:01
  Within system/subsystem:  FACT01    Status:  P       Version:01

  Rerun Instructions

  Restart the job from the beginning.
```

Figure 15-28   Store job/CLI rerun instructions screen.

```
                          Data Dictionary              Date: 8/26/88

                            Store/Modify/Load
                          Job/CLI Program File Info


  Name:  FACT.0101                 Status:  P          Version:01
  Within subsystem:  FACT01        Status:  P          Version:01

  01) Program FACT0101
      Converts RDOS tape format (dispatch system closed calls) to AOS disk format for
      further processing.

      I/O   Filename/File Description     Device   Retention   Format   Copies
      I     FACEXT01S:0                   TAPE     1 YR
            Dispatch system tape (RDOS)
      O     FACTAPEA01                    DISK     EOJ
            FACTS data (AOS format)

  02) Program FACT0102
      Verification against control file

      I/O   Filename/File Description     Device   Retention   Format   Copies
      I     FACTAPEA01                    DISK     EOJ
      O     FACT0101S.W1                  DISK     1 day
      I/O   FACTCTRL                      DISK     PERM
      O     FACT0102.R1                   PRINT                LONG 6   3
```

Figure 15-29   Store job/CLI program file information screen.

Program Analysis.   After the program has been developed and tested, and prior to its placement in the production library, each program must be run against the program analyzer to store the cross-references automatically between the program and the data items, records, files, and copybooks that are accessed by the program in either update mode or retrieval mode. In the case of programs that cannot be run through the program analyzer, the program to data linkages must be established manually through the storage of cross-references in the dictionary. The results of executing the program analyzer against program FACT0105 is shown below. Note that this report shows the activity of the program against only those items that exist in the dictionary.

Date: 9-21-88   Final Program Analysis for: FACT0105   Page: 1

Qualifier: Status: Version: 01 Node:

Name	Ty	Qu	S	Ve	No	Imp	R	U
R199-EXPENSE-REC	03		P	01				U
S199-CALL-NO	01		P	01		I		U
S199-EMP-BADGE-NO	01		P	01		I		U
S199-EXPENSE-GRP	02		P	01		I		U
S199-BILL-CD	01		P	01		I		U
S199-SVC-DT	01		P	01		I		U
S199-SVC-TIME	02		P	01		I		U
S199-SVC-HHMM	01		P	01		I		U
S199-SVC-SS	01		P	01		I		U
S199-TRVL-TO-HRS	01		P	01		I		U
S199-TRVL-FROM-HRS	01		P	01		I		U
S199-DISTANCE	01		P	01		I		U
S199-EXPENSES	01		P	01		I		U
R198-EQPMT-REC	03		P	01				U
S198-LCTN-CD	01		P	01		I		U
S198-CALL-NO	01		P	01		I		U
S198-ACT-REC-NO	01		P	01		I		U
S198-TYPE	01		P	01		I		U
S198-LINE-NO	01		P	01		I		U
S198-DATA	01		P	01		I		U
R048-TIME-REC	03		P	01				U
S048-EMP-BADGE-NO	01		P	01		I		U
S048-FISCAL-DATE	02		P	01		I		U
S048-FISCAL-YEAR	01		P	01		I		U
S048-FISCAL-PERIOD-OF-YEAR	01		P	01		I		U
S048-FISCAL-WEEK-OF-PERIOD	01		P	01		I		U
S048-UNAVAILABLE-DT	01		P	01		I		U
S048-UNAVAILABLE-CD	01		P	01		I		U
S048-UNAVAILABLE-HRS	01		P	01		I		U
R047-EMP-REC	03		P	01				U
S047-EMP-BADGE-NO	01		P	01		I		U
R045-ACTIVITY-REC	03		P	01				U
S045-FACT-SVC-CD	01		P	01		I		U
S045-SVC-DT	01		P	01		I		U
S045-SVC-TIME	01		P	01		I		U
S045-ACT-REC-NO	01		P	01		I		U
S045-STOP-TIME	01		P	01		I		U
S045-CALL-NO	01		P	01		I		U
S045-CONTRACT-NO	01		P	01		I		U
S045-EMP-BADGE-NO	01		P	01		I		U
S045-EMP-OFFICE-NO	01		P	01		I		U
S045-EMP-TERR-NO	01		P	01		I		U
S045-LCTN-CD	01		P	01		I		U
S045-ACCT-TERR-NO	01		P	01		I		U
S045-MODEL-NO	01		P	01		I		U

Qualifier: Status: Version: 01 Node:

Name	Ty	Qu	S	Ve	No	Imp	R	U
S045-MODEL-SERIAL-NO	01		P	01		I		U
S045-UPGRADE-MODEL-NO	01		P	01		I		U
S045-SYMPTOM-FIX-CD	01		P	01		I		U
S045-SALES-ORDER-NO	01		P	01		I		U
S045-CUST-PO-NO	01		P	01		I		U
S045-ISC-NO	01		P	01		I		U
S045-CUST-STATUS	01		P	01		I		U
S045-SCHDL-ID	01		P	01		I		U
S045-REG-HRS	01		P	01		I		U
S045-REG-HRS-BILLED	01		P	01		I		U
S045-PRM-HRS	01		P	01		I		U
S045-PRM-HRS-BILLED	01		P	01		I		U
S045-PARTS-RUN	01		P	01		I		U
S045-PARTS-RUN-BILLED	01		P	01		I		U
S045-FCO-NO	01		P	01		I		U
R044-CONTRACT-REC	03		P	01				U
S044-CONTRACT-NO	01		P	01		I		U
S044-LCTN-CD	01		P	01		I		U
R043-MODEL-REC	03		P	01				U
S043-MODEL-NO	01		P	01		I		U
R042-PART-USED	03							U
S042-LCTN-CDP	01		P	01		I		U
S042-CALL-NO	01		P	01		I		U
S042-ACT-REC-NO	01		P	01		I		U
S042-FRU-NO	01		P	01		I		U
S042-FRU-REV-NO	01		P	01		I		U
S042-FRU-SERIAL-NO	01		P	01		I		U
S042-SYMPTOM-FIX	01		P	01		I		U
S042-HRS-WRKD-FRU	01		P	01		I		U
S042-HRS-FRU-BILLED	01		P	01		I		U
S042-PART-NO	01		P	01		I		U
S042-PART-REV-NO	01		P	01		I		U
S042-PART-SERIAL-NO	01		P	01		I		U
S042-ESP-PARTS-CD	01		P	01		I		U
S042-ESP-PARTS-BILLED	01		P	01		I		U
S042-QTY-PART-USED	01		P	01		I		U
S042-QTY-PART-BILLED	01		P	01		I		U
S042-PART-SHIP-DT	01		P	01		I		U
S042-HRS-WRKD-PART	01		P	01		I		U
S042-SELL-PRICE	01		P	01		I		U
S042-COST-PRICE	01		P	01		I		U
R041-CALL-REC	03		P	01				U
S041-CALL-NO	01		P	01		I		U
S041-CALL-RECD-DT	01		P	01		I		U
S041-CALL-RECD-TIME	01		P	01		I		U
S041-UPDT-DT	01		P	01		I		U
S041-LCTN-CD	01		P	01		I		U
S041-ARRIVAL-DT	01		P	01		I		U
S041-ARRIVAL-TIME	01		P	01		I		U
S041-CALL-CLOSE-DT	01		P	01		I		U

Name	Ty	Qu	S	Ve	No	Imp	R	U
S041-CALL-CLOSE-TIME	01		P	01		I		U
S041-CIA-CD	01		P	01		I		U
S041-STOP-TIME	01		P	01		I		U
S041-TOT-SVC-HRS	01		P	01		I		U
S041-CNTRCT-FLAG	01		P	01		I		U
S041-ERROR-FLAG	01		P	01		I		U
S041-ERROR-FLAG-DT	01		P	01		I		U
S041-REVIEW-FLAG	01		P	01		I		U
S041-REVIEW-FLAG-DT	01		P	01		I		U
S041-EDIT-FLAG	01		P	01		I		U
S041-EDIT-FLAG-DT	01		P	01		I		U
S041-BILL-FLAG	01		P	01		I		U
S041-BILL-FLAG-DT	01		P	01		I		U
S041-CUST-NO	01		P	01		I		U
R040-ARBO-REC	03		P	01				U
S040-LCTN-CD	01		P	01		I		U
STAT-FILE	05		P	01				U
AUDIT.F.CC	10		P	01				
STATUSF.CC	10		P	01				
STATUSS.CC	10		P	01				
STATUSW.CC	10		P	01				
STATUSP.CC	10		P	01				

After the foregoing steps are carried out during the system development process, the data dictionary will have all the data entities documented, all the system entities documented, and the relationships between the system entities and the data entities established.

chapter 16

Data Dictionary Role in Computer Operations

INTRODUCTION

In this chapter the role of the dictionary in capturing and maintaining the operations documentation during the SDLC is highlighted. The on-line access to this information during a failure in operations, as well as other information, are invaluable in maintaining a smooth operational environment. Other extensions of the dictionary in scheduling and resource planning are discussed. Examples from the backup and recovery procedures for the field activity data base development project are given.

COMPUTER OPERATIONS OBJECTIVES

The computer operations department in any company has the responsibility for executing the batch jobs that have to be run on a scheduled basis and ensuring that computers are used to their capacity. The objective of the operations department is to provide the computer resources that are required to meet information processing needs of the organization. The criteria can be further broken down into:

- Availability of applications systems to the end user within reasonable response times
- Timely production of reports from the systems
- Availability of data bases and accessibility through application or utility programs
- All of the above delivered in a cost-effective manner

Any systems or procedures that assist in reaching these objectives will be welcomed by the operations staff. This need becomes especially critical in operations departments that have a variety of machines to operate.

INFORMATION REQUIREMENTS

The average operations department runs jobs that are designed and developed by the systems development organization. Operations may not have had input into the development process if the system was procured from outside vendors. Generally, the operations department is brought into the picture when the system functions are fairly well finalized, and the issue of the capacity to perform the job is brought up. This is the starting point for the operations department to analyze the interdependencies that will be affected by the introduction of the new system and to prepare for all the contingencies. Key information that the operations department will look for will be names of the existing data bases that will be affected, the nature and timing of the new programs that will be executing against the data bases, the recovery steps in case of failure, and any other pertinent data that would have implications for the current way of doing things.

Remember that the operations department is organized to provide a service to existing users, and that service level must be maintained at all costs. If the new application will utilize networks to access data bases on other machines, or have dependencies on jobs that are running on other machines, information pertinent to these must be evaluated by the operations department.

Unlike the DBA function, which is interested in the detailed interaction between programs and data items, the operations department is interested only in aggregate interactions of programs with data files, machines, networks, and so on. Thus the information requirements for the operations department is quite different from that of, say, system development or data base administration. However, the basic data are similar. Let's explore this a bit further.

The main unit of interest to operations is the "job." A job is a series of one or more job steps, which can consist of other job steps or programs and modules within programs. The job has a certain frequency with which it has to be scheduled (i.e., daily, weekly, monthly, special request, etc.). The job also has certain interpendencies with other jobs of the same system or other systems. Thus a job to back up a shared data base would have to be executed before a job that updates the data base. Execution of a job can be manual or automatic, depending on the machine and type of software available. The job also has certain start and stop times designed into it, that is, it must run within a predefined time frame.

The foregoing information is taken into account when a schedule of jobs to be run on a particular machine is made up by the operations department. Under ideal conditions, the jobs would run on a schedule that is planned. However, any one of a number of events could disrupt the carefully devised schedule.

There could be individual failure or combined failure of components that go to make up the system. Whatever the cause of the failure, the first thing that the operations department is concerned with is problem identification and recovery. There are two major levels of failure: A failure in the hardware, operating software, or network is categorized as system-level failure, whereas a failure in an application program or data base is categorized as an application-level failure. If there is network, hardware, or operating software failure, the appropriate personnel have to be called in to fix the problem, and the machine has to be restarted.

The rest of this discussion assumes that this stage of problem resolution has been carried out and the operations department is now ready to perform application system and data base recovery. If there are several jobs going on concurrently, as is usually the case, the discussion applies to every job that has to be recovered.

The operations department will have information on what jobs were in execution when system failure occurred based on information in a master system or console log. The operator has to follow the recovery instructions to the letter to complete the application successfully. In some cases the recovery step is simply to restart the job at a checkpoint or previously defined point where data integrity can be assured. In other cases, the entire data base might have been subject to damage, in which case a backup would have to be reloaded and processing begun.

In still other cases, the problem may neither be apparent to the operations department nor have been covered by the procedures that have been documented. In such cases it is important that the personnel who are part of the recovery team have access to all the information about the system, the job, programs, reports, data bases, and their interrelationships, so that the recovery can be coordinated with access to the common base of information. It has been the author's experience that where all parties to the recovery work form a common base of information, the recovery is smoother.

Another point to remember is that batch jobs are normally run at night, and recovery has to be coordinated, via telephone connections, among a number of people who live in different locations. Thus it is likely that the recovery will be done on-line, provided that one has access to the common set of information. What constitutes this common set of information, and where should this information be located?

The set of information that is required is portrayed in Figure 16–1. The recovery team must have on-line access to these data and be able to traverse the various pieces of data in order to get the information quickly. The persons who originated most

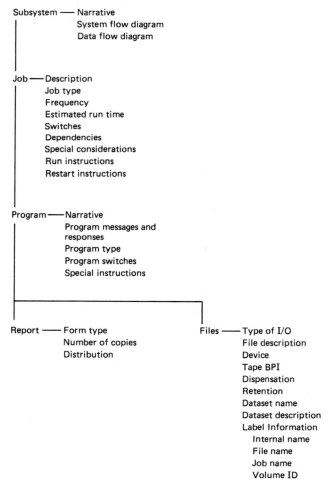

Figure 16–1   Entities, attributes, and relationships required to support operations.

of this information are the system development staff. The users are primarily operations personnel. If we examine the information that is required with the information contained in a typical dictionary, we realize that most of the basic information is already in the dictionary! However, it has to be reformatted and presented in a format that is suitable to the operations department.

DATA DICTIONARY ROLES

The dictionary possesses the information that is useful to the operations department. View access to these data would be necessary for the operations department. This is the first use to which the information in the dictionary is put—as a communication vehicle between the developers of the system and the operators of the system.

As the operations department staff get more familiar with the content of the data in the dictionary, other uses of the dictionary are brought up as applications. In a development organization, revision control of source libraries assumes major importance. Nominally, the operations department is concerned only with systems that have been qualified to be "production" status by the development organization. In the interest of stability, the operations department demands that revision control procedures be strictly followed. This is so that any change in the system is fully documented in the dictionary and its impact communicated to the operations staff in a standard format. This is easy to do in a data dictionary because of the revision control and status control features inherent in the dictionary.

The dictionary plays a more active role in the operation of the application system, when job execution is triggered from the dictionary itself. Since there are several pieces of information about the job already stored in the dictionary, job execution can be triggered by the dictionary with the addition of schedule information. Most commercial dictionaries are not designed to execute jobs, but it could be accomplished as an extension to the dictionary's mainstream functions, once the operations department becomes familiar with all the functions of the dictionary.

Recovery Procedures

The data dictionary is especially useful in planning a recovery from a condition not previously experienced or evaluated. It is helpful when establishing contingency procedures for recovery from any number of unusual failures, thus saving precious time when such a failure occurs. The data dictionary is a point of reference to operations personnel in the following DBMS-oriented procedures:

- Taking a data base save or unload
- Recording the log tape identification
- Starting the TPMS system
- Recovering the systems from various failures
- Bringing the TPMS system down gracefully

The operational information should include detailed procedures to be followed in recovery situations. Previously evaluated failure conditions should be described in the data dictionary, as should the steps to be taken for recovery. The data dictionary can contain information pertinent to the recovery steps that are followed in the operations department. Screens that will be presented to the operator for the information on the FACTS data base load job stream are shown in Figures 16–2 through 16–6.

```
┌─────────────────────────────────────────────────────────────────┐
│                                                                   │
│                        Data Dictionary                 8/26/88    │
│                    Operator Run Sheet Narrative                   │
│                                                                   │
│   Name:  FACTSDB.LOAD                Status:  P          Version:01│
│                                                                   │
│   Within subsystem:  FACT01          Status:  P          Version:01│
│                                                                   │
│   Select one of the following:                                    │
│                                                                   │
│   1. General description                                          │
│   2. Operator run instructions                                    │
│   3. Operator rerun instructions                                  │
│   4. Program file information                                     │
│                                                                   │
│                                                                   │
│   Enter Selection:                                                │
│                                                                   │
│                                                                   │
│                                                                   │
│                                                                   │
└─────────────────────────────────────────────────────────────────┘
```

Figure 16–2   Operator run sheet narrative menu screen.

```
┌─────────────────────────────────────────────────────────────────┐
│                                                                   │
│                        Data Dictionary                 8/26/88    │
│                    Operator Run Sheet Narrative                   │
│                                                                   │
│   Name:  FACTSDB.LOAD                Status:  P          Version:01│
│                                                                   │
│   Within subsystem:  FACT01          Status:  P          Version:01│
│                                                                   │
│   Description:  This job stream takes the calls that have been closed the prior week │
│   in the prior week, breaks them down into separate files by transaction type, sorts │
│   them, then loads the FACTS data base with these files.          │
│                                                                   │
│   Job Type:  Batch                   Programmer:  John Jones      │
│                                                                   │
│   Frequency:  Weekly          Estimated Run Time:  2.5 hours      │
│                                                                   │
│   Switches:  None                                                 │
│                                                                   │
│   Dependencies:  FACTS0106 must have run successfully.            │
│                                                                   │
│   Special Instructions:  None                                     │
│                                                                   │
└─────────────────────────────────────────────────────────────────┘
```

Figure 16–3   Operator run sheet narrative screen.

Scheduling Resources for Computer Operations

The data dictionary assists with computer operations management because it provides a map of the information in the organization and gives a detailed operational view of the systems that are running in the data center's computers. The application systems are processed according to cyclical schedules. In an integrated data base environment, where many application systems may access the same data bases, the interdependencies between various procedures become quite complex. These interdependencies are portrayed in the data dictionary and the information made available to the operations staff.

```
                              Data Dictionary                      8/26/88
                          Operator Run Instructions


Name:  FACTSDB.LOAD                    Status:  P          Version:01

Within subsystem:  FACT01             Status:  P          Version:01

Run Instructions



Set search list to find FACTSDB
QBJ FACTSDB.LOAD
```

Figure 16–4 Operator run instructions screen.

```
                              Data Dictionary                      8/26/88
                         Operator Rerun Instructions


Name:  FACTSDB.LOAD                    Status:  P          Version:01

Within subsystem:  FACT01             Status:  P          Version:01

Rerun instructions:

If programs FACT0103, FACT0105, or FACT0107 abort, the entire job can be started
from the beginning. To do this, just make sure that the searchlist is set to find
FACTSDB; then:

                              QBJ FACTSDB.LOAD

If program FACT0107 is to be restarted, the operator types out the file FACT0107S.A2.
This file will tell the operator which switch to use when restarting the job. Then
the operator will make sure that the searchlist is set to find FACTSDB; then:

                              QBJ FACT0107/s

Where s = the restart switch
```

Figure 16–5 Operator rerun instructions screen.

The information that is required for scheduling consists of dates and times (frequency) of jobs that have to run, and details about the machines on which they are to be run. Figure 16-7 gives the information that is necessary for scheduling.

Information about the different steps in a system, such as frequency, required time, and accuracy, is stored in the data dictionary as attributes to existing entities. This is used as a basis for scheduling systems and determining the impact of new systems on an existing schedule.

It is important that the dictionary be used to actively support the operations environment, for two reasons:

```
                              Data Dictionary                    8/26/88
                             Program File Info

   Name:  FACTSDB.LOAD              Status:  P          Version:01

   Within subsystem:  FACT01        Status:  P          Version:01

01) Program FACT0103
    This program reads the sorted closed call data from the dispatch center and
    formats the data for loading of the FACTS data base.

    I/O   Filename/File Description     Device   Retention   Format   Copies
    I     FACT0101S.W1                  DISK     EOJ
          Dispatch system file with FACT
          Data.

    0     FACT0102S.W1                  DISK     1 day
          FACTS file w/o F53 records

    0     FACT0102S.W2                  DISK     1 day
          F53 activity records

    I     FACT0102S.W1                  DISK
          F53 activity records
```

Figure 16-6 Program file information screen.

1. The data dictionary contains a lot of the information required in the schedule, It is economical to use this information directly, as opposed to asking the system development staff to provide this information in a different format all over again. A dictionary that contains this much information is easily extended to produce the operation documentation.

2. The operations department is the culmination of the entire development activity. By making the operations department rely on the dictionary for its information and support, it will be a driving force to ensure that the dictionary contains information that is up to date, accurate, and complete.

After the information about jobs has been determined and entered into the data dictionary, it is possible to optimize systems throughput by judicious scheduling. Although the improvement of performance is important, the previously defined user requirements must not be compromised.

When schedule adjustments must be made, the data dictionary is consulted to determine the flexibility of each application. If a system failure occurs, affected users can be identified from the data dictionary. If an input data error occurs, the source of the data can be found and corrections made. The routing of output, in itself no small task, can also be facilitated.

Users are generally at least two steps removed from the production of the information that they require. The data dictionary is consulted by operations personnel when scheduling decisions must be made, so that they are aware of users' information requirements. Using the data dictionary views of the information system, it is possible to provide a stable operation with good performance characteristics. Changes in the environment can be planned and implemented with a minimum of impact on existing production systems. Abnormal situations can be anticipated with contingency plans; and as a result, production problems can be reduced.

An illustration of a typical operations schedule for a minicomputer is shown in Figure 16-8. The machine can have three batch streams running concurrently, and the FACTS processing is shown running in stream 1.

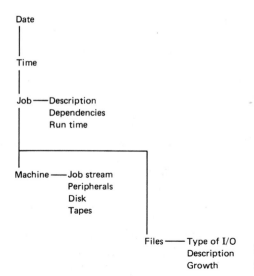

Figure 16-7 Entities, attributes, and relationships required to support scheduling.

DDS1801.R1   FS2C68 Schedule for Sunday, August 24, 1987

Jobname Description	I/O	App Rtm	Jobname Description	I/O	App Rtm
******** STREAM ONE ********			******** STREAM TWO ********		
7:00					

DAILY
  Auto user log/exception report
STATUS –
	N	05	LDS ON
			  Brings up LDS TP monitor
			STATUS –
				N	02

11:30					
FACTS OFF Disables FACTS users STATUS –	N	01			
FACTS.BACKUP/A Backup of FACTDB STATUS –	N	30			
13:00					
FACTS ON Enables FACTS users STATUS –	N	01			

QBJ PRTO401
  Loads corp model/part #
  I/O PARTMSTR
  Dep on DS450 from corp
  Tape #_____
STATUS –
	U	2:00	20:00		

			LDS OFF Brings down LDS TP monitor STATUS –	N	02
21:00					

FACTS OFF
  Disables FACTS users
STATUS –
	N	01	LDSLOAD/I
			  Incremental load of LDS DB
			  from 20:10 from m/c FS2C39
			STATUS –
				U	20

FACT.BACKUP/A
  Backup of FACTDB
STATUS –
	N	30	LDSVER/V LDSDB
			  Verify, chg mode for update
				N	02

21:45					

QBJ FACT.0101
  Disp ctr tapes loaded for
  further process
STATUS –
	U	1:30	LDSDB.J0920
			  Parts picked not shipped
			STATUS –
				U	1:40

Figure 16-8 Typical operations schedule.

Resource Utilization

Most operations departments have limited resources, and organizations need to utilize the hardware and software to the fullest extent possible. This can be done better if the mix of jobs to be executed, and the processing resources the jobs will need, are identified and stored in one place for further analysis. Processing resources include CPU, memory, I/O rates, tape media, disk media, hard-copy media, laser, microfiche, files, records, and data as shown in Figure 16-9. Using information about the current environment, the operations and data base administration staffs reduce contention, route output correctly, assess the desirability of file reorganization, and schedule such reorganization to maintain a smooth production environment.

A data dictionary can be extended to store the cost of the various resources of a production environment. This can be accomplished by storing the cost per unit of each of the resources listed above in the data dictionary as an attribute of the entity. When recommendations are made to introduce new resources, change machine configurations, or alter schedules, the stored data can be used to evaluate the cost impact. In this way, the data dictionary provides the parameters to reduce the cost of an operations environment.

Processing Resource Categories

Machine time
- CPU rate
- Teleprocessing transfer rate
- Channel controller rate

Teleprocessing devices
- CRT
- Data entry
- RJE

Storage devices
- Hard-copy media
- Disk
- Utility storage: tape, laser, microfiche

Data
- Files/data bases
- Records
- Data item

Figure 16-9 Processing resource categories.

Capacity Planning

One of the most difficult and basic problems in scheduling is determination of the availability of the resources needed to execute the application programs. Since each program may use the same data in a different way, the task of assigning resources effectively is difficult, even with automated aids, and is virtually impossible without them. For example, when scheduling two jobs that require access to the same data, several questions must be answered:

- Can the data be shared? If not, should the data base be replicated? On the same machine or on another machine? If on another machine, how do we keep the data consistent between the two data bases?

- Can the possibility of concurrent update be avoided? If so, what happens to the elapsed time between jobs? Can the elapsed time be reduced by getting a faster machine and single threading?

- In cases of concurrency, how should the program that is denied access be handled? What resources are consumed by locking up the record for the duration of the transaction, versus a look-up of the record to see that it has not been changed?

- How should logging be handled in preparation for failure? What is the recovery time for program failure? Is there a backup machine in case the system goes down? Are faster means of backup and reload possible?

It is impossible to provide for each of these questions optimal answers that cover all situations. The recommended approach is to identify the resource that is in short supply and work around that resource.

Considering the cost of each resource individually is not sufficient to analyze the total operational cost. The most significant factor is the overall transfer rate from request to delivery. A model of the anticipated input/output activity can be used; however, actual system statistics must be gathered continuously to evaluate the model and tune the system.

The frequency, time, and accuracy requirements of the requested data functions must be reasonable. For example, it is meaningless to require 24-hour accuracy of a data item that is updated only once a week. Similarly, a request for 20-second query response time should not be honored at the expense of other, more critical considerations when 1 minute would be within tolerable bounds. When very real needs for accurate, up-to-date information are identified, they cannot be overlooked if the system is to satisfy management's needs. User needs should be audited periodically, from the point of data entry to output delivery, to determine continued effectiveness.

Input of actual run times into the data dictionary completes the evaluation loop and enables the operations staff to monitor the performance of systems and machine configurations. The data dictionary data base helps keep these requirements visible throughout other production system planning activities and, more important, makes it possible to evaluate data dictionary effectiveness.

It is not possible to plan effectively for future systems and evaluate their impact on performance without a well-developed model of the existing environment; the data dictionary contributes information to this model. Using this model, the operations and data base administration staffs can reduce job contention, route output correctly, assess the desirability of file reorganization, and schedule such reorganization so as to least affect production jobs.

Security

Security procedures to be observed in the submission of production jobs are incorporated in the data dictionary. The operations and data control staff are responsible for job submission, security profiles of those authorized to submit jobs, when they are to be run, and who has the authority to change the established job submission procedures, so that such problems as unauthorized updates and reports generated with inaccurate data can be avoided. The names of recipients of reports from the operations center are maintained in the dictionary for obvious security reasons.

Automated Run Stream

The operational view of the data base includes the location of the files and the storage devices on which they reside. This information is critical to almost every aspect of operations management. Optimization of throughput depends on the availability of this information, as do the reduction of job contention and the scheduling of file reorganization. The automatic spawning of job streams or run streams is feasible in a multimachine environment if the control program knows where the files are located.

In order to spawn the run streams automatically, the job control language (JCL or CLI macros) used by each production job is stored in the data dictionary and the JCL or CLI is generated automatically from the data dictionary. The benefits that come from this include:

- Control over the production macros establishes accountability.
- Changes in a macro can be applied consistently (e.g., filename or program name).
- Integrity, security, and recovery considerations can best be handled through the use of effective automated tools.
- When the data dictionary is used to generate JCL or CLI, all production CLI that is affected by a change can be updated at the same time. This is a considerable improvement over JCL or CLI that is maintained on separate directories. In such cases, there is no way to determine accurately how many jobs are affected by a change or to ensure that a change is made in the JCL or CLI before the jobs enter the production job stream.

chapter 17

Data Dictionary Role in Data Security

INTRODUCTION

In this chapter we explain the various security exposures and the ways in which data security is threatened. An approach called the "pathways" approach is used to explain the vulnerability of various access points and alerts the reader to the trade-offs that must be made by management between level of risk and security assurance. Next, a security program is presented which includes user training, security administration, access control lists. The dictionary is the place where the access control lists are maintained. The security monitors at the access control points can then query the dictionary directly or use a subset of that information which has been preloaded to verify the security access levels for the individual.

Caveat. It is most important that end-user departments understand and believe in the goals of the security program as well as the measures used to implement it. Only with their acceptance will the program work effectively. Implementing a security program is an all-or-none issue. Taking a "step in the right direction" only causes the need later to reset to zero and start again—but with resources diminished by the cost of the false start.

SCOPE OF DATA SECURITY

Computer security covers the protection of the organization's information (information and data are treated synonymously). Protection from unavailability involves—but is not limited to—logging, recovery, restart, disaster recovery, data integrity, and accuracy. Protection from unauthorized access involves—but is not limited to—user procedures, communication protocols and networks, computer procedures and programs, and file and data element access controls. This chapter deals with protection of data from unauthorized access. After a brief discussion of the different types of data that need to be protected, the pathways approach is described. Potential security exposures along the pathway are presented in tabular format, to give the reader an idea of the breadth of issues that need to be covered. Then the discussion turns to the collection of information related to the data bases that have to be protected: their value to the organization, the relative priority, the assessment of risk, and the amount of protection that can be obtained for a certain amount of money spent. The role of the dictionary is spelled out in relation to the carrying out of security administration functions. Finally, a set of security-level interactions with the dictionary system is presented for illustrative purposes.

Assumption

As a baseline, it is assumed that the data center is physically protected, that is, there are controls to ensure that access to the computer room can be gained only by author-ized personnel. In addition, the usual data center protections are assumed to exist (e.g., fire, electrical, mechanical, humidity, temperature, etc.).

Importance

As the organization increases its dependence on computers for the day-to-day opera-tion of the business, the expense of computer downtime (information unavailability) would be considerable. Extended downtime would become even more costly, to say nothing of lost business and customer goodwill. Unauthorized access to company data could result in disclosure of trade secrets, performance data, customer data, or any of several kinds of proprietary data. Compounding this loss would be the potential for altering or even deleting records from data files. The altered data would have extensive ramifications on other systems and data bases, especially in view of the fact that we are moving toward an integrated data base environment. What makes this risk so large is the fact that subtle alterations to data files would go undetected for long periods of time, making the recovery task extremely difficult. Thus it is clear that an awareness of the risk involved if unauthorized persons gain access to the data is important to have and will be the basis on which further activity can be carried out in the security area.

Types of Data

What do we mean by security, and specifically, data security? In order to under-stand this, we must understand the different types of data that exist, and whether they fall within the umbrella of data security.

- *Production data bases:* contain data that support the mainstream functions of the business from an operational point of view
- *Metadata* (i.e., data about data): data that are stored in a typical dictionary
- *Documents, graphs, charts:* data produced by users and stored in the computers for further processing or transmission (this type of data is less easy to control)
- *Libraries:* data that are organized into directory structures of information; can contain policies and procedures, instructional manuals, source programs used in business operation

The types of data listed above are targets of security concern. However, the only way to access information that is stored on disk is through a file management system. The file management system is the intermediary between the program re-questing the data and the data itself.

An important distinction to keep in mind is the difference between the data base management system and the data dictionary system. The DBMS is a software tool that provides an integrated data storage facility for data that are shared by multiple users, while presenting different views of the data to different users. It features easy access to the data, facilitates the storage and processing of large volumes of data, and most important, accommodates the sharing of data resources among different types of users. The DDS, on the other hand, is a software tool that provides central control of all the data resources in the organization, both automated and nonautomated. Within the automated data files, not all the data may be in DBMS files.

Thus DDS uniformly cuts across organizational and functional boundaries within the organization, and the technical boundaries within the MIS department: namely, the storage of data in different file structures within different types of machines. DBMS is specific to a particular vendor and is related directly to the effective computer processing of the data. Many data dictionaries appear to perform some of the same functions as the DBMS. The thrust of DDS is to provide control over all the data resources, whereas the DBMS provides control over the mechanized data directly, via concurrency, logging, and restart features.

End-User Computing

End-user computing poses data security problems that need to be addressed separately. Two of the major reasons for the differential treatment of this topic are:

1. These systems and procedures allow the end user to have access to data from production files, and these data can be transferred at electronic speeds to other individuals on the network.
2. These systems and procedures allow the end user to create files containing text or data (processed against the data from production files) on an ad hoc basis. Security access controls are thus very difficult to establish because not much may be known about the derived data or the text files that are created by the end users.

The files that are created by end-users have access controls automatically set by the system. These controls enable the creator of the file to modify the contents of the file. The creator of the file can alter the access controls to the file to include access to other users on the system. Thus data files and text files that are very carefully protected on the "production" machines are liable to be outside the purview of security procedures once they are on the office automation or "end-user computing" machines. There is no way to guarantee that end users do not transfer or enable others to view the data that should be protected at the highest level of security. It is a difficult task to educate the end user to the sensitivity of information at the data item level because of the ad hoc nature of the process itself.

Under the conditions where data can be created by end users at will, there are some steps that can be taken to improve the security level:

*   Educate users to the sensitivity of the data that they are working with and point out the need to apply appropriate access controls to the data files that they create, especially where this is done in shared user space.
*   Develop procedures that periodically examine the access controls on user-created files and monitor any violations of security policies.
*   Have a central point of reference that users can contact to raise security issues and obtain clarification.

Approach

The approach used in this chapter is based on the premise that authorized and legitimate access pathways to the data must be protected from penetration by unauthorized persons. As a corollary, other access pathways to the data which are not authorized but can be created by ingenious persons must be identified, and sufficient obstacles must be placed so that these pathways cannot be created and hence penetration attempts are discouraged.

The security program is based on the premise that the pathways to data files can be identified and steps can be taken to minimize the exposure to penetration. The security exposures at each pathway layer are outlined. The steps that need to be taken to strengthen the security at each layer are discussed. The concept of risk is presented so that the costs incurred in developing a security program can be put in proper perspective. Management has to make choices of security options based on risk penetration factors that can be identified through experience and experimentation. A security information system is described that, in conjunction with the data dictionary, would translate user requests for access to data items to the appropriate layers of the pathway in a coordinated manner. This implies that if a user is given access privileges to certain data items, corresponding access privileges at the network, host, program, and file layers would be given to that individual user via the security information system.

PATHWAYS

Attention is primarily focused on file access. Although printed reports can be thought of as files of processed data, attention is focused on access to information that is in machine-readable form. Pathways can be identified for the flow of data to and from the data files. Once all possible pathways are drawn, it is possible to identify the points in the pathway that need to be attended to in order to assure availability. Points at which controls need to be placed to prevent unauthorized access to the data files need to be identified.

The pathways diagram in Figure 17-1 shows the layers of hardware/software that the end user has to pass through in order to get the data. An access control point

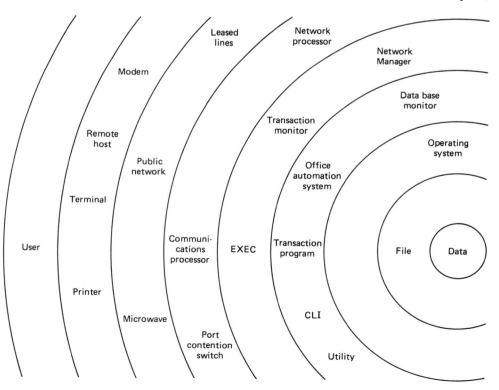

Figure 17-1 Pathways diagram.

has to be determined for each layer. Note that there may be parallel hardware or software routes within a layer; for example, an end user may have access to an application screen as well as a development language. In such cases the impact of having parallel access should be examined independently and then jointly.

Definitions

The definitions of the terms used in the pathways chart are given below.

User. A user is any employee who has an interaction with the MIS computer system. This could be in the form of interactive access to data in the MIS computer system or indirect access to information on reports produced by the MIS computer system.

Network. A network is one or more communications path(s) between a host computer system and either a user or another host, or both. In its strictest sense, a network includes all terminals that are connected to a host. Within this section of the document, ''access to a system'' refers to establishing a communication path to a system, to the point of an EXEC log-on banner or other initial greeting from the system.

Host. A host is the hardware and software that enables a user to execute programs and access files. A host includes the operating system and any processes or programs that are not under the direct control of the user. Note that the lines separating the network from the host, and the host from the application, are necessarily fuzzy.

Application. An application is any program under the direct control of a user. Most applications fall within one of two broad classes: utilities and user applications. Operating system utilities are programs supplied with the operating system and available for general use, such as interpreters, assemblers, linkers, text editors, file editors, or supplied with other vendor-specific products, such as office automation software (All-in-one, CEO), SORT/MERGE, COBOL, PL/1, and FORTRAN77. Other utilities are programs developed by the local systems available for general use, such as LOCK, SECURE, FIND, and PHONE. User applications are programs that perform specific functions for a user or class of users.

File. This category includes directories, files, subschemas (partial views of the data structure) and data items.

Potential Security Exposures

In Figure 17–2, each pathway layer has been analyzed for the types of security exposures that are currently believed to exist at that layer, the security requirements that need to exist, and the steps that should be taken to address the security requirements for that layer. This list is presented to give the user an idea of the breadth of issues that need to be addressed.

Risk Assessment

The probability of penetration by an unauthorized user needs to be estimated at each pathway layer and then conjointly across the layers in order to assess the risk to the organization. The ability to penetrate a particular layer would depend on the obstacles facing the penetrator (e.g., passwords) and the amount of time spent (or number of attempts made) by the penetrator. The probability of penetration is represented by the risk of penetration factor or a risk factor (RF). To assess the risk factors for

USER

Security Exposure	Security Requirement	Security Procedure
1. Security password may be compromised.	Be aware of importance of password.	Maintain a password in addition to badge number. Change password every 60 days.
2. Carelessness in handling reports.	Be aware of sensitivity level of reports.	Instructions for destroying reports after use. Maintain logs.
3. May leave terminal logged on when not in use.	An automatic timeout mechanism must be enforced.	Set up automatic timeout mechanism. Log-out when leaving desk.
4. Terminated employees user ID may not be removed from computer system.	Terminated employees should be removed from computer system.	All security access control privileges for a terminated employee must be removed from the computer system.
5. Employee may not be aware of sensitivity level of data.	Employees must be made aware of sensitivity level of data.	A scheme to identify the sensitivity level of different reports must be established.

NETWORK

Security Exposure	Security Requirement	Security Procedures
1. Direct-connect terminals may not be physically secured, thus allowing for visual eavesdropping or use by unauthorized persons.	Prevention or detection of unauthorized access to terminals.	Unauthorized access to terminals should be reported to their superior and/or a security officer.
2. Terminal wiring passing through cross-connect blocks present opportunities for tapping.	Prevention or detection of line tapping.	Cross-connect blocks must be physically secured.
3. Dial-up modems may be used to access any stream through "blind" dialing.	Prevent unauthorized modem access.	Install call-back or keyed modems. Call-back could be software or hardware controlled.
4. Telephone lines are vulnerable to tapping.	Render line tapping ineffective.	Install encryption device. Encrypt files prior to transmission.
5. A terminal may have access to more than one port via port contention switch (PCS). The PCS does not identify users, only terminals.	Ensure that a terminal has access to only those systems that are required, by the normal user of that terminal.	When a user's location or job changes, or when a user terminates, the network manager must be notified and the network configuration updated.
6. A user on any host in the local area network (LAN) may have access to any other host in the LAN for log-on and/or file access. The carrier (land-line or microwave) may be vulnerable to interception/tapping.	Ensure that a user has access only to those systems that are required, and only the types of access required.	All of the above. Note that there is no way to prevent unauthorized access to systems connected to public data network.

Figure 17-2 Security exposure, minimum requirement, and procedures.

HOST

Security Exposure	Security Requirement	Security Procedure
1. The hardware may fail, compromising data integrity. The operating system may fail, compromising access controls or data integrity.	Minimize the chances of hardware failure. Operating system failure must be minimized.	Preventive maintenance must be performed on a regular basis. Restrict access to OS generation and patches to specific individuals.
2. Operator username is on all systems to facilitate operation of systems, and it has superior privilege. Anyone who can gain access to the system as operator can do considerable damage.	Access to operator username must be strictly controlled. Access to operating system generation and patch files must be strictly controlled.	Password control on operator username should be enforced. Restrict access to OS generation and patches to specific individuals.
3. The log-on executive (EXEC) can only identify users by USERNAME/ PASSWORD. The EXEC cannot detect and reject trivial passwords. The EXEC may be "patched" to circumvent protection.	Additional user identification must be available to all users, with penetration attempt logging. Passwords must be nontrivial. Access to program and patch files must be strictly controlled.	Implement additional password with logging of penetration attempts.
4. The transaction processing monitor (TPMS) can only identify users by USERNAME/PASSWORD. TPMS may fail, compromising data integrity.	There should be penetration attempt logging. Monitor failures must be minimized.	Identify specific individuals for transaction processor management.
5. The data base monitor (DBMS) may fail, compromising data integrity. The monitor may be patched to circumvent protection.	Monitor failures must be minimized. Access to program and patch files must be strictly controlled.	Identify specific individuals for data base monitor generation.
6. The network monitor may be "patched" to circumvent protection.	Access to program and patch files must be strictly controlled.	Identify specific individuals for network management.

APPLICATION

Security Exposure	Security Requirement	Security Procedure
1. Users may use a utility to view or manipulate data in ways that are not authorized (i.e., INQUIRE, SED).	Prevent users from using utilities to view or manipulate data in ways that are not authorized.	Restrict user access to the data and/or utilities.
2. Users may create or modify programs to view or manipulate data in ways that are not authorized.	Prevent users from creating or modifying programs that are not authorized.	Restrict access to program creation utilities and copying utilities.
3. Users may execute application programs that they are not authorized to use.	Prevent users from executing application programs that they are not authorized to use.	Restrict program access to unauthorized users.

Figure 17–2 Continued

FILE

Security Exposure	Security Requirement	Security Procedure
1. Superior directories may have access controls that allow access controls on subordinate directories and files to be modifiable by a user.	All directories and files should be set with access controls that reflect the access level to which the user is authorized. Global access permissions should be avoided where possible.	The security officer must have the tools to list directory structures and examine the assigned access controls and their implications.
2. Location of files within directory structures may be ascertained by browsing or through access to data dictionary.	Access to data dictionary must be on a "need to know" basis.	Data dictionary access controls must be strictly enforced.
3. Record layouts may be known to persons who can then interpret dumped files.	Access to record layouts must be strictly controlled.	Copybook library procedures must incorporate proper access controls.
4. Critical data items may not be encoded.	Critical data items must be encoded.	Critical data files or data items should be encrypted.
5. Tapes containing proprietary information may be reused without erasure of the contents.	Tapes containing proprietary information must not be released into the scratch pool without adequate precautions.	The tape management system must keep track of all files on tape, especially those that are used to store data from sensitive applications.
6. Audit trails may not exist to reconstruct activity at the data item level.	Recovery procedures must be built into programs and procedures that protect the data bases from incorrect update.	Audit trails must be built into system and data base design.
7. Logs of activity against a file may not be available to back out of unauthorized transactions.	Logging facilities must exist for all files that have multiple programs concurrently updating the file.	Logging and recovery procedures must be built into data base design.

Figure 17-2 Continued

different sets of obstacles on a pathway, it is necessary to do some experiments that simulate the penetration attempt through the pathway with different sets of obstacles. The time or number of attempts it would take to penetrate the pathway would be a proxy for the risk of penetration factor (RF).

As more and more experimental data are collected, these can be plotted on a graph. The plots are referred to as characteristic curves and are used to extrapolate from the graph to situations that have not been subject to experimentation. A characteristic curve is a plot of the relationships between the number of attempts at penetration, the number of obstacles, and the probability of penetration. For a fixed number of attempts, it is hypothesized that as the number of obstacles increases beyond a certain number, the marginal probability of penetration would be smaller (i.e., increasing the number of obstacles will not buy greater risk protection). If the plots are standardized, risk penetration factors can be calculated for different sets of obstacles. Conversely, if a certain minimum risk penetration factor is figured, we can arrive at the set of obstacles that are necessary. An example of a set of characteristic curves is given in Figure 17-3.

Data Base Priority

A relative ranking of the importance of data bases must be done by the persons in the organization with the closest responsibility for the data base. The security risk evaluation questionnaire shown in Figure 17-4 provides an idea of the issues that must be probed. The questionnaire elicits information about the value of the infor-

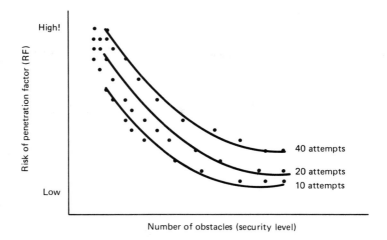

Figure 17-3 Risk of penetration characteristic curves.

Data Security Risk Evaluation Questionnaire

1. Name:_____ 2. Title:_____ 3. Date:_____

4. Dept. Name:_____ 5. Location: _____

6. Responsibility for which functional areas within the company: _____
   _____
   _____
   _____
   _____

7. Responsibility (or major interest) for data systems (e.g., national distribution, central dispatch, payroll, etc.). Please list: _____
   _____
   _____
   _____
   _____

8. For each of the data systems listed above, indicate the potential loss [in terms of as many factors as necessary (e.g., dollar amount, customer service, goodwill, etc.)]

   A. Loss of data due to operational problems, data base damage:

Data System	Loss to Company	How much would you spend to prevent this situation?
_____	_____	_____
_____	_____	_____
_____	_____	_____
_____	_____	_____
_____	_____	_____

   B. Loss of data to a competitive company, individual:

Data System	Loss to Company	How much would you spend to prevent this situation?
_____	_____	_____
_____	_____	_____
_____	_____	_____
_____	_____	_____
_____	_____	_____

Figure 17-4 Data security risk evaluation questionnaire.

mation from the manager's perspective. When the results of the questionnaire are combined with the cost of securing the pathways, decisions can be made as to how to apply selectively the resources that are available.

The responses to the questionnaire must be correlated with other information to get a composite picture. In many cases, it is difficult for a manager to answer the question about the loss to the company as well as how much to spend to protect the information. A typical answer to the latter is "Spend as much as necessary to protect the information." The manager must be pushed for a quantitative answer.

- In a field service organization, managers felt that customer data in systems such as contracts, field activity, warranty, spare parts sales, and customer master must be protected at the highest level of security.
- In addition, data related to the levels of service [e.g., customer satisfaction, employee attitude and skill, problem situations in the field (machine-level problems), etc.] are highly sensitive because access to the data by a competitor would expose the weak points of the organization.

A preliminary prioritization of the major systems/data bases in order to give visibility to the data bases that need the most protection is shown in Figure 17–5.

Category	Systems	Data Base
1.	Contract	Contract, customer
	Dispatch	Open calls, closed calls
	Warranty	Shipped equipment
	Spare parts sales	Order entry
	Customer survey	
2.	End-user computing	Ad hoc data files
	Payroll, personnel data system	Payroll, EIS
3.	Symptom fix, technical assistance, product engineering information	Future
4.	Logistics, repair	LOG, PRC

Figure 17–5 Data base and system priority list.

Cost/Benefit Estimation

Once the risk factor for different sets of obstacles is identified, it is possible to estimate the cost to implement the desired set of obstacles consistent with management's risk preference. The risk preference is used as a surrogate for the benefit. For example, if management was faced with the following options:

- *Option 1:* Set of obstacles A will cost $90,000 and provide an RF of 5 percent (probability of penetration).
- *Option 2:* Set of obstacles B will cost $25,000 and provide an RF of 20 percent (probability of penetration).

A choice can be made as to which set of obstacles to implement given the various trade-offs. Thus we can come up with a list of sets of obstacles 1 through N, and the corresponding RF and cost, as shown in Figure 17–6. The list was developed independent of any particular data system. In general, some of the features that would constitute a set of obstacles would be tailored to the type of data system [i.e., whether it is interactive or batch, number of users, type of users (e.g., clerical versus mana-

Obstacle Set	RF	Cost
1	2%	$190,000
2	5%	$120,000
3	10%	$80,000
4	20%	$20,000

Figure 17-6 Obstacle set.

Obstacle Set	Contract	CDS	NDS	PDS
1	RF $Cost			
2	RF $Cost	RF $Cost		
3		RF $Cost	RF $Cost	
4		RF $Cost	RF $Cost	RF $Cost

Figure 17-7 Security level versus cost matrix. Obstacle set *n* represents a combination of obstacles, RF represents the risk of penetration factor, and $ Cost is the cost to implement a certain obstacle set.

gerial), type of operating system on which the application is resident, data base type, etc.]. Thus we could have different costs and RFs for different data systems. The matrix in Figure 17-7 represents the more general situation where the costs and risk factors (RFs) vary with the data system. Once the matrix is filled with the cost data, it is possible to make decisions based on the amount management wants to spend and the risk that one is willing to take relative to the data system.

SECURITY ADMINISTRATION

The overall technique for security administration revolves around the concept of managing the access controls to the various layers in the pathways diagram. Since the access controls at any one layer have to be coordinated with the other layers, this requires a central coordination and control facility supported by an appropriate information data base. This data base is referred to as the security information data base. Refer to Figure 17-8. The key to an effective security information system is the maintenance of security-related information in a timely and effective manner by the appropriate personnel within the company. Security-related data are comprised of (but not necessarily limited to) the following:

- Layer identification
  - Data item
  - File
  - Program
  - Utility
  - EXEC
  - Communication processor
  - etc.
- Employee identification
  - Badge number

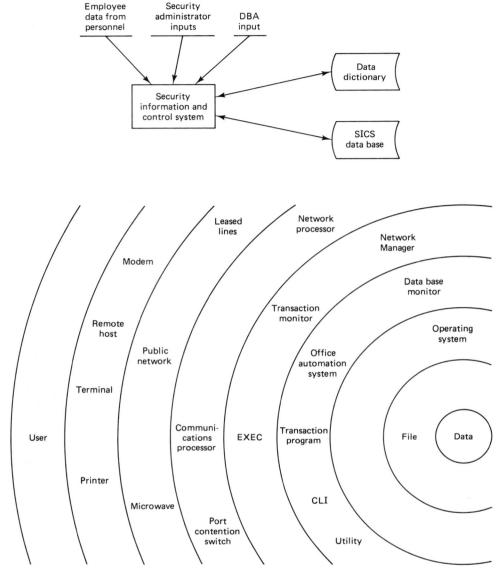

Figure 17-8 Security information system data base.

— Name
— Aliases
— Other identification (voice print)
— Passwords
— Security administrator responsible

Additional restrictions on data access based on organization, level, territory, jurisdiction, and so on.

Data Dictionary Role

Many of the access layers are entity categories in the data dictionary. Since these are already entered and maintained in the dictionary, attributes that are necessary to maintain the security level of users for the various access layers can be added easily. This would be the verification point when access to the layer is sought by the user. Thus a scheme that provides for the entry of security-level information into the dictionary and the mechanism for using that information to verify access privileges is a good starting point for a data security program.

The data dictionary is the centralized repository of information relating to the machines, systems, programs, and data files in the organization. Information about the sources and users of data at the data item level exists in the data dictionary. This could be the basis on which users will be assigned access permissions to use the programs through which they can access the file and data.

The data dictionary contains the relationships among the data items, files, programs, and machines. The entities that are necessary for a security program are shown in Figure 17-9. Detailed attributes are shown in Figure 17-10.

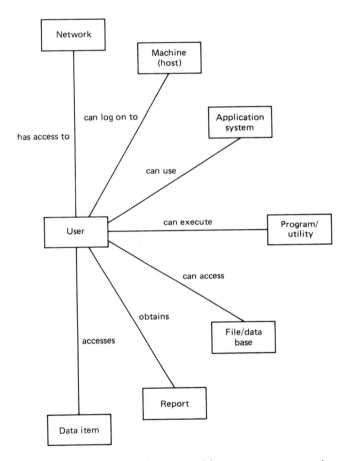

Figure 17-9 Data dictionary entities to support security.

The data dictionary must be fully populated for those data items for which a security program must be established. To assure data security, the existence of that data item in all the files must be identified and cataloged in the data dictionary. A list of all the files and the programs and machines at which access controls must be established is produced. Thus it is possible to ensure that the appropriate levels of access controls are in place to provide a certain level of security assurance.

Security Administrator

The data base administration function within the organization has overall responsibility for the security and integrity of all data. In cases where the security cannot all be maintained by one person, other persons could be assigned the role of security

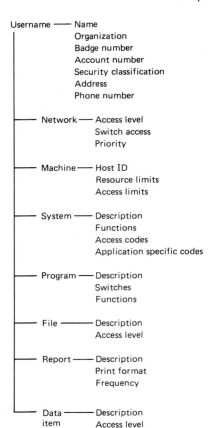

```
Username ── Name
             Organization
             Badge number
             Account number
             Security classification
             Address
             Phone number

        ── Network ── Access level
                      Switch access
                      Priority

        ── Machine ── Host ID
                      Resource limits
                      Access limits

        ── System ── Description
                     Functions
                     Access codes
                     Application specific codes

        ── Program ── Description
                      Switches
                      Functions

        ── File ──── Description
                     Access level

        ── Report ── Description
                     Print format
                     Frequency

        ── Data ──── Description
           item      Access level
```

Figure 17-10 Entities, attributes, and relationships required to support security.

administrator for a subset of the applications for a subset of all the employees. A security administrator (SA) is a person designated by management to be responsible for ensuring that only authorized personnel have access to data for which the SA is responsible. Since the data in the data base contain data from virtually every functional department within the company, each major functional area will have an SA responsible for that functional area's data security. Since an application program is the way for a user to access data, the only way for a security administrator to control access to data is to control the access to execute the program that accesses the data. To put the role of the SA in perspective, the SA is responsible for administering a subset of transaction access capability to a subset of data for a subset of employees in the company.

The DBA delegates authority to the SA to administer security for that portion of the data base for which that SA has been given responsibility. The responsibility that is delegated to the SA by the DBA is very specific in nature and involves the granting of permissions to various employees to access the data base. The SA does not have any technical responsibility and does not need to be technically oriented to perform the job. The DBA is responsible for the technical operation of the data base. What this implies is that there has to be close liaison between the DBA and the SA in order to incorporate the security needs of the user community into the SIS data base. When the user requirements have been entered into the SIS data base, the next task is for the DBA to ensure that the different local security systems (i.e., at the file, program security monitors, etc.) are in synchronization with user requirements as defined in the SIS data base.

The data dictionary administrator can perform the role of security administrator, since many of the data items that have to be updated are similar to what the DDA does on a routine basis. It has been the author's experience that central update of one file and distribution of that file to all computer systems is feasible and desirable with the fast file-to-file transfer mechanisms that are available today. A request for access can be granted on an ad hoc basis for a short period and then regularized on the weekly security file update.

Thus organizational responsibility for data items and systems must be vested in persons designated as security administrators. The SAs are then given the tools to manage their areas of responsibility. The security administrator's responsibilities include:

- Maintaining linkages between users and files, programs, data, and reports
- Maintaining and correlating user employment records, to ensure that employees who have terminated no longer have access to the system
- Verifying that the information in the dictionary is accurate and up to date and is reflected in the actions taken at the various access layers

In addition to the assignment of security administration responsibilities, hardware and software features that have to be developed or purchased to strengthen security at pathway layers have to be identified. Some of these features have been outlined in the charts earlier. They include call-back modems, security monitors, passwords, and so on. The implementation strategy for the pathway layers is to examine critically the exposures and requirements outlined in the chart and put in place action plans to address the requirements. Ultimately, the hardware and software security mechanisms at the layers must be tied into the security information system.

Security System

The set of systems, procedures, and data bases that provide for the storage of security-related information, and the access control mechanisms that relate these data to pathway access points, comprise a security information and control system (SICS). The SICS data base is the data base where information about the employee and pathway access permissions are maintained by the security administrator and the data base administrator. The data dictionary is part of the SICS data base. Figure 17–11 shows the positioning of the data bases.

The SICS data base will contain the governing rules for security that have to be followed at the pathway layers. A match must be obtained with the SICS data base for every layer that the user needs to pass through. Depending on the level of technology available, this match would be manual or automated. This will ensure that a central reference point is checked every time there is an access request against a layer of the pathway. Figure 17–11 shows how the layers communicate with the SICS data base.

The SICS data base will also contain audit trail information regarding the accesses made by users at the various pathway layers. The audit trail will be the basis of exception reports produced by the system.

Initially, the SICS data base will be updated either manually or by data transfer from the local pathway access control point. This means that local security access files will exist at the pathway layers until automated links can be established to the SICS data base. The security mechanisms at the layers will reflect the maximum levels of risk that can be tolerated at a particular layer without jeopardizing the security of the other layers.

Risk

The concept of security boils down to minimizing the risk. Since absolute protection is enormously expensive, what one can hope for in any program is a certain amount of protection for the resource that management wishes to commit to the security pro-

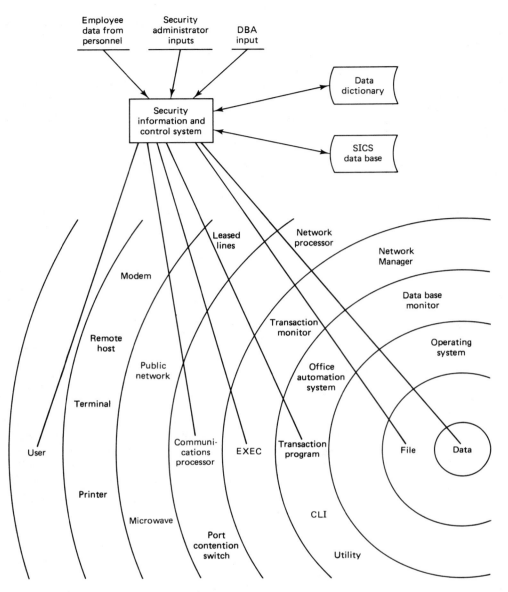

Figure 17-11 Pathways link to security information system.

gram. Management should view the cost of security as a form of insurance premium that has to be paid. In the case of security, the dictum "if it ain't broke, fix it" applies. Once security has been breached, it is too late to do anything about recovery.

To manage the risk, the data bases and systems have to be prioritized in order of importance from management's perspective. A set of experiments have to be designed and implemented that will result in the generation of the characteristic curves. The cost and risk factor (RF) matrix needs to be developed for different sets of obstacles so that management can make security risk trade-offs.

User Involvement

Even the most sophisticated program will not work unless the users support the program. That is why communication of the goals of the security program and the role of the users in that program is crucial to its successful implementation. Therefore, a training program to disseminate the message must be developed. This training can be addressed via different channels:

- Memos and instructional pamphlets to raise awareness levels
- Awareness and procedural training during office automation sessions
- Computer-assisted instruction
- Stand-up training program targeted to specific user groups

Access Control Data Examples

Examples of access control data that are stored in the dictionary are demonstrated through screens in a security monitor application that is tied to the dictionary data base. Refer to Figures 17–12 through 17–16. There are two kinds of security:

1. *Security of the data base:* security that is applied to the data bases that contain the company's data
2. *Security of the data dictionary:* security feature that is a part of the dictionary, and controls the access to the entities and descriptions in the dictionary data base

Security of the Data Base. Refer back to the information list by entity that could be stored in the dictionary to support a security program. Figures 17–12 through 17–16 show the kinds of data that would be available.

Security of the Data Dictionary. The security required to protect the contents of the data dictionary is treated separately because of the sensitive nature of the information contained in the dictionary and the need to provide the widest available access to users in order to propagate the use of the dictionary. The dictionary project manager needs to know how the security system provided by the vendor of the dictionary works, so that he or she can define the security policies and procedures to govern the day-to-day operation of the dictionary.

In the dictionary that was developed by the author, security was implemented at two levels, global and local. The user must have global permission against one

```
                    DB Security Administration          Date:  9/26/88
                                                        Terminal  95
                        Username Menu


                1. Usernames
                2. Username and all access privileges
                3. Usernames by network
                4. Usernames by machine
                5. Usernames by system
                6. Usernames by program
                7. Usernames by file
                8. Usernames by report
                9. Usernames by data item


                        Select:_____
```

Figure 17–12 Security username menu screen.

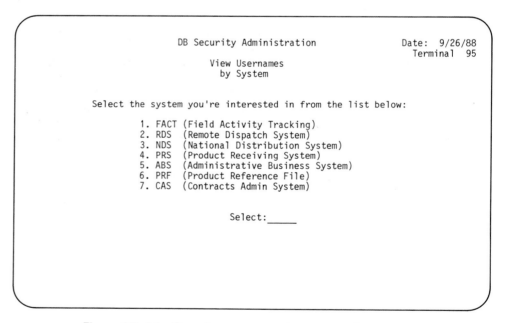

```
                         DB Security Administration        Date:  9/26/88
                                                           Terminal  95
                              Usernames List


        Username        Badge           Dept           Acct         Address
        Barstow, J      24334           Engg           89-2044      MA2122
        Bures, C         9045           Fld Ops        87-3120      CA1013
        Curtin, P       33404           Fld Ops        87-1120      IL1030
        Poitras, W      25345           Fld Ops        87-2120      GA1040
        Powers, M       10967           Fld Ops        87-1000      MA1024
        Ramos, JA       20373           Fld Ops        87-2121      MA1024
        Sikora, K       23569           Engg           89-2044      MA2122
        Weston, A       20373           Fin            82-1014      MA2144
```

Figure 17-13 Security usernames list screen.

```
                         DB Security Administration        Date:  9/26/88
                                                           Terminal  95
                              View Usernames
                                 by System


         Select the system you're interested in from the list below:

                    1. FACT (Field Activity Tracking)
                    2. RDS  (Remote Dispatch System)
                    3. NDS  (National Distribution System)
                    4. PRS  (Product Receiving System)
                    5. ABS  (Administrative Business System)
                    6. PRF  (Product Reference File)
                    7. CAS  (Contracts Admin System)


                              Select:_____
```

Figure 17-14 Security usernames by system view screen.

or more entity classes before that user could access information about an occurrence of an entity within that class. This is a necessary condition. In addition, the user must have local permission (granted by the creator of the entity occurrence) to access the information pertaining to a specific occurrence of an entity.

Global Permissions:

The data dictionary administrator assigns the global privileges when the user is initially assigned within the data dictionary system. The global privileges against an entity could be one of the following:

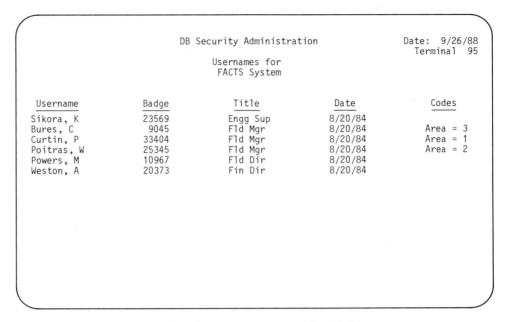

Figure 17-15 Security usernames for FACT system.

```
                    DB Security Administration          Date: 9/26/88
                                                        Terminal  95
                          Usernames for
                          FACTS System


     Username        Badge        Title        Date          Codes
     Sikora, K       23569        Engg Sup     8/20/84
     Bures, C         9045        Fld Mgr      8/20/84        Area = 3
     Curtin, P       33404        Fld Mgr      8/20/84        Area = 1
     Poitras, W      25345        Fld Mgr      8/20/84        Area = 2
     Powers, M       10967        Fld Dir      8/20/84
     Weston, A       20373        Fin Dir      8/20/84
```

```
                    DB Security Administration          Date: 9/26/88
                                                        Terminal  95
                        Usernames by Program
                             FACT0106


     Username            Functions              Switches
     Bures, C        Area view screens          Area = 3
                     Model call statistics
                     Part usage statistics
                     Area personnel             Area = 3

     Powers, M       Area comparative stats
                     Area view screens          Area = 1,2,3
                     Model call statistics
                     Part usage statistics
                     All personnel

     Weston, A       T&M call analysis          Area = 1,2,3
                     All personnel
```

Figure 17-16 Security usernames by program FACT0106 screen.

1. Read (R) permission allows you to read an occurrence of the entity provided that you have local Read access to that entity.
2. Modify (M) permission allows you to modify the content of an occurrence of an entity or permissions associated with that entity provided that you have local Write or Modify access to that occurrence. Modify permission includes Read.
3. Create (C) permission allows you to create an occurrence of the entity class or type for which you have been given Create permission. Create permission includes Modify and Read.

Note that to cross-reference two entity occurrences, you must have at least global Modify or Create against both entity types.

Local Permissions:

Each entity occurrence that is created in the dictionary at first can be accessed only by the creator of that entity occurrence. However, the creator can give permission for one or more authorized users of the dictionary system to access that entity occurrence. Three levels of access can be given:

1. Read (R) access gives the named user permission to view the descriptions and relationship information about that entity occurrence.
2. Write (W) access gives the named user the permission to alter the description and relationships about that entity.
3. Modify (M) access gives the named user permission to alter not only the content of the entity, but also access to the entity. The user who has Modify access has, in effect, all the permissions that the creator of the entity has, including the ability to delete the entity.

A special username category called "General" has been set up within the data dictionary to include any valid user who signs on. The creator of an entity occurrence has the ability to give a general permission, for example, Read (R), to any valid user by giving permission to General. Any valid user then automatically has Read (R) permission. Specific permissions assigned to a user name override permissions given to General. Note that only valid users installed by the data dictionary administrator have the ability to gain access to the entities to which they have been given permissions.

Global and local accesses are not independent of one another. For example, you might have a global create permission for the entity type "system." However, in order to access an entity within that entity type, you must have a minimum of Read (R) at the local level. The matrix in Figure 17–17 shows the possible pairings of global and local accesses and the permissions that result from each combination. From the matrix it is clear that it is the lesser of the two permissions that applies in any combination of privileges.

Access to Data Dictionary

To gain access to the data dictionary system, you must complete a user permission request form. A sample of this form appears in Figure 17–18.

Filling out the User Permission Request Form

On the user permission request form you must specify the names of the entity types you wish to access, the global level at which you wish to access each type, the reason why you will be using the data dictionary, and your choice of a username

		GLOBAL		
		Read	Modify	Create
LOCAL	Read	Read	Read	Read
	Write	Read	Modify content	Modify content, create entity
	Modify	Read	Modify permissions, content	Create entity, modify permissions

Figure 17–17 Global and local access matrix.

```
┌─────────────────────────────────────────────────────────────────────────┐
│                          Data Dictionary                                  │
│                       User Permission Request                             │
│                                                                           │
│  1. Name of Requester: _____     Date of Request: _____ │
│                                                                           │
│  2. Position _____      Manager/Approval: _____ │
│                                                                           │
│  3. Department _____           Phone: _____ │
│                                                                           │
│  4. Badge No. _____                                │
│                                                                           │
│  5. Entities Requested/Permission (Read (R), Modify (M), Create (C))      │
│                                                                           │
│        System           _____                                           │
│                                                                           │
│        Job/CLI          _____                                           │
│                                                                           │
│        Program          _____                                           │
│                                                                           │
│        File/Data Base   _____                                           │
│                                                                           │
│        Record           _____                                           │
│                                                                           │
│        Data Item        _____                                           │
│                                                                           │
│        Report           _____                                           │
│                                                                           │
│        Schedule Date    _____                                           │
│                                                                           │
│        Schedule Time    _____                                           │
│                                                                           │
│        Machine          _____                                           │
│                                                                           │
│        Peripheral       _____                                           │
│                                                                           │
│        Copybook         _____                                           │
│                                                                           │
│  6. Manual Issued/Date _____       Manual No. _____  │
│                                                                           │
│  7. DDS to be used for:                                                   │
│                                      Job Functions                        │
│                                   1. Data planning                        │
│                                   2. DBA                                   │
│                                   3. System development (SDLC)            │
│                                   4. Operations                           │
│                                   5. Security administration              │
│                                   6. End-user computing                   │
│                                   7. DD project implementation            │
│                                   8. DD administration                    │
│                                                                           │
│  8. User Name Requested    _____       │
│                                                                           │
│  9. Password Requested     _____       │
│                                                                           │
│                                   DBA/DDA Approved _____ │
│                                                                           │
│                                   Date: _____│
└─────────────────────────────────────────────────────────────────────────┘
```

Figure 17–18 Data dictionary user permission request form.

and password pair. In selecting your username, please adhere to the following standard: If you already have a username that you use on a system other than the data dictionary system, you must use that username. The password, of course, is your choice and may be changed to ensure security. Once completed, have your manager sign the form and then submit it to the data dictionary administrator, who will enter the pertinent information.

Changing Your Password

To change your password, you must enter your username exactly as you normally would. Then enter your password, but instead of pressing the New Line key after your password entry, press the "Modify" function key. You will then be prompted to supply a new password of your choice. Please note that the new password will not echo on your screen (i.e., you will not see your new password as you type it); therefore you should be very careful when entering it.

chapter 18

Data Dictionary Role in End-User Computing

INTRODUCTION

The evolution of end-user computing has been fueled by the extraordinary growth in low-cost personal computers and the increasing frustration of end users in getting systems from the MIS department in the face of large backlogs of system requests. Thus users have asked for access to the data bases and have either purchased off-the-shelf programs or developed applications on their own. The role of the dictionary is one of answering questions about the data and applications that are available. The end user can then use this information to get access to the data and then use application tools to process the data to get the information. Since the data act as the common link between the data bases in the production environment and the end-user environment, it is important that the same data definitions be followed as in the MIS department, for obvious reasons.

WHAT IS END-USER COMPUTING?

"End-user computing" refers to the capability of end users (managers, analysts, ad hoc users, administrative personnel, etc.) to use computer hardware and software tools to gain access, manipulate, and communicate data to do their jobs more productively. There are other terms used in conjunction with end-user computing: namely, information resource center, departmental computing, and office automation systems.

- *Information resource center:* a unit that provides end-user services such as training, demonstrations, use of equipment, and application development and execution facilities.
- *Departmental computing:* a term promoted by minicomputer vendors to include the computing that is done within a department. This is intended to include a group of end users sharing a common computer and using that computer to

communicate to one another. This does not preclude the end users having terminals that may be intelligent workstations or personal computers on a local area network (LAN).

- *Office automation systems:* provide functions such as mail, messaging, calendar, and word processing, and have gateways to other applications and networks. Since more and more end users have turned to office automation systems to do their desk-bound work, it is a natural platform to perform other kinds of computational tasks that could be classified as end-user computing.

Benefits of EUC

The ultimate objective of placing computing power at the hands of end users is to improve the productivity of individuals within the organization. This is done primarily by enabling individuals to access the information and data that they need to support their job activities and giving them the tools (processes or programs) to act on the data. Examples of tools are:

- Word processor
- Electronic mail
- Teleconferencing
- Electronic calendar
- Telephone message store/forward
- Spreadsheet (e.g., Lotus 1-2-3)
- Statistical analysis packages (e.g., SPSS, BMD)
- Software application programs
- Decision support systems
- Data base manipulation software (e.g., dBASE, Focus)
- Compilers and translators to execute natural language instruction
- Application generators
- Computer-assisted instruction
- Data dictionary
- Application directory

Reasons for EUC

There are certain reasons for the evolution of end-user computing. These can be broken down into hardware costs, software tools, and trained personnel. The "end-user computing environment" has come about for a number of reasons. First, hardware prices have come down drastically, so that processing power can be downloaded to users directly instead of being scheduled and optimized centrally. The reduction in the unit cost of computing through such developments as desktop workstations and personal computers has made it feasible to have computer workstations with memory and storage at the individual or small-group level.

In addition, developments in telecommunication technology and local area networks have made it feasible for end users to access remote resources such as printers, plotters, data bases, and other applications easily and inexpensively. The many software packages available for use on popular operating systems such as MS-DOS can be operated by persons with lesser amounts of computer training, and in many cases these applications are menu driven and self-prompting. This means that users with little computer background can quickly become proficient in utilizing software application packages.

Many employees have had computer training as part of their educational background and so are able to use programming languages to meet the data manipulation requirements of their jobs. The programming languages used for certain types of applications are so specialized that it would not make business sense to support them from a central technical support function. An example of this is a mathematical programming language called APL.

Another reason for the proliferation of end-user computing is that end users are being asked to develop systems themselves because the MIS department generally has a large applications backlog, and the end-user computing requests do not fall within the priority projects of an MIS department. When end users take a larger role and share of the computing burden, the MIS department is freer to focus on projects that are major in scope without the interruptions caused by end-user requests for minor processing assistance.

Functions of EUC

To promote the end-user computing process within the organization, EUC functions have been set up and staffed within most companies. This function is generally a part of the MIS department and is chartered with the role of encouraging end users to take increasing responsibility for their computational needs. A typical role statement might read as follows: "To promote a self-service approach to computing, so that end users can become self-sufficient in achieving their individual business information objectives." The major subfunctions within the EUC function are:

- *Provide EUC resource access.* This consists of providing access to the hardware, software, and data resources requested by end users to enable them to perform self-service computing.
- *Promote EUC.* Generate a demand for and increase in the utilization of personalized computing, and to promote its benefits and efficiencies with specialized offerings.
- *Provide EUC assistance.* Address user questions and business needs by providing options, recommendations, alternatives, assistance, and training.

EUC and Production

The mechanized information processing within an organization was generally confined to the MIS department. With the advent of end-user computing and office automation systems, the information processing is being distributed to departments, and thence to workstations on an individual's desk. Thus a drastic change has been taking place. This change is being recognized by individuals in both the end-user computing world and the traditional MIS world. Since data flows freely between these worlds, distinctions between the two are fuzzy. The end-user computing environment is not intended to displace the production systems that are used to support the day-to-day operational processing of business information needs, including scheduled report servicing. The central MIS organization, with its responsibility for timeliness, accessibility, security, and administration, will continue in that vein. In view of the fact that there is relatively less control on the end-user side, it is predicted that data transfer will initially take place from the controlled central production environment to the end-user environment but not vice versa.

As end users become more sophisticated in the types of applications that they develop and operate, and the data become central to the operation of the business, the end-user-developed applications will be subjected to the standards applied to other "production" systems, and incorporated into the "production" environment.

COMPONENTS OF EUC

The things that have to go together to make EUC a successful venture are the identification of the components necessary, and the provision of the resources to make it happen. If there are several options to handle data transfer from the production data base to the end-user workstation, the option that does it speedily and with simplicity is the one that should be promoted. It is important to realize that end users have a low threshold for frustration, and any technical problems will quickly turn them off. Problems with resource availability, such as response-time delays and availability of hardware, are other things that will prevent EUC from being successful.

The key components are hardware (i.e., microprocessors, terminals, communications equipment), software (i.e., application programs, utilities, translators, compilers), data (i.e., data extracts, data bases, data about data), and training/consultation.

- The hardware that would satisfy the needs of the end user would be determined by the potential processing power, memory, input/output power, and storage needed to process the data, and then to output to devices such as printers, disks, or tape.
- The software that would satisfy the needs of users would be determined by the application logic that would be required and the need to program such applications (if such applications have not already been developed in the software marketplace). In many cases the application software may have built-in restrictions on the kind of operating system (e.g., UNIX, MVS, VM, OS/2, etc.) that the application system will run on. The operating system that is required will predicate the hardware that is necessary.
- The data requirements would be expressed in terms of the set of input data items required for the software application system to perform its designed function. The data item conventions would correspond to the data dictionary conventions that apply to MIS-developed systems. This promotes the use of standards throughout the end-user computing environment.

End-User Application

Thus the definition of what constitutes an application from an end user's perspective is a combination of hardware, software, data, and training/consultation in the right proportions, as shown in Figure 18–1.

TECHNOLOGY

Technology comes into the picture because advancements in technology provide choices to the end user in the ways in which data can be accessed from the data bases, and the different types of tools that can be used to access the data. Some considerations in selecting the appropriate technology are discussed in relation to the computer network.

Computer Architecture

The computer architecture has to accommodate a multitude of hardware and software requirements in a convenient and timely manner. The architecture must be flexible enough to accommodate growth. The first decision that has to be made is whether the hardware should be centralized or decentralized. Centralized hardware implies that the end user's terminals would be tied directly into a minicomputer or mainframe. There could be potential contention problems if the demand outstripped the resource.

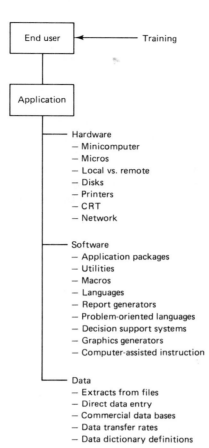

Figure 18-1 What constitutes an application from an end user point of view.

Another issue to be addressed is whether a single operating system will meet the needs of all the users. If a single operating system can meet the needs of all users, a single-machine solution may be feasible. However, situations arise where a multicomputer setup may be needed, depending on the nature of the work being performed. For example, data processing applications make a heavy demand on the input/output processor, whereas scientific applications make a heavy demand on the central processing unit. Specialized or finely tuned operating systems give the end user the power and throughput needed to do the job. If it is decided that end users need the capability to use more than one kind of operating system, this raises the issue of communications between the different operating systems.

In another situation, the application program and data are downline loaded into the personal computer for word processing or other PC-based application, since this would relieve the load on the mainframe. Once the processing is completed at the desktop computer, the resultant data are transferred to the mainframe. The reason for doing this would be that the backup and recovery procedures can be enforced more easily on machines in a data center than at individual workstations.

Local Area Network

With increasing use of personal computers as desktop workstations, end users want the connectivity to minicomputers and mainframes via the PC. The connection of several PCs to each other and to minicomputers is achieved via local area networks (LANs). Before setting up a LAN for a group of PCs, research has to be conducted about the number of users, physical distance separating them, types of applications to be supported, and so on. Based on the responses to the considerations noted above, consideration has to be given to existing equipment, cost, cabling, data transfer rates, and expandability. The LAN, in turn, will need to have access to wide-area networks that bring together computers that are many hundreds of miles apart. The wide-area networks are connected through a common carrier, specialized carrier, or private communications links.

In the general case, different types of workstations will be used to perform local processing, connections to a minicomputer hub are required for communicating and data base processing, and several minicomputers or mainframes may be linked to the minicomputer hub via a wide-area network. It is possible to provide the end user with access to a large number of computing resources through the network. Depending on the kind of application that is being executed by the end user, it is possible for the end user to execute that application on the computer where the resources are available, and to direct the results back to the user's PC. The user of the network thus has access to the entire network of machines in order to complete the task.

In Figure 18–2, each minicomputer is connected to the other minicomputer or mainframe (M) in a wide-area network. Each minicomputer acts as a gateway host or hub that services the PCs on that local area network. Each minicomputer serves many different functions, including shared file and print services, application execution facility, data dictionary service, network routing, and control.

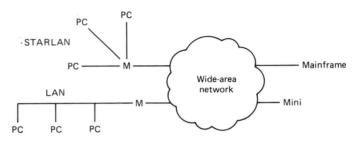

Figure 18–2 Computer architecture.

DATA STRATEGY

The strategy for the provision of data also involves choices. In the simplest case, the requestor is presented with the list of data items available via the dictionary. The user then prepares a request that is handled by the MIS staff. A data extract is prepared from the production files, and the file extracted is loaded on the user's PC or minicomputer.

Several of the foregoing steps can be automated. For example, the dictionary could be used to format the end user's data request. The formatted data request can be subject to checks to ensure that the end user has the appropriate access rights to the data items. If the data exist in another extracted form, the dictionary would know about this and direct the user to the appropriate extract file. In the extreme case, the data dictionary can be used as the central cross-reference mechanism for translating a logical data request into a physical file and record definition. The role of the data dictionary comes into play in two different modes:

1. As a resource of the data items that exist in the organization
2. As a tool to facilitate the retrieval of information from the data bases

PROCESS MODEL

In most instances of end-user computing, the end user will want to work with data that exist in the central data bases that are managed by the MIS department. In the next few pages we present a model of the process of specifying the data to the persons charged with the data base administration responsibility and getting the data in a format with which the end user is comfortable.

Data Items

To obtain data (whether raw or data strips) successfully, you must specify the data standard name for the item(s) for which you require data strips. You should use the Query function in the data dictionary to identify the data items that you are interested in. After you have done this, you may submit the end-user computing request. Before the steps necessary for completion of this form are discussed, an overview of the people and concepts involved in end-user computing is given.

Hardware

To supply end users with the hardware they need, a determination of the processing and input/output power requirements is made: What will be required for the end user to obtain, store, process, and output the data (to devices such as printers or mass storage)?

Software

The software necessary for accessing or manipulating data is the responsibility of the user. If users encounter problems (or have questions), they ask the DBA for assistance.

Format of Data Request

The data requirements are submitted by the end user on the end-user request form. Once the request is filled, the end user is supplied with a data file, which is composed of multiple records in a flat or sequential file. The format for the file is shown in Figure 18–3.

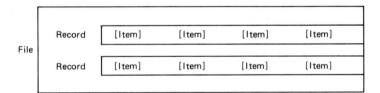

Figure 18–3 File format for data extract.

Parties Involved

Following is a list of the persons and groups involved in end-user computing and a brief description of their roles.

- *Data base administrator (DBA):* manages data base activity, including data definition and specification, access control, data base design, data base processing
- *Data security:* reviews user requests to determine "sensitivity" of data required; approves or disapproves requests, based on review
- *Computer operations:* provides data center and facilities management
- *End users:* create or acquire their own software to manipulate the supplied data strips; use existing software utilities

```
┌──────────────────────────────────────────────────────────────────────────┐
│                        End-User Computing Data Request                     │
│                                   Part I                                   │
│                                                                            │
│                         Request No. _____      Date ___/___/___ │
│  Requested by _____   Tel. Ext. _____   M.S.____│
│  Department Name _____   Account No. _____│
│  Username _____                                   │
│  Describe Request _____│
│  _____│
│  _____│
│  Hardware Requirements:  CPU:_____                          │
│  Memory: _____                                         │
│  Disk Storage: _____                           │
│  Software Requirements:  Operating System: _____                 │
│  Application System: _____   Frequency of Run: _____│
│  Retention Days (default is 30) _____                                 │
│  Requesting Department Approval _____    │
│  Data Security Approval _____   Date ___/___/__│
│  Security Level: _____                                        │
└──────────────────────────────────────────────────────────────────────────┘
```

Figure 18–4   End-user computing request form: I.

End-User Computing Request Forms

The end user computing request forms consist of two parts. In Part I the enduser supplies identification and authorization information, as shown in Figure 18–4. In Part II the end user specifies the data required, the selection criteria, and the output formats, as shown in Figure 18–5.

Filling out the End-User Computing Request

The following information must be supplied on the form:

- *Request number:* a sequential number, assigned by the DBA, used to identify the request throughout the process
- *Date:* date of the request
- *Requested by:* your name
- *Tel. ext.:* your telephone number and extension
- *M.S.:* your mail stop
- *Department name:* name of the department in which you work
- *Account number:* name of the department in which you work
- *Account number:* your department's account number for chargeback
- *Username:* your username as you type it to log-on to the E-mail system
- *Request description:* brief explanation of why you need the data you are requesting

```
┌─────────────────────────────────────────────────────────────────────┐
│                     End-User Computing Data Request                   │
│                                 Part II                               │
│                                                                       │
│                      Request No. _____    Date __ / __ / __ │
│                                                                       │
│   List of data items:                        Data source (if available): │
│   ─────────────────────                       ───────────────────────── │
│   ─────────────────────                       ───────────────────────── │
│   ─────────────────────                       ───────────────────────── │
│   ─────────────────────                       ───────────────────────── │
│   ─────────────────────                       ───────────────────────── │
│   ─────────────────────                       ───────────────────────── │
│   ─────────────────────                       ───────────────────────── │
│   ─────────────────────                       ───────────────────────── │
│   ─────────────────────                       ───────────────────────── │
│   ─────────────────────                       ───────────────────────── │
│   ─────────────────────                       ───────────────────────── │
│   ─────────────────────                       ───────────────────────── │
│   ─────────────────────                       ───────────────────────── │
│   ─────────────────────                       ───────────────────────── │
│                                                                       │
│   Selection criteria:                                                 │
│   ─────────────────────────────────────────────────────────────────── │
│   ─────────────────────────────────────────────────────────────────── │
│   ─────────────────────────────────────────────────────────────────── │
│                                                                       │
│   Special instructions:                                               │
│   ─────────────────────────────────────────────────────────────────── │
│   ─────────────────────────────────────────────────────────────────── │
│   ─────────────────────────────────────────────────────────────────── │
└─────────────────────────────────────────────────────────────────────┘
```

Figure 18–5 End-user computing request form: II.

- *Hardware requirements:*
  - *CPU:* System type you will use
  - *Memory:* Estimated minimum amount of memory needed to run the application
  - *Disk storage:* Estimated in 512-byte disk blocks
- *Software requirements:*
  - *Operating system:* Specify operating system (i.e., AOS/VS, CP/M, MS-DOS)
  - *Application system:* Specify application system (i.e., sed, super comp, utility, language, etc.) to be used
  - *Frequency of run (usage by user):* Times per day/week that these data will be processed
  - *Retention days:* How long you want the data strip source tape to remain in the library? The default is 30 days
- *Security clearance:* This is a combination of your department's director and the data security officer:
  - *Requesting department approval.* This must be signed by a director or anyone in your department who reports directly to someone at the level of vice-president or higher.
  - *Data security approval.* You must have data security approval before you can submit the form for access. The data security officer will assign a security level.

To the completed form you must attach a separate sheet listing the data items you require. The correct names for these data items can be found in the data dictionary. This list must conform to the standard names found in the data dictionary.

List of Data Items

The end-user computing request form must be accompanied by a list of the data items for which you require data strips. If the data item you require is not in the data dictionary, inform the DBA and the items will be added to the dictionary. In specifying data items, you may group them together using group names. For example:

```
DATE
            MONTH              PIC 99
            DAY                PIC 99
            YEAR               PIC 99
```

Groups of fields may also repeat. This should be indicated by an ''occurs'' clause as is normally represented in the COBOL file definition. For example:

```
QUANTITY-USED OCCURS 13 TIMES  PIC 9(08)
   DATA ITEM  TIMES REPEATING  LENGTH
```

The extract file produced from the request will have the following characteristics:

- File type will be sequential.
- Maximum record size is 8192 bytes.
- Record will be a fixed length supplied by the DBA.
- Block size maximum is 8192 bytes; integer number of records per block will be accommodated based on the record size (supplied by the DBA).
- Data items will be of the ASCII character set.
- The decimal will be implied in the case of numeric data items. *Example:* Dollars 9(04)V99 = 0000.00.
- For signed numeric items the sign convention will be a trailing overpunch. *Example:* Quantity S9(06).
- It is the user's responsibility to account for missing data and apply the appropriate scale conversion factors.
  Example:
  — *Cost:* $100.5631
  — *Unit of measure:* Each, or per dozen, etc.

Data Groups

While a request may specify groupings of data items and repeat occurrences, the extract produced will consist of data items at the elementary level. Thus the physical positioning of data items will not be affected by groupings. Other kinds of format requests can be fulfilled. For example, if your application requires an MS-DOS file format or a dBASE or a WORDPERFECT format, it can be produced by the system.

Note: If an extract file is to be accessed by a text editor, a line-feed character can be inserted at the 80th or 132nd character position so that the text editor is easier to operate.

Selection Criteria

When applicable, you must also supply a list of selection criteria for the data items you require. Both upper and lower bounds must be set using standard Boolean operators. For example,

```
CUST-NO > 0 AND < 2000
```

indicates a customer number greater than 0 and less than 2000. Carefully defined selection criteria saves both processing time and file space.

Data Extract

After the DBA receives the end-user computing request, the process to create a data strip is initiated. The necessary program(s) are generated against the data bases where the data exist, and data extraction runs are scheduled against those data bases. The data bases could be located on different computers at different locations. All data extracts will be presented to the user in the format requested. Additionally, all extracts will be stored on labeled magnetic tape(s) in the library for the retention period specified (default is 30 days).

Directory

Immediately after the extract is created, unless otherwise requested, the data extract will be loaded onto the end-user system in the directory :EUCFILES. You will be notified that your file has been loaded, together with the number of records, the name of the file, and the record layout. The DBA will update the end-user log, close out the request, and generate an acknowledgment to the end user via E-mail. For example, the file EUC0001 is structured as follows:

- Block contains 2 records.
- Record contains 256 characters.
- Label records are omitted.
- Part queue information

```
PART-NO              PIC X(10)
VOLUME-CD            PIC X(01)
ABC-CD               PIC X(01)
CONT-EXP-CD          PIC X(01)
PART-REPAIR-FL       PIC X(01)
PART-MAKE-BUY-CD     PIC X(01)
ICA-CD               PIC X(04)
PART-COST            PIC S9(07)V9(04)
```

- STCK queue information

```
QTY-ON-HAND-E        PIC S9(08)
QTY-OWED-E           PIC S9(08)
QTY-WIP-E            PIC S9(08)
QTY-ON-HAND-W        PIC S9(08)
QTY-OWED-W           PIC S9(08)
QTY-WIP-W            PIC S9(08)
```

- HIST queue information

```
QTY-P1-SHIP-E        PIC S9(08)
QTY-P2-SHIP-E        PIC S9(08)
QTY-P3-SHIP-E        PIC S9(08)
QTY-RET-E            PIC S9(08)
QTY-REP-E            PIC S9(08)
QTY-INTL-SHIP-E      PIC S9(08)
QTY-SPS-SHIP-E       PIC S9(08)
QTY-MISC-SHIP-E      PIC S9(08)
QTY-P1-SHIP-W        PIC S9(08)
QTY-P2-SHIP-W        PIC S9(08)
QTY-P3-SHIP-E        PIC S9(08)
QTY-RET-W            PIC S9(08)
QTY-REP-W            PIC S9(08)
QTY-REC-NEW          PIC S9(08)
FILLER               PIC X(66)
```

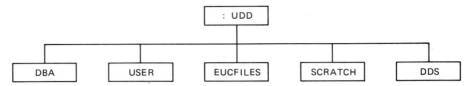

Figure 18-6   Directories used in end-user computing.

DIRECTORY STRUCTURE AND USAGE

The following directories are used in end-user computing, illustrated in Figure 18-6.

- USER:
  — Assigned to each end user.
  — Provide for the development and storage of tools (text editor, programs, etc.).
  — Space requirements can be monitored.
  — Backed up daily and can be recovered by operations (via a special request) in the event of accidental file deletion.
- EUCFILES (directory containing the data strips)
  — Supplied by the DBA.
  — Retained on tape for 30 days unless otherwise specified on DDS-98.
  — Names are formatted with the prefix EUC followed by XXXX, where XXXX is the number of the request.
  — Access control list (ACL) is set so that the user has read/execute access only.
  — Data files in this dictionary are backed up daily.
  — Data strips will be deleted after 30 days unless otherwise requested.
- SCRATCH (common work directory for all end users)
  — All work files are in this directory.
  — Files are deleted weekly (over the weekend).
  — No backups are done.
  — Space is limited.
  — All sensitive files should be stored on tape.
  — Files must be deleted by the user when not in use.
  — It is not to be used for storage. All historical information should be dumped to tape to be retained for a specified number of days.

The data strips are loaded in :EUCFILES with your ACL. You will have read and execute privileges only. You must then create a link to the data strip in order to access the data. You create this link by typing at the prompt:

```
CLINK ''DATA STRIP NAME: :EUCFILES: ''DATA STRIP NAME'' (NL)
```

This enables the program to find the data strip file. All work files will be used in :SCRATCH to avoid space problems. To work on these data strips, you must first position yourself in :SCRATCH by typing at the prompt:

```
DIR :SCRATCH ''NEWLINE''
```

You may now manipulate the data as you wish.

Work Files

The work files you create must be deleted when not in use. This is very important in maintaining and monitoring space requirements. The :SCRATCH directory is deleted weekly by operations. Any files that you want to save must be stored on tape, as they will automatically be deleted from :SCRATCH at the end of each week.

Space

The DBA has the responsibility of monitoring space and its use for the end-user computing system. Initially, this task will be performed using a macro. The macro reads through all the user directories and :EUCFILES and creates a report. The report is broken into two sections:

1. *Listing of user files:* This listing contains all user directories and files within those directories, identified by username. This listing contains the name of each file, the amount of space used, the date and time the file was created, and the date and time of the last modification of the file. *Example:*

   ```
   Filename 2000 10-Oct-88 13:00:01 20-Oct-88 09:30:56
   ```

2. *Listing of files modified prior to DD-MMM-YY*: This listing consists of only those files that were loaded prior to the date specified. (Note that the month is represented by a three-alpha-character abbreviation (e.g., Oct, Dec). This listing reports on file name, amount of space used (in bytes), and the date and time the file was created. *Example:*

   ```
   User Filename 2000 10-Oct-88 8:30:25
   ```

The listing file described above is read by a program with preestablished parameters for space used and amount of time the file has existed. Users who are using excessive amounts of space or who have had a file in a directory for more than 30 days (for example) will receive a memo notifying them of this. This memo specifies username, the file name, and the amount of space used. The user is asked to verify that a need still exists for the data being stored. A copy of this memo is send it to the DBA. Initially, this process will be performed weekly in order to effectively monitor all user directories and data strips (:EUCFILES).

Housekeeping

End users are responsible for taking care of their own "housecleaning." You must delete any files not in use. Notify the DBA once you are finished with the data extracts supplied to you. The DBA will then ensure that adequate space is available to all end users by deleting those files that you no longer need.

Backup

A complete system backup will be performed daily. This includes the entire data dictionary system, all data strips, and the complete contents of all user directories. As stated previously, the SCRATCH directory will be deleted each weekend. Any files you need to save must be loaded to tape and then stored in the library.

To recover from an accidentally deleted file, you must fill out a special computer run request form and send it to the DBA. When describing the request, write "Please load from user backup file: USERNAME:FILENAME from dd-mm-yy." You must give the full filename path to the deleted file and the date of the backup. This request will be reviewed by the DBA and your backup will be restored to you.

chapter 19

Trends in Dictionary Development and Usage

INTRODUCTION

Data dictionaries have been around for over two decades and are packaged in many different ways. In some cases the dictionary is a stand-alone system, whereas in other cases, it is tied into a vendor's DBMS product. With the proliferation of 4GL packages, the dictionary is often embedded within the package. The expansion of information processing and the trend to distributed processing often require the user to pay much closer attention to the characteristics of the dictionary that is acquired. Vendors make many claims for a dictionary and it is often difficult to evaluate the importance of these claims. With the pressures on productivity that currently exist in the information systems world, it is important to understand the role of the dictionary in managing information processing activities.

The objective of this chapter is to review dictionary concepts in simple terms, define the contexts in which dictionaries are used, and present a network dictionary model for further analysis. To help the reader put the dictionary's role in context, three perspectives on dictionaries are presented. These will help the reader understand the current issues in implementing data dictionaries and will assist in evaluating products in relation to the intended directions in information processing and priorities within the organization. Thus the selection decision can be made with a full understanding of the dictionary's functions as well as its role in meeting the needs of the organization.

DICTIONARY CONCEPT

When a user or computer application requests data, the computer must know what data are stored in the data base, how they are organized, and how to access the data from the data base so that the correct data are returned to the requestor. These rules may be contained in a file layout, an include file, a copybook, a subschema, a relational table, or a data dictionary. To give a primitive example, a data dictionary can be thought of as a file layout that is part of an application program (i.e., an FD in a COBOL program). The FD contains basic information about each data item, including the size, the relative position within a record and file, and the access methods. However, all this information is embedded within a section of the application program source. For other persons to make use of this information, they would not only have to know the specific programs that contained the FD, but also the rules coded within those programs. Figure 19–1 shows the position of the FD within an application program; note how each application program has its own area for the FD.

In a typical data base management system (DBMS), the subschema (or user view of the data) may be located in a separate file and occupy a different segment of memory. Changes to the subschema can be made only by authorized personnel such as data base administrators, and more rules, such as security access, can be incorporated in this type of dictionary. This is shown in Figure 19–2.

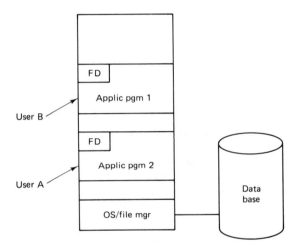

Figure 19–1   FDs within an application program.

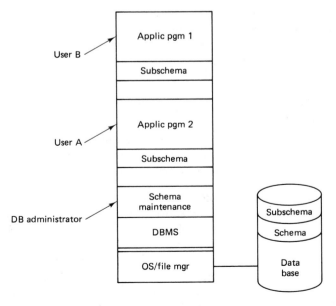

Figure 19–2   Location of subschema with respect to application.

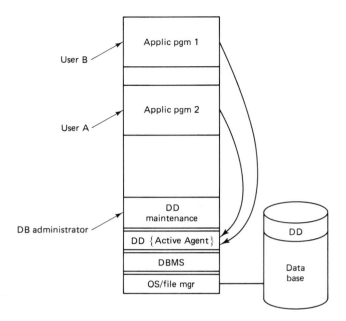

Figure 19-3 Dictionary in relation to application.

In the complex case, the data dictionary is the focal point for all data access; that is, the data dictionary not only tells the computer where the data are located in the data base, but also which application programs process the data, and closely coordinates with the DBMS in controlling access to the data base. Figure 19-3 illustrates this situation. In the diagram the dictionary agent (DD{Agent}) is the process that intercepts data dictionary requests and ensures that the requestor has the right levels of access before passing the request on to the DBMS. Note how the dictionary functions become more differentiated and distinct from the application programs.

Problem.   As the number of computer applications grows and the data bases increase, the number of data dictionaries in the organization will continue to grow substantially; however, if the dictionaries are not synchronized to a common set of rules, they will tend to be different from one another. Thus a data base system that follows one set of data dictionary rules will not be able to communicate with another data base system that follows another set of data base rules. There are two major problems when this occurs:

1. Users tend to lose confidence in the data when they follow different rules in different data bases.
2. Data-based systems tend to be duplicated, and proliferate unnecessarily, because it is often easier to create a new version of the data item than to resolve conflicts between existing ones.

Solution.   The solution to this ever-growing problem is to disseminate the rules from one authoritative source or repository, and make that the reference point for all other dictionaries in the organization. Such a repository is often called a global dictionary. This would ensure that users get data that are consistent and follow one set of dictionary rules. However, the implementation of this simple notion gets complicated because of the need to interface different types of dictionary systems to one another and to organize information flow along certain directions to ensure consistency. All of this has to be done at the same time that definite forces and trends taking place in information processing and the underlying technology are accommodated. In practice, the implementer is faced with a moving target and must be nimble enough to maneuver through the pitfalls and obstacles that arise.

THREE PERSPECTIVES OF THE DICTIONARY

Design, Control and Communication Tool

Design

The top-down approach to data design is to develop the business or logical data model that reflects the rules of the business as well as the direction of the business. The data model is then translated into data base designs that support the portfolio of applications for the company. Although many efforts at top-down implementation of a data model have been initiated, the traditional momentum of development resulting from the applications backlog requires a close coordination between the applications that are being developed currently as well as the planned implementations resulting from the model.

The business data model is the end result of codifying business rules and is depicted in terms of data definitions and use, data model diagrams, and standards and procedures pertinent to the above. The physical structure of the data bases, and the rules for access and distribution, are also included. Once the business data model has the approval of senior management, it can become the yardstick against which projects can be measured for conformance to the technical standards as well as progression to a corporate data plan. The dictionary plays a pivotal role in the dissemination of this information to the project teams throughout the company and as a reference and control point to ensure that progress is made toward the plan.

Control

Once the overall plan and standards are put into the dictionary, there are a several ways in which these can be enforced:

- *Active enforcement through the dictionary's role in the system development life cycle (SDLC):* This is the ideal situation, because checks can be built into the SDLC to ensure that the data model for the application is consistent with the planned data model.
- *Enforcement through the data base administrator's (DBA) role in data base design.* This is a good way to enforce the data model; however, it requires knowledgeable DBAs in the application development organizations.
- *Enforcement through audit of data base designs.* This is the least desirable alternative because there is extreme reluctance to change a design once a significant amount of effort has been put into it.

Communication Tool

One of the significant problems in dealing with multiple project teams is trying to keep up the level of communications between the groups. The temptation is always there to skirt the data conflicts that arise by developing new data standards and building interfaces between the old and the new when it would have been appropriate to use the old one in the first place. In addition to the dictionary's role in communicating the existing data standards and models, it is important to realize that these data standards are not absolute. Circumstances will arise that call for these standards to be modified. Thus the communication has to be a two-way process.

The dictionary can be used to propagate standards as well as to "sniff" out the changes that need to be made to the standards, by having utilities that enable a user to request a change in the standard. Once users get the feeling that their concerns are being heard and addressed, their commitment to the process of which the dictionary is a part will increase.

Management Information System Data Base

Evolution

As the usage of the dictionary evolves within the organization, and the various applications to support other MIS activities are implemented, the dictionary's importance within MIS will continue to grow. Under these circumstances, a question that may arise is: How is the dictionary data base any different from an inventory, or accounts payable, or customer data base? The answer is that it is not. The population and maintenance of the dictionary data base will be just as important as maintaining any of the other data bases that are supporting the company's business. The dictionary in effect becomes the data base that supports the MIS side of the business.

Role of DBA

It has been stated earlier that the automation of MIS data via a dictionary is a formal recognition of the importance of the MIS function by the senior managers. Most such efforts start off primarily as data bases that support data base administration activities within the organization. That trend will continue to grow with the increase in the different types of data that are being automated and the increasing quantities of data being generated by end users. As the quality of the data in the dictionary improves, other users will be interested in utilizing the data in the dictionary for other functions within MIS, such as systems life cycle support, operations, and security.

Life Cycle Support

Since the ultimate objective of the dictionary data base is to be a proactive support tool for the MIS development and support activities, the trend will be to include dictionary updates as part of the system development process. The integration can occur in one of two ways:

1. As part of a new development methodology that automatically includes dictionary updates as part of the process
2. As a migration tool to the new development methodology

In either approach, the system that provides for capture of the relevant data into the dictionary as part of the process will be the one that will become popular; the dictionary that requires a lot of "perceived overhead" activity will become less popular over time. Therefore, there will a tendency on the part of vendors to develop tools that extract information from the process itself to populate the dictionary.

DDL vs DML

In the current products in the marketplace, a distinction is made between data definition language (DDL) and data manipulation language (DML). DDL is the syntax used to update the data dictionary data base, while DML is the syntax used to update the application data base via the DBMS. If the dictionary data base is just another data base in the MIS portfolio of data bases that have to be managed, the distinction between DDL and DML should fade. It is likely that the unique syntax of the dictionary DDL will be absorbed into the DBMS DML. There are two major benefits from this:

1. It enforces the use of the dictionary as part of the DBMS, similar to the situation with recoverability and security controls.
2. If a standardized syntax for dictionary DDL is developed and used by vendors of DBMS products, it is possible to tie different vendors' DBMSs to a global dictionary and obtain the benefits of a dictionary in a consistent manner across all applications.

Active Data Base Management Agent

Role in DBMS

Most vendors of DBMS and 4GL products assert that their products are dictionary driven. This implies that the dictionary data base is referenced during the process of accessing data from the data base. Since the dictionary function is embedded in the DBMS or 4GL, this forces the customer to look to one vendor to supply both the DBMS and dictionary capability. In some organizations, policy decisions have been made to stay with one vendor's products, and this makes it easy to interface various copies of the DBMS to the dictionary. In other organizations, DBMS products from many vendors may be in use, each with its own version of a dictionary. Since the linking of a dictionary data base to the DBMS or 4GL requires proprietary information on the internal workings of the DBMS, a dictionary that plays an active role in one DBMS will not be able to play an active role vis-à-vis another vendor's DBMS because of the restriction noted above.

A way to address the problem is to have the active component of a dictionary that is needed by the DBMS extracted from a global dictionary data base. Under this scenario, the active component of the dictionary data is extracted from a global dictionary to support the DBMS at run time. The drawback to this approach is that multiple copies of the metadata will exist: once in the dictionary data base and once with each copy of the DBMS. All the problems associated with multiple copies of data now apply to the metadata. The updates to the dictionary need to be synchronized, either manually or automatically, to be a worthwhile solution.

Role in Distributed Data Base Environment

Most organizations have distributed data bases simply due to the fact that they have data bases that cannot all fit into one machine. Whatever the cause of this situation, issues that have to do with a distributed DBMS environment arise. Some of the issues are:

- How do you maintain consistency between active dictionaries that control different subsets of data on the DBMS data base?
- Should there be a single point of reference for all the active dictionaries?
- How should the dictionaries be organized so that there are no concurrent update conflicts?
- What interfaces are necessary in a distributed dictionary to present a unified view to the end user and the MIS users?

Role in Network

With the advent of high-speed communication links that are available today, the role of the dictionary in a network is becoming more prominent. When networks are brought into the equation, there are several ways in which to distribute the dictionary.

It is possible to organize the dictionary into a machine that serves only as a

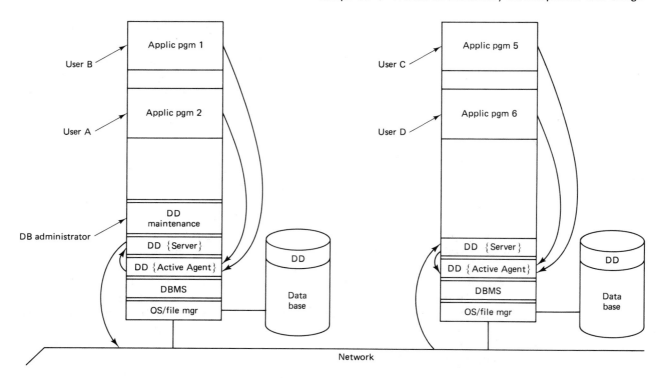

Figure 19-4   Dictionary in a network.

dictionary processor, with all other machines in the network communicating with this processor for active as well as passive system components. Such a processor would have to be extremely fast to avoid contention. However, if the dictionary machine were to be a specialized processor, it could be the hub around which all data access would take place. Such a machine could be linked into the network as a dictionary server, utilizing a standard protocol that all vendors could then follow.

The dictionary could be a virtual dictionary; that is, it could contain views of the data in the local data base, and also contain pointers (addresses) to other dictionaries in the network where definitions of data could be found. The system would look up the pointer address for the data item, and then access the other machine in the network for the information. Figure 19-4 illustrates how this would work, with the DD{Servers} performing the functions of DD access across the network.

Another variation of the above is to have the dictionary at a node contain only the definitions and addresses of data existing on the local node; the DD{Server} process would query the local DD and if the data item could not be found in the local node, a query would be formulated and sent to other DD{Servers} on the network. Obviously, this is a complicated solution to implement, but one where the dictionary maintenance burden is restricted to the local node.

RECONCILING PERSPECTIVES

Data Needs

It is apparent that dictionaries can be used with differing levels of emphasis on each of the perspectives presented or in combination. There are trade-offs with emphasizing a particular perspective. The common thread through the various perspectives is the fact that the data that are needed to support the three perspectives overlap.

It is evident that a common data base to support the functioning of the dictionary is desirable. Whether the data are maintained in a consolidated data base or can be distributed depends on the vendor's appreciation of the problem and support to a particular perspective.

Process Needs

Another aspect that is evident from the discussion above is that the dictionary can be used as both a static and a dynamic data source. For the active data base management agent functions, the dictionary data should be in a static mode because the metadata that control data base access cannot be allowed to change at will. For the planning and system life-cycle views, the data in the dictionary will be subject to change to accommodate business changes and design iterations. Under these conditions, the dictionary has to support multiple versions of data.

Change Control

Another conclusion that can be drawn from the discussion is that a change made to the design or life-cycle view will have an impact on the active data base management view. Therefore, a mechanism that predicts the impact of a change throughout all the other perspectives is essential in order to propagate change in an orderly manner from the planning stage to application implementation.

A Model

A model is presented that would try to reconcile the different perspectives. It consists of four types of processes that would be necessary:

1. DD{Design} process, which would enable the data administration personnel to enter and change the business data model and report on the impact to the existing data base structures
2. DD{Life Cycle} process, which would enable MIS personnel to utilize the dictionary actively during applications development
3. DD{Active Agent} process, which would provide the run-time support to the DBMS data bases
4. DD{Server} process, which would enable communication among the three processes above using a common syntax and protocol

The data that would be required for each process to function adequately could be stored in one data base in a very simple implementation, or be distributed across several processors, to support a distributed data base environment. Figure 19–5 illustrates the situation for three machines running production applications. One machine is used for design and life-cycle development functions. That machine is part of a local area network consisting of workstations that run software that supports data design, life-cycle development, and DD maintenance. All these workstations need access to the dictionary data base that resides on the host machine within the local area network. This data base is the global data base from which dictionary definitions are propagated to the production machines in the network.

The host machine is connected via a network link to the three production machines, each of which have data base applications that are being run. There is a DD component in each of the machines that reflects the local data base environment. Any changes to this environment are first made at the global DD level and are then downline loaded into the production machines at the appropriate time. This ensures that there is consistency between the design and life-cycle version of the DD and the production version.

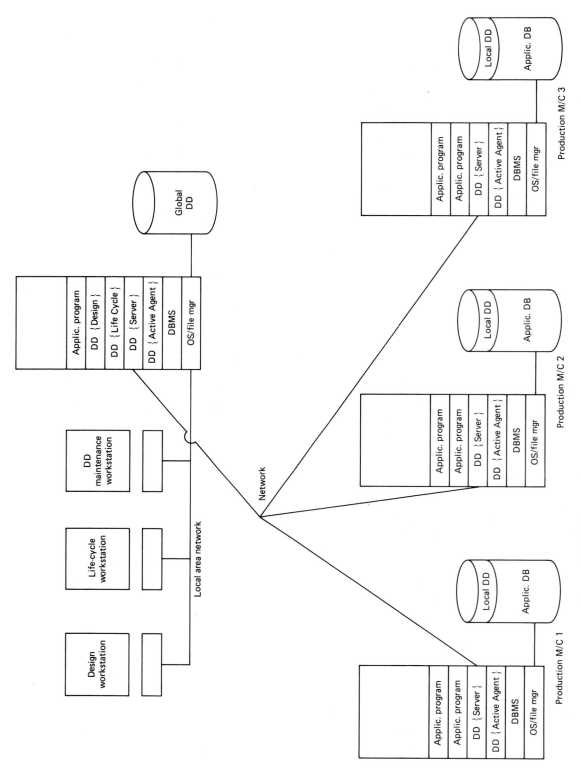

Figure 19-5 Proposed model of a dictionary in a network performing different functions for different users.

Note how a DD{Server} process is available in each machine to provide the dictionary functions requested by the application or the DD{Active} agent. The same DD{Server} process is active on the workstations to provide the interfaces to the design and life-cycle development functions on the global DD computer.

CONCLUSIONS

From the discussion above, it is clear that there are several ways in which dictionaries are implemented by vendors, with varying levels of emphasis on design, life-cycle activities, and DBMS/4GL support. It provides a basis for information systems managers to ask relevant questions before committing to purchasing decisions. In addition, this discussion emphasizes the importance of the network in a distributed data base environment and presents a model that can reconcile dictionary requirements across a network. This is just a starting point. Much more work needs to be done in this area. There is also a need to develop standards for interdictionary communication, so that users can use DBMS and 4GL products from different vendors to suit the business, without having to worry about data incompatibility.

Glossary

access key: Set of values that can be used to retrieve records from the data base.

access method: System routine external to an application program that performs storage and retrieval of physical data. The operation of seeking, reading, or writing data on a storage unit. A technique for moving data between a computer and its peripheral devices (e.g., serial access, remote access, indexed access).

access path (logical): Route taken through the logical structure of the data base, in terms of the data relationships utilized by the system, in order to locate a desired logical unit of data.

access path (physical): Physical reference paths and related access methods used by the DBMS to perform storage and retrieval.

active: In connection with data dictionary usage, refers to the closeness of the linkage between the DD and DBMS.

alias: Names other than the official name by which an entity is known.

attribute: Known characteristic of an entity. A field containing information about an entity. The values associated with an entity.

candidate key: Attribute or combination of attributes of a relation such that for each tuple of that relation, the value of the key uniquely identifies that tuple, and no attribute in the key can be discarded without destroying this uniqueness.

canonical schema: Model of data that represents the inherent structure of that data, and hence is independent of individual application of the data and also of the software or hardware mechanisms that are employed in representing and using the data.

checkpoint: Act of recording the state of units of data and those application programs operating on them, for the purpose of reconstructing the data and restarting the programs.

communication network: (also referred to as data communications network) Collection of transmission facilities, network processors, and so on, which provides for data movement among terminals and information processors.

conceptual schema: Overall logical structure of a data base.

copybook: File that contains the source code that can be directly copied into a program by reference. The source code typically contains file and record descriptions. Also contains program segments, edit/valuation routines, global tables, declaratives, and so on. Also known as an "include file."

data: (a) (noun, plural) often constructed as singular, things known or assumed; facts or figures from which conclusions can be inferred (Webster's *New World Dictionary*); (b) representation of facts, concepts, or instructions in a formalized manner suitable for communication, interpretation, or processing by humans or by automatic means (ISO); (c) any representations, such as characters or analog quantities, to which meaning is or might be assigned; (d) symbols, written or stored on some recording medium, representing certain things, ideas, or values and conveying meaningful information in particular contexts (Everest).

data administrator: Person with an overall responsibility for defining the standards and policies with respect to an organization's data.

data base: (a) Generalized, integrated collection of company- or installation-owned data which fulfills the data requirements of all applications that access it, and which is structured to model the natural data relationships that exist in an enterprise; (b) collection of interrelated, largely unique data items or records, in one or more computer files, which may be processed by multiple application programs; (c) collection of interrelated data stored together with controlled redundancy to serve one or more applications; the data are stored so that they are independent of programs that use the data; a common controlled approach is used in adding new data and retrieving existing data within a data base.

data base administrator (DBA):   Person or group of people responsible for definition of an organization's data base(s), and for the monitoring and control of operations against the data base.

data base management system (DBMS):   Functions that support the semipermanent storage of user owned data and provide access to that data. Also includes features that provide concurrency control, restricted views based on access control lists, recoverability, and transaction atomicity.

data base structure: Field, record, and interrecord relationships which collectively define the format in which data are stored. The content of the structure is made up of data items.

data base synchronization: Process of ensuring that the component parts of a distributed data base are logically consistent.

data description language (DDL):   (also referred to as *data definition language*) Language used to (a) describe the characteristics of items, aggregates, records, sets, and areas of data base to the DBMS; (b) describe the characteristics of data items, aggregates, records, sets, and areas within a subset of a data base as viewed logically from within an application program.

data dictionary: Software facility that maintains data on data base structures and processes that affect the data base, and provides utility services, such as file and record descriptions to the user. A data dictionary capability is sometimes integrated within the DBMS; it is essential for the development and control of an operational data base environment.

data dictionary system (DDS):   Program or a group of programs for implementing a computerized data dictionary.

data independence: Concept of separating the definitions of logical and physical data from programs, so that programs are not dependent on where or how physical units of data are stored or accessed. A characteristic of data base systems arising from the segregation of data structure definition (i.e., DDL) from data access (i.e., DML).

data integrity: Concept that all units of data must be protected against inadvertent or deliberate invalidation. Data accuracy and consistency.

data item: Single named data entity containing no substructure; the lowest level of addressable data in which data value(s) are physically stored.

data manipulation language (DML):   Language of the DBMS whose statements are used by programmers to invoke the DBMS facilities from a host language (COBOL, Fortran, PL/I, etc.). The commands required to create, access, and change the content of a data base.

data model: Architectural or conceptual description of data objects, relationships, and their attributes in a general rather than a specific sense. A data model is converted into a data structure by using a DDL. In the relational model, a data model is the set of all relations—that is, all data stored in the data base.

data name: Name (term) given to units of data (item, aggregate, record, set) for the purpose of uniquely identifying that unit of data.

data record: *See* Record.

deadlock: Situation where two or more run units are competing for the same resources and none may precede, as each run unit is waiting for one of the others to release a resource the latter has already claimed.

distributed data base: Single logical data base which has been implemented in more than one physical segment, attached to more than one information processor.

distributed data base environment: Computer network in which processing can take place and data can be stored at the same or different nodes; a computer network of nodes connected with a communications facility; a collection of two or more interconnected nodes, each with computing facilities sufficient for any of the following: to execute user processes, to execute a data base request, to execute a network access process, or to store data and their definition.

distributed processing: Technique for implementing one logically related set of information-processing (application-related) functions within multiple physical devices. A data base under the overall control of a central data base management system, but where the devices on which it is stored are not all attached to the same processor. A hardware configuration in which a large centralized computer is augmented or replaced by two or more smaller machines, intercommunicating, and located near the application's users.

domain: Set of all possible values for a data item type from which attributes are chosen (relational model).

elementary data item: Smallest named unit of logical data available to a program.

encryption: Involves an algorithm that maps data into an unintelligible bit string which can be transferred into its original form with an inverse algorithm.

enterprise name: Name by which an entity is known throughout the enterprise (generally, the nonabbreviated form).

entity: (a) Person, place, thing, or event of interest to the enterprise; (b) any person, object, event, or abstract concept about which data can be stored (Everest); (c) concept or object of interest to an organization; something about which data are recorded; an entry in a data base (MRI-System 2000); (d) something about which data are recorded (Martin).

entity category: Generic classification of an entity (i.e., programs, jobs, files, records, etc.).

entity name: Symbol by which a person, place, thing, class, or any object of thought is known.

entity type code: Alphanumeric codes to associate with an entity category.

file: (a) Physical portion of the data base managed as a single entity by the operating system of a computer (Ross); (b) set of related records treated as a unit (e.g., in stock control, a file could consist of a set of invoices) (ISO); (c) set of record occurrences of similar logical structure and data type (Cardenas); (d) set of similarly constructed records (Martin).

flat file: (a) Single-level record array with only one record type; a relation in normal form; (b) collection of records containing no data aggregates [i.e., no "nested" repeating data items (vectors) or repeating groups of data items].

global dictionary: Dictionary that contains dictionary data that applies to all systems in the enterprise and is an authoritative source of information for other local dictionaries in the enterprise.

group: Named collection of zero, one, or more data items within a set or entry. They may vary in frequency, format, and relationship. Relationships are: subordinate, peer, superior (also segment, data aggregate, periodic set, detail group, item).

hierarchy: Set of directed relationships between two or more units of data, such that some units are considered owners, while others are considered members.

host language: Computer language (e.g., COBOL, Fortran) in which the DML for data base access is embedded.

identifier: Unit of data, usually a data item, that serves to identify the data record uniquely.

index: Collection of unique descriptors (keys) and related data addressed for use in storage and retrieval.

information: (a) Meaning that a person assigns to data by means of the known conventions used in their representation (ISO); (b) data evaluated in a specific situation, applied to solving a particular problem or used in decision making (McDonough, 1963); (c) that which is or can be derived from data (Everest); (d) data transformed through the infusion of purposeful intelligence; communicates meaning or knowledge inspired by observation (Hanold, 1972); (e) any kind of knowledge or message that can be used to improve or make possible a decision (Langefors, 1966).

information network: Interconnected set of hardware and software components, including communications facilities, configured to meet some or all of the application work load requirements of an enterprise.

information processing: Hardware and software functions which provide computation, decision making, and data manipulation, supporting the execution of computerized applications.

information system: (a) Interconnected set of hardware and software components, and procedures, which together meet the application work load of the enterprise; (b) system in which the data stored will be used in spontaneous ways which are not fully predicted in advance for obtaining information.

inter-entity relationship: Relationship that allows entity occurrences of two different entity types to be connected.

internal schema: Physical structure of the data.

intra-entity relationship: Relationship that allows entity occurrences of the same entity type to be connected (typically, in hierarchical fashion).

inversion: Access technique in which data values from individual records are segregated into a separate area of storage, which points back to the original area.

inverted access method: Storage structuring of an index, whereby a given key value is associated with a pointer array to all similarly valued records.

journal: System file, usually on magnetic tape, wherein an audit trail of changes to the data base is kept, largely for the purposes of recovery.

key: Any field upon which access to records may be effected without searching records themselves for a match on a data value; also, a field used to facilitate the physical access of "related" records or to physically order records in a set. In the relational model, "key" is short for "candidate key."

keyword in context (KWIK): Word taken from the context of the full name of an entity, that is used as a key to access that entity and its associated information.

linkage: Mechanism for relating one unit of data to another by means of associating the disk address of the target (pointed-to) record with the source (pointing) record. Links may be embedded within the data unit itself, or by relating external pointer sets to each data unit (non-embedded links).

linked list: (also referred to as "chain") Set of records in which each record contains a pointer to the next record in the list.

list: Method of relating an owner record to member records of the same type, in which links pointing to each member are embedded in or associated with the owner record.

log: Recording (journal) of all environmental changes relative to the data base. It may include copies of all transactions, before/after images of updated records, time and date stamps, user and terminal ID, security breaches, and so on.

logical data: That data which the application program presents to or receives from the DBMS.

logical data structure: Set of relationships that exists between two or more units of logical data as viewed by the user.

logical record: Collection of one or more data item values as viewed by the user.

metadata: Data that describe other data. The data are organized in the form of entities, attributes, and relationships, and are generally stored in a data dictionary.

minicomputer: "Small-scale" information processor capable of operating in an office or hostile environment (i.e., with minimal environmental control).

multiprocessing: Support for application systems by two or more processors; the processors themselves are treated as resources for improving overall throughput.

multiprogramming: Support by an operating system for two or more programs to occupy main memory at the same time and to share the resources of a single processor.

multitasking: System able to support multiple tasks at once, largely by overlapping I/O.

multithreading: Code in a program so designed as to be available for servicing multiple tasks at once, in particular by overlapping I/O. Multithread code must be reentrant.

network (processing): System of intercommunicating processors through which "distributed" processing is supported; also, a configuration of distributed processing in which every processor communicates directly with all other processors.

network (structure): Data structure characterized by the membership of records in sets, as either owners or members.

normal form, first: Data in flat file form.

normal form, second: A relation R is in second normal form if it is in first normal form and every nonprime attribute of R is fully functionally dependent on each candidate key of R.

normal form, third: (a) A relationship R is in third normal form if it is in second normal form and every nonprime attribute of R is nontransitively dependent on each candidate key of R. (b) The entire candidate (or primary) key is needed in order to identify each and every other data item in the tuple, and no data item is identified by a data item which is not in the candidate (or primary) key.

normalization: (a) Decomposition of more complex data structures into flat files (relations) (Martin); (b) process of altering the format of relations in order to improve their performance in user operations, especially updating. A flat file is in "normal" form; the third normal form is deemed best for relational operations (relational model).

null item: Item for which space is allocated in a record but no value currently exists.

occurrence: Specific representation of a given data item, aggregate, record, or set.

operating system: Software that enables a computer to supervise its own operations automatically, by calling in programs, routines, languages, and data as needed for continuous throughput of different types of jobs.

ownership: Characteristic of a data record relative to its participation within a defined "set," in which records of another type exist as members, subordinate to it.

physical data: Those data that the DBMS stores on or retrieves from a storage medium.

physical record: Unit of data accessed by the hardware from some storage medium.

physical structure: Set of relationships that exist between two or more units of physical data.

pointer array: Data record that participates in set relationships as an owner, and which contains within it the disk addressed of all members of the set.

precompiler: Program that interrogates an application program and replaces DML statements with CALLs to DBMS routines.

primary key: Key field that uniquely identifies a record, used to physically order records in some file organizations (e.g., ISAM) or to provide primary access in randomized storage structures; in the relational model, one candidate key in a relation.

privacy key: Facility specified as a literal, a data item, or a procedure, used to unlock an operation that is locked (Date, 1975).

privacy lock: Facility specified as a literal, a data item, or a procedure used to prevent an operation unless the matching privacy key is presented (Date, 1975).

program: Set or group of computer instructions.

qualifier: Value for a data item that combined with other items that comprise a key, makes the combined value unique.

record: (a) Unit of data that is retrieved from or stored into a file (CODASYL-COBOL); (b) occurrence of a named collection of zero, one, or more data items or data aggregates (CODASYL-DDL); (c) group of related fields of information (data items) treated as a unit by an application program (Martin); (d) collection of related values treated as a logical unit during any operation of the data base management system (e.g., during data collection, processing, or output) (logical) (FIPS-TG24); (e) unit of data to be placed on, or taken from, a storage device in a single operation (physical) (FIPS-TG24).

recovery: Process of reconstituting a data base to its correct and current state following a partial or complete hardware, software, network, operational, or processing error.

recursive structure: Data structure characterized by the relating of records of the same type, typically in the sense of components (substructure) and where-used (superstructure); often used in bill-of-materials applications.

redundancy: Situation where there are multiple occurrences of a particular data item replicated in the data base environment.

relational: Way of modeling data structures by relations. Relations are usually represented as a collection of tables where each table contains the occurrences of a particular relation. Each column of the relation corresponds to an attribute, and each row is an instance of the relation (FIPS-TG24).

relational model: Theoretical approach to data management based on tables and their manipulationl proposed by E. F. Codd and others.

relational operator: Named operation (e.g., JOIN) on one or more tables (relations) in the relational model.

relationship: Definition of a single association between two entities in the dictionary. (*See* Inter-entity *and* Intra-entity *for further types of relationships that can exist in the dictionary.*)

run unit: Execution of one or more programs. Each run unit is a separate process serviced by the DBMS with its own user working area and communication locations.

schema: Complete internal representation of a data base—includes all named entities: sets, groups, data items, areas, sort sequences, access keys, and security locks.

set: Named relationship between two or more record types, in which one record type participates as the owner of the set, and one or more records of other type(s) participate as members.

subschema: Subset of the schema, representing a portion of a data base as it appears to a user/application program. Identifying names may vary, and the format may differ in a manner consistent with the schema.

transaction: Named collection of one or more related data items representing a unique event or occurrence. The event may involve input, output, or a request for processing.

transaction controller: There is a transaction controller at each node which serves as the interface between processes at the node and the communications facility.

transparency: The shielding of the application from changes to the data base structure. Can be accomplished via the use of I/O driver routines.

tuple: Ordered collection of one or more domains (data item) which constitute an occurrence of a record.

validation: Checking of data for correctness, or compliance with applicable standards, rules, and conventions.

virtual sequential access method (VSAM):   IBM file mechanism, which provides independent indexed sequential access method.

working storage: Portion of storage, usually computer main memory, reserved for the temporary results of operations.

References

BELKIS, W. LEONG-HONG, and BERNARD K. PLAGMAN, *Data Dictionary/Directory Systems: Administration, Implementation and Usage.* New York: Wiley, 1982.

CODD, E. F., "Future Normalization of the Data Base Relational Model," in *Courant Computer Science Symposia,* Vol. 6. Englewood Cliffs, N.J.: Prentice-Hall, 1972.

Cullinet Integrated Data Dictionary Network Reference, Rev. O.O., Rel. 3.0, September 1982.

Cullinet Integrated Data Dictionary User's Guide, Rev. O.O, Rel. 3.0, December 1982.

Data General Field Engineering, *MIS Data Dictionary System Administrator Guide,* 1982.

Data General Field Engineering, *MIS Data Dictionary System User Manual,* 1982.

DURRELL, WILLIAM R., *Data Administration: A Practical Guide to Successful Data Management.* New York: McGraw-Hill, 1985.

HOLLAND, ROBERT H., "DBMS: Developing User Views," *Datamation,* February 1980.

HOLLAND, ROBERT H., "Developing the Corporate Database Plan," *Data Base Symposium,* Washington, D.C., April 1980.

Honeywell Level 66 Data Dictionary/Directory System Planning and Design Guide, DM11-00, October 1981.

IBM DB/DC Data Dictionary Planning and Design, I0115, December 1981.

IBM OS/VS DB/DC Data Dictionary Administration and Customization Guide, SG20-9174, March 1984.

IBM OS/VS DB/DC Data Dictionary Applications Guide, SH20-9190, March 1984.

IBM OS/VS DB/DC Data Dictionary General Information Manual, GH20-9104.

IBM OS/VS DB/DC Data Dictionary Installation Guide, SH20-9191, September 1984.

LEFKOVITS, H., SIBLEY, E., and S. LEFKOVITS, *Information Resource/Data Dictionary Systems.* Wellesley, Mass.: QED Information Sciences, 1980.

LOOMIS, MARY E. S., "Aspects of Database Design in a Distributed Network," *Data Communications*, May 1980.

MARTIN, JAMES, *Computer Data Base Organization*, 2nd ed., Englewood Cliffs, N.J.: Prentice-Hall, 1977.

NARAYAN, R., "Design of Data Structures for Migration to DSE," *Proceedings of the 5th Honeywell International Software Conference*, 1981.

ROSS, RONALD G., *Data Dictionaries and Data Administration: Concepts and Practices for Data Resources Management*. New York: McGraw-Hill, 1984.

WERTZ, CHARLES J., *The Data Dictionary: Concepts and Uses*. Wellesley, Mass.: QED Information Sciences, 1987.

Index